AMERICA IN THE FIFTIES AND SIXTIES

AMERICA IN THE FIFTIES AND SIXTIES: JULIÁN MARÍAS ON THE UNITED STATES

Translated from the Spanish by
Blanche De Puy and Harold C. Raley

Edited and with an Introduction by
Michael Aaron Rockland

THE PENNSYLVANIA STATE
UNIVERSITY PRESS
University Park and London

The following works by Julián Marías are available in English Translation:

Generations. A Historical Method, trans. Harold C. Raley (University: Alabama University Press, 1971).

History of Philosophy, trans. Stanley Appelbaum and Clarence C. Stowbridge (New York: Dover Publications, Inc., 1966).

José Ortega y Gasset: Circumstance and Vocation, trans. Frances M. López-Morillas (Norman: University of Oklahoma Press, 1970).

Metaphysical Anthropology, trans. Frances M. López-Morillas (University Park: The Pennsylvania State University Press, 1971).

Miguel de Unamuno, trans. Frances M. López-Morillas (Cambridge, Mass.: Harvard University Press, 1966).

Philosophy As Dramatic Theory, trans. James D. Parsons (University Park: The Pennsylvania State University Press, 1971).

Reason and Life: The Introduction to Philosophy, trans. Kenneth S. Reid and Edward Sarmiento (New Haven: Yale University Press, 1956).

Library of Congress Cataloging in Publication Data

Marías Aguilera, Julián.
     America in the fifties and sixties.

     "The fifties originally was published as Los
Estados Unidos en escorzo (1956) and The sixties as
Analisis de los Estados Unidos (1968)."
     "Epilogue: The United States in 1970. Trans-
lated from the Spanish by Harold C. Raley": p.
     Includes bibliographical references.
     1. U. S.—Civilization—1945–   I. Marías
Aguilera, Julián. Los Estados Unidos en escorzo.
English. 1971. II. Marías Aguilera, Julián.
Análisis de los Estados Unidos. English. 1971.
III. Title.

E169.12.M34   917.3'03'9   77–157770
ISBN 0–271–00556–4

International Standard Book Number: 271-00556-4
Library of Congress Catalog Card Number: 77-157770
Copyright © 1972 by The Pennsylvania State University
          All Rights Reserved
Printed in the United States of America
Designed by Marilyn Shobaken

CONTENTS

INTRODUCTION

With the publication in English of his two books on the United States in one volume,‡ the Spanish philosopher, Julián Marías, joins the ranks of those foreign intellectuals and travelers to these shores who have always been the most significant commentators on our developing society. Such writers as Alexis de Tocqueville, Frances Trollope, Frederick Marryat, Charles Dickens, Harriet Martineau, James Bryce, and Denis Brogan have examined the American forest when our own writers have been detained among its trees. Approaching America from the advantage of a comparative point of view, the foreign writers have explored the common denominators and unity of American civilization. They have looked at the big picture. In forcing us to do so as well, they have brought about major breakthroughs in our knowledge of ourselves.

At the same time, the foreign writers have had the effect of reinforcing American provincialism: first, because from their bird's-eye view they have concentrated on the predominant White Anglo-Saxon Protestant culture; and also because, with the major exception of Tocqueville, we have in turn concerned ourselves almost exclusively with what the Anglo-Saxon commentators have had to say about us. *To whom* a civilization listens indicates much of *what* is important to it, and it is clear that, until recently, Americans have cared mostly about what Englishmen have thought of them and have placed a premium on British civilization. We are Anglophiles more than we would care to admit, and we have yet to declare our cultural declaration of independence from England.

Our affinity for England has been matched by an almost

‡ *The Fifties* originally was published as *Los Estados Unidos en escorzo* (1956) and *The Sixties* as *Analisis de los Estados Unidos* (1968).

total ignorance, if not avoidance, of Hispanic civilization.
Julián Marías points to this in Chapter 18, entitled "Provincialism," where he discusses the fifty-four volume *Great Books of the Western World* published by Encyclopedia Britannica. Of the seventy-four authors included in *Great Books*, twenty-five are Anglo-Saxon, while Cervantes alone represents all of Hispanic civilization. In the United States, Marías continues, "there is an overemphasis on Anglo-Saxon culture—going far beyond the inevitable and justifiable weighting in favor of one's own that is normal in every society."

Lack of interest in Hispanic civilization is especially evident in our attitude toward Spanish and Latin American commentators on the United States: most of us have never heard of them; their works have remained untranslated into English.

But this is changing. The appearance of Marías' writings on the United States follows on the heels of translations of the Caribbean's and South America's most important commentaries on the United States, written by Jose Martí and Domingo Faustino Sarmiento.‡ If America is now interested in reading what Hispanic writers have had to say about us, it is because Hispanic civilization itself is increasingly of interest to us. At the same time, a reordering of our notions about ourselves is taking place as part of which we are assigning greater significance to some of the heretofore "invisible" subcultures constituting these United States while reevaluating, and perhaps even downgrading, the significance of the Anglo-Saxon mainstream.

Attention to the subcultures of the United States is having a profound effect on current historical writing and on our geographical imagination. In the past, students of American

‡ *Marti on the U.S.A.*, trans. Luis A. Baralt (Southern Illinois University Press, 1966); *Sarmiento's Travels in the United States in 1847*, trans. Michael Aaron Rockland (Princeton University Press, 1970).

civilization were nearly obsessed with Puritan civilization and with the cradle of that civilization in the area around Boston. This obsession was an extension of the cultural apron strings which bound us to England and which are becoming increasingly frayed as "new" areas of the country, such as the Southwest and California, with their radically different civilizations, are becoming historically fashionable.

Paradoxically, the obsession with Puritan and Anglo-Saxon civilization has existed side by side with the conception of America as a melting pot. This is because, as we have seen increasingly in recent years, the melting pot has meant not so much a blending together into one of all the civilizations which make up the country, but a melting or absorption of the other civilizations by the predominant White Anglo-Saxon Protestant one. The melting pot offered full citizenship only to those who accepted White Anglo-Saxon Protestant values. One had to *melt* to join the melting pot.

Black people were the first to question the melting pot concept on a grand scale and to dramatize its conformist, if not totalitarian, aspects. After living for 350 years as aliens in America, Blacks, in the late fifties and early sixties, simultaneously began to recognize enhanced possibilities of acceptance by America and to question whether they really wanted acceptance if it meant assimilation. Militant Blacks rejected the dominant culture and began to do their own thing. "Just when we were almost white," they found, "it was better to be Black."

The gesture of the Blacks became the cutting edge of the Second, or Cultural, American Revolution in which we presently find ourselves. The most dramatic (and surely the most permanent) feature of this revolution has been the reemergence of pluralism and diversity when we were already convinced that our lot in the decades to come could only be increasing standardization and conformity. The melting pot is being replaced by the salad bowl as the dominant metaphor for American civilization. The salad, which replaces the stew or soup which presumably was in the melting pot, is made up of distinct, as opposed to homogenized, elements. Whether American unity can survive this newly emerging variety will be determined in the coming decades; but if it does, the United States will be a more interesting country.

Of course, the Blacks have not been alone in bringing about these changes in the way America perceives herself. The Hispanic communities in recent years have been particularly conscious of their separateness and have begun to engross the rest of us in their rhetoric and in their history. They have dramatized the extent to which all Americans share in an Hispanic legacy. There is a relationship between reading the Hispanic commentators on the United States today and our involvement on the domestic political scene with the needs and demands of Mexican Americans, Puerto Ricans, and Cubans. Increasingly viewing the Hispanic world as our own, we are beginning to read the Hispanic commentators on the United States precisely because what they have to say is not foreign but is, instead, central to our concerns.

Of those Hispanic commentators currently writing on the United States, none has so involved himself and written at such length and with such understanding as Julián Marías. And, luckily, since he is still vigorous and is a prolific writer, we have undoubtedly not heard the last from him on the subject. Born in 1914 in Valladolid, Marías studied with and was soon the principal disciple of Ortega y Gasset. Later he distinguished himself in his own right as a philosopher and, indeed, in recognition of his contributions to learning, he was named to the Spanish Royal Academy several years ago. Coming to intellectual maturity on the eve of the Spanish Civil War, he has, since that event, led a Pasternak-like existence in Spain, refusing exile but also avoiding association with the Franco regime, going so far as to decline offers of teaching positions at the University of Madrid. The object of criticism from both the Right and the Left, Marías has steadfastly aligned himself with a liberal Center which, in Spain today, has few open partisans. Almost alone, politically, in Spain, his annual lecture trips to the United States have, no doubt (partly because of his need to find a viable alternative to the regime he has coexisted with during the entirety of his adult life) been important to him for political and moral sustenance. Of course, the seesawing of American foreign policy vis-a-vis Spain during and since the Spanish Civil War has, over the years, been particularly trying, if not painful, to a man with Marías' views. However, he has been able to take some pleasure in seeing his philosophical works become standard texts in this country in recent years; and, together with his lectures, they have made him a familiar figure on our campuses since the early 1950s.

But what Americans have not known until now is the extent to which Marías has been studying and writing about us since that time—and with such splendid results! "There are places and countries that impel me to write about them," he exclaims on the first page of *The Sixties*, "and the United States moved my pen . . . from the very first weeks." It also inspired some of the best writing Julián Marías has done, not only as a philosopher, but as an artist. Few writers have described so well how things *feel* in the United States as, for example, in a sentence like, "In the deserted [railroad] station, muffled by the snow's cotton padding, a telephone rings away." The philosopher also is very much apparent in such sentences as "Do Americans smile because they are happy? Or in order to be happy?" and "Half the things that man has invented are to console him for having to die; the other half, to protect him from despair while he lives." Marías brings a formidable talent and versatility to his investigations into American uniqueness.

However, unlike most other European commentators, especially since the emergence of the United States as a superpower, Marías has not allowed his desire to say something unique about the country to compromise his objectivity. He approaches the United States without preconceptions. Whereas, as he tells us himself, "most travelers who come to New York from the other side of the Atlantic and then publish a book about the United States bring that book under their arms already written," Marías is unafraid to discover in the United States a country very much different from what Europeans and even Americans conventionally imagine about it:

> Ordinarily it is feared that life in the United States will be hectic, and it turns out, rather, that it is calm. People speak of the crowds, and actually the great danger that continually threatens is loneliness. There is the myth of the country's noise, but in two years I did not hear a radio in an adjoining house, and not infrequently I cocked my ear avidly to catch the sound of footsteps in the street.
>
> When one really understands the situation, what he finds deficient in the United States is not private life but, rather, social gatherings for conversation and the exchange of ideas. Instead of instability, he finds that what changes occur are not always, through a lack of imagination, profound enough. Far from seeing "imperialism" in the Americans, one discovers that they have but scant talent for leadership, insufficient in present circumstances; and also that they display too narrow a concept of themselves—a trait quite compatible with a certain annoying and disturbing self-sufficiency in directions where it is little justified.‡

Rather than reiterating that the United States is a place dominated by modernity, by the invasion of private life, and by aggressive materialism, Marías is charmed by "the flavor of age" he finds permeating the country, surprised by its "essential loneliness," and impressed by the basic spirituality of the

‡ In *As Others See Us*, ed. by Franz M. Joseph (Princeton, 1959), pp. 28–29.

American people who, in contrast to the Europeans, have already begun to reach a point of saturation in their desire for material goods. In our contemporary image of ourselves as an harrassed nation, Marías offers consolation by reminding us of aspects of the national life we tend to forget and which other European commentators have found it convenient to ignore.

Marías also differs from the majority of European commentators in his enthusiasm for the United States. Most European commentators seem to have achieved recognition in direct proportion to the strength of their criticism. Marías, on the other hand, "must confess, arch-European that I am, that, after making the attempt to live within that form of life —experiencing it from the inside—I found it endearing." When he was first invited to the United States in 1951, he was

> sure I would find many surprising things, different from the European, perhaps even valuable ones. What I did not anticipate was that those things would prove personally attractive to me. . . . It turned out . . . that scarcely had I arrived in the United States when I felt myself keenly attracted. Frequently I was amused, charmed, deeply and unexpectedly moved. Why? Simply because I discovered something that I had never been led to expect: in the first instance beauty; secondly poetry; and finally the charm of everyday life.‡

Not that he is an apologist for the United States. At one point he states: "Personally, I do not believe the United States to be superior . . . in many areas the advantage would be ours." It is in the United States, one suspects, that he has discovered what he likes about Spain: contesting the virtues and shortcomings of the Western World's most dynamic society with one of its most traditional ones, he declares the result a draw.

‡ *Ibid.*, pp. 26–27.

But although Marías' enthusiasm for the United States is not unqualified, in *The Fifties* he occasionally seems too intent on seeing the United States in a favorable light. As a visitor for the first time to the United States, he is overawed by the gadgets, drugstores, and other paraphernalia of the consumer society which are no longer novelties for us. Of course, considering the standard of living prevailing in Spain in the early 1950s, Marías' fascination for American material culture is understandable. Nevertheless, his treatment of the Negro is sometimes patronizing, sometimes naive (though, at the same time, peculiarly Spanish and European and, because of this, sometimes more realistic than Americans are capable of being), and it is difficult to agree with his contention that "the United States almost goes too far" in its commitment to equality and social justice. When he celebrates Thornton Wilder ("I hope for the imminent flowering of a movement in American letters, the most illustrious precursor of which might be Thornton Wilder's *Our Town*") at the expense of Evelyn Waugh (*The Loved One*, he tells us, is "impiously written, very misleading in its deliberate omission of all perspectives"), we realize how much Marías' sensibilities in the 1950s echo those of Middle America today.

Of course, when he tells us in *The Fifties* that "There is no poverty in the United States," or that "Many people in certain countries cannot forgive America for having received so much from her," we are shocked into the recognition that these very views were regarded as rather advanced among Americans in the 1950s. The reader of *The Fifties* will find embarrassing, if not painful, the extent to which views he held so short a time ago have already taken on an antique, if not *campy*, quality; he may well conclude that, of all historical periods, it is our most recent past with which we are least in touch and in sympathy. One great virtue in reading *The Fifties* today is its dramatization of how radically the conventional wisdom in this country has changed in only a decade and a half.

The Marías of *The Sixties* has become, like the rest of us, a different man. When he first came to the United States, Americans still had a great deal of innocence about their country and confidence in its future. "Above all else," he writes in *The Fifties*, "the United States is a country where confidence predominates." In the 1950s Americans had not yet "discovered" poverty, had not begun to acknowledge the pervasiveness of racism in their country, and were not spectacularly involved in and depressed about the most unfortunate war in their history. They were still doctrinaire believers in "progress" and did not see it as intimately linked with pollution. When Marías first came to the United States the present crisis in our institutions and in ourselves had not yet set in. *The Sixties* reflects this crisis.

In *The Fifties* Marías suggested that what distinguished Americans from other nationalities was their moderation, their tolerance, and their easy acceptance of compromise. "The exploitation of the spleen," by which he meant the tendency toward excessive argumentativeness, over-politicization, and divisiveness, was less evident in the United States than in almost any other country. "If the time ever comes when Americans truly look with mistrust at each other," he wrote, "what we think of as the United States is finished." In *The Sixties* it appears to Marías as if America's spleen has already become enlarged:

> When I first came to the United States a tone of complacency prevailed in the country. . . . Today, after a generation, the criticism raised by the United States about itself is so frequent, intense, broad, and publicized as to be unimaginable in other places. . . . Compared to the United States, *all* European and Latin American countries are incredibly conformist.

What has changed about Americans in the period between the early 1950s and the late 1960s is their temperament. "The propensity to criticism," Marías says, "has been developed." Criticism, of course, is necessary and beneficial, and Marías is pleased to find the complacency of the 1950s modified. What concerns him is the excessiveness of the criticism and the fear that it will destroy more than it will reform. Marías points out that "there were similar or even greater causes before and there was less criticism. Now criticism has become widespread even regarding matters where some general satisfaction would be in order." Having personally witnessed the excesses of the Left in the Spain of the 1930s bring on the massive repression of the Right, Marías fears that the United States, like the Spanish Republic, may be losing its balance. After all, he exclaims in the Epilogue to this volume, written in 1970, "Almost everything *real* is better than before." An optimist, Marías feels that not only are most of America's problems of her own creation: some are even products of her imagination. He does not, however, lightly dismiss these problems: in the Epilogue he writes that "certain dark clouds, threatening and seemingly borne closer by the wind, now hover ominously over this land and darken its sky." But the dark clouds are at least partly the product of the "budding belief" that, regardless of obvious improvements in the United States in recent years, the situation is somehow worse. "And if people continue to believe it," Marías warns, "it *will* be worse."

Nevertheless, Marías sees a light at the end of the tunnel of present despair. "The United States," he writes, "like Cervantes, prefers the journey to the destination, the road to the inn." The present ferment, even the exaggerated self-depreciation which has been its by-product, is all part of the one constant in the American experience: the almost obsessive commitment to change.

Marías has an intriguing thesis about change in America.

"At times," he writes, "I think that *everything* changes so much in order that the *country itself not change*. . . . For if only a certain thing were to change . . . this would cause a *disfiguration*." The United States changes, therefore, "so as not to change fundamentally."

So, although Marías is presently concerned about the United States, he is still basically hopeful about her future. Being a philosopher who bets on mankind's possibilities, he is particularly committed to the success of the United States which, in the last chapter of *The Sixties*, he calls "the prow" of the Western World. At a time when malaise is so widespread in the United States, reading Julián Marías can be a very good tonic for Americans. He awakens a sense of wonder about our country, and confidence in its future, which we have been too fatigued of late to feel by ourselves.

MICHAEL AARON ROCKLAND

PART ONE

THE FIFTIES

Translated from the Spanish* by
Blanche De Puy

* First published as *Los Estados Unidos en escorzo* (Buenos Aires: Emecé, 1956). The translation is taken from Volume III of the *Obras Completas* of Julián Marías (Madrid: *Revista de Occidente*), published in 1964.

PREFACE

This book springs from personal experience: three stays in the
United States—in the east and in the west—the first of a year's
duration, the second and third, a semester each. This experience has nothing to do with traveling, because I was not a
tourist; nor is it concerned primarily with the exercise of a
profession, even though during those periods I was a professor
at Wellesley College, Harvard, the University of California
at Los Angeles, and Yale. No, the point is that for a certain
time I *lived* in the United States, so when I speak of years and
semesters, you must understand that I mean fragments of my
life.

What I am trying to say is that the United States represents
something that actually *happened* to me—and for that reason
something that will in some way stay with me always. The
traveler never really lives in the country he visits; his life is
temporarily suspended and he is limited to a kind of tangential
contact with the foreign world through which he passes "in
transit" but in which he is never at home. That is why a trip
—this also explains its potential pleasures—is always a vacation. Professional activity in a strange country likewise is
often carried on without establishing any real relationship to
the place in question: there are many European professors
who for long years perhaps have been located not in the
United States but in their respective departments—of Spanish,
French, German, Biology, or Art—which just happen to be
situated in America.

Such has not been the case with me. I first went to the
United States thanks to an unexpected invitation from
Wellesley College. The drift of my personal affairs at the time
was not carrying me toward North America. I was strongly
convinced that the United States does represent a reality

which must be comprehended in order to understand the world in which we live, but such a possibility was not within the foreseeable limits of my horizon. When an immediate opportunity presented itself, however, after a moment's hesitation, I accepted it. About that time—in the spring of 1951 —I had already decided to take a brief trip to Peru and Colombia during the coming summer; as I was en route to South America, I had to fly over the United States—Boston and New York—for a few brief hours. From the plane I looked down with great curiosity at the city of Boston, its port and its surrounding countryside, at all that was to be, a few months later, my world for the space of a year. Yes, with curiosity and with a bit of anxiety, for there are sufficiently few years in a life-span for one year to loom large and importantly. How would that strange world seem when seen from within? I questioned the landscape as one scrutinizes the features of a face, and its traits gave me a reassuring answer: yes, it probably would be possible to live twelve months on that piece of the planet.

When I arrived once more in the fall, not to pass through this time but to remain, all that unfamiliar world began tentatively to be mine: first, Wellesley; from there, neighboring Boston and Cambridge; then all of Massachusetts, the whole of New England, and the Atlantic states from Vermont to Florida. By now, after each trip through those regions, the return to Boston was a homecoming. My life was creating itself there, being made, day by day, among the features of that world—trees, houses, sunny days and snowy ones—and among its people; evolving now not only from my own essence but through the experience that I inescapably carried with me. Later the same story was repeated when I returned to the States, crossing the country this time from East to West and in various other directions—Illinois, Ohio, Wisconsin, Minnesota, Utah—and took up daily life in California; and still again when I lived once more in the now familiar

Atlantic states, and another time when I had a window on the South from Louisiana.

These are the reasons why I say that the United States *happened* to me. And all this transpired as I spent my time living an American kind of life—without, of course, trying to convert myself into an American (which would be a dangerous self-deception), without ceasing to be both a Spaniard and a European. This trial of American life was a question actually of making myself at home therein, of transferring myself wholly into a new manner of life with all its resources, its desires, its expectations. In other words, I attempted to overcome the loneliness of the outlander and to arrive at companionship with someone alien and strange, with "the other." But, of course, this is the process we call *friendship*: to be companionable with someone who is not and can never be the same as oneself, to use one's imagination in order to understand him, to feel the live warmth of his hand in our clasp, to be left with a prick of pain and nostalgia when bidding him goodbye, and to know that one now can never entirely forget him. These pages are then the story of my friendship with the United States.

Julián Marías

Wellesley—Madrid—
Los Angeles—New Haven,
October 1951—June 1956

1 THE EUROPEAN IN THE UNITED STATES

Each day ships and planes cross the Atlantic and deposit their human cargo on the docks and airstrips of America. A majority of these passengers find themselves in a new world very different from the one they have just left behind. The impression produced—whether on a man or a woman—varies considerably according to a person's country of origin, his age and condition in life, the expectations with which he has arrived in the United States, and, naturally, it depends also upon the regions and levels of society that he encounters. Many of these men and women keep their impressions to themselves, unexpressed, or allow them to serve some purely personal end. Others, on the contrary, capable of giving form to their impressions, make them explicit; thus they possess not only the mute impression but also its manifest expression or, in other words, an interpretation of the United States. Some, lastly, share this interpretation, extend it to others, perhaps write it down and publish it. The latter are usually of an intellectual bent: writers, journalists, teachers, artists, politicians, diplomats, researchers, technicians, businessmen. It is these Europeans—much more than Americans themselves—who project an image of the United States in Europe, and it is that image with which we Europeans prefer to deal. The meaning that the expression or nametag "United States" has for us arises chiefly from the accumulation of such interpretations that has been offered us. Finally, this composite concept becomes a mirror in which Americans see themselves portrayed: apart from their own manner of conceiving or of understanding themselves, their own way of living, their own reflections of themselves, they encounter this other image, beamed back to them from the far side of the Atlantic, and it affects their own realities far more than is common-

ly thought. Thus the impression the European is beginning
to form as he passes through the triple barrier of the Departments of Health and Immigration and the smiling and
meticulous United States Customs does acquire a certain
importance.

Underlying all other differences, the one which seems most
important to me with respect to European visitors in North
America is the time factor. Some "take a trip," that is, they
pass briefly through certain cities or areas of the country.
Others stay for some time, that is, they reside temporarily in
the United States. A third group is comprised of those who
definitely establish themselves or, at least, plan to stay indefinitely. The European image of the United States is a
product mainly of the first group for two reasons: because
the first is the most numerous and because it is customarily
made up of people who go, whether for professional motives
or not, to *see* America and to talk about it. The third group,
because its members do remain in the United States keeping
less in touch with their European origins, contributes less
than either of the others to the formation of the European's
image.

Almost all the books I had ever read on the United States
left me with a feeling of dissatisfaction. After having resided
there, I confess that the dissatisfaction has frequently turned
into downright irritation. Why so? What is the explanation
for their deficiencies? There are two chief sources of trouble:
the information presented and the author's prior assumptions.
Let me begin with the first, less important factor. What is
most surprising in almost all such books on the United States
is the paucity of information on what the author saw. Anecdotes are recounted, statistical data are provided, what certain people have said is duly reported: in other words, the
author fills many pages with material that he could easily
have put together in Europe, saving himself the crossing. Is
all this because information is hard to come by? In general,

the answer is "yes" in two senses. Taking the first sense—quantitatively the less significant one—the majority of those who write about the United States have spent only a few weeks in the country—sufficient time, of course, to do what one does in other places, see the historical monuments. But in the United States there are scarcely any monuments to see and those that do exist are generally uninteresting. The hurried visitor usually sees hotels—which are more or less the same everywhere—various means of transportation, which in such a large country use up a considerable amount of available time, and certain "picturesque" features: the skyscrapers, some huge factory, a couple of places of entertainment such as a drive-in movie, and a Negro quarter. Such a traveler also sees the passing landscape—generally, only at one season of the year and thus fixed and unchanging—through his plane window or better yet from a train or a car. But how about the streets? Yes, of course; but it must be borne in mind that the American street does not serve the same purposes as its European counterpart. It is not, for example, a place to walk, far less a background *pour flâner*; and it is only fully comprehensible, therefore really visible, when it is part of the life of someone capable of taking account of its own peculiar functions, when the passer-by *uses* it, and thus brings into relief and clarifies its properties.

And so we come to the second sense in which information is precarious: human life can only be understood from an inside point of view, never when it is considered merely as a spectacle. This is why being a tourist reveals something to us about a given pattern of life only when that pattern coincides in general with the one already familiar to us. This is the case, more or less, within the various countries of Western Europe and to some extent—but only *partially*, and one can fall into serious error by forgetting that point—within the countries of the Hispanic world. American life in both halves of the hemisphere has developed structures very different from those of Europe; in the case of the United States, these differences are of the essence. What one "sees" is disorienting because it is only possible to understand these structures by living within them; if one projects over them another life pattern such as one's own, one misunderstands them because then one sees something different from what is there. For that reason, as I have said before, a valid view of the United States requires a considerable amount of time and, even more important, a true immersion in the new forms. What I imply by that is an effective participation in the functioning of all phases of life: earning money, having a house and running it, buying, traveling, going back and forth from one place to another, having neighbors, making friends, and above all working.

A small instance may perhaps make clearer what I wish to say. If there is anything that theoretically can be done anywhere at all, without ever leaving home, it is to read the newspapers of any given country. However, reading American newspapers in Madrid or in Paris is an entirely different matter from doing the same reading in a city of the United States. Because a newspaper is not an autonomous entity: after all it has its role along with all other papers, it articulates with the other media of communication, and each paper represents something particular and peculiar within a given segment of life. The European reader tends to project onto the American paper his image of its European counterpart. An immediate consequence is that he credits it with more importance than it actually has in the United States. Besides, the European assumes that the relative weight of the various elements in American life to which the paper refers corresponds to their importance in Europe, or else to the amount of space dedicated to them by the daily paper, not realizing that a newspaper is by now almost everywhere an attention-getting device or system dealing preferentially with certain matters considered to be particularly "newsworthy." For example, a reader would be mistaken if he believed that politics play as significant a rôle in American life as in that of Europe, or as important a one as that described in the daily papers of the United States. The same is true of the reader who thinks that the limited amount of newspaper space given over to literature is an indication that literature doesn't count in the United States, when the fact is that it counts in another way, and in another sector of that life.

A further example illustrates even more distinctly the difficulties engendered by undigested information: let's take the question of the American economy and standard of living. Everyone knows that the standard of living in the United States is much higher than anywhere else, and besides, any recent arrival in the country can see that this is so. But this coarse statement of fact should be refined, and herein lies the problem. If we start with average income in the United States, the impression of wealth is overwhelming: an average monthly wage of less than $300. is very rare, and it is not too difficult to find an average of $800., or even of $1000. or $1500.—without yet mentioning certain highly-paid professions such as medicine or big business—all of which means that in Spain the comparable range would be from 15,000 to 80,000 *pesetas* monthly. Of course, the land of milk and honey! But look at the other side of the ledger: a traveler takes the subway in New York or the bus in Boston and the minimum fare costs him 15 cents, or about 8 *pesetas*; as he glances casually at a display window on Broadway he sees a man's fur hat, a millionaire's whim, with a price tag of $100. The poor traveler decides that hat would infallibly produce an automatic headache and, the next moment, reflects that there is no such place as El Dorado; that prices in the United States are correspondingly as high as incomes; and that the final outcome must therefore be much the same as everywhere else. Is this conclusion justified? Not at all. Because as a matter of fact many prices—independently of any relation to income—are very little higher or are *even lower* than in Spain, including the pricetags on normal, ordinary hats. A college professor can buy a new automobile, the latest model, for four months' salary; or for two months' if he can be satisfied with a three-year-old used car. A secretary can buy a luxurious fur wrap with two months' pay; with a year's salary she could achieve the maximum degree of ostentation—a mink coat! Display windows on the Gran Vía of Madrid are filled with many objects that cost more—regardless of other factors, I repeat—than those offered in New York, Boston, Washington, or Philadelphia, and this despite the fact that Spanish average incomes are 10 to 15 per cent of their American counterparts.

Where do we stand? A seeming Utopia viewed as a mirage which quickly disappears, and then reappears. The traveler, faced with hotel bills, sporadic shopping trips, entertainment and invitations, slips easily into a state of tremendous confusion from which he could only be rescued by a team of economists or several months of actual living in America under entirely normal conditions. Only as he attempts to plan a budget and live within it can he investigate in fact the American standard of living, what one can allow oneself and what is beyond reach, what privations and what treats are threaded into life. A tourist may only choose between intelligent perplexity and insolent error.

I stated earlier that defective information was the less important factor and that the most serious problem in most European books about North America has to do with the authors' presuppositions. What are these underlying assumptions? Is it possible to reduce them to some kind of unity despite the diversity among authors with regard to country of origin, intellectual background, and political bias? I shall try to list some of the assumptions, the more persistent and pertinent ones, that seem to me to contribute most heavily to the creation of the United States' image in Europe.

The first presupposition—parent to all the rest—is that one already knows all about the United States. There is no more deeply rooted conviction. Even the authors who pretend surprise usually do so only to highlight the fact that they were really already party to the secret. This is the most telling reason why such books as those to which I refer say little of what the author sees and a great deal of what he knows or opines. I have just finished reading an essay on American cities produced by one of France's first-rate contemporary writers. In it he speaks of speed in construction work, of the rapid rate of city growth, of the temporary quality of cities —the facility with which Americans replace or displace them —all things which no one can witness during a stay of six weeks in the United States. On the other hand, he never mentions the vegetation which fills American cities, which indeed constitutes them and lends them all their character. Well and good, it is difficult to familiarize oneself with the United States; not only does one *not* know all about it without having to budge from Europe, but even after some length of time when one has managed to learn a few things, it is still necessary to count up exactly what one does not know—how much is lacking, how much is not mastered and filed in one's hip pocket. Naturally, mistaken belief in prior knowledge paralyzes all fresh investigation and invalidates even the accurate information which one may absorb *velis nolis*, because all data are forcibly lodged under the shelter of the a priori ideas from which one departed. I have met Europeans who, after residing ten or twenty years in the United States, still remained faithful to the image they brought with them, although that image might have been given the lie a thousand times over by the real facts, and despite the enormous changes which came about during those decades.

Other presuppositions, and principal components of this prior knowledge, may be summarized as follows: lack of originality, emphasis on modernity, colossalism, uniformity,

vulgarity. The inevitable consequence, completing the chain
and linking it to the initial assumpton, is lack of interest. But
all these assumptions are eminently arguable. The fact that
the United States has a European heritage does not indicate
any lack of originality. I believe, on the contrary, that something essentially and vigorously new has slowly been produced there—but not being any kind of concrete, tangible
thing, it is difficult to see—a way of life. The unassailable fact
that America has a relatively brief history does not imply
modernity in the sense of a timeless living for the moment:
again for me, on the contrary, the United States held a flavor
of age, as though permeated by history. And if one affirms
that in the context of the Modern Age this is a modern country, is that admissible? Is there any sense to a Modern Age in
a place where there were no Middle Ages? And so we see to
what point we can debate this presumed modernity, a concept
usually considered obvious and old hat. With regard to
colossalism, though evident certainly in some aspects of life,
it is counterbalanced by such a tally of areas and aspects in
which just the opposite occurs that inevitably it becomes
necessary to reconsider the opinion. Against New York,
Chicago, or Los Angeles, one must put the reminder that
four-fifths of all Americans live in small towns. And this is
the way it goes on all scores.

It is undeniable that many things are standardized in the
United States, identical throughout the entire country—"na-
tionwide," as they say: I have held that it is this very
uniformity in elements or objects familiar to the whole enormous country that forms the basis for its unity, and that these
well-known standard features are what really tie the country
together. Clearly this uniformity brings to the fore certain
similarities in the inhabitants, but from that admission to the
platitude that Americans are mass-produced, there is quite a
distance to leap. According to the image popular in Europe,
Americans are practically identical, or at least interchange-

able; repeatedly European authors have stressed the "impersonal" quality in the beauty of American women, suggesting that one is therefore as good as another. (And lately some try to convince us that such beauty as there is is in short supply besides.) If one discounts the element of ill-humor in this accusation of sameness, what remains is the real semblance of men and women who belong to an established society. To a stranger, the children of a given family all look alike because what the outside observer notices above all is the family resemblance; seen at close range, these children look no more alike than do any other brothers and sisters. There are indeed two pressures toward uniformity in the North American species of humanity that are not often taken into account: the first is that, thanks to adequate means, hygienic resources, sanitation, and nourishment, one sees much less frequently here than elsewhere biologically defective human beings, the abnormal, the lamentable cases. (They exist, of course, but in lesser numbers; one can spend months without seeing such a case, and in some cities they simply do not appear.) Second, in Europe one of the factors that makes for great differences—group differences, that is, not differences among individuals—is the considerable distance maintained between social levels: in the United States, the distances are far shorter. In Spain, for example, the difference between a fashionable lady of the upper classes and her cleaning woman is enormous; in the United States much less so, not because the upper level is lower, but because the inferior level is extraordinarily higher—and not only from the standpoint of economics. In other words, the tremendous distances between social groups is attenuated in North America. (In many South American countries the differences are even greater than in Europe, and this alone is enough to explain why the two Americas resemble each other so little). In the United States, nevertheless, fashionable ladies, department store clerks, carpenters, truck drivers, or priests are not any more homogeneous within their own groups than are their counterparts in any country of Europe.

All this automatically explains the stereotype of vulgarity: the hurried traveler demands of one and all, given the generally high human level each has attained, the last word in refinement—something which in his own country he would be very careful not to expect except in a few hundred select persons—and when he is disappointed, he declares that everyone is without taste.

To these general characteristics of most books written about the United States, we must add two more. One we might call the "sophism of the accidental" or, less pedantically, the search for the picturesque detail. Certain authors select some existing detail of American life which appears amusing or unusual to them and focus all their attention upon it without questioning—or at least without informing the reader—what place that detail may have in the total picture. This is what happens in Evelyn Waugh's book, *The Loved One*, about certain cemeteries in California, and what was common in certain books twenty years ago that insisted monotonously on speakeasies and Prohibition. It is the equivalent of what we call *La españolada* in books about Spain which talk exclusively about bull-fights and gypsies—real elements which certainly do exist but which matter not at all to some twenty million Spaniards.

The other phenomenon, of rather recent vintage, is a certain resentment felt towards the United States. Many people in certain countries cannot forgive America for having received so much from her: in independence, in economic resources, in potential. Others are in too great a hurry to declare Europe superior to North America. Personally, I do not believe the United States to be superior either—in many areas the advantage would be ours—but I cannot deny that a peremptory proclamation of superiority such as this: "between the two barbarisms, Russian and American, our exquisitely civilized refinement . . . etc." causes me to react with a flood of distrust. A man who is sure of himself is not bothered by competition: quite the contrary, he is not distressed to learn that someone comparable to him exists in the Western World. (The same sort of thing is happening with some countries of the New World who are trying to hand old Europe her severance pay and relegate her to a glorious past.)

The outcome of all this is that in the great majority of European books on the subject, the United States is simply not interesting. And since these books deal with the subject of the United States, they themselves turn out to be uninteresting. To tell the truth, I cannot understand how people of intellectual bent who would give a right arm (perhaps even a vital organ) to be able to contemplate the beginnings of the Roman Empire do not, however, feel any stirring of interest in the formative stages of one of the three or four most formidable creations that in all history it has been man's privilege to observe—a creation which, by great good fortune, is happening directly within range of our distracted vision.

2 GLASS HOUSES

In the United States houses are made of glass. The ancient dream has been realized, and the *limping devil** would have very little trouble. But, the European reader may ask, how is that possible? No one has said they are, it hasn't been in the newspapers, and the movies are proof to the contrary.

---

* *El diablo cojuelo* (1641) is a picaresque novel written by Luis Vélez De Guevara in which a limping demon lifts the roofs of houses so that the reader may observe the goings-on inside—Trans.

Anyway, he may add skeptically, they're probably only made of plastic. And, as a matter of fact, the houses look to be made of wood: when you pound on them, your fist produces a friendly and familiar sound; people live haunted by the specter of fire and so they are on the alert, ready with an exterior iron fire-escape—and if they don't have that. . . . In my house, as I entered the bedroom the first thing I saw was a thick rope coiled and hanging from a stout iron ring; I must confess that I was startled. Is it possible, I thought, that maintenance service is so well organized that even desperation is planned for in advance? Can it be that this device will allow a man to hang himself comfortably at home on his first impulse, rather than having to go to the hardware store or "Five and Ten" to buy a rope with the attendant risk that something or other—the splendor of an autumn-colored tree, the latest model refrigerator, or the smile of a girl who passes by—might reconcile him to living and make him change his mind? No, that wasn't it: the rope was there in case of fire, to slide down to the ground after first reading the instructions.

The houses look to be made of wood, and incidentally, they are charming; I mean the ones which first became part of our inner consciousness when we saw Thornton Wilder's *Our Town*. We began to sense something of the profound poetry of the American cities—of which scarcely anything has been said, of which it is time to speak. It was, to be precise, in a movie-house that I first realized that our quarters were made of glass. It was the first United States movie that I had seen in its own sauce, so to speak; an insipid film like so many others in which the houses were the same as have appeared a thousand times on all the screens of the world, with their two storys, their lawn, and a grumbling but cordial grandfather who is slowly pruning an elm tree or a horse chestnut. But before entering the house, before the camera focused on the interior, I had already seen it; and when the bustling mother went to the refrigerator to take out things for breakfast, I saw without her opening the door all that was in it, all that she was going to remove: tomato juice, a receptacle made of thin wax-covered cardboard with a small opening at the top from which a cuckoo's head might feasibly emerge but instead comes a white stream of pasteurized milk, the tray where a dozen eggs are resting each in its own compartment, and a cellophane filing folder—yes, a folder—where the sumptuous slices of bacon lie shimmering. Everything is transparent, everything is made of glass, everything is the same as in my house or in that of any of the spectators. They tell about the man who when he heard the roar of the Metro-Goldwyn Mayer lion, exclaimed impatiently: "I've already seen this movie about the lion," and walked out of the theatre. That was my feeling exactly, and I did as he did. I had already seen that movie.

A little more than a month ago a friend of mine, an admirable Argentine lady with clear and curious eyes, was using them rather furtively, blushing a bit, to peer through the lighted windows of the old quarter of Madrid—Calle de Puñon Rostro, Plaza del Conde de Barajas, Calle de la Pasa, Plazuela de San Javier—and she excused her indiscretion by explaining to me that she took great delight in interiors, in surprising life in moments of unpremeditated spontaneity. Since I have always been a victim of the same disease, it was no effort for me to understand and justify her conduct. But here in America no one has to peer inside because everyone already knows how everything will be and the insignificant walls really hide nothing at all.

Everything is made of glass, then. Everything? Faces and foreheads included? That's the belief in Europe, at any rate. And there are the magazines which put out five million copies; the films which are showing simultaneously in all the movie-houses; the commercials which indefatigably give the same advice to fifty million people; radio and television, both of which penetrate every single house and every apartment in every large city. All these well-known channels toward uniformity must of necessity permit us, within certain limits, of course, to prefigure what lies hidden behind the American's smile. Yes, but after much reflection, that is, after repeating over and over what many others have thought—all of which means falling into a practice highly disdained in Europe—one does not come out with any feeling of satisfaction. The question arises as to whether this is all true, whether things really are just that way; and even if they were, would it be admissible simply to note the fact and let it go? Doesn't the situation rather invite us peremptorily to take a few steps forward, to attempt to see whether it all really does work this way, and if so, why and to what purpose? As the Archpriest of Hita said some six hundred years ago, if I remember correctly: "Let's peel off the rind and get to the sweetmeat."* And since, fortunately enough, the skin is made of glass this time, it may well be worthwhile to go looking for trouble, to allow our eyes the pleasure of truly enjoying the transparency.

3   THE FAMILIAR SHARED

Millions upon millions. Millions of dollars, of course, but above all of people and, therefore, of all kinds of objects. And this is the decisive factor: one of the underlying assumptions of American life is that the majority can't be wrong. "Do as a million others do, buy X shirts," says one advertisement. Often a cigarette is touted simply as being the best-selling brand, and this is considered a sufficient proof of its excellence. And it is a known fact that a book which sells in quantity—a "best-

---

* Juan Ruiz, Archpriest of Hita, (1283?–1350?), author of the classic *Libro De Buen Amor*—Trans.

seller"—is for that reason a good book, and one which will therefore keep on selling, a kind of snowball effect managed by the publishing industry. A million identical copies are made of every object manufactured, and these are on display simultaneously again and again all over the country. The movies go over and over a limited repertory of topics, of emotions, of compelling gestures, or at least of gestures considered to be attractive which therefore have the same force as though they were authentic. All the fabulous apparatus of the advertising agencies serves to render certain persons—relatively few in number—very well known, naturally with traits that are at once homogeneous and distinctive. What I mean to say is that on one hand there exists notoriety or celebrity, and on the other an interpretation, or at best a pair of contrary interpretations (this is especially so in the case of a politician) both of which are so familiar that as a consequence they neither complicate nor interfere with a train of thought. Yet together with this phenomenon, the American feels some obscure uneasiness about his gregariousness—which in another light he cherishes—and thus aspires to "personalize" himself. "Your personal product," whispers the ad for a make-up used by something more than three million young women. "Personalize your lighter or your handbag," and the personalization consists of attaching to the standard product some initials (which, by the way, usually cost more than the original object). The only problem is that since the initials themselves are standardized, they should really be personalized themselves, and so on *ad infinitum*.

Now this degree of homogeneity usually produces on the European countenance a disdainful smirk of superiority. We've seen the same expression flourish on hundreds of pairs of lips belonging respectively to French writers, German professors, English politicians, Spanish journalists—especially when the latter do their reporting without budging from Barcelona or Madrid. So it becomes a standard smirk: anything can be contagious. Sometimes one is tempted to ask them to personalize it!

And thus the question arises as to whether that European expression is truly European, that is to say, whether it is intelligent. (Because Europe represents Intelligence.) Understand me, please: I am not saying that the European is *ipso facto* intelligent—unhappily the way things are going, just the opposite seems to be true—but rather that Europe has no other salvation than to be intelligent, that it cannot permit itself the luxury or the comfort of not being intelligent because it has no other hope; and therefore stupidity is treason, a crime of "*lèse-Europeanism*." It might be worth our while to consider, if only for a few moments, this uniformity and homogeneity of life in the United States, and to attempt to analyze what these qualities mean and what purposes they serve.

To me, the outcome seems apparent: it is all a matter of insuring overlap of experience through a repertory of shared familiar elements. Try to imagine what we mean by the United States. (The first thing to do, like Lope with his list of precepts, is to lock up with six keys all ideas that have to do with European countries, because this is literally, another world.*) Its area is slightly less than that of Europe, according to the books, but if you subtract Russia, which is another kettle of fish, and hold to the countries which, outside Geography class, we really envisage as European, then the area of the United States becomes almost twice that of Europe. And peopling that vast surface are more than 160 million inhabitants of various origins who began by speaking different languages, people of the most disparate races, religions and customs, with a national past of a maximum of three centuries and in many regions of the country only one or two centuries.

* Lope Félix De Vega Carpio (1562–1635), one of Spain's greatest dramatists, affirmed in a manual in verse called *El arte nuevo de hacer comedias* (*The New Art of Playwriting*): "Cuando he de escribir una comedia/encierro los preceptos con seis llaves." (When I must write a play/I lock up the rules with six keys.)—Trans.

Isn't it worthwhile to ask what it is that holds these people together? Or is it such a simple matter to weld millions of people into a nation? In Europe, "these great bodies which are the nations," as Descartes put it, have been evolving step by step, gestating like some kind of organism in the dark womb of the enormous and delicate Middle Ages; they have been crystallizing like small gemstones, they have been incarnated century after century in their kings: and despite all that. . . .

The uniformities which call forth a smile on frivolous lips are the artifacts and products of a colossal, creative, historical enterprise. Shell, Kodak, Freud, Clark Gable, Einstein, Gillette, MacArthur, the 5,200,000 copies of *Life*, Camels, the Constitution, the sculpted and rhythmical legs of Ginger Rogers, the Pilgrim Fathers, Ford, Bob Hope, Cardinal Spellman, the Corn Flakes of Mr. Kellogg (who died at ninety-odd after having furnished hundreds of millions of Americans with their breakfasts); all of this is familiar to everyone and known by each one to be familiar to all the rest. This is the familiar shared. And this repertory of shared familiar experiences which operates automatically creates the underlying assumptions which support the life in common of the New York Jew who has just arrived from Poland, the Arizona rancher, and the Texas cowpoke in San Antonio whose name is Fernandez, spelled, of course, without its Spanish accent. Thanks to all these different shared, familiar elements, which range from the venerable to the grotesque, thanks to the Bible and the characters created by Walt Disney, thanks to an elementary faith in democracy and an equally elementary admiration for the aggressive bosom of a certain actress, to the automatic obedience to traffic regulations, and to certain decisive moral standards, the United States today stands as the *United* States. As things are today, that fact would seem to have a certain interest. And it perhaps guarantees that a smile is still possible on both sides of the Atlantic.

4 THINGS, DEATH, AND THE DEVIL

Every day the world grows fuller of man's manufacturing. Nature is about to be covered over and supplanted by a layer of artificial objects. At the dawn of the Renaissance, the kings of Castile could still improvise a palace with a few furs, some cushions for the ladies, and a brace of tapestries to hang on the austere walls of Coca, Turégano, Madrigal, Segovia, Tordesillas, or Medina. They were not too far as yet from the bedouin's tent, as quickly pitched as folded. Afterwards, things became more complicated, but we Europeans are still only halfway between carefree Arabia and blessed America. We all know how many objects, apparatuses, gadgets, and utensils have been invented and put into use in the United States; any newspaper or magazine overwhelms us with proof, but when one actually sees these things in operation, when one takes in the enormous number there are of them—only a tiny fraction appears in the ads—then one can begin to measure their influence and scope.

What ends do these devices and objects serve? Of course, each one has its own purpose: an elevator chair on which the lady of the house goes up and down along the bannister from one floor to another; a magnetized box in which to put house keys and then hide in some strange corner; a gadget that measures the number of miles one has walked during the day; another that provides the motorist with a cigarette it has lighted and puffed on three times; an alarm clock that wakes us not with a grim bell but with winks of light and, if we are invincible sleepers, decides to try a melody that should predispose us to wake up smiling; and also a device to open boiled eggs, and another to press garlic, thus eliminating its Celto-Iberian crudities. A whole book could be filled just by listing all these ingenious gadgets. All of which means that an American hardware store is one of the most enjoyable and amusing places on the planet.

But my question is of a different order. What are all these objects good for? That is, what purpose do they serve in their totality, in their crushing superabundance, within the way of life that both produces and consumes them? There is no use attempting a utilitarian explanation because even if it were revealing, it would be less than definitive. These gadgets and accessories represent the height of superfluity; no one wants them except when he sees them; they are beyond our craving and very likely it is they themselves that arouse our appetites. At this point, one's mind grabs on to that idea as though it were a life-line. That's it! It's all a question of luxury, of the excessive economic well-being characteristic of the United States. Industry, based upon the demands of ever-increasing production, hurls forth new objects to be desired as a consequence by millions of American consumers. All this is undoubtedly true; but it is, I fear, nothing more than a secondary truth. Being truths, they quiet us; but being subsidiary, they also allow the substance of whatever we are trying to comprehend to escape us.

Obviously the question we should have posed is that of why American luxury consists of gadgets. This is not the first time in history that luxury appears as a phenomenon in society; indeed I believe that today's version can scarcely compare with the standards of Rome, the Renaissance, or the seventeenth century. The difference is that this time luxury is majoritarian, and in this fact lies its novelty. I have wondered over and over about the mysterious virtue of such gadgets, and therefore have searched for their purpose over and above their own specific use.

What all the American devices, accessories, and paraphernalia have is—a plot. Just as novels do or plays; or as does life itself. Their tremendous profusion converts their acquisition and enjoyment into a step-by-step enterprise of great fascination. The average American sees before him a broad horizon of possibilities for acquisition; a walk through the streets window-shopping or simply a weekly perusal of the Sunday paper is equivalent to all the forces of temptation deployed in a painting by Bosch. (Parenthetically, could it be merely a coincidence that Bosch's name should have lighted here on this page?) The first impulse—the one which Catholic theology sagely grants is innocent and not sinful—is to buy each and every thing in sight since all that is offered is usually most entertaining. Second thought, which takes the form of adding up dollars and pricetags, restrains the primary impulse and converts it into a long-term project. First comes the refrigerator, then the television; in February those pillows that seem to be made of the very foam from which Venus emerged; in the Spring, remodeling the kitchen—one of the sacred places in American life—though it then may be necessary to wait until fall to trade in the car.

But, the European asks himself, whatever for? Isn't the car comfortable, luxurious, very roomy, fast, safe, in perfect condition with bright paint and shining metal work? Why change cars? And here we come to the heart of the matter. Despite their prodigious number, American objects are nonetheless finite; they multiply like rabbits, but they can still all be counted. I was struck by the ad: "The ideal gift for the man who has everything." Could it be possible? Could there actually be unfortunate souls who had reached the outermost limit of the possibilities? And at that moment I realized I had uncovered the American beggar, the indigent American: he is not the man who has nothing, but rather the one who has everything, the one who lacks incentive. One cannot imagine greater poverty, and I shivered compassionately as one does before the conventional picture of the ragged man in the snow who devours with his eyes all that he sees in the shop window. But for these American needy, the spirit of charity has invented "the newest model." And, besides, a magic word, one of the four or five secret well-springs of American character: *features*. In most dictionaries, *feature* means trait or distinctive characteristic; but when speaking of a gadget, its *features* are its possibilities, its refinements, its new resources, its accumulation of improvements, or, in a few words, its power of attraction. The machine on which I type has more *features* than any other because it is the latest model. An American would use it with pleasure; but within a few months some obscure malaise would seize him: he would have seen in a magazine that next year's model was out and that it had two new *features* which this machine does not possess, and that in America is one guise in which unhappiness appears. The only cure is to acquire the newer model as soon as possible. Thus affairs go into gear, thus the secret of perpetual motion has been discovered, and so doors open onto the good life.

Objects thus displayed, like promises to be fulfilled one by one, are a great consolation, and life needs always to console itself since at best it is a constant struggle to throw up dikes and build protective walls in a vale of tears. These objects serve also as a means to avoid thinking about death. As do all diversions—you will say. Yes, but other diversions, the European variety, seem to take us right back to death, though perhaps via a detour; and it is true that in America people think less about dying than anywhere else. (Can you imagine Unamuno* in the United States? What a topic for a fantasy or a novel!) Of course, death does arrive here as well as in other places; but year after year the charitable gadgets—perhaps they are pious traitors—distract one's thoughts from the inevitable end. And from the devil who also is conspicuous by his absence—and who, when he does dare appear, must disguise himself as a psychoanalyst. It is true, of course, that

* Miguel de Unamuno (1864–1936), poet, novelist, essayist and philosopher, Rector of the University of Salamanca. Preoccupied obsessively with the problems of death and immortality—Trans.

the devil continues to be ostracized the world over; death has been rehabilitated and even has publicity agents among the existentialists, but the devil remains out of fashion and, as always, is taking full advantage of our forgetfulness.

In the United States, however, this forgetfulness assumes a different aspect; I believe really that here it has to do with a kind of perennial innocence. Gadgets, after all, are such simple things, so child-like. One plays with them; and children's games scare the devil away. Well, it could be that just this is the hidden purpose of American paraphernalia. We must not forget that it was Franklin who invented the lightning rod. Can it be that they have also managed to discover a rod which averts transcendental lightning?

5 FOREHANDEDNESS

Every morning I buy the *Boston Evening Globe*, that is to say, the afternoon edition of that Boston paper. Of course when I say *afternoon* I mean the afternoon to come and not that of the preceding day. On Fridays I pick up copies of *Life* and *Time* which bear the dateline of the following Monday. The reader need not think that I have struck up a friendship with the little old man from beyond the grave who in René Clair's film *It Happened Tomorrow* managed to give the journalist a copy of tomorrow's paper on the night before its publication. No, all I have to do is go into the nearest drugstore, pick up my ration of future time and leave a few cents on a tray—following the *honor system*, an ingenious means of saving money by counting on people's honesty. And that is not the end of it. It's quite likely that on some day in March a friend may ask, "Could we have lunch together on May twenty-second at twelve sharp?" My answer ordinarily would be: "How do we know we'll still be alive?" But since this attitude is too Spanish to express in English, instead I take out a little notebook—without which it is just as impossible to live in the United States as without a refrigerator and for parallel reasons—to check whether or not I have any other obligation noted down for that date. And if the page is blank, it thereupon ceases to be so, and I am committed to lunch in two months on a day which is as precise in the agenda as it is hazy in my imagination and with a friend with whom I should very much like to lunch right now, or maybe tomorrow, while I have his smile before me, while I can count on his good humor, his cordiality, or his wit. But this is not possible; and one day among all the other days, called forth by the automaton of the calendar, he will suddenly turn up, whether it's hot or cold, whether he or I are happy or sad, hungry or dyspeptic, whether we have something to say to each other, or whether we are inclined to be taciturn. The last definite entry in my little notebook happens to be for the twenty-third of August; from then on my future takes on an air of dark uncertainty such as the textbooks tell us enveloped the reign of Witiza.*

In order to get a job, to give a course in a university or to take one, you have to make up your mind at least eight to ten months in advance. A few days ago a young lady told me that at Christmas-time she had purchased the wedding gown she intends to wear in June. In January, with two feet of snow and temperatures which go well below zero, it gives me the shivers to look at shop windows where a whole collection of straw hats is displayed along with "tropical" sandals, beachwear, and bathing suits. And exactly on the 26th of December the huge piles of Christmas cards are replaced by stacks of Valentines which, in turn, disappear as if by magic on the

* Witiza was the next to last of the Visigothic kings in Spain—Trans.

14th of February to make way for Easter cards. And so on
ad infinitum.

There is one exception, however: death. With its traditional lack of consideration, death persists in turning up in-
opportunely, in giving no notice, in slipping in silently, "with
the velvet step of a bare foot" as Unamuno marvelously puts
it, without any forewarning. For this reason death assumes in
the United States the air of an undesirable alien and has therefore made no progress towards citizenship. Still it is interesting to watch efforts there to domesticate it, to oblige it to be
foreseen, to insist that it conform to the customs of the country. All this, of course, primarily through the use of statistics
—thanks to which death enters into the realm of figures, mea-
surement, and prediction. There is only one trouble: the
death that is thus dominated and rendered inoffensive, as it
were, is someone else's, not mine nor yours nor that of a third
person dear to the heart. The latter kind of death, individual
death (I dare not say *personal* for that is still something else),
is also anticipated insofar as possible. In hospitals there comes
a moment when the name of a patient goes on the critical or
danger list, from which it may pass to the terminal or *dying
list*. And then the family begins to deal with the mortuary to
arrange for all that is necessary to wipe out the anomalous
situation that is imminent.

I believe that here we have the perspective from which to
view American punctuality, their desire to do everything on
schedule, on the dot, and their tendency toward forehanded-
ness. It is something that goes very deep; it has to do with the
desire for security in a nation which feels itself ultimately
troubled simply because life in its surface manifestations is so
extremely secure. If I have a luncheon date for the 22nd of
May, it is as though I had in hand the time between now and
then; my commitment for next year allows me the illusion of
thinking I have bought a goodly portion of the future. In this
way, what with dates made long in advance, far-off amuse-

ments and contracts, one shores up the fragile structure of one's life and strings the bridges which lead from today unto tomorrow. And this explains the necessity for exactness. While a Spaniard would suggest we do something "one of these days" or "next month," holding off the notation of an exact date until another meeting and further confirmation, the American fixes the day and the hour—he says that he is going to be married, not in the spring or next summer, but the 14th of April or the 21st of June. Naturally, it is one thing vaguely to anticipate certain plans within a kind of blurred outline which bit by bit comes into focus, with an awareness of contingency and insecurity. It is something else again to build bridges whose steel or stone supports rest firmly on a specific outcropping of the terrain. An American would feel himself out of sorts, disquieted, and unhappy if he could not count on an immediate future staked out and marked down in terms of definite appointments and due dates—even though among them he must number an obligatory income tax payment or his departure for Korea.

Nothing points up the fundamental difference between American and Spaniard more than the form which the latter's desire for security tends to take. Spanish life in its entirety is subject to hazards, happenstances, and ups and downs of all varieties. At short range, there is no way of life more beset by chance. Yet there are two areas in which every Spaniard desires to be fixed, two things which affect his existence in its total figure and so must be "for one's whole life": the first is marriage; the second, a government job, a professional position, or a guaranteed place on some lifelong payroll—and he calls this latter goal, of all things, a "*destino*."* Naturally, a Spaniard always takes off in the direction of eschatology.

---

* Destiny or destination—Trans.

6 FROM ROBINSON CRUSOE TO HENRY FORD AND BACK AGAIN

One of the symbols or even myths of the Anglo-Saxon race at the beginning of its historical fulfillment is Robinson Crusoe. (Those who read Spanish might be interested in the story of Pedro Serrano, a Spanish Robinson, told by the Inca Garcilaso de la Vega in the *Comentarios Reales* a century and a half before the English story and incorporating some very curious differences.†) But because all human impulses when prolonged tend to swing toward their opposites—for instance, we go from the radical pessimism of Calvin to Rousseau's no less radical optimism—from Robinsonism, over the centuries the road has been towards the division of labor, expertise, and specialization to the point where a worker performs nothing more than a single precise operation: an exact half-turn of an eternal screw. The symbol here is Ford: the myth takes the form of a caricature etched in acid, Charlie Chaplin's *Modern Times*. First, in solitude and during difficult times, whether on the island of Juan Fernández or in the plains of Nebraska, to know how to do everything for and by oneself; then, in prosperity and in the midst of the multitude, to have everyone do just his part which should, if possible, be reduced to a single motion. (I really believe that all American magazine articles are products of the joint efforts of an entire team, the Minerva Trust, Inc., or some such combine.)

There is no doubt that this division of labor is the means by which the United States has achieved its fabulous economic potential, still more immense than one is led to believe by all the figures, statistics, or anecdotes. We have all read hundreds of times that American workingmen own cars, but we have

† See my article, "El otro en la isla: Robinson Crusoe y Pedro Serrano," *El oficio del pensamiento*, Madrid, 1958 [Obras, VI].

always thought that this statement should be taken with a grain of salt, that probably only certain workers of a special category were car owners. But no, the statement must be taken quite literally. Every few days I go by a construction job on a large building and I see a late-model car parked nearby that is identical with one we admired last winter in Madrid which belonged to a friend who happens to be the general manager of one of the principal Spanish banks. One day the proprietor of the car climbed into it, taking the wheel in a most natural manner. It was one of the masons whom I knew by sight from having watched him in the mornings as he vigorously hefted the structural beams. And when it isn't a mason, it's the locksmith, or the clerk in the supermarket, or the janitor—forgive me, but our janitor has *two* cars. Even high school teachers, equivalent to our instructors in *Institutos*, can afford automobiles. And, of course, refrigerators, electric mixers, television, and those irresistible heating systems.

Labor is highly paid. Income is extremely high. (I remember that in Spain when something costs ridiculously little, one usually says "The work alone is worth more than that!") But since reality has its own imperious laws which man cannot subject to his desires, the result is that the American worker can afford to buy anything except labor. And labor becomes the supreme luxury which scarcely anyone can permit himself. Forget about domestic help (a tremendous subject on which, though much has been written, almost everything remains to be said; its absence being one of the decisive factors for good or evil in American life). You cut your own hair, shine your own shoes, make all kinds of repairs, paint a door. A friend who is a university professor in the neighboring state of Rhode Island pointed to his house and said to me: "It has to be painted, but do you know what that would cost me? A thousand dollars. So, I think that during the next vacation . . . ." So he will probably give up writing a chapter of his latest book and instead will buy himself a Duco spray gun, and he may even have a good time. Thus each man is his own plumber, carpenter, and shoeblack. His own barber too? No, that is a little too difficult; but for twenty-nine cents he can buy an article that is a kind of hybrid between comb and razor, and this will help him delay having to hand over to Figaro his inexorable tribute of one hard, round dollar. But how much does all this self-help cost? Doesn't it represent, rather than a luxury, the greatest collective extravagance?

Thus, as a result of specialization, division of labor, profits, and wealth, it turns out that each man must be a jack of all trades. In the heart of an enormous city, a desert island. Inside his own house, each American daily relives the myth of Robinson Crusoe; at best, if he is married, he can count on the help of a female Friday, and in the middle of the island the process of division of labor is germinated again, for she washes and he dries—or sometimes vice versa. And this is how the pendulum of American life sways back and forth between Robinson Crusoe and Henry Ford.

7 WELLESLEY AND THE FOURTH CÁNTICO

I have just finished reading in the very place where he wrote it Jorge Guillén's fourth *Cántico*,* the last such, if we take his words to be true, and thus the "First Complete Edition" of the whole work. At the bottom of its last page, two place

* Jorge Guillén (1893—) eminent Spanish poet, native of Valladolid, who spent the years following the Spanish Civil War teaching at Wellesley College. Retired, he now divides his time between Italy, Spain and the United States. His book of poetry, *Cántico*, grew with each succeeding edition until in the fourth, here cited, it contained 334 poems—Trans.

names and two dates appear: "Tregastel, Brittany—1919; Wellesley, Massachusetts—1950." What a distance in time and place! And despite the acknowledged evenness of his poetry, in the middle of this book, like a river running under two bridges, there flows half the lifetime of Jorge Guillén spanning two generations in history, from Versailles to Korea, and an entire era of Spanish poetry. And, in between, adding its own silent presence, is the solitary Atlantic.

I once said that Guillén by preference deals with the stuff of daily life and of it recreates a new world, a true world, which is the imaginary poetic correlative of the one in which we live, of the ones the poet inhabits and experiences. And so he transfigures the landscape, never actually presenting it nor describing it, so that we can only recognize and uncover it when we finally identify his emotion or when we find duplicated in the feeling of the poem the emotions—lived or imagined—of our own lives. So it is that this time with an unheard-of abundance of allusions—Spain, and more exactly, Valladolid, appear in the poem entitled "Luz Natal"* which represents perhaps a foreshadowing of what Guillén may give us after his *Cántico*.

So now I have given myself the pleasure of tracking down through the swirling metaphors and the bright verses, those virtual reflections of the real landscape which today surround me. This is one more joy to add to the many other complex delights that *Cántico* offers. There is a rain of hurried golden leaves, which as they cover the ground, lay the carpets of a New England autumn. They fall from unreal trees where a subdued green allies itself to red-tinged gold. Small plump birds with long blue tails hop from branch to branch. Every once in a while the landscape explodes with red trees, rust and yellow ones which print their reflections on the quiet waters of Lake Waban, on whose shores a dark-bricked Gothic tower stands watch. It is almost easier to be-

* Native Light (or Light of Birth)—Trans.

lieve in their existence as reflections, a spectral kind of being after all, than when they implacably assault one's eye in all their chromatic reality—waving there in front of us so real and so unlikely in our common air.

And on the green paths, winding toward ivy-covered buildings, unforeseen encounters and unawaited marvels: a squirrel that arches his tremendously long tail and climbs up a tree trunk; an angel on a bicycle—one that Alberti* missed —with rosy flesh under the curls and rhythmical bare legs still childlike in conformation; youthful silhouettes in the distance; a fresh young profile where tomorrow is incarnate; hair blowing in the wind like leaves—hair that brought forth from our poet a poem now gone to dwell with the old, hallowed ones which are traditional and well-known in Spanish: "La cabeza," "Beato sillón," "La rosa."

> "¡Oh melenas, ondeadas
> A lo príncipe en la augusta
> Vida triunfante; nos gusta
> Ver amanecer—¡doradas
> Surgen!—estas alboradas
> De virginidad que apenas
> Tú, Profusión, desordenas
> Para que todo a la vez
> Privilegie laesbeltez
> Más juvenil, oh melenas!"**

* Rafael Alberti (1902—) well-known Spanish poet of Guillén's generation who wrote an entire book of poetry dedicated to rather unusual angels, *Sobre los ángeles* (1927–28)—Trans.
** Freely translatable as follows:
> Oh, long manes of hair,
> Coiffed like a prince triumphant
> In his splendid life; how pleasant
> To see dawning—in a golden surge—
> These bright virgin waves
> Which even you, Profusion,
> Can scarcely disarray—
> So that everything at once
> Must favor most
> Youthful slenderness, oh manes!   —Trans.

Jorge Guillén, within his melancholy, with certain sober, imperceptibly sad notes, in five vibrating lines of blank verse called "*Nosotros*," maintains an ever-mounting sense of joy in the things before him, of pleasure in the realities, a tremulous and cautious delight in all that exists or passes at our side: tree, night plane, radiator, love shared daily, pain so acute it must be silent, a woman in her automobile—perhaps the lightning flash of beauty that is ever-fascinating—a child, a squirrel, a young girl coming into flower.

And this is the moral basis—yes, moral—which underlies the always authentic, never capricious poetry of Guillén. It is the ethic of a man who sees death in the distance— "Alguna vez me angustia una certeza" ("At times I am anguished by a certainty")—but who calms himself with the thought that there is as yet no need to hurry; that "lo urgente es el maduro fruto" ("what is most urgent is the ripened fruit.").* And one may well ask whether this tranquility, this happiness in the simple things, the final substance of all Jorge Guillén's poetry and the vital matter of his *Cántico*, can well be made of other stuff than an absolute and unlimited confidence in reality; that is to say, in hopefulness.

8 OUR CITY

A snowfall has forced us to take possession of this small city in Massachusetts, has drawn us away from the splendors of the landscape by slowly enclosing it within invisible bulwarks. Now the city has a feel of intimacy; it has turned inward upon itself, is truly a city, our city. The snow has been

* Marias is here quoting from a poem of Guillén's—Trans.

falling tenaciously for hour upon hour. Its first effect, even before creating the ghostly refulgence of blanketing white, was to impose a marvelous silence. The city now moves on tiptoe, and the elms, the immense chestnut trees, the erect pines dare only rustle in a whisper. The frame houses, carrying a soft white burden on their peaked roofs, seem closer to each other, cinched together by the new snow. The generous streetlights no longer limit their brightness to one patch on the dark earth: now their beams mingle as they shimmer along large stretches of ground. The whole city—silence, murmurs, neighborly warmth, lights blinking from corner to corner—becomes a secret.

Intimacy. Inside her window, Mrs. Webb is reading in the lamplight; near her is the baby grand piano, while from his portrait on the wall, Abraham Lincoln looks down on the reader and magically transforms the book into *Uncle Tom's Cabin*. In the interior the radiator is singing—a veritable "winter nightingale"—and a tall grandfather clock is peacefully ticking off the seconds. Just opposite, two children already in pajamas and ready for bed are rubbing away the steam that clouds the windowpane.

There are few people left hurrying along the streets. Reddened faces, and on each a smile. No, these are not the lands of agora and small plaza, of tranquil conversation as one soaks up sun or sits in the shade of a mimosa tree under the violently blue sky. Here one smiles quickly at one's neighbor, without breaking step—perhaps this is the reason one does always smile at him. And over a period of time, smile after smile, one begins to fashion a pattern of shared living. The man who goes by with his bundles, which he has collected in a wire-mesh cart in the grocery store and has paid for as he left; the woman who slips a nickel into a meter at the place where she has just parked her green car, and another woman—with a red coat, high boots, heavy gloves, and shining eyes—who is vigorously wielding a shovel as she removes the snow from her doorway; and the street cleaner free of class-consciousness but with a true professional conscience who efficiently cleans the walks and leaves them bare, and glances cordially at the people who walk over them; and the physician who crosses the street, bag in hand, ready to give a sick man a leisurely and friendly examination and to prescribe for him some simple remedy that may remind us of our grandmother, remedies which present-day pedantry has perhaps forgotten too quickly (true or not, Marañón* my friend?); and two girls loaded down with books and notes, lively and smiling in blue slacks and red socks, each with a flaring blond forelock on her forehead; and that oldster, greatly resembling Don Benito Pérez Galdós,** who goes to the eleven o'clock mass at St. Paul's Catholic Church, and his compatriot whom he has greeted for sixty years as the latter leaves the Congregational Church.

This then is the city, our city. Not mine, really, nor anyone's; nor does it belong to that vague entity we call the municipality or the government. For it is not an inert space in which houses have by chance been built, nor a battleground, nor a petrified mass of cement, envy, and indifference. It is the ambiance in which our homes reside, acknowledge each other, and grow old together, in the midst of which they are engaged in tracing out their biographies. These houses have seen each other born—rapidly, by means of huge machines, obstetrical instruments whose size belies their gentleness, in the hands of good-humored workers dressed somewhat like Popeye or Harpo Marx. They have contemplated each other daily with eyes wide open and shades undrawn; in all confidence they have revealed their inner secrets each to the other. They have been cheered when a stork rested once more on a neigh-

---

* Gregorio Marañón (1887–1960), an internationally known specialist in Endocrinology who was also a celebrated man of letters and a prolific author of critical works in the fields of science, history, biography, social problems—Trans.
** Benito Pérez Galdós (1843–1920), a great Spanish novelist whose "presence" continues to influence Spanish letters—Trans.

boring roof; they have whispered earnest words of sad compassion when the shadow of death appeared unexpectedly; they have trembled when one of their number has been snatched up by fire, leaving only charred trees and twisted iron stairways. It is here, only here, that the poetry of everyday life must be written.

On this December night, while the snow falls thick and heavily, the railway station, usually so close, has become extraordinarily distant. Shall we ever learn that there is more to distance than can be measured? That a step on asphalt is not equivalent to a step in the snow? The station is closed and empty, alone in a mass of white; above, the sky is grey and dark; the parallel rails stretch out this way toward Boston, that way toward Worcester, Springfield, Albany, New York, everywhere. In the deserted station, muffled by the snow's cotton padding, a telephone rings away. And the surroundings, all by themselves, have begun the first chapter of a detective story.

In some houses the Christmas trees show faint lights—flashes of blue, red, green, and yellow. Wreaths with scarlet streamers. Santa Claus has just arrived with his sleigh and reindeer. In an unlighted window behind the panes, there is a brief glimmer of light: Miss Virginia Clark, who did not receive a letter today from Korea, has just lit a cigarette and is fixedly watching the snow which continues slowly to fall.

9 A CLUSTER OF SOLITUDES

American life can only be understood from the perspective of solitude. Scarcely is the sentence written, and already I can hear the reader's protest. Doesn't the United States have a population of 160 million? Haven't we agreed that this is the land of the masses? Isn't the country full of those enormous cities, colossal piles of heaped-up humanity: New York, Chicago, Philadelphia, Detroit, and Los Angeles?

For Europeans, and for us of the Mediterranean countries especially, a town *is* for all intents and purposes a plaza. In other words, an enclosed space surrounded by houses whose sole mission is to form a cloister shutting out the encircling countryside. What I mean to say is that what is of importance in the city is not the houses themselves, but whatever there is in the midst of them. Whoever may doubt that statement has the proof today closer at hand than ever before; let him go someplace in Germany where there are no houses left, but only cities. It is sufficient if there are only a few facades left standing, mirage-like borders around the gaps that are the plazas, markers for the channels of coming and going that we call streets. This indicates that a city is first of all shared living, presence, company; and since man is a talking animal, that implies conversation. Agora, forum, marketplace, plaza. For people to see one another, to gossip, to rant, to admire, disdain, envy; to buy and sell—bargaining, of course, spending an eternity arguing back and forth, in thrust and parry, in the pleasure of talking; to stroll slowly around the arcades again and again, the men clockwise and the girls counter-clockwise, repeating the ritual gestures—avid glances, furtive looks, cocksureness, and timidity—under the impassive Cyclopean eye of the municipal timepiece.

American cities rarely contain plazas worthy of the name, and when they do the place is usually empty, available perhaps for certain infrequent gatherings, a blank space, or simply a means of cutting across from one point to another. Their very names are indicative: they are called the Square, the squared plot which separates the houses; or the Common, the land belonging in common to all the citizens; or the Green, the green lawn which brings a gentle country flavor to soften the dark brick houses.

Don't forget that the United States is a country still in the making; though it is in the finishing stages, there are still hundreds of details to be taken care of. And the country has been created from two different starting points, one on the Atlantic and the other on the Pacific, as though there were two crews working to construct a tunnel and hoping to meet halfway through in the Midwest. Americans have gone on daily pushing forward their frontiers; they have always lived in outposts, whether fort or trading station, and that means alone. We in Europe started from shared society. The old villages banded together in a city whether because of some outbreak of violence, for a sacrifice, because of a place of worship, or for political reasons (-*polis* is the root of *politics*, things of the *city*); so did the medieval towns bound about by walls, with streets for each guild and the maternal naves of the Cathedral whose bells call the living, toll for the dead, and stave off the menacing lightning. In the United States life has been lived in hunters' and trappers' outposts, among the herds lost in the middle of the vast plains, in the log cabin surrounded by endless fields of corn, in the desolate oil fields, in the placer mines where hopefully or doggedly they wash the sand for gold. The American soul is a lonely one; its ultimate substance is that of solitude. From time to time joy or desperation may push individuals toward their fellows and so a party is organized, a fair, a civic celebration, or an orgy, in church, saloon, fairgrounds or meeting hall—all single swallows which never a summer made.* Then two almost legendary powers —Law and Industry—caused the cities to spring up. For though it is indeed true that there are many large cities in the United States—in 1950 there were 106 with a population over 100,000—it is no less true that these cities are of recent birth: in 1880 only 19 exceeded the 100,000 mark. Many of the 106

---

* The author probably has in mind Cervantes' statement that: "One swallow does not make the summer." *Don Quixote*, Part I, Chap. 18 —Trans.

did not even exist in 1880; others were merely crossroads. The city does not therefore offer a springboard towards an understanding of American life. When the cities came into being, that way of life had already been formed and, in its deepest strata, hardened. For that reason also the cities are not defined by their plazas; they are acephalic, headless, or even more to the point, amorphous, because what is most characteristic of the urban zones in America is that they consist of huge "metropolitan areas" made up of many almost indistinguishable cities, each with residential districts that are more or less cramped, more or less spread out. No one lives close to the members of his own circle; to see one's best friend means covering many miles, before by horseback but now, thanks to Detroit's horsepower, on steel and rubber.

American life in its entirety, in every walk and aspect—religion and politics, intellectual and economic life, fame and entertainment, love and literature, virtues and vices—is conditioned by the fact that the most appropriate definition of those enormous cities of iron and cement could serve easily as the title for a small volume of lyric poetry: *A Cluster of Solitudes.*

10   ANOTHER WORLD

If there is any country which is unprofitable for the tourist, it is the United States. Perhaps that is why in Europe people usually have an idea of America which is inaccurate and out of focus, so over-simplified, so stereotyped, so picturesque and, at the same time, so barren. The United States has been badly "narrated" to Europeans. And it is not easy to see any remedy close at hand. The two chief sources of information on the subject are the movies and the reports of visitors. Films have a justifiable tendency, legitimately beyond criticism, to deform reality; what can and should be thoroughly criticized, however, is the manner in which they carry out that presentation. The artistic mission of the moving picture, as in all branches of art, or all kinds of interpretation, is to exaggerate, to emphasize, to bring into full potential. It is apparent that Cezanne's apples do not exist in nature, but his apples have more apple to them than do the ones we see on trees or in the fruit dish on our table. The trouble with American movies—but not only with the American ones, let's avoid the stock complaint —is that they are going through a phase of recurrent stupidity. And their presentation of American life, which is the aspect of the problem that interests me here, usually tends either to propagandize for "the American dream" or to debunk it, to make it seem more trivial and less serious than it is.

When propagandizing, the film tries to convince the spectator of the marvels of American life not by showing, but by arguing and attempting to persuade on the basis of ideological principles considered admirable by certain mediocre groups. These circles, by the way, are usually made up for the most part of *parvenus*, generally recently transplanted Europeans who have lost their own personalities and are therefore trying to be "pluperfect" Americans simply because they realize that they are not, nor will they ever be, Americans pure and simple. At best, this kind of film deals with the beliefs on which a large number of Americans "think" their lives are founded, and not with those which, in reality, do rule their actions and which, quite logically, often go unrecognized. In other instances, the movies diminish, dilute and impoverish the American way of life, converting it not into a caricature of itself but into something worse—a comic strip, a primitive platitude —ultra-vulgarity. The process through which this result is obtained is a curious one. A few centuries ago (four centuries, more or less) it was discovered that a fictional hero did not necessarily have to be a man of exceptional outward appearance; it was sufficient that he be in fact an exceptional man. That was the first step; the second was the discovery that not even this requirement was obligatory; that any man could be a protagonist because every human life is replete with interest, and that what converts an ordinary man into a hero is precisely that art of the novelist or dramatist or (in the case at hand) the skill of the actor, none of whom could be run-of-the-mill people. It often happened in the movies that actors or actresses who were outstanding examples of splendid humanity could lend their quality to some simple, ordinary character and thus with singular effectiveness communicate those lives to us. Today this is not the case; now, more frequently than not, the actors or actresses are in themselves completely trivial and stultefying, and they offer us a drained and graceless version of the life they are trying to incarnate. Any reader, if he is a habitual moviegoer and not too young, must have noticed that where before the actors used to delight us regardless of the merits of the film, now it is most unusual for an actor in himself to offer us any enjoyment. I spoke once of the pleasures to be found in some of the very bad pictures made by Greta Garbo. Today, unfortunately, all this human magic is supplanted by photographic technique, sound track, "special effects"—poor substitutes for talent—and the outcome is often a yawn.

But what about the other source of information? What about the visitors who actually see the United States? I truly believe that most travelers who come to New York from the other side of the Atlantic and then publish a book about the United States bring that book with them, under their arms and already written. Then why do they take the trouble to come? Only to "authenticate" their work, to slap a few hotel stickers on it and give it a rubber stamp or two. Almost all Europeans think they already know all about the United States; at best they seek merely to confirm prior assumptions.

The few who admit to their possible ignorance usually take such a whirlwind trip, a Cook's tour, through the country that their experience is little better than useless. To gain some intellectual profit from a quick trip through North America, one would have to enjoy an extraordinary degree of perceptiveness and most unusual powers of analysis. Why all this difficulty? After all the United States is a new and simple country, isn't it? Yes, doubtless, but its form of society is totally different from that of Europe, its underlying assumptions and general structure are distinct; and so long as they remain unrecognized, it is impossible to comprehend correctly any of the particular, easily visible, phenomena which in and of themselves are not especially complicated or mysterious. What I mean is that each detail, each element has a function different from that of the corresponding element in European society; conversely, if we seek in the United States for correspondences with some European reality, we must be careful not to fall into the same error. What in the United States could possibly "correspond" to the Sorbonne? It is not an easy question to answer (though it would be worthwhile to try to find such an answer) but, naturally, one can immediately reply that no such university exists here. Thus it goes. The only way to arrive at some kind of understanding of American life—is to live it. This means the experience of total immersion in daily life, going through the same simple actions time after time, familiarizing oneself with one piece of the country. (And since it is a relatively homogeneous country, at least within certain broad zones, it is much less to the point than one might think to cover it all—the essential thing is to become a part of it.)

When one does not enter into the American way, life becomes a continual deception in the two senses of disappointment and ensnarement. One finds nothing that one looks for; one cannot evaluate or comprehend any of the facets one encounters. It is necessary to adjust one's viewpoint, one's perspective, to situate oneself within some pattern by means of which everything acquires a measure of sense and reality. This is why the man who limits himself to "recounting" the United States without ever altering his own point of view, though he may be truthful, is invariably misleading. Despite himself, he falsifies everything he reports. Long months ago, when I began to transmit to a Spanish public some of the observations I have made here, I was very fearful and found my sense of intellectual responsibility rising up in alarm. One is dealing here with sensitive material that raises serious methodological problems. The solution I eventually found might be briefly expressed in this formula: impressionism plus analysis; to pay attention especially to the surface manifestations of things, to their physiognomy, to their purest and simplest expressions; and, at the same time, to make the analytical effort to refer each thing to its context, to perceive its true function, its effective mode. On many things I had from the very beginning a sufficiency of information. In some cases this was because certain kinds of reality are so elementary that they stand out at first sight—ads, the way in which women drive cars, going shopping, eating habits. Nevertheless, I felt that all that seemed so apparent really was not; that one had to know about many, many more things before interpreting anything, even the most insignificant of all, as, for example, the particular vegetation that fills innumerable American cities, or, without journeying further, this small corner of the world called Wellesley.

11 REMEDIES FOR DESPERATION

Too often we forget that life is constantly threatened by despair which lies in wait around every corner. Distracted by other dangers and ills, and also by our pleasures, we lose sight of the enemy and only realize its presence when we find ourselves defenseless against its attack. But since this experience is the most anguished and crushing there is, mankind, without being aware of so doing, concerns itself with despair and attempts to exorcise it. Half the things that man has invented are to console him for having to die; the other half, to protect him from despair while he lives.

As it happens, Europe has been relatively successful in this effort. I mean that collective despair, despair as a way of life—not as a personal condition that descends upon us unexpectedly—is rather infrequent. Why so? Europe is too crowded, and despair is, above all, solitude, devastation, desolation, human emptiness where there should be companionship. By this last statement I mean that despair is not loneliness pure and simple, but alienation from others, disconsolateness among other people. Despair, if we take the extreme case, is the opposite of the communion of the saints. And pursuing this train of thought, we might perhaps understand what hell is. (And, incidentally, perceive the frivolousness contained in Sartre's famous thesis —because he neglects Descartes' advice against precipitousness and prejudgment—that "Hell is the others.")

But have I not contradicted myself? If despair truly thrives only when one is among the many, how can being crowded protect Europe? Doesn't despair hover over the great cities— for example, those of South America, which are full of hundreds of thousands of people, but which have about them nevertheless a feel of vacant lots and houses under construction

with white XXX's on their windows? Cities where an in-
flamed imagination finally sees an immense "For Rent" sign
stretched from one end to the other of the city limits. Indeed,
I did forget to mention with *what* Europe is crowded—it is
with history. And that implies that it is also filled with its
dead. My friend Gabriel Marcel has said with great feeling:
"The world would be uninhabitable if there were no others
except the living." In Europe we have with us and behind us
the numberless legions of the dead with whom Quevedo*
lived "retired to the peace of these desert lands." Those who
have lived before us in the same houses, on the same ground.
The lodgers described by Galdós, who lived and died in the
Calle del Pez and applauded or insulted Espartero;** the men
who bowed to pale ladies in the halls of the Prado, tipping
their bowler hats; others who went to pay their respects to la
Calderona*** or to celebrate the latest sallies of Villamediana.**** And all the past inhabitants of the Rue du Bac, for
whom Balzac still serves as medium, the ones whose super-
imposed spirits give lustre to the Place des Vosges, and those
who for centuries like so many locusts have made the Nea-
politan street named Toledo hum with loquacious chatter;
and still others who have walked arm in arm over each generation of dry leaves fallen from the chestnut trees on the
banks of the Neckar.

When no one exists other than the living, we are alone. And
despair overwhelms us easily. This is the problem in young
countries, new countries, officially supposed to be carefree. I
am moved more than I can say by the things man does to elude
despair. As, for instance—with a surprising degree of success—

---

* Francisco De Quevedo (1580–1645) poet, prose writer, satirist, secretary to King Philip IV—Trans.
** General Espartero, Regent from 1840 to 1843 for Isabel II—Trans.
*** "la Calderona" (María Calderón) famous actress of the seventeenth century and mistress to Philip IV—Trans.
**** Juan de Tarsis, Count de Villamediana (1582–1622), court poet
and master of intrigue—Trans.

in the United States, or at least in New England, the part of the country I know best. Human beings in this region have gone out of their way to find means of impeding or curing despondency. Probably without being aware of what they are doing, or perhaps realizing it only dimly, deep inside. The smile, for example. Do Americans smile because they are happy? Or in order to be happy? Granted, in order to appear so, since melancholy is not held to be in good taste and sadness is somewhat frowned upon. A smile can even be made into a slogan—as mindless as all of them—*Keep Smiling*. But in its true and deeper sense, a smile is the expression of communality, a sign of recognition that one's fellow man exists and should be loved as oneself—or only a little less—a pledge to shared living that is almost like a blessing.

And, in like manner, the fabrication or improvisation of a history. The United States is said to be a "very modern" country, aseptic, "chrome-plated," with no niche in time. And sometimes so it is, but more as a matter of entertainment, to while away a few hours, or as an eccentricity. When it is a question of life in earnest, the American turns decidedly evocative. What a vogue for antiques! Colonial houses with all the left-overs from olden times—a restaurant called "The 1812 House" installed in a delightful home of that era—nineteenth-century Gothic on the college campus, where at dusk a carillon pours out its tenderness over lawns like those trod by William of Ockham, reminiscent of Oxford or Cambridge with their load of seven centuries of Latin; but no, this is Wellesley, or perhaps Cambridge, Massachusetts.

And it is the same thing with all the rest of the vegetation as with the college greens. Indeed this is the significance of the delightful landscaping which embellishes American cities. Chestnut trees, elms, maples that turn scarlet in the fall; trees and shrubs of deep crimson; ivy that is green or red, a climbing calendar that tells the season as it winds up the brick walls; flowers of all hues—yellow, blue, purple, red—raised with great care in each unwalled garden, paradise open freely to all. The busy American with so much to do applies himself assiduously to his garden and works all year so that for two weeks the city may enjoy the golden splendor of the forsythias. And rooted in the greenery, amid the chromatic brilliance of all the flowers, stand the frame houses painted white or maize or pink, or, even better, allowed to retain the honorable color of weathered wood. Where no history exists, or very little, nature should be made welcome; and lovingly imposed on nature, culture—and I use the word in its original meaning of agriculture. The entire city is alive, vibrant in the passing winds; it keeps us company with its foliage, smiling with winks of light and shade among its leaves; it greets us with the familiar good smell of new mown grass pressed by the rollers, or it surprises us with the unanticipated perfume of its morning glories. This is the vegetation that is the equivalent of ancient stones. And it has the same tonic effect on our spirits as a walk down the Segovian street called "Death and Life," through the arches of San Juan de Duero, or to the romanesque tower of la Antigua, or under the eaves of Toledo where a small lamp's glimmer always throws mysterious and gallant shadows. On the banks of the Tajo or the Pisuerga, the Seine or the Saar, the Charles or the Hudson, amidst granite or greenery, the problem is the same—to salvage man's spirit from despair, implacable enemy of this world.

12 "OLD-FASHIONED"

Again and again the word crops up; with an air of conclusive-
ness, as a definite verdict beyond appeal: "old-fashioned," literally "antiquated" or "out-of-date." Well, naturally, in the
United States, the country mad for novelty and the latest
model, it is understandable that if something is called "antiquated," nothing more remains to be said. Fine, but now from
here on please notice that "old-fashioned" indicates the highest praise. An excellent ice cream, sold in cartons decorated
with the figures of a woman in hoopskirts and a man in a cut-
away with high hat in hand, is said to be "old-fashioned"; so
are the candies—exceptionally digestible and even faintly tasty
—made by Fanny Farmer. (The greatest failure in America is
its candy and pastry, which brings tears to the eye as one
thinks wistfully of the *yemas* of San Leandro, the *segovianas*
sold by the aqueduct, the yellow custard that decorates the
Sorian *collados*, the almond paste one orders in the morning
in Zodocover so as to pick it up fresh in the afternoon, the
puffs and the buttery shortcakes of Andalusia.) Shoes, jew-
elry, glassware, furniture—all with "old-fashioned" quality.
Even the Baltimore and Ohio Railroad, besides its speed, safe-
ty, comfortable Pullmans, and good food, advertises as a supreme lure "old-fashioned courtesy"—antiquated manners.
Which is rather alarming. Is it possible that courtesy truly is
out of date, since it is thus advertised without qualification or
hesitation by a major railway?

The adjective "old-fashioned" fits in with a passion for
antiques—things of antiquity which truly are not very ancient
—sold everywhere, generally in frame houses probably built
after Hiroshima, in tiny villages or right on the side of the
highway, and not in the extremely old Rue Saint-Jacques, nor

in the charming Rue du Cherche-Midi which would itself figure as a terrific "antique," nor in the Calle del Prado. The phrase ties in with the children's Yankee and Rebel caps—reproductions of the uniform caps of the Northern and Confederate armies during the war between the states—which are offered for sale in store windows (incidentally, an unmistakable indication that the Civil War has really passed into history). And with the microscopically painstaking attention paid to American history.

Let us wander into a bookstore in the United States; if it sells old books, so much the better. Bookshops dealing in old books, or in second-hand books picked up at auction, are among the most expressive realities of any country, revealing of many secrets. How few foreign books! (Yet, for the record, there are similarly very few books in foreign languages in the bookshops of the Latin Quarter or in the stalls along the Seine.) And books of a vintage earlier than the nineteenth century are very rare indeed. As everywhere else, a vast number of inexplicable books—ones that nobody can understand why they were ever written and ones never read except by the author and the typesetter. (This subject deserves to be taken more seriously; if someone were to analyze everything published in a given country during a certain era, the results would be enormously enlightening.) And in all these American bookstores—in New York, Boston, and Cambridge—shelf upon shelf of books about the United States. But make no mistake—they are not over-all syntheses on what the United States represents and what it has in sum accomplished—tomes such as these, let me call them narcissistic books, are of very recent date and still very scarce. No, here we find books on minor topics of all kinds: the witches of Salem, the life of Dolly Madison, the explorations of Narváez, Soto, or Champlain, the Maine landscape, the Gettysburg address, New England furnishings in the eighteenth century, accounts of what ex-presidents have done after leaving the White House, the daring deeds of Kit Carson, the first days of Wall Street, the ideas of Jefferson or the notion Martha Washington had of her husband, the history of Harvard, Yale, Wellesley, or West Point told in minute detail and, even better, the story of the Colt revolver—called "the peacemaker"—or of the double-barreled pistol invented by Deringer which was called a derringer, doubling its r's along with its firepower.

All this means that the supposed mania of Americans for living in the present is a fiction propagated by hurried travelers. The United States' past is active everywhere and every moment, and in tangible ways; for that reason I have persisted in noting down the smallest, often miniscule, topics which are of interest. Grand rhetorical appeals to the past are something else again. Sagunto, Numancia, Lepanto, the 2nd of May.* But one can "name over" all of these and still be essentially ignorant of Spain's vital background. With the exception of the local historian, what does a Spaniard know about the city in which he lives? Is he familiar with the lives and deeds and sayings and letters of the men who lived before us? Granted that those who condemn traditionalism would like to begin over again every day at zero, but what about the others? The immediate past is unfortunate and one must turn away from it; the nineteenth century is a period of ridiculous nonsense; the eighteenth sought foreign models and was Frenchified, Voltaire-ridden; the seventeenth is the century of decadence. There still remains the sixteenth century, but since some peo-

---

* Sagunto, a town allied to Rome but attacked by Carthage in 219 B.C.; the inhabitants resisted a long siege and finally burned the town, many immolating themselves and their goods. In Numancia, a city which was near present-day Soria, the inhabitants resisted the Romans until exhausted by a long siege. In 133 B.C., they set fire to the city and sought their own deaths in combat or in the flames. Lepanto (1571) was the great naval battle fought by the Spaniards under the command of Don Juan of Austria that turned back the Turks and saved Europe from the threat of Islam. The 2nd of May (1808) was the day of the revolt of the common people of Madrid against Napoleon's forces that began the War of Independence—Trans.

ple don't care for Charles V and others don't like the *comuneros*,* tradition thins out more and more until all that is left are the Catholic Monarchs, Ferdinand and Isabella. Because, after all, the Middle Ages—what with its Trastamaras and its Moors and its Jews—scarcely offers more than two or three footholds: the Cid's beard; the tent of Miramamolín; and perhaps the name—but only the name—of Ferdinand the Holy.

So it is that the United States is a three-dimensional country. Not only does it fall within a physical longitude and latitude, stretched between the two great oceans and between Canadian frigidity and Caribbean warmth, but it also has temporal depth, solidity, consistency; in other words, it enjoys social reality and therefore historical potential. People generally do not realize how significant it is that the American when he wishes to vaunt his product, whether it is vanilla ice-cream or courtesy on the tracks, thinks of the label "old-fashioned."

13 GOING SHOPPING

There are three customary ways of going shopping in the United States. The first, traditional and universal, is a matter of starting down the street, looking at store windows, going in and out of shops and department stores, having one's curiosity aroused, getting loaded down with packages, and returning home without having bought any of the things one needed but with other unanticipated and superfluous purchases which are for that very reason eminently more desir-

* The comuneros were a group of democratically-oriented citizens of the Spanish cities who revolted against Charles V. Their movement was crushed in 1521—Trans.

able. The second procedure is much more typically American: it consists of getting in the car and transferring oneself to one of those places called a *Shopping Center*, or more stylishly, *Shopper's World*. A center or a world, if you will, dedicated to shops or to the person going shopping. These centers are nowhere; what I mean is that they are not part of any town but exist rather alongside some highway. (Some day I should like to write about the world represented by the American highway, which has a substance all its own, where one can find everything, even a rare book shop! Near Wilmington, Delaware, a few miles from the fabulous gardens of the Du Ponts—where an infinite number of orchids bloom at the expense of Nylon—I was able to search and glean among old books just as though I were on San Bernardo Street in the shadows where a few years ago Baroja* was usually to be found.) These mercantile worlds are composed of innumerable shops in juxtaposition: simple buildings, enormous plates of glass, reverberating lighting, and, within the compound, everything that God ever created—a movie house, various drug stores, and a colossal parking lot for the shoppers' cars. The inhabitants of many different cities gather in these markets situated outside the city where it is possible to circulate freely, to leave the car; where one can go in with empty hands and emerge with the furnishings for an entire house, with provisions for a year, a boat for the summer, or—naturally—another new car.

The third shopping method is the simplest, most efficient, and most American of all: you sit at home with a copy of the *New York Times*, for example, and you write letters. In a few days the amazing United States mail, which consists mainly of things other than letters, begins to bring you packages from all over the country: hats, shoes, suits, café curtains for the

---

* Pío Baroja (1872–1956), eminent Spanish novelist, was trained as a physician but abandoned medicine for literature and produced over one hundred novels—Trans.

windows, books, television sets, marmalade, ham, seeds of exotic plants, furniture, ingenious gadgets for hunting and fishing. The mainstream of United States commerce can thus flow into the smallest hamlet in Idaho. And, to tell the truth, shopping by mail order offers unsuspected pleasures.

But there is one fact that surprises a European who goes shopping in any American city, and that is the fluidity of the prices, the price differences that exist between one store and another and from one date to another. Sometimes it's a question of very similar articles, sometimes of identical ones. Our friends, the economists, usually tell us that in an efficient free market with many buyers and sellers—where there is no monopoly or cartel or other villains I leave the reader to imagine —prices are self-regulating and uniform. Well that is doubtless so; yet there is no doubt either that Campbell soups cost eighteen cents in the supermarket, and a Greek grocer at five minutes distance sells them for twenty; and corn flakes for twenty-seven as opposed to twenty-one, and so on. A friend of mine conducted a thorough comparative examination, cloth with cloth, fur collar with fur collar, lining with lining, of his storm coat with one I had bought for forty percent of the price he had paid; a suit of the identical material costs exactly double on the right hand side of a street in Boston of what it is worth on the left side; and, lastly, for a very tricky gadget I found these three prices: $39.50, $14.95, $4.95—the last price, of course, being the one I paid! Even within the same shop, prices vary; usually at the end of each season they go down, but it does not always work that way: a pair of shoes marked eleven dollars went down to eight for one or two weeks, and then went back up to the regular price.

I believe that there are explanations for these anomalies which are not strictly economic ones; that is to say, they are economic reasons but they belong to the outer fringes of economic science (where, by the way, the most fecund nucleus of ideas may possibly be located). In my opinion, the Greek can sell Campbell soups at a higher price—despite the fact that his are the same cans as those found from Maine to Montana and from Florida to California—for two reasons: for one thing, he closes his shop very late in the evening and he is open on Sundays; for another, he stocks a great variety of exquisite fruit. Thus he can count on an assured number of steady customers who pay for the privilege of buying good fruit at off hours by tolerating slightly higher prices on all other items.

But there is, above all, another general reason which justifies instability and fluctuation in prices: the standard uniformity of the vast majority of American goods. What I mean is that surprise and discovery, the unexpected, almost cease to exist and with them disappears one of the primary incentives to buy: the exciting sporting element. American merchants are clever enough to realize this so they arrange for variety and surprise to occur not in the products but in their prices. Going shopping for many people becomes a bargain hunt; and, indeed, the word *bargain* is one of those which appear most frequently and insistently. In Boston, one famous and enormous chain of department stores has a "Bargain Basement," a cellar of markdowns that brings Dante to mind with multitudes of people who look over the stock, try things on, buy, pay, and have a cup of coffee, a sandwich or an insipid drink at a circular bar. In that atmosphere better than anywhere else I think one comes to understand what Ortega means in the famous first chapter of his *Revolt of the Masses* by the rise of the mob or crowd. Well then, this Bargain Basement is run on the following principle: all merchandise is displayed with a dated price tag and that price is automatically lowered twenty-five per cent with each week that passes. If you want a bargain, almost a gift, even a gift as a matter of fact, it is just a matter of waiting—unless, of course, someone else has beaten you to it! And so the whole thing is converted into a kind of stock exchange where one can bet on the ups and downs; this is where the excitement comes in, the amusement, and, therefore, the mob. Because, as Pascal realized a long while ago, the man who gambles would not enjoy it if he didn't have the chance of winning a little money, but if you were to give him a sum of money without his gambling for it, he would not enjoy that either.

14 THE MIDDLE AGES
IN NEW ENGLAND
(UNCASTILLO* IN BOSTON)

No, that is not a typographical error. It's not a question either of any castle in Boston, but rather of something even rarer and more anachronistic: a piece of far-off Aragon grafted onto the homeland of the Pilgrim Fathers in the very heart of New England.

I cannot shake off the memory of the abrupt shock I received. I was peacefully wandering through the galleries of the Museum of Fine Arts in Boston, experiencing from time to time an occasional glimmer of esthetic pleasure. Without any major excitement I turned from the dark Egyptian obsidians to the white Venuses; from the delightful varicolored Chinese porcelain horses to landscapes of the Middle West or of Massachusetts painted a hundred years ago by romantic Americans who were moved and touched by each snow-capped mountain and each waterfall; from the rhetorical tremor of Fray Félix Hortensio Parravicino as he was portrayed by El Greco to the couple—yellow hat and beard, red bonnet and passion contained—that Renoir painted as dancing

---

* Uncastillo literally means a castle (un castillo) but here Marías is playing on a place name—Trans.

in Bougival. And suddenly, as I turned a corner and went through a door into one of the large rooms, the unforeseen, a hallucination, perhaps the magic retable of Maese Pedro! Through the enchanted power of an unpretentious Romanesque portal, the neutral walls of the Museum vanished. In their place was a plaza with dark brick and adobe houses, an inn with mule carts at the door, sashes, sandals, bodices and shawls, a fountain—surrounded by water jars—which threw its jet over greenish stone and a trickle of water running off in a furrow of the dry earth. Spain! When I finally managed to return to Boston, I went closer and read the card beside the ancient stonework. And, in fact, I *was* in Spain: the Church of San Miguel of Uncastillo in the province of Zaragoza.

In the land of no Middle Ages, a twelfth century church. Nonsense—the impossible, plus my Spanish talent for reconstructing an entire world on the basis of a few modest building blocks. But why so great a shock? Why should the portals of a small Aragonese church produce such a violent reaction in a museum where Persia, Chaldea, Egypt, and China live in harmony with Venice, Flanders, the Austrian court, and Verlaine's Paris? Why, in the unreal space of a museum wherein everything is valid and compatible, was it impossible for me to slip indifferently or pleasurably by the church of San Miguel?

The point is that we cannot shuffle all the arts together and make no distinctions. The name of art—ambiguous at best—covers many different things. A picture is not the same as an urn or an engraved sword, a marble torso, a sonata, a sonnet, a gothic cathedral. Some are objects, others are not; and even among those that are, how many differences of degree and kind exist! For the time being, let us categorize as though making an inventory and distinguish between fixed and movable goods. And there it is. Paintings, statuary, bronzes, glassware can come and go; buildings cannot. But isn't the church from Uncastillo presently in Boston? That is the trouble: things happen which should not happen; and houses, instead

of living and dying where their foundations were laid, are uprooted and travel over the globe, crossing the ocean or perhaps just the road. (A friend of mine once stood stricken with
terror when someone said to him in the most normal of tones:
"When this house was on Washington Street. . . .")

A house is a serf on its terrain. It has to be rooted in an environment—it demands that for it acquires the ambiance it invents. An ancient building evokes an entire world of the past.
The charm of old cities is not only or chiefly a matter of esthetics—esthetics is often a great cover-up—but rather their
attraction lies in their power to resurrect worlds that have
gone by. And each city has its own age, legible in its houses
as is ours in the lines of our faces, an age which traces the span
of its biography and puts boundaries to the life it has experienced. This gentleman never went to the palace of Congress
to hear Castelar,* that young lady was never an habituée of
the Royal Theatre, the city of Boston never had its Middle
Ages, its pilgrims to Santiago or Rome, its guilds, its news of
the Moors, its courtly songs, its tourneys. (How clearly the
nostalgia for that alien world shows through in the English
verse in which that romantic Bostonian Longfellow relived
the *Coplas* of Jorge Manrique!**) And for that reason, the
Romanesque portal of San Miguel de Uncastillo transplanted,
carried by boat across the Atlantic (why if we have a sunken
cathedral, should we not have a seafaring church?) has all the
disquieting drama and the equivocal delight of the absurd, of
that which simply cannot be and, yet, is, since there we have
it before our eyes.

---

* Emilio Castelar (1832–1899), historian, politician and great orator
—Trans.
** Jorge Manrique (1440?–1479) was a Spanish soldier-poet whose
masterpiece was translated into English by Henry Wadsworth Longfellow in 1833—Trans.

15 INTELLECTUAL LIFE
IN THE UNITED STATES

As soon as any two people bring up the topic of American intellectual life, disagreement emerges. For that matter, why two people? One will do, because as soon as someone in his inner thoughts arrives at an opinion on the subject, he is usually forced to contradict himself. This is the explanation for the swing of the pendulum between admiration and disappointment, confidence and scepticism, astonishment and disdain, and at times between cant and sarcasm. Usually one rounds up facts which bear on the problem: the best books on symbolic logic are American ones; so many thousands of extremely learned doctoral dissertations are being written each year; 97.3 per cent of all the students at X University are ignorant of the location of the Danube, and 84.8 per cent have never heard of Calderón;* there is a prodigious number of experiments underway in the United States on *ACTH*; while you can read the complete works of Dilthey in Spanish, only a few fragments of his writings have been translated into English; a baker's dozen of the greatest names in the world today are teaching in American universities; the pride and joy of such a university is not its three Nobel prize-winners but its football team.

It is easy to conclude that the facts taken by themselves tend to be confusing—because if we assume that they are all equally trustworthy, where do we stand? I believe that the only thing which can orient our point of view is a clearer idea of the forms intellectual life takes in the United States. And above all, one decisive fact—and this one we can accept at face value since, more than a fact, it is a structure: American intel-

---

* Pedro Calderón de la Barca (1600–1681), greatest dramatist of the Baroque period in Spain—Trans.

lectual life is not public, but professional in character. I mean to say that the American intellectual is not normally a man in the public eye, that is, not necessarily so, and if he is, it is probably for reasons other than his function as an intellectual: maybe his picture has appeared in *Life*, he has been on TV, he has attacked Senator McCarthy or Senator McCarthy has attacked him, he has been granted a whopping prize, he has issued an opinion as to whether or not the United States should appoint an ambassador to the Vatican, or he is director of a foundation which distributes fellowships. In all these cases the intellectual is converted into a man in public life and thus acquires the kind of celebrity that in European countries one sometimes achieves through writing and thinking. Naturally enough, his fame has little to do with his ideas and the public does not bother to inquire about them. It would be interesting to learn how many American intellectuals are known to the general public; probably someone knows and there may even be statistics, but it is summertime and I don't feel in the mood to search them out.

Who does know the intellectuals? Whence comes their prestige? By what devices do they obtain their positions, their reputation, their influence? Naturally, the people who know the intellectuals are other intellectuals. But even this is saying too much: an intellectual is known only by those who share his special field of interest. The chemist is known to other chemists, the philologist to other philologists, the Egyptologist to other Egyptologists. American universities are not divided into European faculties or schools, but rather into narrow departments which might better be called hermetic compartments, and transmigration from one to the other of these units is extremely difficult. Thus it is unlikely that a philosopher should be well-known to the Hispanists, that psychologists have some acquaintance with a historian, or that scholars of the classics will be aware that the discoverer of an important theorem is working alongside them in the next office. The patron saint of American intellectuals might well be Juan Palomo.*

The social prestige enjoyed by the man of science, the professor, or the serious writer arises from the social element in the individual's life: his position in such and such a fine college, the fact that he is a highly-placed technician at General Motors, or that he is the author of books published by a respectable publishing house and reviewed in the Sunday literary section of the *New York Times* or in certain specialized magazines. All these things generate prestige, condensing it and pouring it automatically over the head and shoulders of the beneficiary, but *not* conferring it on his own name or true personality. In Spain an admirable and admired man may happen to occupy a professorial chair, but none of this admiration flows on toward his successor—perhaps because people there believe that merely holding a chair does not prove much of anything; in the United States the man holding an illustrious professorship is deemed by that fact to be illustrious himself even before one is acquainted with him—and often there is no time later to check the evidence.

I ask you to try to imagine what this simple explanation of the basic fact—the opposition of professional life and public life—implies with regard to the functioning of all intellectual affairs. This is the structure we must bear in mind whenever we ponder the degree of intellectual freedom existing, the intellectual potential of the United States, or the amount of influence exercised on his country by the individual intellectual. At the same time we must not forget that the vast majority of scientific centers and schools of higher learning in the United States are private institutions not connected with the state;

* Juan Palomo is the hermetic hero of a Spanish folk saying:
"Así dice Juan Palomo:
yo me las guiso
y yo me las como"
(The sense is that he cooks and eats his own beans and has no truck with anyone.)—Trans.

that is to say, they are run by society and not by the public power of government. It would be too idealistic to hope that in North America a man like Menéndez-Pidal* should be well-known or popular when all he has done in a lifetime is to pour over medieval texts; or a man like Zubiri,** who speaks softly and writes about things which scarcely a few dozen readers understand; or a man who writes simple intense verses about the swelling hills of Soria, as did Antonio Machado; not to mention even richer and more complex figures such as Unamuno, Ortega, or Ramón Gómez de la Serna, Valle-Inclán, or Ramón y Cajal.*** Now in Europe, the public quality of intellectual life, though offering many risks, is a fine means of defense; in America the wheels go around because institutions are in the black and because the status system is founded on sane norms. Think, however, what might threaten if the system broke down and if the intellectual could not count on the court of appeal of public opinion, on a society (always much slower and surer than the State) which has the power, if the instance should arise, of conferring social status

---

* Ramón Menéndez-Pidal (1869–1969), dean of Spanish intellectuals in the twentieth century; foremost critic and literary scholar; director of the Spanish Academy—Trans.
** Javier Zubiri (1898–   ) eminent Spanish philosopher, student of Ortega and Heidegger—Trans.
*** Antonio Machado (1875–1939), one of the greatest modern Spanish poets; though a native of Andalusia, he adopted Soria as his spiritual home.
   Miguel de Unamuno (1864–1936), see earlier footnote.
   José Ortega y Gasset (1883–1955), foremost modern Spanish philosopher and man of letters, Professor of Metaphysics at the University of Madrid until the Spanish Civil War, founder of the prestigious journal *Revista de Occidente*.
   Ramón Gómez de la Serna (1888–1963), novelist, dramatist, and essayist, creator of a new form *la greguería*, short definitions in prose combining poetic imagery with elements of wit and irony.
   Ramón del Valle-Inclán (1869–1936), novelist, dramatist, and poet of the Generation of '98, a truly literary figure who created the *esperpento*, a form which attempts to communicate an effect similar to that of the disfigured reflection in the "fun house" mirror.
   Santiago Ramón y Cajal (1852–1934), world-renowned Spanish histologist awarded the Nobel Prize in 1906—Trans.

on a nonentity and shrugging off the existence of a man who seems to be at the very top.

Few examples bring more light to bear on the intellectual situation in the United States than a consideration of what is happening in America with regard to Spain and Hispanic studies. But this is a topic which deserves full attention on another day.

16 HISPANIC FERVOR
IN THE UNITED STATES

The first point to emphasize is the tremendous volume of concern among North Americans with Hispanic affairs; in no other country is our culture so widely studied—probably not even in Spain. There are in the United States over a thousand centers of higher learning (universities and colleges); and we must add to that total some five hundred slightly more elementary institutions called junior colleges. The vast majority of all these schools have programs for the study of the Spanish language and culture either in autonomous departments or within a Department of Romance Languages. Spanish is studied as well in innumerable high schools and secondary schools. Perhaps it is sufficient to record, for instance, that in 1950 institutions of higher learning conferred 2541 degrees in the field of Spanish (in French, the runner-up, only 1825). Dissertations and theses on topics drawn from Spanish culture are very numerous; the journals in the field are remarkable both for their quantity and their quality.

But up to here we have been dealing only with facts which do not in themselves afford a basis for evaluating the status of things Spanish in the United States. Opinion falls into two principal camps; often one passes from one idea to the other, after discovering the error of one's first view, but the sad truth is that both ideas are in error so one is unable to remain in either position. If one notes also that in addition to the students who major in Spanish there are many others (in some institutions up to twenty per cent of the student body) who learn our language and follow courses in our culture, one might conclude that Spain is completely familiar ground for North Americans. But immediately disillusionment sets in, because the average American has in fact a very hazy idea of our country. Our geography is fuzzy in his mind, he knows very little about our history; from our cultural heritage he has salvaged only a few names: Velázquez, Goya, Cervantes, Ortega, Lorca.* No, the American masses know very little about Spain. (It is quite apparent, of course, that no country is widely known to the majority of the citizens of another; let us each examine his own conscience and fund of information about the outside world—how many of us could summarize the historical development of Poland? How many English poets are familiar to the average Spaniard? Could he locate the various states of the Union? If anyone looks into the hiatuses in the geographical and historical knowledge of Frenchmen, Englishmen, or Germans, the results will be equally terrifying.) All this means, however, that the effect that this North American fervor for things Spanish has upon its coun-

---

* Diego Velázquez (1599–1660) court painter to Philip V and one of the world's greatest artists.

Francisco José Goya (1746–1828), world-renowned painter whose work evolved from a colorful, decorative classicism to a bitter and brilliant portrayal of the horrors and injustices he saw around him. His etchings alone would guarantee his place as one of the greatest Spanish artists of all time.

Miguel de Cervantes Saavedra (1547–1616) Spain's outstanding literary figure who won a permanent place in world literature with his novel *Don Quixote*.

Federico García Lorca (1898–1936), poet and dramatist extraordinary, a cult figure outside of Spain, killed in the early days of the Civil War—Trans.

try of origin is far different from what the situation would imply in a European country, since in any country of Europe so much work in and concern for a foreign culture would signify that that culture had become as familiar as the home civilization.

Noting all this, we fall into the second idea: utilitarianism. Of course, we tell ourselves, North Americans want to learn Spanish not because Spain interests them but because they want to do business with Spanish America. Regretfully, I cannot install myself comfortably in this other interpretation either. Because it is obvious and evident that North Americans do conduct business with South Americans, but *in English*. I wonder just how many letters in commercial Spanish are exchanged between the two Americas. Further proof lies in the direction taken in Hispanic studies. A couple of universities which tried the innovation of teaching Spanish by using newspapers both failed resoundingly. Those who wish to be initiated into Spanish prefer to read Galdós, Valera, Unamuno or Machado, Cervantes, Lope De Vega or the picaresque novel, Rubén Darío or Rómulo Gallegos. When Harvard University invited me to teach two courses, what was the suggested subject matter? Romanticism in Spain for the first, and for the other, Unamuno and Ortega. The two theses which I have directed in the United States dealt with Unamuno and Machado. And when the Department of State suggested that I give a series of lectures at Georgetown University in Washington, they were not interested in my speaking on politics or economics or Spain's relations with Spanish America, but rather on "Ideas and Letters in Spain Today." And these personal experiences of mine serve merely to confirm the general picture.

What conclusion may we draw then? Once more we arrive at the profound differences between the structures of European and American society, and the professional rather than public quality of intellectual life in the United States. Familiarity with things Spanish is thorough and often deep-felt among those who devote themselves to the field, but this knowledge does not pour over sufficiently into society as a whole. The field lacks impact and publicity—in the sense of public character and not in that of *propaganda*, the great plague of our times. And one of the reasons for this lack of effect—only one of them, of course—is that we Spaniards take so few pains ourselves to intensify the impact and, in fact, care so little about what may or may not go on in the United States which is in our interest. I remember one year that the Cultural Attaché of the French Embassy visited Wellesley College to pin the insignia of the Legion of Honor on the lapel of an American professor. What had she done to deserve this? Nothing other than teach French literature in exemplary fashion for some thirty years. She had not been involved either with Vichy or with the Resistance movement; she was not concerned with French politics. Thanks to her efforts, thirty classes of young women had learned to know and love not Messieurs Auriol, De Gaulle, or Herriot, but François Villon, Racine, Baudelaire, Proust, Stendhal, Bergson—France.

Despite all, I believe that the intensiveness with which Spanish culture is treated in the United States, the Spanish fervor of a goodly number of Hispanists, the touching enthusiasm of the majority of students in the field, and especially certain changes in the social structure of the country that are now only in the initial stages, will combine eventually, whether or not our actions justify it, to bring about a sense of Spain's energetic presence—a notion of the value of that way of life with which for some centuries we have been experimenting in our small corner of Europe and that occasionally turns out rather well.

17 AMERICAN LIBRARIES:
THE TWO SIDES OF THE COIN

In the middle of the campus, cushioned by green lawn or crusty snow, stands the library.

Through spacious windows whose shades are never drawn its many books are on view. How many books? A hundred thousand, three hundred thousand, a million, perhaps even six million. At night—for the library is open at hours convenient for its readers rather than for its personnel—entirely lighted it glows beneath the high stars or the lowering clouds; it shines forth among the dark trees and seems almost to call to us in the silence.

An American library is not a ticket window nor a counter nor even a catalogue placed in front of an impenetrable wall behind which presumably books are to be found. It is truly a library; that is, a building housing many volumes—real books, visible, palpable, succulent, tempting—capable of seducing even those who most resist the idea of going there. There are books of all eras, in every language, on all subjects; collections which are constantly added to, that do not come to a halt, say, in 1850; books that take their places on the shelves because a would-be reader has so desired it.

American libraries operate according to three principles: visibility, accessibility, trust. The books are on their metal shelves in great rows of stacks or in small rooms, always in evidence and in open sight. They signal to us with their lettering, they provoke us, they invite us to read. If one prefers not to use the immense card catalogues and goes searching in the stacks, great discoveries lie in store. As you push a button, long tubes of neon light gradually brighten the multi-colored shelves that flank you. You may circulate freely through the entire library, upstairs and down, lose yourself in a forest of print, go everywhere, remove books from their places, take them to a nearby table (not to some remote reading room), work with as many as you please: five, ten, twenty at a time. You may take books home—if you are a teacher or a student, no matter which—simply by signing your name on a card. (Contrary to our custom, books are never sequestered in some inaccessible holy of holies, a castle of no return where only the initiated are permitted to enter, guarded by "a watchdog who never sleeps and a huge dragon"; they are merely placed temporarily "on reserve," which means that they must be used in the library and not taken out of the building.)

I ask you to imagine what this situation can mean in terms of the possibilities for study, research or reading for pleasure. With few differences, the numerous public libraries all operate on the same basis, always ready to acquire the books desired by various readers, as do the cooperative libraries whose books are used in common by a group of members. Nothing could seem to be more perfect, more convenient, more desirable. Indeed they are delightful and responsible, besides, for certain decisive advantages in American culture. Yet reality is always so multi-faceted. . . .

These marvelous libraries lead to one result which particularly distresses me: the disappearance of privately owned libraries. People own few books. Even intellectuals, university professors, usually keep only a few hundred volumes at home: books sent as gifts by their authors; a few journals; that limited number of indispensable books which one uses all the time; books that one has already read in the library and found to be of permanent value. But, people say, American books are very expensive. Of course they are, but it is true also that personal incomes are higher than anywhere else. No, I am not convinced by the economic argument. The sacrifice an American has to make to buy a book is no greater than that required of his opposite number in France, England, or Germany. What really happens is that the public library with all its ready facilities takes care of temptation. Why *buy* books? A recently published work will already be on the library shelf, and, if it isn't, all one has to do is fill out an order card giving the title, and a few days later (or weeks if the book comes from overseas) it punctually arrives.

But does this add up to the same thing? I have greater confidence in books one has at home, the ones that are read and reread, that are filled with hieroglyphics and underlining—perhaps with notes in the margins—the books that one picks up by chance late at night when it is already past bedtime and stays up with for another wakeful hour. I believe that these familiar books are the ones which truly and indelibly shape an intellectual personality. The Spaniard devoted to letters slowly accumulates his personal library at the cost of heaven knows how much effort, how many sacrifices, how many suits with shiny trousers. A thousand volumes, two thousand, five, or sometimes ten or twenty thousand, that represent journeys to book fairs, delvings into the shadows of second-hand bookshops, catalogues of foreign books thumbed over with shivers of envy in search of bargains—bargains ever rarer and more adulterated now that the search has been systematically taken over by the great hunter-dealers. Finally there is no more houseroom; books spill over everywhere invading the tables and chairs, the floor. Naturally there is no car, no electric refrigerator, nor anything else of that sort: just books, books, and more books.

But the disappearance of private libraries is not the only unfortunate consequence; there is also the surprising difficulty encountered when one wishes to publish a book. The costs are very high (top quality paper, luxurious habits in the production process, expensive binding, extremely generous salaries) so the only books which can profitably be published are those which will sell around ten thousand copies, with an absolute minimum of five thousand. And since it is the great libraries rather than individuals that purchase the books, the market for them is unexpectedly low in proportion to the population and the wealth of the country. People do not buy many books, especially works of highly intellectual content, because they feel no need for them, because they can always read them in the library. But since the libraries alone, numerous though they are, cannot guarantee a sufficient sale, many interesting books (perhaps the most interesting ones conceived) are never published and so cannot be read either at home or at the campus or public library. Only the university presses can absorb the probable loss entailed by the publication of a scholarly book, and even these organizations sometimes request the author to subsidize publication of his work, to the tune of one or two thousand dollars.‡ Thus we have the paradoxical situation that in Spain, usually regarded as a poverty-stricken nation, many books can be published which could never see light in the richest country in the world—where there is, incidentally, no single publishing house with a list comparable to that of the *Revista de Occidente*. And for this state of affairs, which constitutes a grave threat to the intellectual future of the United States and, eventually, to that of the whole world, the blame must fall upon the incredible development of the American library which, thanks to its own perfection, may well find itself unable to shelve some of the best books which have been or could have been written.

‡ The practice actually is for the author to seek a subvention from a foundation or a scholarly institution—Ed.

18 PROVINCIALISM

Several weeks ago,† *Time Magazine* devoted a feature article (and what is even more impressive, its multicolored cover) to Professor Mortimer Adler. Over the ensuing weeks, I carefully followed the Letters to the Editor dealing with the story. With the comments and reactions long gone, I still find that no one ever brought up what I thought needed to be said. Furthermore, the very absence of comment on one specific point removes the focus from Adler, and from the author of the article, and transfers the problem into a more important area—American society. At that juncture I find myself becoming much interested.

What was it all about? Professor Adler is a shining light, one of the most brilliant of American intellectuals. (The adjective *brilliant* is chosen with particular care.) He is or has been associated with some of the most active and promising groups in American cultural affairs: the University of Chicago, the Ford Foundation, the seminars in Aspen, Colorado (which drew inspiration from our problem-beset Institute of Humanities in Madrid), the Encyclopedia Britannica. Under the auspices of the Britannica, Mortimer Adler, with the help of an imposing general staff, has been preparing a collection of works known as the Great Books of the Western World, which come September are to sell in the popular edition for some three hundred dollars. There are 54 volumes with 74 authors represented and a total of 443 works. The magazine is pleased to add for the delectation of its readers further quantitative data: the collection comprises 32,000 pages, 25 million words, and, above all, will take up five feet and one inch on the library shelf. In addition, Adler will present a colossal

† In the spring of 1952.

two-volume subject index, called the Syntopicon, where the
102 Great Ideas are identified, together with the 1792 terms
subordinate to them, including also cross references to the
passages in each author's work in which the ideas appear. It
must be granted first and foremost that we are dealing here
with an enormous effort to open up the intellectual horizons
of American readers, with an aggressive maneuver on the part
of the humanities against the narrow cults of rarefied science
and logical positivism, against certain strait paths of thinking
that influence American universities more than is realized and
through them pervade the country.

But our momentary enthusiasm falters as we check the list
of authors included. Who are they? It is scarcely necessary to
mention that Spain is conspicuous by her absence because this
is so commonplace as to cause little surprise. Only Cervantes
figures as one of the 74 greats of the Western World. Against
his solitary figure are ranged 25 Anglo-Saxon names which
proclaim the assumption that the English-language culture
represents one third of all the West has to offer in ancient,
medieval, and modern times, including the flowering of
Greece and Rome. This seems ever so slightly optimistic,
don't you agree? That point aside, there are other frequent
surprises. Right at the beginning we encounter Appollonius
and Nicomachos, but not Cicero, whose shadow spread over
Europe for some two thousand years—in the fields of politics,
law, philosophy, and rhetoric—nor Seneca, who has conquered time again and again to reappear at decisive moments
in the history of ideas: at the birth of Christianity, when the
Middle Ages were about to take shape, in the Renaissance
world, and in the Baroque period when Seneca offers one
hand to Descartes and the other to Quevedo.

On Mortimer Adler's list appear Hamilton, Madison, and
Jay, the men who drafted *The Federalist* a century and a half
ago, but we look in vain for Petrarch, master of the European
lyric and the art of love, unexcelled craftsman at work within

Europe's intimacy for two long centuries; for Erasmus who incarnated an entire era; for Luther, without whom no one can understand either the German language or the history of Europe; and for Voltaire, who filled the eighteenth century to overflowing. Nor are these all the omissions. If one were to choose a single name to symbolize the whole of western culture, that name might well be Leibnitz—with his particles and monads, his dynamic physics and theology, representing the fusion of the Churches and the Berlin Academy. Well, incredible though it may seem, the name of Leibnitz does not appear on the list where we do discover Gilbert or Huygens, probably with a slight blush on their pale dead cheeks. And John Stuart Mill, discreet and clever as he was, would probably feel the same shame were he to seek and fail to find the name of his teacher Auguste Comte, founder of positivism and of sociology—the keystones of nineteenth-century thought and the two principal systems on which the United States has been nourished even to the present day.

Fielding, Sterne, Boswell. Very well, but must we pay for their presence with the absence of Herder, Fichte, and Schopenhauer? Faraday is welcome, of course, but not as a replacement for Planck. Can Western thought of the last hundred years be comprehended through William James and Sigmund Freud alone without including Kierkegaard, Nietzsche, Dilthey, Bergson, or Husserl, to mention only those safely dead? Can the West be understood without taking into account its mystics, whether Eckhardt or Saint John of the Cross? Can one really do without the whole of lyric poetry and the modern theatre (except for Shakespeare, of course) overlooking Lope and Calderón, Racine and Molière, Schiller, Ibsen, and Pirandello?

Readers of *Time*, some in admiration, some with antagonism, wrote in their letters to the Editor about various "intra-American" aspects of Adler's enterprise: his polemic with Dewey, his disdain for the existing universities, his possible influence on the educational system of the country. No one, apparently, was surprised at his projected image of the western world in whose name, of course, all the indicated reforms were to be made. And the sad thing is that his picture of western culture is decidedly provincial. The recrudescence of provincialism in so many places is particularly alarming because we have just begun to rid ourselves of all chauvinism in the intellectual sphere, realizing that all nationalistic prejudice represents a strictly provincial attitude insofar as it is unaware that nationalism in any western country is necessarily provincial in character. And the appalling thing is that this apparition springs not from the ultra-conservative ranks which traditionally affect archaic views, not from among intellectual pygmies or prefabricated scholars, but from a source whence we have reason to expect the newest advances, an area equipped with fabulous resources—and so provincialism reappears like a ghost, a specter that steps down from the latest model supersonic jet plane.

Though it may seem strange, this phantom would have met some serious obstacles in Spanish intellectual circles, just as is happening with other, similar cases. I should not like to be misunderstood: my objection does not have to do with the list of Great Books in itself, but rather with the criteria for selection. In Spain, for instance, where so many things slip by, no man of intellectual stature would ever tolerate a list so grotesquely favorable to authors of the Spanish language, so forgetful of what has in actual fact laid the ideological basis for the world in which we live. We cannot afford to do without a large number of books by a multitude of authors born outside our boundaries, who did not write in Spanish, who are not "of the family," who do not belong to our domestic traritions, but who do represent essential ingredients of the authentic reality we share with Europe and the West. And when the moment arrives to take a responsible role in world affairs, the first necessary condition is to know how that world is constituted and not to confuse world realities with the special interests, legitimate though they may be, that may be of primary concern in La Coruña, Gerona, Bordeaux, the Palatinate, Calabria, Wales, Tucumán, or Illinois.

19 THE UNIVERSITY AND SOCIETY IN THE UNITED STATES

The United States is crowded with universities: from the Atlantic to the Pacific, from Canada to the Gulf of Mexico, they have been strewn throughout the length and breadth of the land. It is true that they tend to bunch somewhat in the northeastern section of the country, in New York and New England; that they grow close together in the old and flavorful state of Massachusetts, around Boston; but nowhere are they lacking because, whether they are called universities or colleges, there are a thousand of them. And if we add the five hundred junior colleges, that comes out to one institution of higher learning for every hundred thousand inhabitants. Using the same scale, that would mean in Spain having some two hundred and eighty such schools. This quantitative information alone leads us to think that an American university must be different from its European counterpart and, above all, that it must play a different role in the life of its country. What is an American university, what purposes does it serve, how does it "live" in the United States?

THE CAMPUS

First of all, its physical presence. The American university can scarcely be called "a house of learning" but might better be referred to as a "countryside of learning" because its physical reality is characterized by its vegetation. In appearance, the university is a park or a forest, a field, a campus which, as in the case of Wellesley, may very well comprise some 400 acres and a lake. As for trees, the walnuts, elms, maples as the academic year begins glow their reddest and then shade into rust, purple, violet, and gold until they seem to converge into one of Juan Ramón Jiménez's early poems. And in the midst of all this vegetation stands the stone or the dark red brick of the scattered buildings, usually nineteenth-century Gothic in style. When trees are not the dominant feature, when buildings are no farther from each other than those of a European university center, then Americans dare not use the word *campus* and they say *yard*, as in the solemn, venerable, and leafy case of Harvard. But the squirrels are everywhere the same.

Damp earth, the softest of lawns, thick branches loaded with birds; and the walls, hung with ivy that is red in the fall as the term begins and green for commencement. For two or three months the snow mutes the campus, hushes the sound of footsteps, changes the color to tones of diffuse, rising light. Nature. But does this constitute the University? Is it not rather quite the contrary—that is, nature in opposition to culture?

This opposition is always problematical in the United States and especially in its universities. One does not *go* to a university to do something—for example, to study science—one *stays* at a university, lives there, resides in its environment. That is the essential point: most universities are residential in character. Many of them are close to small towns which serve merely as their periphery; even the others, the urban schools, constitute closed worlds in themselves—a campus with houses where one eats, sleeps, converses, reads, studies, plays, and prays. These are the backdrops of a life in common, and that is the chief function of the American university: to provide for shared living.

THE TWO SUPPOSITIONS

All this would seem to imply that in the choice between education vs. instruction, Americans have opted for the former and Europe the latter—with England, as always, taking the middle road. But is that the way it works out? What about American utilitarianism? And over-specialization? And the kind of preparation for highly specialized, practical functions that turns out experts in the infinitesimal? All of this has some truth in it and exercises considerable influence, but that part comes later. In Europe we see that ambiguous coexistence of two kinds of "faculties"—the professional (or vocational) and the more strictly intellectual divisions. Except when protected by a tradition of long duration, the professional schools—of engineering or veterinary medicine—do not impress us as truly belonging to the university. In the United States, where there are universities dedicated exclusively to the liberal arts, specialization tends to come after the completion of a formative period which culminates in graduation from undergraduate status. Such specialization is almost always a matter of postgraduate work, training that a student takes once he has finished his basic college courses, and it is usually comparatively brief after four years of undergraduate work which lay the important groundwork.

This situation reflects the differences between American university departments and European "faculties": in the United States, "faculty" is used to mean the entire teaching staff of the college, the total of all instructors, the group responsible for the academic program. There are multiple departments —each, therefore, with a highly restricted field: chemistry, mathematics, music, English, philosophy, Greek, zoology, sociology, Spanish, astronomy, religion. The departments tend to separate the instructors, and only secondarily the students. That is to say, a professor belongs to the department of physics or the department of psychology, but the student takes courses in many different departments; and his decision to major in one of them means only a minor amount of specialization, or rather an intensification, an act of preference in order to concentrate more time in a particular field. Thus we can contrast the "system" of studies in a European faculty, characterized by a more or less rigid schedule of courses, and the lack of "system" one discovers upon investigating the American B.A. program, which is based solely upon a certain number of credit hours, some structure of prerequisites taking account of necessity and incompatibility, and a final concentration in one or another discipline. The American university is concerned with a "level" of learning rather than with a coherent system of studies. Now we can explain how it is that the European sometimes finds his American colleague scandalously ignorant, and vice versa. The European discovers the holes in the American's training, gaps in the systematic mastery he would expect to exist; the American is shocked by the ignorance of the man holding a doctorate in science with respect to the humanities and by the total absence of acquaintance with physics or biology on the part of the lawyer or the man of letters.

The whole picture becomes clearer if we can bring into relief the two different suppositions which underlie university life in the United States and in Europe respectively (and by Europe, I repeat, I mean the Continent). In Europe, the task of the university is to offer instruction in a science or art; in North America, to educate and form a personality. How can two such distinct aims animate the "same" kind of institution? Simply because of the difference in the basic assumptions mentioned before. The European supposition might be stated thus: "The formation of personality follows as a consequence of systematic scientific instruction." The American tenet could be expressed as follows: "The formation of personality requires (among other things) scientific instruction." This means that while in Europe it is assumed (surprisingly enough) that the study of philology, civil law, or chemistry will induce the individual student to become a *person*, Americans hold to the belief that in order to become a *person* the individual must undertake various activities, among them the study of botany, Latin, philosophy, *or* mechanics—and I underline the *or* because if you press him closely, an American will not hesitate to admit that it makes little difference which, much to the horror of the old-world intellectual.

Naturally, therefore, the American university must be residential; one must be able to *live* there. In Europe, training is thought to be the duty of the family; in the United States, it is believed to be the responsibility—each according to its level —of the institutions of learning. The task is a difficult one which requires an abundance of means, time, and "expert" attention: it is not a job for just anyone. Can the family possibly train its children? Is the family itself educated to the task? Does it possess the knowledge, skills, techniques, abilities, and resources necessary to personality development? All this seems highly questionable to the American mind.

WHAT THE UNIVERSITY OFFERS

The university transmits three things: the knowledge necessary in a given discipline, a synthesis of the dominant ideas of the era, and a system of beliefs and norms of behavior. In the United States the latter is the most important: in and around that mission the other tasks find their places. Therefore science is valued no more highly than is the honor system, because of which no examination need be proctored since the student whose word is accepted as the truth neither cheats nor gives aid. Therefore the student is completely free to choose his own courses, and what is evaluated with regard to him are his personal reactions, his customary manner, and his talent for living together with others. For the same reason also, mind and body are trained not equally, I should say, but at least without the tremendous imbalance usual in Europe. At a women's college, I attended a swim show that could have sparkled in *The School for Sirens** and, a few weeks later, an excellent production of Sophocles' *Antigone*—in *Greek*! The purpose of the University is to provide for the acquisition of every kind of essential tool, including those necessary to research. And I say *including* with no irony intended, because research is esteemed as only one possibility offered the student *among others*: the exercise of a profession (some of little intellectual hue, such as nursing, secretarial work, or commerce); the educational field; social life; political activity. If an individual does choose research, then it is that the university takes on the strictly *scientific* complexion that in Europe seems its essential and almost exclusive reason for being. I must add also, that when the university does take on this air it is a real, not a fictitious, manifestation.

The American student is indeed ignorant about many areas in which he has not taken courses; sometimes, of course, it seems absurd to us that he has not done so. But it is extremely unusual for him to have only a vague idea about what he *has* studied—something that frequently occurs elsewhere. Take, for example, the field of languages, ancient and modern, and the many European university graduates who have passed courses in a half dozen of them, yet still do not know any one language well enough to be able to read a book in it or to sustain a conversation. American students of Spanish write in Spanish and put together in our language theses of two or three hundred pages; the same phenomenon occurs, of course, among those taking other modern languages. Two traits characteristic of the American university are a kind of

* An Esther Williams swim film—Trans.

intellectual modesty and a minimum of pretense. Yet at the top levels, initiates realize very well that every year the university presses do put out a good number of books (in all disciplines) of the important kind that must be taken into account.

DANGERS

Unfortunately every human reality has its inherent risks; even its very virtues may often be lying in wait ready to convert themselves into some form of temptation. What are the most obvious dangers associated with the American university? The one most in evidence which today seriously concerns many educators is utilitarianism. They fear, and perhaps with good reason, that attention (and therefore money) is being diverted from the humanities and liberal arts toward scientific investigation and the development of industrial or politico-social techniques. This is indeed a grave danger, but it does not originate within the university; that is, even though it may exercise a decisive influence, it originates outside the institution and is therefore not a danger *of* but a danger *for* the university.

The inherent danger is rather what I would call the excessive "professionalism" of the faculty. The American instructor tends to be very competent and able. He is thoroughly familiar with the discipline he teaches, he keeps up with new developments by constant reading of books and journals, and he fulfills his duties with a truly surprising conscientiousness and dedication evidenced by his lack of absences, strict punctuality, fidelity to his planned teaching programs, concern for his students, and knowledge of them as individuals. (On this point I shall have more to say later.) One of the factors that makes such behavior possible is the large number of universities and the quantity of professors in each, or conversely, the small number of students in each class. If we look at the ratio of instructors to students, we find that it is almost always higher than 10 to 100 and, in many instances, there may be 20 or even 25 professors for every hundred students. Statistics for the year 1950–51 show the following totals in some of the better colleges and universities for student population and teaching staff: Harvard, 10,632 and 2,481; Yale, 7,317 and 1,505; Princeton, 3,500 and 522; Wellesley, 1,718 and 210; Smith, 2,276 and 259; Columbia, 25,637 and 2,825; Georgetown, 5,027 and 764; Cornell, 10,191 and 1,427; California, 44,260 and 4,437.

But all this has another side to it. The astronomical number of instructors leads us to wonder whether they can be anything more than merely excellent functionaries. It would be impossible for them all to reach beyond that and useless to ask them to try. Yet the basis of dynamic teaching is an effective intellectual life; the only "contagious" professor who can pass on the germ to his students is the instructor whose life outside the classroom and beyond the campus is in its own inwardness decisively intellectual in character, affected by all the problems and difficulties of the man of intellect. The student should witness the drama inherent to the real function of intelligence in its most authentic form. This experience is the essential factor in education. If that experience is missing, then everything else, regardless of how good or useful it may be or how well it operates, is invalidated and discredited. It is my fear that the American university may not be offering that kind of ferment in the necessary proportions. The concern for mechanics, the unchallenged hypertrophic growth of bureaucratic "administrations," the attention given (indispensable attention of course, but perhaps excessive) to the proper fulfillment of teaching duties, may lead an instructor to believe that that is all which is required of him—and many professors are simply and only "professors," a situation that cannot bear scrutiny. There is an adjective which typically occurs to American students when they wish to describe a teacher in whom they can make out some intellectual hinterland over and beyond his professional functions: "inspired." It would indeed be an excellent idea to season professional competence (as bread is fortified with vitamins) with a good dose of "inspiration."

Another inherent danger has to do with the already noted lack of system in student academic programs. Doubtless there is something healthy about the prevalent lack of confidence in rigid "plans" of study, about the emphasis on the student's inclinations; however, as a result the blank spaces on the resulting intellectual maps of the cosmos frequently go beyond the permissible limit. Students know well what they do know, to the extent that it is possible to learn something without knowing about other related things. For instance, a student may have had a course on Plato, another on Berkeley and Locke, and a third in mathematical logic. He has worked dutifully, he has read a dozen good books, and he has written various papers of surprisingly high quality in careful fashion and with complete honesty. Yet he has no notion of the history of philosophy, he has no idea of what happened after Plato and before Berkeley, nor does he suspect how we arrived at symbolic logic. With all his fine learning, he truly has no conception of what it is all about, of what the real problem—or better, *drama*—is that underlies all three of those courses he selected from the splendid catalogue offered by his university.

SOCIAL IMPORTANCE

What is the social role of the university in the United States? Is it an important one or not? The answer is not an easy one; or rather there are several to offer, and at first glance they seem to contradict each other. To begin with, a European perceives a lack of universality in university activities. A professor, no matter how eminent, has no reputation outside his narrow professional circle (and if he has, it is for reasons other than his professional status or his character as an intellectual). The causes of this situation are many and demand a lengthy explanation. In large part, the problem derives not from the university itself, but rather from the general structure of the United States—its enormous expanse, for example, and its lack of any true "center." (As is the case with its cities and towns, the country itself also has failed to establish a "Plaza Mayor.") Thus it is that there is no such thing as a truly national newspaper, for only two or three make any such pretense or achieve even minimal success if they do; and practically all Americans read local papers. Similarly, philosophical and scientific journals as well as literary magazines have very limited circulation, and the mass-circulation slicks measure out their doses a drop at a time when it comes to news of an intellectual nature, particularly when reporting on life in the university.

There are, however, other causes which arise from the university itself—primarily from its *private* and *professional* nature, as opposed to the *public* character of its European counterparts. The majority of colleges and universities (and almost all of the prestige-laden ones) are private institutions; even the government-sponsored schools are under the jurisdiction of a given state and not of the national government. There are many advantages to this arrangement, some especially appealing when observed from within the European system; but this fact does tend to help "hide" the university. (It can, of course, be argued whether this is a danger or merely another advantage—possibly a proponent of the latter view would win out.) The American university enjoys considerable autonomy. It is best, of course, to avoid exaggeration when speaking of autonomy or independence in the middle of the 20th century, but if we compare the American with the government-run European institutions, great differences do exist in this area. The American university also operates on terms of cordial rivalry with its fellow institutions and therefore cannot dispense with the struggle for prestige. Any student may choose from among innumerable institutions; nor is location a decisive factor, since students from all sections of the country pour into the better schools. A university cannot allow itself to rest on its laurels, because it cannot count on funds which are automatically granted but depends, rather, on its endowment, gifts received, and tuition paid by the students. So it is that universities usually recruit their teaching staff directly and without restriction via an appointment generally of temporary nature which becomes permanent (after considerable time and in the light of long experience) only when tenure is granted to the professor in question. Thus they avoid the risk of granting a candidate a professional chair which then remains irremediably "occupied" in name only for forty years' time: a mistake, if one has been made, is immediately rectifiable. Each professor has therefore a market value on the open exchange, and his range of quotations is a decisive factor within the university hierarchy.

All this is true to such an extent that social standing originates within the university and is acquired automatically. A professor in an illustrious college enjoys high social prestige even though no one knows who he is, what he has done, or how he thinks. This explains the comparative ignorance outside a tight circle of specialists regarding work done in the university; even among the intellectual minority it is infrequent for a man's reputation to be widespread. There is then an indisputable lack of resonance in public affairs, but social prestige, impersonal and uninformed, functions thus in a safe and certain manner.

It should be noted that the American university professor is poorly paid, if we compare his income with those obtained by other professional men in the country. Despite that handicap, his salary alone will permit him to lead a fairly solvent life and, in the upper ranks, to reach a level of some luxury—especially in the economically more prosperous universities. (There is, of course, a strict hierarchy: Instructor, Assistant Professor, Associate Professor, Professor—and the last step is none too easily reached.) But going along with this relative freedom from economic problems is a heavy, intensive work load. The much-used phrase "full-time" is not just a manner of speaking: a professor must invest his entire day in his professional occupation; he does not need any other job, nor would he find it easy to undertake one. For his duties are not limited to giving a few more or less fixed classes per month: not only is absolute assiduity in instruction expected without exception, but there is also the obligation to participate actively in the life of the university as a whole: department meetings, faculty councils and committees, teas, student invitations, reports and a certain amount of other administrative paperwork, and, above all, prompt correction of work assigned and meticulous attention to the student. A teacher knows his students as individuals; he meets with them during set office hours during which he remains in his study at their disposal to guide their efforts, check their progress, dispel their doubts. Often, when mutual confidence has led to friendly relations, the professor exercises a kind of personal tutorship. Students invite their teachers to dinner with some frequency; the professor often has his students come to his home to chat over a cup of tea or coffee, and sometimes he too invites them to a meal, in small groups or one or two at a time. This extremely human kind of relationship is considered to be at least as important as an exposition of the laws of thermodynamics, Greek verbs, Aristotelian categories, or Cervantine prose, and from such a relationship, solid and durable friendships often come into being. To direct a thesis does not mean two or three interviews with the candidate, but rather, for student and director, thirty, forty, or fifty work sessions together ranging in purpose from orientation, discussion, and extremely scrupulous verification of work accomplished, to checking over the incredibly detailed requisites in matters of form and even proofreading for errors in typing.

All of this tends to put a mute on the sounds of university life; lives lived in the university are slightly obscure, having little access to either notoriety or fame, but they are accompanied by security in prestige—that magic prestige to which the American is so sensitive, the prestige of the expert. In every university there are innumerable files wherein is kept the entire history, and the rating, of every student who passes through. There is also a professional Vocational or Placement Office to which graduates address themselves when they wish references for any potential employers and whose dicta carry very considerable weight. Furthermore, when an announcement of engagement or marriage appears in the society section of the paper, one item never left out is that the groom is a graduate of Harvard, Yale, Princeton, or Columbia, and *above all* that the bride has her B.A., M.A., or perhaps even Ph.D. from Wellesley, Smith, Radcliffe, or Bryn Mawr. Otherwise, the splendor of the union would be slightly dimmed.

WOMEN'S COLLEGES

It is common knowledge that a good number of American colleges are either exclusively for men or for women; although the tendency towards coeducational institutions is growing stronger, today the most characteristic pattern is still that of the men's or women's college which does not admit students of the other sex. The idea of men's colleges is not especially surprising, since up until the last few decades institutions of higher learning the world over were open only to men. Women's colleges, however, give rise to a feeling of some doubt on the part of a European. Isn't it rather absurd to separate the sexes?

The apparent absurdity is explainable in terms of two conditions, one historical and the other functional. The historical condition has to do with dates: the original and most revered women's colleges (such as the Seven Eastern Colleges) which are models for all the others, were founded in the nineteenth century—Wheaton in 1834; Mount Holyoke in 1837; Wellesley in 1870; Smith in 1871; Barnard in 1890—during the era when women still could not enter the existing universities. Such colleges made possible the incorporation of women into fields of higher learning through institutions designed especially for them. The second condition, a matter of function, is based on the fact we have noted that the American university emphasizes education rather than instruction and is therefore residential. This pattern, if it does not impose separation of the sexes, nevertheless tends to favor the development of two separate types of institutions.

PROBLEMS

Even in such a swift glance at what the university represents in the United States, we have noted a respectable number of problems arising from among the many germane to the character of the institution, and there are still others. There is, for instance, an over-emphasis on Anglo-Saxon culture (going far beyond the inevitable and justifiable weighting in favor of one's own that is normal in every country) that results sometimes in an otherwise cultivated group being completely unfamiliar with the name of a first-rate man whose works do not happen to have been put into English. There is also a deliberate delight in spontaneousness which may lead in turn to the willful fabrication of a false "spontaneity" that develops into nothing other than vulgarity affirmed and confirmed. It is sought out for its own sake, insolent and smug, and forcibly demonstrated in such phenomena as the spring riots which take place from time to time in the men's colleges, taking the form perhaps of a noisy panty raid on a neighboring women's college (or on the female dormitories if this happens in a coeducational institution). I remember my struggles to explain in English what we mean in Spanish by that quality we call "la chabacanería";* it seemed almost impossible to find an English equivalent for the term, or an example to illustrate its significance, until I discovered a perfect instance: the spring riots.

But the most interesting and most serious problems are new ones: I mean the problems that are arising today, the ones that are going to force the university to examine itself thoroughly and to introduce important changes. Until now the best men in the United States have gone into industry, business, and administration. I believe they were right to do so since they were answering their country's most pressing need: putting the nation into operation, building toward effectiveness, security, and a high standard of living. Strictly speaking, culture (and especially the liberal arts) was largely left in the hands of women, who have long been the educators of the United States. It is only fair to say that they have done their task rather well—as in Argentina up until a few years ago, and in most of the rest of Hispanic-America—but the situation should not be allowed to continue, not because it is time for a relief shift or because men should replace women in the field, but because men also are needed in an area which demands their best efforts. Related to this problem is that of the "importation of ideas" from abroad, especially from Europe. For many years "ideas," and "culture" in the United States have been in the custody of women and transplanted Europeans.

All this cannot—must not—continue as before. The United States must invent some program for its collective life. But— the objection may come—hasn't such a program long been in effect? Certainly, and a most attractive project it was—to

* Self-complacent and rampant vulgarity—Trans.

bring into being the United States of America. But since this entity is now formed, since the country can no longer live only within its own boundaries but must cohabit in the world at large, functioning as it were as a single personality engaged in dialogues with others, it is now incumbent upon the United States to search out and find a plot for its further history. The return in Hollywood to the Western, the vogue for recalling the country's origins, seem fine indeed—always providing that they do not represent turning one's back on current problems or an appeal to the memory of a past life-program as a recourse against the difficulties attendant upon the imaginative creation of a new one, one that is urgently needed. And this life-project which represents a country's inner intimacy can only be invented by the country itself. Foreigners may serve as gadflies or stimuli; they may present for consideration by Americans other systems and manners of approaching reality, other enterprises, other human configurations, so that through contrast and comparison what is needed may be discerned; but that need must be autonomous and authentic, for a vocation in that sense resists being imported and naturalized.

So if I am not mistaken, within the next few years the American university is going to have to change its course. Industry and administration get along very well now on their own steam without any great need for major improvements; invention is now called for in other aspects of life. At the moment there is on the horizon a mirage of what is regarded as most important: physics, and particularly nuclear physics. There is no doubt whatsoever that the area is decisive in importance, but since certain teams and groups already in the field will continue to exist and develop without grave difficulty, that is sufficient answer to the need. The areas which are now beginning to appear as unexpectedly urgent are those of history and metaphysics.

20 PHILOSOPHY AT YALE

Often while crossing the great square at the heart of New Haven, I have stopped and wondered what it would look like had it been the Spaniards who arrived in 1639 in the bay and on the banks of the Quinnipiac, instead of Thomas Eaton, the merchant so caught up in thoughts of heaven, and John Davenport, the clergyman so attentive to the things of this world. New Haven's Green would undoubtedly be called the *Plaza Mayor de Puerto Nuevo*. Probably there would be arcades, the buzz of incessant conversation, slow and dilatory passersby, cafés—with terraces for when the snow departed and tables could be brought out—and, on one side or another, a baroque cathedral with gilded altars and carved saints.

Instead of which there is mostly lawn and elm trees. In the United States, the landscaping dominates even urban settings, and New Haven is the city of elms. On one side of the Green are the business establishments; on another, a huge drugstore, the neo-classic Post Office building, and various banks; on the third, the Court House, the Library, the University Press, the Graduate and Faculty Clubs. In the middle are three small colonial churches: Trinity Church, Center Church, and United Church. The Green is usually covered with snow four or five months out of the year, and only in May does it really take on color and become truly green. In New Haven, in Connecticut, in all of New England, as in Antonio Machado's Soria, "Spring lags but is so beautiful and tender when she arrives." The Green in its vast void is almost always lovely; automobiles and blue busses cross through it; hurried pedestrians circle it; the stars and stripes flutter at the top of the memorial to those who died in the First World War; perhaps there is a man selling multicolored balloons. One day it is suddenly filled with men, women, and smiling young girls in colorful dresses all with blurred crosses on their foreheads: it is Ash Wednesday. Then when the sky turns deep blue and the sumptuous grass springs up, when the spring bonfire of yellow forsythia flares, when the pink and white dogwoods lend the entire city an air of unusual delicacy, the Green begins to come alive. Children play under the elms, college students take their break there, lonely old men spend the useless hours puffing on their pipes or getting together on the green wooden benches to talk over old times—perhaps pulling out, as one disinters from the moth balls an ancient frock coat kept in an unused trunk, the Italian, Armenian, or Polish language of their youth, long buried under an English which they still resist.

The fourth side of the Green is a boundary; what bounds the huge square common is one of the sides of the Old Campus (the oldest part of the college) of Yale University. The dark stone—thick walls, austere windows in dormitories for the young, turrets reminiscent of the Châtelet in Paris—both isolates the city from its university and affords a means of communication between them, and the University is in turn the border beyond which New Haven fronts the world.

Universities worthy of the name are open to the world and for that reason have no choice but to seek out a cloistered retreat, the material representation of a spiritual turning inward. Yale, which is more urban than some other American universities, which lies within the city and is a part of it (city streets cross and divide its campus) is nevertheless the very epitome of withdrawal and retirement.

Its many roads have a flavor of the cloister about them: they end in various squares, green or white with the changing seasons, such as the one which stretches toward the great Sterling Library with its four million and some volumes; they lead through a series of such sheltered squares which culminate finally in the enclosed and self-contained Old

Campus. Here is old Connecticut Hall, built in 1752, and nearby the statue of Yale's young hero Nathan Hale, standing with hands behind his back waiting for death. Beyond is the statue of former president Pierson and the ever-present elms. There are no bells to toll, but at dusk the Old Campus is filled with the music of the carillon pouring down from neighboring Harkness Tower, a gothic edifice beside which, in the wrought iron gate to one of the colleges, are the letters which form the students' motto: "For God, for Country, and for Yale," elucidated in turn at the entrance to the campus by the shield of the university bearing the legend: "*Lux et Veritas.*" For only through enlightenment and the search for truth can a university serve God, the country, and itself; and any other form of servitude amounts to treason.

I taught philosophy for a full semester at Yale. It may not be entirely idle to note down the semester's substantive content: a graduate seminar on "The Theory of Human Life"; another, also for graduate students, on "Imagination and Fiction"; a third course for undergraduate majors on contemporary European Philosophy; and a series of lectures dealing with the latter theme. It is not an idle effort because Europeans tend to believe that North American universities are interested only in mathematical logic or, at best, in epistemology. At Yale, where there are usually some fifty graduate students preparing for their doctorates in the field of Philosophy, in 1955–56 in the Graduate School alone, some thirty-two courses were offered in Philosophy. In eight of them, in the title or course description the word "metaphysics" appears, and some are courses or seminars on Aristotle, St. Thomas Aquinas, Duns Scotus, Ockham, Leibnitz, and Kant (and not only on Peirce, Whitehead, or Dewey). If we include the thirty-three undergraduate course offerings spread over four college classes, we arrive at a total of sixty-five courses and seminars (year or semester) in Philosophy offered every academic term. This elementary piece of arithmetic might surprise not only many readers outside the United States, but also many people within the country's borders. Where else in Europe or in America is philosophy taught more generously or more abundantly?

I should say further that at Yale, philosophy may be cultivated at a leisurely pace. There is, it seems to me, no more propitious approach. The problem of philosophy in America is a particularly touchy one. Philosophy was not born in America, nor, as yet, has it been *reborn* there. That is to say that society as such, whether in North or South America, has not yet arrived at the radical need for philosophy. (In passing may I say that I cannot understand why some Americans, particularly South Americans, prefer to believe that this moment has indeed already come and are thus ready to give up without a struggle the future miracle which will take place on the day that truly brings the moment of recognition.) Nevertheless, what is true of society is not necessarily true of individuals; many North Americans feel the call of a vocation for philosophy, the personal necessity for a way of life within philosophy—and this in as authentic and intense a fashion as anyone anywhere. On the other hand, society in America derives from European society, carries European society in some form inside its own structures, and European society in certain of its aspects is constituted of and by philosophy: in other words, philosophy does belong as part of the tradition of American society and is an ingredient of that society. In an article written for the *Yale Alumni Magazine* of June, 1956, Hendel convincingly insists that philosophy played its part in the heritage of the United States, assuming importance even before the Revolution. What his thesis amounts to is that the United States was not forged without philosophy, but rather in a certain measure, with the conscious help of that discipline. Nothing could be truer. But when the time arrives to forge a philosophy in what is now the United States, then the situation becomes highly problematical. In America philosophy is on hand (that is, available as part of one's heritage); while in some parts of Europe (and only in certain parts), philosophy is being created in a different form. Philosophy, then, belongs to the traditions of the Americas to the extent that those societies derive from and contain those of Europe. At the same time, philosophy comprises the common mission of the West, of which the Americas are an essential part. This state of affairs may explain, I think, some of the many misunderstandings which cluster around the much-debated question of philosophy in America.

Peril has always lurked in the sense of urgency, in the various shapes of haste. The worst of these engenders a kind of protective coloration which at times has gone to the extreme of simulation: an apparent philosophy which is only apparent (precisely the Aristotelian definition of sophistry, *PHAINOMÉNE SOPHÍA OÛSA D'OÛ*), and which in Spanish we may describe with an idiom colloquially translatable as "to make like one is making something." Haste is betrayed also by the attempt to arrive immediately at an "American" philosophy—without being clear as to whether or not the structures of the several western societies prohibit such a development; without being sure whether or not it is possible today to have an English, French, Spanish, or German philosophy, or even, in the strictest sense, a European philosophy. A third manifestation is the urge to be in on "the last word" which, ironically enough, usually causes one to be stuck with the next-to-last (Existentialism, for instance). Finally, another subtler indication of hurry, this one more usual in the United States than in Hispanic America, is the drive to "liquidate" traditional philosophy in the name of "Scientism" and *reduce* it to symbolic logic or "epistemology." Both of these are honorable fields honorably cultivated in the United States: what seems harmful to me is the effort thus to limit philosophy. I tend to believe that such an attitude is European and not American in origin; that it represents a flowering of separatism. Let me explain. Certain European proponents of philosophy, conscious of their own limits within traditional bounds, have upon transplanting themselves to the New World thought that they might attain greater recognition if they identified what is only a part of philosophical knowledge with its totality and negated the value of all that was overlooked. At the same time, they have played to the bias in favor of "science" which exists in a considerable sector of American society.

To this kind of "separatism" has been added another variety also uncommon in terms of the most meaningful American traditions: "Anglo-Saxonism"—isolation within the English language. Although the beginnings of philosophical discipline in the United States, in the nineteenth century, reveal profound French and German influences, the last years of the 19th century and a good part of the present one have witnessed a pernicious return to isolation (parallel to that produced on the continent of Europe). There are many instances of exclusivism in the English language: even today there are books on philosophy in circulation which devote page upon page to the thinkers who have written in English but never mention Brentano, Dilthey, Husserl, Blondel, or even Comte (if my memory serves, Russell does not include his name in his Englishman's *History of Western Philosophy*). Similarly there are numberless books in German, French, Spanish, or Italian which scarcely mention Peirce, Royce, Whitehead, or Alexander. Almost the only exceptions to this double and general neglect are Bergson and William James. And if we take the case of living philosophers, the same situation obtains.

As I was saying, however, at Yale philosophy may be pursued without haste and in the midst of abundance. It is amazing to see, despite the fact that in that university are teaching some of the most distinguished figures in the country—Hendel, Blanshard, Northrop, Margenau, Fitch, Weiss—with what respect, indeed reverence, the entire legacy of occidental philosophy is gathered in and tended. (Nor is the Orient forgotten.) I admire the way in which those excellent teachers at Yale efface themselves, to put it that way, in order to provide free access to the wealth-in-common of which they consider themselves to be custodians. All past philosophy, from the Greeks to the present day, is there represented. If Locke and Dewey are studied, so are Descartes, Leibnitz, and Hegel; Kierkegaard, Husserl, Jaspers, Unamuno, Ortega, Marcel, or Heidegger weigh in equally with Russell, James, Schiller, or Pierce.

The consequence of all this is evident in the profound receptivity of the students in what I would call their intellectual readiness. I have seen them, armed both with confidence and a critical spirit, both trustingly and energetically enter deeply into forms of thought which until then were completely alien to them, managing to master them to a degree far beyond what one would expect them to attain in so short a time. Other teachers at Yale have testified that this impression of mine is not an illusion, reporting that in their own seminars they have often found after very few months traces of that manner of philosophizing adhering to the minds of their students.

The growth of the Department of Philosophy at Yale is astounding. One year when the loss of a privileged position in the required academic program led to the expectation of a decline in registration in introductory courses, there was instead the highest enrollment ever. In the last fifteen years the number of students selecting philosophy has gone consistently up: today that number equals half the student body. There are multiple reasons for this, some historical but some peculiar to Yale, since the same phenomenon has not occurred everywhere.

It is certain that the United States, as is true in a different fashion of the rest of the Americas, is coming closer to philosophy, beginning darkly to sense a need for it. This is the youthful form of approaching the problem. I remember my own state of mind at age 17; not only did I not know what philosophy was all about, but I had only vague notions of its existence. I was much more at home with physics and the natural and mathematical sciences, and I believe my vocation was carrying me toward those fields; but nevertheless, I began to sense a strange stirring of disquiet, an almost imperceptible uneasiness. There was something "there" that bothered me, something I was missing that attracted me most mysteriously. Perhaps that something might be philosophy. And so having recently acquired my Baccalaureate in Science, I began that summer, as though moved by some presentiment, to improvise the Baccalaureate in Letters so as to be on the safe side. And that academic precaution soon turned out to be well justified.

I believe that the United States biographically—and that means historically—finds itself in a very similar situation. Soon —sooner than expected—Americans are going to need philosophy in order to be the people they are; that is, the people they *must become*. Philosophy, which up to now has figured only as an element in their tradition, will in the near future be a part of their destiny. But the risk is great that on the day when that necessity actually finds full outlet, when man in America truly needs philosophy, there will be no philosophy for him there to find. Don't mistake my meaning: I am not saying that he would not be able to locate an already constructed philosophy. But a ready-made philosophy does not serve us, for it is never our own. A philosophy must be constructed with one's own tools, as one's own task. My fear is that he will have had his authentic philosophy falsely supplanted.

I never suspected that my experience at Yale, especially the meetings of the Department of Philosophy, was going to provide me with new hope for the future of the United States. For in those long, spacious meetings, once more unhurried and luxurious, that entity called philosophy was handled with a respect as much in evidence as bathos was absent, with a gravity as obvious as the lack of pedantry, with lively cordiality, with freedom and friendly disagreements, with enthusiasm and good humor. And philosophy was polished and burnished as thought was given to the eager, open, impatient minds of the boys who would approach her image with questioning and hope—boys no one wished to flatter, defraud, or deceive because they represented, no more, no less, a considerable fragment of the United States of the future. And all this took place under the fraternal and paternal captaincy of Charles W. Hendel, the man who, if I had expounded at Yale on Aristotle's *Nicomachean Ethics*, would have afforded me a living illustration of how all the ethical virtues may dwell with the dianoetic ones in peaceful reconciliation.

21 THE AVERAGE MAN

When in Europe people begin to discuss America's ideas, tastes, preferences, and sentiments, the attitude assumed is usually one of disdain. Sometimes it is a smiling disdain, such as that provoked by a group of naive youngsters; sometimes the reaction is more bitter and less direct, double-edged as it were. A European tends to find Americans elementary—in their publications, their magazines, their movies, their concept of democracy, their pleasures, their ideas, their very religion. And from his vantage point of twenty-five centuries of complexity and refinement, the European feels a certain amount of pity. Valéry and Matisse, Vittorio de Sica, Jaspers, Toynbee, and T. S. Eliot (who, of course, is an American), "organic democracy" and the *"troisième force,"* the "Tour d'Argent," spirituality and the *"témoignages,"* the moral stockpile of Western culture. In short, superiority. But assuming this superiority, there comes to mind an innocent query: who is the subject and who the object? In other words, who is superior to whom? I am afraid that we have here a strange incongruity; that the average man of the United States is being compared to a member of a meager minority—truly not even a minority but a small group—in Europe. When they contrast the true vulgarity of the *Saturday Evening Post* or the much less serious tastelessness of *Life* with the presumably exquisite *Hommes et Monde* or *Les Temps Modernes*, Europeans overlook the elementary fact that the first pair of magazines are read by some tens of millions of persons and the second group by only a few thousand. When they categorize the American way of life or way of thinking as primitive, they have in mind by way of comparison Bertrand Russell or Guardini, the professors at the Sorbonne or the members of the Academy, the fifty, one hundred, or two hundred families in each European capital that constitute the top stratum. What would be the result if we were to attempt a valid confrontation with similar social groups in Europe? If we were to investigate the actual reading habits of eight million Spaniards or fifteen million Italians or twelve million Frenchmen? What is the "way of thinking," the world view, the ideas on life, politics, and religion of the peasants in Extremadura and the miners in Wales; of the petty bureaucrats in Madrid, London, and Rome; of the ladies of the house wherever they do still stay in their houses? Do they read Kafka and Vicente Aleixandre? Do they like Marcel's theatre, or do they perhaps prefer their "folklore" and the kind of play where the son turns out not to be the son after all and you can discreetly pull out a handkerchief? Does their religious life draw its nourishment from Karl Adam—or Karl Barth, if you prefer— or from other quite different sources? And the reigning political ideas—the notions really controlling the multitudes: are they not somewhat comparable to the uncouth formulae which come out of the inquiries of the Gallup Poll?

The fact is that Europe (and this is the case even in the least democratic of countries) is a "represented" continent. All that the European keeps telling himself about Europe has to do with a few select minorities which "represent" vast submerged masses whose actual presence is customarily dispensed with. (Parenthetically, for that reason it is fatal when the public scene is invaded by a group which has not arranged for the necessary selective representation, and so like a pipe from a well brings to the surface all the vulgarity and mediocrity which under normal circumstances remain below ground where they are less operative.) In the United States, however, that entity called "the average man" or "the man in the street" is not a conventional fiction with traits assigned to him that really occur only in the upper ten per cent of society; he *is*, no more, no less, the entire population. Certainly in various large sectors of the country, in the northeastern states for example, it is a question of the integrity of the whole social organism. It is not just a matter of economics, although that factor is a decisive one. The janitor with two cars; the television sets in the houses of laborers; the plumber who turns down a college scholarship of eighteen hundred dollars a year for his daughter preferring to leave it "for someone who really needs it"; the man we may ironically call "the Boston beggar" who asks for a handout at the edge of Park Square while wearing an elegant cheviot suit, an immaculate shirt and, in his long cigarette holder, pulling on a Philip Morris. All this, of course, represents a point of departure.

But the point of destination is quite another matter; or perhaps things are not so simple as they seem and there is a virtuous circle. (Why should circles always have to be *vicious?*) I am thinking, for example, of the universality and spontaneity of good work habits—in an entire year I never had a single student who did not perform at least satisfactorily all the work assigned to him; of the level of competence in language and manner of expression; of the correctness generally displayed in social intercourse; of the high stage of biological development (apparent even in physical appearance); of the street outside (that amazing phenomenon so different, so comforting or oppressive, as you travel from one meridian to the other or leap back and forth among the parallels!); of the honesty so customary—except in large cities where there are professional groups of delinquents—that you never need lock the door or be afraid to leave a valuable parcel outside (for example, a package on top of a mailbox whose slot is too small for it), and you can forget that car keys are ever kept elsewhere than in the ignition.

What about the minorities? The summits? Well, that is another story and we shall leave the orography of the United States for another day. Because we should first have to look into the local relations between the peaks and the plains before we could compare American eminences with the Pyrenees or Mont Blanc.

22 A CIVILIAN NATION

After living a short while in the United States, a European begins to sense a certain trait or characteristic, vague and somewhat atmospheric, which is difficult at first to pin down because it is noticeable, if at all, in that it contrasts with something customary in Europe, or at least on the continent. Then one fine day he suddenly realizes that it is a perfectly simple thing: the United States is a civilian nation.

But what does that mean? Are there not other civilian countries? Naturally, the immense majority of the inhabitants of any country are civilians: almost all Spaniards, Frenchmen, Germans, Italians, Argentines, Peruvians, Indians, or Australians enjoy civilian status. But the term usually appears in a negative form: notice how little the word is used, its negligible linguistic prominence betraying its status in history. "Civilian" means—what is neither ecclesiastical nor military. Thus at first glance it becomes something that has no positive force, something peculiarly private, a kind of left-over, at best, even though paradoxically that remnant may include almost the entire population. It is interesting that in Spanish the living word used to designate that which is civilian is not *civil*, but *paisano* (peasant), and the paired terms are "military" and "peasant," so that if you are out of uniform you go dressed as a peasant. Now the usual synonym for peasant (*paisano*) in Spanish is *campesino* (field hand), and that term carries with it a slightly pejorative connotation. All of which leads to a situation wherein whatever is civilian does not appear to have any inherent virtue, or to be anything particular, determined, or fixed with a definite personality or a sharp profile, but rather presents itself as amorphous, inert, and ineffective.

The underlying causes of this condition are not particularly mysterious, but they do involve lengthy explanations. Contributing factors have been: the predominance of the forces of the Army and the Church; the feudal nature of the monarchies of continental Europe; the relatively continuous state of war which has existed in Europe; the frequency of revolutions and uprisings; the influence of a "heroic" kind of rhetoric; the public acclaim over military or ecclesiastical merit—and the rarity of such meritorious acts in civil life. The historical birth of the United States reveals an entirely different genesis and helps explain the tremendous variation in consequent development. Again to take a very concrete linguistic example, think of the different clusters of meaning surrounding the words "Law" and, in Spanish, "*Ley*."

American life (and here I refer only to North America, since the situation in Hispanic-America, despite its comparatively more peaceful history and the relatively minor influence of the church, is much closer to that of Europe) is resolutely civilian in character. Far from being something secondary or marginal, civilian status is a national fact of life —unless someone cares to prove the contrary. "Civilian-ness" is the positive, substantive aspect of society, the very trunk of the body social. And anything that is not civilian in nature —something exceptional, something private—must in every case justify itself and arrive at some configuration of its own. That configuration is based on a civilian pattern, it depends for support upon civilian life and receives from that source both its force and its right to act upon the body of society. A member of the military or ecclesiastical world, if he is to leave his own sphere and deal with the whole of society, must take out "citizenship papers"—in other words, justify his role in public affairs in terms of the civilian structure. An American feels himself positively a civilian. The expression "American citizen" is not merely a juridical status useful for obtaining passports and naturalization papers; it is rather a real, historical condition carrying a resonant echo (for the person whose ear is attuned to the sounds of history) of that other designation *civis Romanus*, which reflected the collective consciousness of a people who, though prodigiously gifted warriors and administrators, formed always in their finest era a civilian nation.

Of course you must remember that I am writing this at the end of the year 1952. It is impossible to predict what may happen even in the near future. Some day the United States may cast aside its civilian rhetoric, may feel that the mufti worn by a *paisano* gives too little distinction, may take up the vogue for uniforms or habits and feel lost or disqualified out of such dress. But that moment has not yet come. Eisenhower, in order to cease being merely a military ornament and assume effective national power, had to be "de-militarized"; that is, he had to become a civilian, a *paisano*, and only then—paradoxically, it seems to the average European—could he assume supreme command of the military forces of the nation. And I remember that one day while strolling along 15th Street in Washington, D.C., I saw at the entrance to a doorway a card which read: "L. H. Hemingway—Bishop." And on another, smaller card on the door itself: "From 3 to 5." And this anecdote, a slightly extreme example, caricaturizes if you will the civilian mentality of the United States.

23   THE TEMPER OF LIFE

That things go wrong can be a great consolation. Because then as you bump into each problem, you can rage a bit—or a lot—and think that if it weren't for the fact that things are always going wrong, life would really be marvelous. If there's no hot water when we want to take a bath, if the drains are plugged, if the bus doesn't come, if we don't like the places our tax money goes, if it takes two hours and a quarter to get from Madrid to Toledo, or if our salary doesn't carry us to the end of the month, we feel depressed, irritated, or impatient and we think that if things were only otherwise, we'd be delighted. Since it is difficult to arrange to experience the ideal, but since on the other hand we always trust that someday we may reach such a state, that hope salvages the present situation and allows us a refuge therein—permits us to live, as it were, on whatever credit the present offers us.

But if you go to the United States, you undertake the interesting and dangerous experiment of living in a country where, generally speaking and by and large, things work very well. The plumbing is a marvel; it is extremely rare to have the electricity cut off; the means of transportation are admirably comfortable and punctual; you can trust letters and packages to the mail, even without registering or insuring them, and be reasonably sure of their arrival; the taxes are high but their results "show," and the average American has the impression that his tax dollars are being directed to the right place—in fact, the place they are supposed to go. When something does seem to him to be going wrong, the American writes a letter to the editor of a newspaper or a magazine, and the editor (though not always) publishes it, and they both are confident that the evil will be remedied. Naturally if he has a profession (and he needs only one) he manages nicely to get to the end of the month without having to scurry around as though he were doing six different jobs in order to scrape up enough to live on. In other words, ninety-five per cent of everything normally works beautifully; therefore irritation, discontent, and complaints are truly exceptional: you can go for days and even weeks on end without finding even a slightly reasonable pretext for becoming annoyed or exasperated.

And then one makes the discovery that, despite all, life does have its inconveniences. Not everything about living is encouraging; one does not always have the desire to face life. Very well, life then is replete with limitations. Sometimes it is a very sad thing, sometimes unfortunate, occasionally insipid: and the worst of it is that there is no one or no thing to hold responsible. In other words, the lack of accidental ills clearly highlights the irremediable deficiencies intrinsic to life itself.

I think that the exploitation of the spleen reached its greatest peak in Victorian England: things were going too well in the British Isles, there was too much security and ease, more honorableness and confidence than our species apparently can tolerate. In Shakespeare's England the spleen probably did not flourish; and today, when there is a problem to be met around every corner, no one talks much about it either. Only the enormous youthful vitality of North Americans has saved them so far from the disease which so afflicted the Victorians; they all feel as though there is a great deal still to be done, and what they don't find in the way of an obstacle, they invent in the form of a task. Still there are already a few signs that the saturation point is being reached. When an American takes occasion to examine his own life and the internal structure of his country, he experiences a sense of satisfaction, a comforting feeling of security, that "tranquility with regard to domestic arrangements" that Cervantes enjoyed in Salamanca and that today is easily available in New England. But as the fruit conceals a worm, this whole picture carries within it the threat of boredom. From time to time the fatal question timidly comes forth: "Is this all there is to life?"

Luckily, Providence appears to watch over the United States and has arranged for a whole series of guardian spirits to keep diseases of the spleen at a distance: Korea, China and the Russians, Tunis, Jordan, Iran, the Saar, the ones who do not want to be armed and the others who want to over-arm, those who desire to remain *au-dessus de la mêlée*, those who are perfect and, therefore, a unique problem, those who in every corner of the globe want to play at being great powers. No, it is hardly likely that the temper of American life will verge on melancholy satisfaction. Without counting the Negro problem, polio, and the national search for a place to park, it is enough to read the papers in order to find that comforting consolation which sustains us and allows us both to mistrust and to look forward to what the next day will bring: the happy thought that things around us are going badly.

24 EIGHTY-NINE PER CENT

If ever the subject of conversation among Spaniards turns to religion in the United States, the two ideas which crop up immediately, one on the heels of the other, are these: first, irreligiosity (enormous de-Christianized masses, total forgetfulness of the other world and unchecked appetite for this one, complete lack of belief); and second, religious chaos (an infinity of sects and denominations, doctrinal anarchy, the atomization of faith). Statistics, one is told, bear this out. Usually when someone talks about statistics he doesn't have them at hand, but this time I am going to bring them bodily into the discussion. In October of 1951 there were no more and no fewer than 265 religious bodies existing in the United States, and I emphasize the date because since then a few of them may have died out or others been born. More recently I came across another statistic which is rather more surprising: someone wanted to determine what proportion of North Americans believed in a triune God, and it turned out that 89 per cent professed that belief. And, the report adds, that is only 10 per cent fewer than the total of all those who believe in God.

Apparently, then, only 1 per cent of all Americans are atheists, and only 11 out of every 100 do not believe in the Trinity. These results invite us to read over the other statistics a little more slowly and try to understand what they mean. (That is not so easy as it seems. One example shows why: everyone is always talking about the divorce rate in various countries and citing statistics on the number of divorces which occur, but not once have I seen the elementary fact stressed that people who obtain one divorce are likely to divorce more than once; that there are some people who never divorce and others who have an entirely different idea of marriage which leads frequently to the dissolution of marital ties. In other words, among the divorce figures, the "repeaters" probably should be discounted, and the total number of divorces received should probably be divided by two, three, or four to obtain the true number of couples who are divorced.)

There are then, in fact, 265 religious bodies in the United States, but that does not mean that there are 265 religions or faiths. There are groups which have only 47 members, or 29, or 24, or even 8—fewer than those who make up a Spanish *tertulia* meeting regularly at some café. These groups are simply religious associations or local congregations. The number of different "faiths," that is, bodies conscious of distinct substantive beliefs, is very small. Among a total of 90 million persons whose recognized religious creeds have been counted by census, seven major religious bodies account for 73 million people. (The most numerous persuasion, of course, is the Catholic Church, with a membership of more than 28 million.)

How can this be possible? How can there exist side by side this unanimous belief in God, an overwhelming majority of believers in the Trinity (that is to say, orthodox, heterodox, and even residual Christians) and at the same time an unimaginably capricious and picturesque multiplicity of forms and distinct ways, offered in any large city, to celebrate Easter or Christmas? To answer this question properly would mean an analysis of the deeper meaning of American religion, an inquiry, so far as I know, still to be undertaken which would entail long and arduous explanations. Reserving for another time such an attempt, I should like here to present one or two indications which may help orient the discussion.

First of all, an American does not see religion primarily as a matter of doctrine, as a repertory of opinions or theses—dogmas—with regard to which the most important question to raise is that of their truth or falseness. I don't mean to imply by that that he does not believe his religion to be true—and in the case of a Catholic, share in the belief that his religion is the same the world over—but rather that religion appears to the American primarily in the guise of *worship*; that is, adoration, reverence, the tribute that one pays to God. To be religious is above all else to *worship*, to fulfill the demands of a cult, to offer adoration to the deity—and this may be done in many ways. Twelve years ago Franklin Roosevelt listed religious freedom as one of the four basic liberties in these words: "the freedom of each individual to worship God in his own fashion." Thus it would seem that religious pluralism in the United States reflects (though not exclusively so) a diversity in forms or ceremonies and, upon occasion, in the kinds of devotions.

The result is that positive elements are everywhere emphasized more than negative or differentiating features, that people take doctrine into account rather than the errors of its forms, and faith rather than its imperfections. The initial religious pluralism evident in American history, and the fact that the United States has been developed by religious dissenters from all over Europe, explains the existence of this dual characteristic: widespread religious conviction and a minimum of hostility among different faiths. I do not say that hostility does not exist: merely that it is minimal. In the United States you may observe any religion you like, but you will meet disapproval if you have no religion at all. One might almost say that an American surveys the variegated panorama in his country through the eyes of a historian in religion: everyone seeks God, in better or worse fashion—gropingly, as St. Paul put it—but each after his own manner.

25 THIS WORLD
AND THE HEREAFTER

Some years ago the great aircraft carrier *Leyte*, anchored in Boston Harbor, was ripped by a tremendous explosion. Columns of flames flashed through the hatchways, burning many members of the crew. A group of sailors found one officer so badly burned that they could not recognize him. The lieutenant got these words out: "I am a Catholic. Get me a chaplain. My blood type is A." When they explained to him that the whole group was trapped inside the ship and that they could not escape themselves nor do anything for him, he instructed them to knock out a distress signal in Morse code by banging on the bulkhead. The sailors did not know the Morse code so the officer, in agony, taught them how to hammer out an *SOS* with a monkey wrench and a piece of wood. When they had managed to start signalling, he then said: "Let's pray." And he led an "Our Father" without once mentioning his pain. For half an hour, at intervals, the sailors continued to knock out an *SOS*. At the end of that time a rescue crew heard them and was able to free them. But the lieutenant died a little while later.

This was the story told in all its simplicity and without any posturing by the American press. It is assuredly true that the grandiose gestures and phrases so generously poured out in other places à propos of some administrative or technical event would hardly square with the sober efficiency of that American naval officer. But his attitude seems to me to reflect an entire mode of being. At the point of death, destroyed by fire, he disregards both suffering and fear and simply takes charge of the situation. Pragmatism, someone will remark. Yes, but a complete, authentic pragmatism and not a half-way pragmatism, myopic or mutilated. The situation is that he and the group of sailors are about to die. Something has to be done. What? First, naturally, try to save oneself. But in this world and in that of the hereafter; or rather, first in the hereafter and, if possible, in this one. So the lieutenant asks for what he needs clearly and without risking the danger of confusion: he is a Catholic and his blood type is A. He wants confession and a transfusion. But since the crew is trapped and unable to get out, it is not enough to ask: he must do something. And since one enters the hereafter through this our world, and because, after all, this world is important too, the lieutenant calls technique into play in order to get his message through to some temporal saviors and immediately thereafter directs the great transcendent plea to the Savior beyond.

Nothing seems more characteristic to me than the behavior of that American officer, behavior that undoubtedly strikes a Spaniard as very strange. But if you hold American history up to the light, from the Mayflower to the Constitution, from the Constitution to John Foster Dulles or Fulton Sheen, you will see that moving scene aboard the *Leyte*—moving, not pathetic—repeat itself a thousand times. I said moving and not pathetic because that is exactly the nature of United States history, the tone of American life. It represents what ours in Spain has never been. We Spaniards have always inclined to the belief that all that counts is the world of the hereafter, and we have neglected this world; often we have been content merely to explain this, using the hereafter as a pretext to abandon the immediate problem or to perform in a distracted fashion whatever seemed most convenient for us here below, while with insistent gesturing we point to the heavens.

A human situation is composed of many planes: a foreground, intermediate zones, and a far-off horizon of finalities. A man who reacts to the situation in its entirety and attempts to master it cannot overlook any of those planes. If he does, he is not a pragmatist nor a practical man. There is no doubt that Americans have occupied themselves more with this world than with the hereafter, caring more about the first floor of life than the upper storys—for, contrary to popular belief, the United States is not a country of skyscrapers, but rather of small houses with good solid foundations.

The slender tower driven into the blue is gallant indeed even when all around it the houses are of adobe, but one cannot remain satisfied with adobe. Besides, I suspect that we slip easily into error because the tower and the hovels surrounding it are almost never of the same period: when the tower was built, the houses constructed of brick or stone were humanly livable. When the village fell to the level of adobe, its poverty was excused by pointing out the tower raised by others, ancestors of the present incumbents. Some momentary aberrations aside, the United States has realized that although man is a citizen of two spheres, he must begin first with the world down here, because otherwise nothing will be accomplished. But he knows that the story does not end there: first an *SOS* in Morse code, then the Lord's Prayer. We in Spanish say: "A Dios rogando y con el mazo dando,"* but we rarely act in accordance with the proverb.

26 ESSAYING A NEW KIND OF LIFE: THE UNITED STATES

When a European disembarks in the United States two contradictory impressions usually enter his mind. One impression is a sense of similarity with Europe: so many standard homogeneous things exist in this world, so many identical objects; and since they are all passed back and forth from continent

* "Call on God but put your shoulder to the wheel"—Trans.

to continent, the traveler normally experiences as a consequence both confidence and disillusionment at the same time, because "It's the same all over." The second impression springs from his habit of fixing on certain details which are especially picturesque and for that reason more noticeable than others. The appropriate expression here is an exclamation which may be uttered either in amusement or in irritation, depending upon the traveler's character: "What a way to live!" The tourist and the visitor who, though not a tourist, allows himself to be similarly distracted, remain prisoners of these impressions. For of course we must take for granted that a foreigner arrives with certain expectations built up from the movies, from the books and magazines he has read, from the talk he has heard. These expectations are confirmed through a series of isolated encounters which correspond to the cinematographic details: the policeman, so incredibly stocky, smiling, and Irish, who seems to have stepped out of a Hollywood film; the drugstore, where in fact you can buy everything in creation from coffee and ice cream to pens, books, magazines, cigarettes, toys, and (why not?) even medicines; the drive-ins where automobiles go to the movies; the skyscrapers, Coca-Cola, the parking meters. "That's the American way of life for a fact!"

But the possibility does exist of getting inside that outer layer, or epidermis, and taking a close-up look at the United States. Even this approximation is ambiguous, however, since it offers two very different perspectives: the first, from the standpoint of life in Europe; the second, from a point of view which has penetrated United States life and regards it from within.

The European who observes the United States without ever abandoning his own point of view finds every day bringing new disappointments. This is especially so because many things are lacking in the United States which the European sorely misses, looks for, and fails to find: cafés, and particularly cafés with terraces; *tertulias*; places to stroll; "literary activity," newspapers with articles featured in the French, Spanish, or Hispano-American fashion, and so on. It is true in the second place because many of the things which do exist are different from what they are "supposed" to be. A minor illustration may help clear up what I mean. When I tried various Californian wines, and friends asked me whether or not I liked them, I answered that I liked everything except the labels. Because the label reads *Sherry*, *Port*, or *Burgundy*, and the person about to taste the wine therefore starts from a definite expectation; and since the liquid he tastes, though very good indeed, bears no resemblance at all to European Sherry, Port, or Burgundy, his reaction is one of disappointment. If the label read *Golden Gate*, or *San Diego*, or *Pasadena Red*, the wine itself would impress us as of excellent quality. And the same sort of thing happens in almost every sphere: Harvard is not at all like the Sorbonne; books in the United States serve an entirely different purpose from in Europe; eating well in Boston is not the same as eating well in Paris; to be famous means something entirely different on each side of the North Atlantic.

Both European and American citizens predictably start from value judgments, from esteem or contempt. On one side, people speak of the American way of life; the others talk of the refinement of the old world or of European *esprit*. With the exception of the very discreet, most partisans on both sides tend to interpret whatever is unfamiliar as inferior —backwardness, poverty, prejudice or, perhaps, improvisation, vulgarity, rudeness, poor taste, mass culture. Take, for instance, that rather unprophetic book of Georges Duhamel, *Scènes de la vie future*, in which a quarter of a century ago he asserted contemptuously that the American people were headed for the worst possible decadence, that they would be incapable of carrying out a long-range task (*de longue haleine*) or of improving themselves even to the slightest degree through energy or intellect. An equivalent error is made by the American in Spain who sees nothing but the beggars, who interprets even the rich peasant's way of life as "misery," or who notes that the average Spanish family does not possess either a car or an electric refrigerator, while failing to observe that they do have domestic servants, that they use linen tablecloths and napkins every day, and that the man of the house—if he is an intellectual—has a private library of five to ten thousand volumes.

Naturally, there is more than one possible point of departure; there is a much more interesting viewpoint open to the person who installs himself inside the forms of American life and lives that life himself. Such an action does not, however, imply accepting and appropriating for oneself the famous American way of living and thinking (which some impetuously hasty United States citizens would like to export to South America, to Europe, to Africa, and to the Orient)—a "way" that consists of certain techniques plus a repertory of ideas on which many Americans say (and some even believe) they base their lives. No, aside from the fact that almost no aspect of that mode is exportable or translatable (a very delicate problem indeed to be touched on so lightly here), we are dealing rather with the "real" forms of American life, of which Americans (but no more so than other men elsewhere) are themselves generally ignorant. Nor is it desirable that they should *not* be.

How is this form of life different from the European? First of all, by virtue of being a form, of having a structure. Strictly speaking, Europe no longer offers a form of life: such forms existed once, and they were splendid ones, but they have been broken up and lost. The result today is that no one can "install" himself, and this is the chief cause of our instability. Various subterfuges are called into play to explain the situation: the hollowness of tradition, the tendencies of literature, narcissism. From all this arises an awareness of oppressive air and darkening horizons, a feeling of temporariness, a sense of the insuperable difficulty of national problems, of stagnation. The situation in Europe, especially since the close of the last World War, is similar to that in a theatre when, intermission being over, the curtain for some reason does not rise: after a few minutes the spectators become impatient or bored; some leave, others forget their manners and begin to be rowdy. (In some countries of Hispano-America, the situation is about three-quarters the same; in others, four-thirds!) The great novelty of the United States is that there is form to life there, and that form is precisely a "new life," life with a structure.

Thus the United States strikes us as an "old" country—an amazing impression, but unmistakable if one observes closely. We arrive at this sense of "oldness" because the old way of life in Europe was that of living within certain forms. It is often thought that North Americans have no such forms, that they are *sans façon*; but this is not the case, they are not at all *sans façon*—what happens is that the *façons* are simply different from the familiar European forms. (Notice the different nuances when we compare the French expression I have just used with the word "informal" in English and with what the word *informal* means in Spanish;* the tremendous distances between each one of these three negations of "form" indicate that what "form" is differs substantially in each case.)

Fashions, social customs, the style of various institutions: all of these have a form in the United States, and most are living forms as is evident (in society as well as in nature) by their adaptability.

In many European countries the sense of ceremony has been lost, and ceremonial occasions have become either antiquated

---

* In Spanish the word is applied to one who does not obey the conventions either in the business world or in social intercourse, or to someone who is simply rude—Trans.

masquerades or cheap shams, or both. I shall never forget the mixture of dignity, joviality, friendliness, and real feeling that accompanied an academic procession in cap and gown at an American women's college, nor that of the commencement ceremony and granting of degrees at the poignant moment in June when the students say farewell to their magic world and look to the future: *incipit vita nova*.

I have sometimes wondered why the most timely as well as the most intelligent book written on America is the one done by de Tocqueville in 1834—*La democratie en Amérique* —a book infinitely less antiquated or *démodé* than the work produced by Duhamel a century later. And I believe that the reason for its success, quite apart from the author's astonishing talent, was not only that he was writing at a time when the French were "collectively" intelligent and, therefore, at a moment when it was easier for individuals to be so, but also—and more importantly—because there was then in existence a European way of life with which de Tocqueville could compare and thus "understand" the American way. Because the spark of comprehension comes from the friction caused by the contact of two such forms, and thus de Tocqueville was able to seize the significance of the American undertaking, the germinating collective enterprise. At many points it is sufficient merely to elongate the lines of his inquiry in order to arrive at the United States of today; for that reason, de Tocqueville's book provides so many dire prophecies now come to pass.

Within the American way of life, happiness is a possibility. Never fear that I am falling into the cliché that Soviet Russian propaganda has been pounding into us for some time; the one about "millions upon millions of happy people." No, happiness is a personal matter. Our happiness depends upon our having good health and some working capital, upon whether or not the woman we love says "Yes," whether or not our children live contented lives, whether or not our

books are praised. It depends upon our not experiencing serious remorse, upon our not anguishing too much over an
idea that crosses our mind—nor over a setting sun. No, here
I am dealing with the "alveolus" of happiness, a particular
structural environment in which individual happiness may
lodge. To be an American citizen is not a guarantee of personal happiness—far from it. But in the United States—as in
Europe before—*given the necessary personal conditions*, happiness is normally and statistically a common state; in other
words, "many" people are happy for "long" periods of time.
Does that imply that happiness is no longer possible in Europe? I am far from believing in such a lamentable situation.
The thing is that happiness in Europe today is never obvious
or easy; even after having all his personal conditions fulfilled,
the individual must "invent" happiness—he must know how
to create its alveolus, the structural host in which it may
lodge. It is difficult to be happy in Europe, not only because
of the usual obstacles, but because it requires a special talent;
perhaps for that reason when a European does find happiness it is twice as delightful for him, for it is shattered so
frequently!

In the United States, what is there, really *is*. You can rely
on what there is (money, cars, machines, public services) and
get along without what is lacking (domestic help, the talent
for improvisation, special things that are one-of-a-kind). That
fine Spanish expression *venido a menos* could be turned
around and applied in inverted fashion to North America:
the United States is a nation of people "*venido a más*."* What
I am trying to say is that every moment they become more
than they were before: they are on the upsurge in every
aspect and order of life and, like adolescent boys, they are
constantly growing out of their clothes. They are a complete
people—with no gaps showing—living in dynamic tension: for

* *Venido a menos*—come down in the world; literally come to less vs.
venida a más—gone on to bigger and better things—Trans.

that reason they are always "in peak form." The field of reality here has clearly marked borders and does not overlap into that of fiction. Almost everything that is supposed to be real *is* real. You can count on, and indeed must take into account, the quality of most products, the sufficiency of salaries, the efficiency of services, and also the effectiveness of work done, the lack of such an attitude as "let's not and say we did," the validity of promises which are carried out without fail. For all these reasons American life holds a minimum of failures and disappointments: for the same reasons, and because it is meticulously thought out in advance, it offers a minimum of undefined hopes and surprises.

But of what does this form of life consist? I should say it is constituted primarily by the firmness of its governing social usages. American society is the most solid and stable of any I know. (I hope you will allow me occasionally to follow a linguistic usage that is essentially an abuse—but an unavoidable one by now—and that is to apply the unqualified adjective "American" to all that pertains to the United States. The usage is both unjust and inexact, but there is no ready remedy for it, since the adjective "North American" fails to solve the problem, as it implies an invasion of Mexico and Canada; and the Spanish adjective *estadounidense* would sound silly in English.) Rigorous sanctions exist in many areas of American life. But what about liberty or freedom? We must bear in mind the widespread lack of rebelliousness among Americans who do enjoy a great deal of freedom but use it with extreme caution. (Perhaps this is the reason the American has his liberty—because he seldom calls it into play.) In every sphere of life there are demanding norms: strict punctuality; the rules of the road; the manner of ordering in a restaurant or of making a purchase in a store; the detailed instructions for the use of a device, including even how to open one of those remarkable American cans; bureaucratic regulations issued, for instance, by a university administration—all of this wraps

American life in a net of restrictions, of soft, elastic norms which are nonetheless strong and stubborn. (Certain universities put out an entire booklet which dictates in incredibly minute detail exactly how research papers must be prepared and presented: how much margin must be left on the page; how direct quotations must be handled—according to whether they are longer or shorter than five lines; the order in which the first and last names of the authors cited must be placed; the way to decide whether to use a comma or a colon before a short or long quote.) Is this tyranny then? Not at all—at least the American does not feel it to be so. His attitude is rather conformist: he believes in the experts, he accepts the rules, he adapts to the climate, as he does indeed to his bony structure or to the restrictions unavoidably imposed by his firm young skin. An American does not evince a temperamental need to "do it some other way." (In this, the Spaniard probably represents the opposite extreme.) He thinks that when someone has gone to the trouble of figuring out the proper way to open a package and has explained this method at length, then that must indeed be the best way of doing it. The Spaniard considers these instructions impertinent and opens the package in some hitherto unsuspected fashion. However, we must not assume on this basis that no critical spirit exists in the United States of America. On the contrary, it flourishes; every magazine editor receives hundreds of letters from readers who criticize everything from foreign policy to Mamie Eisenhower's charming bangs; from the country's religious orientation to the proper spelling of Dolly Madison's name. What happens is that this criticism arises from a presupposition of incredibly extensive and profound agreement. The very existence of criticism depends precisely upon this basis of agreement on fundamentals—agreement, for example, that such criticism should be permitted.

Of course we may inquire about the implications of a large part of contemporary North American literature, with its evident preference for subjects and themes which seem atrocious, somber, abnormal, off-center. The image of American life created by many novelists and playwrights—from O'Neill and Lewis through Faulkner or Caldwell to other younger writers—could lead us to conclusions very different from what I have suggested. Then does what these authors describe not really happen in the United States? Doubtless it does, because almost all such things happen everywhere. The important point is to find out "how often?" and "how come?"; in other words, whether each of these things which happens is significant. In such literature authors seek out "the exceptional" because the discovery comes late that ordinary life is worth writing about—that it is perhaps the most worthwhile theme. Steinbeck is a borderline case in point. I hope for the imminent flowering of a movement in North American letters, the most illustrious precursor of which might be Thornton Wilder's *Our Town*.

The facile conformity I have mentioned makes for a minimum of instability. But wait, doesn't that conclusion contradict all that is most apparent in reality? Isn't change, constant and rapid variation, the visible pattern of United States life? Isn't the country transforming itself under our very eyes? Yes, by all means; but such movement does not imply instability any more than does the flight of an airplane, which is only unstable, by the way, when it comes to a stop. Society, like the plane, is designed to be mobile and to change constantly but with continuity. North American life is noticeably less spasmodic than that of any other variety of humanity. American society resembles the grasshopper least of any other, or shows, if you prefer, the fewest possible traits of the adventurer (bearing in mind the comparison Ortega made between grasshoppers and adventurers). This is true of society despite the fact that an individual American life may have a high coefficient of adventurousness—a quality that has not entirely perished from the scene.

The underlying basis of many of the characteristics I have cited is American "utilitarianism" (for once I wish to support the cliché, but only on condition that we understand what we are talking about). Utilitarianism is a fact of American life, but it is not synonymous with "materialism" or "good business"; it indicates instead the reign of *convenience*. A basic assumption in American life is that if you offer someone something that is good for him, he will take it; in other parts of the globe this assumption does not hold, and serious errors arise when we forget that. The opposite attitude is graphically expressed in our Spanish saying *"Quedarse uno tuerto por dejar ciego a otro"*;* which is exactly what the American does *not* do. This spirit is what gives rise to a lack of hostility that one can actually breathe in with the air (one does breathe it in because it makes for a revivifying atmosphere); at least this is so in the Eastern areas that I know best. I am here thinking of that gratuitous, spontaneous, baseless hostility that flourishes in other latitudes and longitudes. The American is capable of hostility, naturally, but almost always for some specific reason, and normally he prefers to exude benevolence.

One explanation for this state of affairs is the situation with regard to social classes. There is no doubt that they exist—although there is also a certain leveling effect, especially since the lowest level is very high—and the problem of determining their origins and their functions is a delicate one. But that is not the aspect that interests me here. In Europe we have just witnessed the destruction of social classes and their transformation into debris. In the United States we find a peculiar sense of belonging, of self-satisfaction, on the part of each social class or segment. The chief distinction between the "common man" and the "proletarian" is that the former possesses a way of life within which to install himself and to which he adheres; he believes his condition an honorable and estimable one, and he aspires to what he desires within that

* To lose one eye in order to blind someone else—Trans.

framework. We can better comprehend "proletarianization" when we think of it as the general phenomenon of loss of social structure or form and consequent discontent; in this sense the word applies to *all social classes*, including the aristocracy, and constitutes a grave danger for Europe. I believe that it is from this point of view that we can adequately bring the Negro problem into focus, a situation far too complex to be dealt with summarily. It is futile and frivolous to reproach Americans, as many countries do so frequently, for the existence of a Negro problem. It is permissible certainly to criticize their solutions—diverse in character—but the problem does exist there and perhaps, like so many other problems, it may simply have no solution. In my opinion, however, any remedy must be directed toward the satisfactory installation of the Negro within his own condition and form of life. This group is unique in American life because it is probably the only important segment which does not enjoy the same general situation as the rest of the country and, therefore, reflects unusual manifestations of proletarianism in the European sense of the word.

The rareness of exceptions to the general rule can be demonstrated by a glance at the respective status of men, women, and children. In the United States, the custom common in many societies of minimizing and passing over women simply does not exist. For that reason American women enjoy so much freedom, such exuberant vitality. (Nevertheless, one may stop to wonder why it is that certain women—a considerable minority—harden as they approach their forties without, apparently, any clear biographical reason. This is a physical toughening, evident in their glances, in their carriage, in the way they handle the wheel of an automobile.) Nor is the child a victim of oppression; on the contrary, there is unlimited respect for childlike spontaneity. Short of killing themselves, children may do whatever they please—and we all know what children like to do. Therefore the great national task is to transform the child (whether male or female, it makes little difference) from a wild hooligan into a "person"; for example, into that refreshing and delightfully well-wrought person called "the college girl." The United States goes almost too far: the upper classes are somewhat downtrodden, and manual labor is too well compensated—even from the strictly economic point of view based on the sizable investment necessary to procure a very costly education. Women are favored under the law and through social custom; children go beyond the pale—one has only to recall how much is written on the dangerous problem of the teen-ager, the adolescent between thirteen and nineteen.

American life is "hard" but "sweet." (*Sweet* is not an antonym for *hard*, but rather for *sour* or *bitter*.) People work hard. Making a living costs a lot of effort—you have to run here and there, suffer through the cold and the heat, take care of the house and the garden, shovel snow, raise the children. But there is a certain sweetness in all of that. Perhaps an instance will show why. The job of carrying to the laundry a bag of clothes which are to be subjected to the manipulations of the washing machine is in itself physically demanding and a thankless task. Yet it is very likely that the road from the house to the laundromat leads along a delightful street with many lovely frame houses, greenery, ivy, and purple flowers, and that the street is also lined with neighbors' smiles and greetings (which grow more cordial in proportion to the weight of the load) and, at the end of the road, another smile, even broader and more encouraging, bestowed by the laundry employee who takes the bag and weighs it. The human environment is hospitable and smooth. Hardness is an attribute of things or of impersonal factors: the cold, the snow, the heat, rules and regulations, and taxes.

A structured and limited life, a life absorbed in itself, its substance permeated by everyday habit: this is the joy of American life. Seen from a European perspective, it is doubtless a deficient form of life, because the European misses many things not in the picture. The American born within its framework who does not compare it to other forms and who does not hail from another world fits into it as though it were a cradle. I must confess, arch-European that I am, that after making the attempt to live within that form of life—experiencing it from the inside—I found it endearing. I am not capable of perceiving only what it lacks nor of overlooking what it can offer us that today we do not have. Using Unamuno's remark, I may say that I enjoy "the plenitude of its limitations." And I consider it unintelligent to cast aspersions at such limitations in the name of certain "superior spirits" because the structure or form of life, like religion, like the world itself, is for the benefit of all—not for that of "the masses," but for that of each single individual. The American level of economic and industrial development allows 160 million people to live in a human fashion. Consider what that fact signifies for some in terms of potential, moral possibilities included, and in terms of justification for others. Here is a problem more pressing than abstract art, the literature of engagement, or "matters of principle." And all this without even taking into account that the superior men *are* superior and that they exercise their function of guidance without requiring that others wear themselves out in the attempt to pamper them.

The whole question boils down to a matter of mentality: the American knows what to count on and where to turn. But there are challenges in the offing and, mark it well, most of them are of an intellectual order. For the present moment there is no depression, no poverty, no weakness, no insecurity, no material danger of a serious nature. What is happening is that the American today has to think about new things: he must get out of his shell, make room in his life for other ingredients. Will these new condiments give his life a flavor which the demanding palate today finds lacking, or will they ruin the recipe? The American form of life must open out

and stretch itself. So long as it has sufficient elasticity, it can
do this, but it may rend and break if it is allowed to become
rigid, which is to stay, stupid) The best one can wish for
Americans—and for everyone else, for that matter—is that
they may keep clear heads today and even clearer smiles.

27 SUNSET INDUSTRIES, INCORPORATED, USA

In an ancient city of Castile there is a sign affixed to the building occupied by a very modest industry which reads: "The
Intimacy Ice Factory." I remembered that lettering and what
it suggested when I noted the title of a new U.S. corporation
recently established in New England, its first plant being
opened in Haverhill, a small city in the state of Massachusetts
which for some time now has been my home. The name reads
"Sunset Industries, Incorporated"—translated into Spanish it
might suggest "Industrial Twilight, Inc." or, more literally
rendered, "Industries of the Setting Sun." What is original
about this corporation is that it hires *only* men and women of
sixty or over. The women who are employed in the Haverhill
plant are between sixty and seventy-eight years of age. One
of them is a great grandmother.

This company is simply taking seriously a situation characteristic of our times, the consequences of which are, in part,
easily foreseeable—but which we must force ourselves to envisage—and, in part, difficult to imagine. The fact is that men
and women of the twentieth century do not easily decide to
die, or even to go into a decline. Up until a few decades ago,
the large majority of people died before completing their
sixtieth year. Those who remained were elderly "survivors,"

and I use the word in a double or even triple sense: 1) they were very few in number; 2) for that reason, the ranks they had formed in other times were dispersed and battered; 3) they were, with a few special exceptions, in a state of avowed physical and moral decadence, especially the latter. Old age began very early, partly for physiological reasons, partly as a matter of attitude. When a man begins to say, first jokingly and without believing it, "I am an old man now" or "at my age," after a while it all turns out to be true. Eighty years ago the Carlist princess Doña Nieves de Braganza, because of the hazards of civil war, arrived in the Catalonian city of Ripoll. There she lodged in the home of a family where the lady of the house, a woman of great beauty, was known as "The Blonde of Ripoll." The princess in her memoirs expresses her admiration: what loveliness, what a firm skin, what golden hair; then they told her that the Catalan beauty was twenty-eight years old, and she could not credit it. She could not believe that at twenty-eight a woman could appear so young and handsome, that she could have that fair skin and shimmering hair—because at twenty-eight, she insists, one can simply not say that a woman, even a married woman, is young any longer. At the age of twenty-eight the Blonde of Ripoll was duty-bound to pass into the twilight and her golden hair to reflect the fading light of sunset.

In rough figures, the average life-span in 1500 was twenty-two years; in 1700, thirty-four; in 1800, forty-six; in 1900, forty-nine; in 1953, sixty-nine. It is evident right away that there is something mysterious occurring in the twentieth century. But these statistics serve little purpose because they are too complex to interpret. Obviously, it not only is a question of longevity, but also of the enormous decline in the rate of infant mortality, the disappearance of many serious diseases, and the reduced threat of those which do last on—domesticated as they are by surgery and the use of antibiotics. It is more to the point to observe what is happening only to old people: in the United States, insurance companies calculate that the average life expectancy today for a man is 68.6 years, and for a woman, 72.1. The probability in 1930 that a child should reach sixty-five was figured as 52%; for the child born in 1953, the percentage is 64 if he is a boy, 74 if a girl. And that is not the whole story: those sixty-five years do not represent an end-limit, but almost a median. It is expected that more than half of all men of sixty-five will live another twelve years, and a fifth of them, twenty years more. In the case of women the prospects are incredibly favorable: half of those who are sixty-five today will reach eighty, a fifth will live to be eighty-eight. There are today in the United States thirteen and a half million persons who are over sixty-five years of age, and by the end of the century that age group is expected to number twenty-six million.

All of this implies that there will be solid generations with their ranks intact, with their own formations: rather than isolated individual survivors from the tremendous shipwreck of old age, *rari nantes in gurgite vasto*, there will be *an additional generation* on history's stage. Given this new situation, it then becomes imperative to examine the dynamics of such generations, their duration and the gaps between them—elements which may change as the pattern of age groups alters perceptibly and so affects the empiric structure of human life.

It is not the collective aspect of the question which interests me, however, but rather the changed conditions which this statistically common longevity may introduce into an individual life, because now man will begin to count on that longer life-span, and it will operate as a factor in our horizon. The term used by American insurance companies, "life expectancy," has one abstract statistical sense, which is what interests the actuarial departments, and another concrete, imaginative, and emotional one which represents what each individual anticipates as the probable, uncertain limit of his life on earth.

Until our day it was taken for granted that life terminated around sixty, or at least that vital activity then ceased. Think for a moment of the sentimental overtones of the word "sexagenarian," and of the annoyance those overtones cause real-life sexagenarians today. The structures of collective life are based on outdated assumptions; it used to be expected that a man who had achieved "a certain age" (between sixty and seventy) would cease to operate. That is the time for retirement, for conversion into what we call the inactive, passive elements of the population. But today it seems that such "passive groups" are not that at all; they feel themselves capable of full activity. But that activity (and, therefore, the design of their lives) turns out to pose a problem.

There are two possible but quite distinct approaches which may be labeled as "to continue" and "to begin over again." In some instances the tendency is to postpone official retirement age: in many American universities it is sixty-five, in others, sixty-eight; in very few is it seventy, the usual age in Europe. The task now is to establish a peak retirement age and then look beyond it. An even greater innovation seeks to eliminate obligatory retirement at any age. After such and such a date a committee decides whether or not a worker should retire or continue on the job: this means that age, any age, is no longer the determining factor in retirement from full-time activity, but rather the qualities and capacities of the individual person. There will be numerous difficulties in applying it, but the principle itself is hopeful and encouraging: not to assign any preordained limit to a man's active life; not to prescribe any "liquidation period" during which a man, exiled from the job or the profession which has constituted his world, must await death passively, literally in a state which an administrative Gallicism customarily terms "a extinguir."*

There is, however, another tendency clearly evident in the

* Waiting for extinction, on the way out—Trans.

United States toward a paradoxically early retirement. The average American enjoys a sufficient income, he owns his own home and acquires other means at an early age, he has a savings account and insurance—all of which makes it economically feasible for many Americans to retire at sixty or earlier. There are a good number who do retire early and many more who wish to do so.

Still the question arises: retire *from* what and *to* what? Because we should not smoothly allow a purely negative interpretation of retirement to go unchallenged. The point is to retire from the profession one has engaged in to date, not in order to await a melancholy extinction, but to begin new activities. This is the substance of the matter, the idea of a *new life* which begins at a time when previously we thought of life as ending.

It is likely that even before finding official acceptance, this point of view had germinated among the women of America. American women marry early—before twenty-one on the average—and in a country where there is no domestic help the care of house and children is a very heavy task. Women are forced to work hard for many years. But then the moment comes when the children are grown and are independent; perhaps they have married or, in any case, they are in their college years and almost always in a distant city. Their mothers, thanks to an excellent racial heritage, an adequate diet, proper exercise, and the cosmetic arts, find themselves a comfortable distance from any symptoms of old age. At that point they may enter on a second life, with time to themselves, with freedom to plan their days without having to sacrifice their lives to the demands of child care. Many couples, left more or less alone again, begin to regard each other in a different light and make new plans. Widows or divorcées usually feel along with their freedom a certain emptiness which carries them into a number of activities: clubs, committees, get-togethers, or social groups often catering only to lone women and not always to very discreet ones—"pan con pan . . . ,"* as the Spanish proverb goes.

When the moment comes to make plans for the new stage, a man tends to undergo a kind of crisis. Why keep on doing the same old thing? (We have to take into account the fact that Americans have a greater propensity for change—in occupation, job, or residence—than do Europeans, one explanation for which is the greater similarity that exists among American cities than among European ones. The difference between living in Providence or in Baltimore is not comparable to the differences between residing in Granada or in Oviedo, in Munich or in Heidelberg.) Perhaps a certain couple has lived for years and years in a harsh and inhospitable climate, in Iowa or in North Dakota. Why not, then, try California or Florida? All these thoughts bear the impress "to begin over again."

But that attitude has underlying it some fairly ticklish assumptions. One of these has to do with the capacity of the individual substantially to modify his life program; and this capacity in turn requires, on the one hand, a certain willingness to break with the past and, on the other, a youthful brand of resilience and flexibility. Besides which, this orientation brings to light with unaccustomed honesty the fact that most men do not live in accord with their inner callings. There is an infinite number of tasks in the world to which men do not feel themselves *called*. People carry out these labors, of course, because they are necessary (for the collective good) and, in individual terms, because they must earn a living; but they nourish no great illusion concerning their work. Most men are willing to accept these things as they are. Some wind up feeling a certain hope or pride in their daily occupation; they work *con amore*, they put a good deal of themselves into their task, and through self-esteem come to esteem the results

* "Birds of a feather"—Trans.

of their labor. Others become embittered and sour, fermenting rancor and discontent; still others never give a thought to the problem because it never occurs to them that their lives might be different. Many Americans as they reach sixty, and perhaps before, abandon their "work" in the strict sense of that word—imposed labor, professional, required, unpleasant, boring, without spark—and dedicate themselves to what Ortega has called the "pleasure-bearing occupations" which, for the most part, involve another kind of work perhaps equally demanding.

Work, yes, but another *kind*. A chosen task, not one determined automatically by the circumstances. Thus a man's vital impulse renews itself, as with a projectile whose flight is restored by firing a new rocket. The trajectory, which was on the downward curve, which would soon touch the ground, flattens out again and begins to head for a more distant horizon—a new version of the elixir of youth.

For what I am trying to say is this: as the average life span increases, and as individuals are better preserved in their advanced years, we are of necessity arriving at new social structures designed for those who are "to begin over again." For example, take the case of retiring university professors who are immediately rehired by other universities engaged in rounding up splendid faculties of "old hands" who will youthfully set their sails for a second voyage. Another instance: the university in Massachusetts which offers special courses only for women of sixty-five and over. Moreover, this constructive reaction to the vital statistics will tend to prolong longevity. This reorientation of individual lives will offer those lives fresh exuberance for still further decades. It's not merely that men and women "do not die," that they remain on the earth for more years than they expected; but rather that they are going to have a more abundant life, to supplement their vitality, so that they may truly look forward to the second part of a life program and to the vital projects

which give it significance. On his eightieth birthday a great
Spanish scholar demanded from his doctor sixteen years more
to live; he needed those years, neither more nor fewer, to
finish off the tasks he had in hand. I do not doubt that God
will grant him his request; five years have gone by and he has
shown no sign of weakening.† Besides, knowing what intellectual work entails, I am sure when that gentleman reaches
ninety-six he will still have many things left to do. He will
have come across new and exciting topics for investigation,
and he will need a reprieve. At times the sunset is very slow
and very lengthy. I anticipate decisive changes in the structures of society and of human history, simply because of the
moral behind the story of "Sunset Industries, Inc.," a new-
born firm in New England.

28 THE FEMININE HALF OF THE U.S.

Why such an odd title? Why not speak simply of "the North
American woman"? Indeed, for two very different reasons.
The first is that the alternative suggestion represents a huge
topic which I do not feel at all capable of tackling here, because to do so would require abundant meditation and extensive documentation, which I am far from possessing. Almost
everything written about women is incredibly incomplete,
and what is said about American women is even more so.
Therefore, because they seem easier to understand from a
distance, and because they would as a matter of fact insist on
that distance being maintained, I renounce all right to such a

---

† By now [1964] fifteen have gone by, and nothing is changed [Marías
is undoubtedly referring to the Dean of Spanish intellectuals at that
time, Don Ramón Menéndez Pidal, who died in 1969—Trans.]

fascinating subject and prudently abstain from promising to say something about it when I know I cannot fulfill my promise.

The second reason is more positive: I wish to imply in my title something, rudimentary as it is, that seems to me the principal point to be made: that in the United States women do constitute a *half*, not of the population, for that is true almost everywhere, but *of the country*. In almost every other country they are less than that; in some instances it seems as though the country were made up entirely of men, who, of course, "have" wives.

Antonio Machado speaks in his poetry of the "cities of womanless streets," in his native Andalusia; in the United States, this line would be incomprehensible: women are all over, in the streets and everywhere else. How can there *be* so many of them? This is the question inevitably asked by a European. The reason is clear enough: American women, in the immense majority, are "in circulation," in several senses which we might well enumerate. In the first place, in many regions of the United States and especially in the Northeast, there is scarcely anything that might be called "the lower classes," groups which never cross over the outermost threshold of social life. In most European countries and on other continents, large sections of the population remain "outside," in a kind of social exile, and have no access—or very occasional access—to normal forms of community life such as strolling, going shopping, attending a performance, sitting in a café, traveling, studying, or listening to lectures or concerts. And immediately we must add to that statement an all-important observation: ascending the social scale to the point where a kind of social life begins, it is apparent that this entry is for men only, and that women of the same social stratum must still remain in the shadows on the outer fringes—which in this case means they are relegated to the dark interiors of their homes.

In the second place, in the United States domestic life is much less absorbing and requires less seclusion. In countries where domestic service exists as a matter of course, a large number of women are occupationally bound as domestics with no hope of egress; and even in countries which have lost their servant class, women spend a great deal of time in household duties, undertaken still in a fairly primitive fashion, and in child care. Think, for example, of the number of hours a French, Italian, or Spanish housewife devotes in the kitchen to the time-consuming preparation of complicated dishes. In the United States, where for all intents and purposes there is no such thing as domestic service, women are relieved from their tasks by the knowledgeable assistance of their husbands and grown children, through mechanization and the use of many helpful devices, by the excellence and efficiency of service industries (heating, maintenance, plumbing), and by the simplicity of the national cuisine. Another small but decisive detail: the American timetable operates earlier than the European or South American counterpart, not to mention Spain: dinner at six o'clock means an end to household tasks and leaves a portion of the day which even in the worst of circumstances allows for some free time to be freely spent.

In the third place, age is a factor in the number of North American women whom we see all over the place. In certain countries—France—women bloom late. The *jeune fille* hardly figures at all; only the married woman who is approaching her thirties really exists for society. In other lands, on the contrary, a woman must withdraw from society at a very early age; she has scarcely entered upon maturity before she is relegated bit by bit to domesticity. In the United States girls develop their personalities and their roles from early youth onward, and they do not withdraw from society until forced to do so by extreme age or death because, normally speaking, there is no such thing as retirement from the scene. Activities may vary but they never cease, and this variation is one of the most interesting aspects of American society.

But above all, the reason American women are everywhere to be seen is that in United States society men have not monopolized all initiative as essential to their masculine rôle: women as well as men may take the initiative, though not in exactly the same way nor in the same directions. For to be fair it must be said that what exists here is not "equality," but a subtle differentiation in masculine and feminine aspirations without any subordination of the latter to the former. American women are everywhere because they are themselves. Let me put aside for the moment the question of what the consequences may represent for women's portion of reality.

The situation of American women represents a novelty for almost all the rest of the Western world, because we tend to forget that the presence of women in European life is fairly well confined to the larger cities. As soon as we shift out of the metropolitan European city, we are back again in large measure among the various men-only forms of society. In the United States this is simply not possible: at work, at play, in social life as a whole, the American world is always ambisexual. In fact, there are some departments of life where feminine predominance is so persistent that the traditional arrangement is inverted; for example, concerts, some species of lectures, and other "cultural" activities. (This phenomenon is also taking place on a lesser scale in South America.) The fact that marriage is common among the very young—between girls from eighteen to twenty-three and young men generally two to three years older—and that from six o'clock on in the evening, when the day's work is done, couples tend to go out together, also adds to the omnipresence of women that is so immediately evident to a new arrival in the country.

I must confess that such evidence is extremely pleasant because, taken statistically, the North American woman's good looks and grooming are very impressive indeed. This is the necessary starting point because it is the first thing one observes, and at the same time it is a most important factor which explains many other things. I say "statistically," because my interest at the moment is not whether or not the beautiful women of the United States are more handsome than the beauties of other lands: it lies rather in the quantitative situation—there are so many more of them, and this is what enables them to impose the coloration they do on society, on the street, and in public places. An excellent racial mixture, an adequate diet, a sense of cleanliness more widespread than almost anywhere else in the world, frequent attention to body care, and, above all, a tremendous rise in the level of lower social groups—all these may be counted as contributing factors to the end result. But then we must add another cause of a different order: the existence and dominance of an ideal of femininity which affects a very large number of women. What I mean is that the majority of American women function as women, they are conscious of being women, they work at being women. This is true to such an extent that the exceptional cases (numerous, naturally, but exceptions nonetheless) wear an unmistakable air of having "given up," of "quitting," of "surrendering." Sometimes this takes on an embittered aspect (the woman who, despairing of her feminine condition, chooses to become an eccentric); other times, it takes the form of jovial resignation (the middle-aged lady who decides to block out the bathroom scale's report to her esthetic conscience and devote herself happily to butter and sweets, even though she knows she will come to look like a pouter pigeon). Except in such cases as these, American women circulate: lithe and secure, very slender, yet with the marks of their femininity quite apparent, wearing halos of shining hair, serene and smiling, confident, sure of themselves and of their world. You can see them coming and going, entering the shops, filling the colleges, working in offices, stopping in at the drugstore for lunch or a quick cup of coffee, praying in the churches, sunbathing in their gardens, clearing the snow away from the door, pushing a baby-stroller, commuting on the train that will take them to their jobs in the city. Or you see them go by like the wind in their enormous shiny cars, right hand on the steering wheel and a cigarette in the left, as they pass between the elms and the chestnut trees bordering the asphalt road.

I have spoken of the beauty and of the excellent grooming of North American women, and this matter of grooming requires some elucidation. The woman "on active duty" who has not "given up" pays particular attention to her person: extreme cleanliness, care of hair, make-up rarely neglected, careful checking of weight and proportions. (In the case of some women, actresses for example, measurements are published revealing their bust size, waist, hips, and thighs to the exact inch.) And how do they dress? Here we must make a distinction. The American woman's situation differs considerably from that of her European counterpart, because in the United States there are scarcely any seamstresses or *couturières*, so that women therefore do not have their clothes made for them but instead simply choose them. It is possible that the truly well-dressed American woman is not *as* well dressed as her colleagues in Europe, but on the other hand, in America there are many, many women who dress rather well compared to the very few who do so in Europe. But this, despite all, is not the most important point. There are three other things which should not be overlooked: first, that American women do not always dress well, but only when they dress up. What I mean to say is that they do not hesitate upon occasion to wear a grubby raincoat, jeans, and a cowboy jacket, or shorts and a man's shirt with the tails hanging out. But a few hours later they transform themselves back into models of distinguished femininity. Second, they do not seem to be bound by any sense of consistency or uniformity in details. For instance, below a fur coat that looks as though it may have cost three thousand dollars you may observe someone wearing flat-heeled loafers and white socks. Third, American women dress much more for men than for other women, and are therefore more interested in finding clothes that are becoming and attractive than in being "original," striking, or marked by the touch of some famous *couturier* (who is, naturally, either unknown to or despised by the entire male population anyway).

Interpreting this information will lead us to the conclusion that the American woman's attitude toward her own person and her relations with her own sex and with men simply do not coincide with such relations as they exist in other lands. She is not very conceited, much less so than her opposite number in Spain, France, Italy, or South America. She is not always on the defensive nor engrossed in myriad details; she rarely dresses over-fastidiously, and so enjoys a greater capacity for spontaneity. On the other hand, she never forgets that she is a woman (as occasionally seems to be the case with a German or an Englishwoman); she is habitually conscious of her body and aware that it is attractive, but always without insisting on it, without censurable intention. This is the reason why, in the Catholic churches of America, well-dressed and impeccably groomed women go to mass and take communion in sleeveless summer dresses with low-cut necks—in summer women wear almost no other kind—to the astonishment of no one and in an attitude of poised composure. If one wishes to measure modesty in terms of square inches of skin revealed in the hot summer weather, then, of course, North American women are less modest than many Europeans; but I sometimes wonder whether modesty may not be considerably more difficult to assess, because next to the undoubted generosity with which legs or shoulders are shown we must place the matter-of-factness and relative innocence of the manner in which they are shown (and not *exhibited*). I can remember only one woman—one hot afternoon in August on Washington Street in Boston—who made what we might call "European use" of her bare shoulders in conjunction with a long mane of coppery hair.

In Europe the consensus is that American women are lovely, of course, but all alike. I believe this opinion to be the result of a bird's eye view which retains in its glance only the traits, common to the country visited, which are different from those of the country of origin. It does not seem to me that American women of the same social level are any more similar to each other than are Argentine, French, or Spanish women of the same class. A resemblance does occur—but this is another story—among various social groups, because in the United States the ground floor of society is much reduced in size and, besides, it is not very far down: there is as a result less distance between the extremes, but no fewer *individual* differences. The American woman is undoubtedly characterized by a certain straightforwardness in manner, a certain lack of reserve which may look like simplicity or superficiality. But with that statement we arrive at the most interesting part of the discussion, and also at an interpretation fraught with the greatest possibility of error. I shall try to clarify my impressions and offer a few conjectures.

I remarked before that American women are everywhere because they are themselves and at one with themselves. I meant in that expression to suggest their relative independence, their freedom from want, the fact that to a much greater degree than elsewhere they live from their own centers of balance and so do not lean on men. They show more initiative and offer less argument. They live with men on a common ground, in a world where they feel themselves to be legally established. They do not feel precariously positioned in an alien world, a man's world (within which women of other cultures fabricate in a somewhat clandestine and mysterious manner "their" world—which is, by the way, an enormously fascinating creation), but rather they relate to men from an equal footing and "share" the world with them. This lends a special flavor to the dealings between men and women in the United States. We might say that between the sexes there exists a "Good Neighbor Policy" which presupposes recognition of respective areas of sovereignty. The American woman reacts to a man first of all with attention and interest; her attitude implies that she counts on him. The relationship, as a matter of principle, is cordial and constructive; women "approve" of men, they take pleasure in their existence and in their presence. (This is something which traditional European convention hides and occasionally attenuates, or alternatively overemphasizes and spoils.)

An American woman who feels any measure of liking, admiration, or affection toward a man expresses it with complete naturalness in a way which—excepting the idea of "surrender"—recalls the traditional attitude of the European gentleman towards his lady. This lends a uniquely cordial, comfortable, and friendly tone to male and female coexistence in the United States.

I do not intend to imply that there are no defects or limitations in this state of affairs. If I had to condense into one line the greatest difference I find between American and European women, I should say that it is the same difference as that which distinguishes the Hudson or the Mississippi from the Duero, the Seine, the Rhine, the Arno, or the Danube. American women, like American rivers, have had fewer things said to them. Rivers in America, I once wrote, channel more water than those in Europe, but less poetry. European woman has been created, century by century, with the words poured into her ears by her men: madrigals, sonnets, gallantries, streetside compliments; and with the help also of hats with feathers that swept the dust, jalousie windows, scrupulous chaperones, idolatry, and disdain. That is to say that man has in large proportion invented the European woman; he has proposed her—and to a great extent imposed upon her—as a projection or figure incarnating the character he has created. The North American has cooperated in another sense in the creation of his female partner. Much has been said of the *self-made man*; with greater fitness we might speak of the *self-made woman* of the United States who has "invented" and projected her own image without a great deal of assistance—and, in any case, with *assistance* only.

All of this confers upon the American woman, as seen by European eyes, a singular novelty. A European finds her to have (let no one doubt it) a good dose of spontaneity, frankness, and sincerity to which he is not accustomed. He verifies happily that she lacks many feminine traits—primness, affectation, vanity—which, though justifiable at the time of their origin, have usually degenerated into vestigial, inauthentic forms that hinder vital dealings and meaningful communication between men and women. The American woman has a kind of aura that is refreshing and vivifying, a youthfulness at any age like the air in the early hours of the morning. At the same time one has the feeling that this woman, to whom as yet few things have been said, has not yet been completely interpreted and consequently is not yet entirely realized. Her potential goes far beyond the point at which she now finds herself. Since she has—to a great degree—created herself, since she is so self-contained, there are vast unawakened areas in her personal reality which must be discovered, found out, elicited, and roused by men. To say that a woman is self-contained is at bottom an error because not even a man can be thus described, much less a woman, who is in a sense a triple distillation of human kind. Woman does not exist in a state of nature: at most only the female breeder does. She is an artificial construct, a work of art, and in order to be finished she needs the cooperation of both sexes. The American woman is interested in men—I have already made that point—but once she becomes the person she is to be, self-contained, she does not alter in form, though she becomes interested in others and is interesting to them. From this condition springs the peril of egotism which hovers over women in the United States; from this also arises an over-confidence which is often dearly bought at the price of renouncing certain very deep and intimate levels of being at which to be a woman implies *insecurity*. Finally, this also is the explanation for the fact that American women, normally demanding and justifiably so, are often willing in some matters to be content with very little. Obviously, since they are less subject to their husbands, a poor marriage is of less consequence to them than to a Spanish woman, for instance. But for this very reason they consider matrimony as less decisive (for better or for worse), and therefore an American marriage is less risky, less vulnerable, less exposed to frustration and unhappiness, but also less open to the intensity and perfection which can only be achieved when one is willing to risk everything on one card.

All of this leads us to the conclusion that women in North America, marvelous as they are, are still on the road, still under construction. And the danger is that, because of their comfortable niche in society and because of their undoubted perfections and charm, they may fall into a state of self-sufficiency, of satisfied complacency. This would be a tremendous mistake because man, and woman even more, is substantially "insufficient." If it were to happen thus, the American woman might become petrified in these transitional forms, in which, delightful though they are, she should not remain indefinitely, like a morning hour which refused to make way for noontime. A large part of the creation of the United States has been the almost exclusive responsibility of women: they have been the educators, the movers behind considerable portions of national culture. I believe that they have done their share admirably. While men, for their part, were seeing to the development of the economy, of agriculture, industry, and management, women were cooperating with them in outstanding fashion. There would be no United States, for example, if there were no secretaries, an amazing truth. But things today are very complex; to accomplish anything, everyone is needed. And especially so when the task is to achieve a full measure of humanity. Women in the United States are going to have to demand more of American men: not more service, more effort, more wealth, more technique, more courtesies, or greater assistance; but rather more human quality, more male perfection, more imagination. American men must learn to say more and better things to their women; and the latter, to listen to them. Women, thus interpreted, invented, revealed, could throw themselves into a great colonial enterprise—colonization of their selves. It has been justly said that until a man awakens her, a woman is always a Sleeping Beauty. American women do not appear to be asleep because they are full of youthful vigor and activity; but one might risk the query whether or not such a woman in some hidden corner of her soul is not a "beautiful somnambulist" who walks, moves, stirs about, works, and smiles, but who is at heart asleep.

If one fine day American men discover in their imaginations the right words (not words learned elsewhere) with which to speak to their women, they will find themselves in the midst of unexpected riches, with unsuspected lodes, in an incredible paradise. But in order to come to this state of perfection in America, there must be millions of hours of dialogue between man and woman—friendly, jocund, moving, passionate conversation.

29 THE DEFENSE AND SURRENDER
OF A WAY OF LIFE

Seven years ago† while I was investigating a subject so remote as the origins of philosophy in ancient Greece, I came across a fact which I thought contained the germ of nothing less than a law of history. Ever since then I have looked at present-day reality from that point of view, and few ideas have so helped me in attempting to understand what is transpiring in our world or what may happen in the next few years, and above all the peril that hovers over the United States and, therefore, over the entire Western world.

The story is familiar. The Persian wars brought about a general crisis in Greece at several levels. First, because of the implicit threat: the ever-increasing power of the Persians presented the risk that Hellenic life might be totally transformed. If the Greeks had been defeated, there is no doubt but that their way of life would have been destroyed and replaced by an entirely different form. The Hellenes were perfectly well aware of this; they knew that their existence as a people was at stake and the very sense in which they customarily understood the verb "to live." But this is not the whole story: the mere threat itself, even before it could materialize or be fulfilled, brought about a change in the Greek world. Because when the Greeks came truly face to face with another way of life, another concept of society and of man's nature, the Greek universe which, in fact, had seemed to them *the* world, the only possible world, was changed into *a* world, one of at least two possible universes between which one could choose. That is the decisive point: even though the Greek naturally found his own world preferable, he would now *have to* prefer it, to choose it. His world would no longer be the only

† Written in 1954.

reality for him, but rather a state limited by certain determining factors; a conditional and insecure world that might well have been or become entirely different. Lastly, the seriousness of the wars with the Medes was such that the Greeks were obliged to make an all-out effort toward victory involving new techniques, a different use of resources, the incorporation into active social processes of large segments of the population, and a shift in basic assumptions and in human relations. Finally, after the victory, when the Greeks believed that they had saved the traditional, national way of life for which they had battled half a century, it turned out that that form of life had dissolved, that it no longer existed. It was not a question of Persian patterns imposed on Hellas, because the Hellenes were the victors: the new structure was a way of life the Greeks had not known before, that they had neither desired nor sought, a result of the Persian threat and, especially, of their own energetic defense efforts.

"Each time that man truly risks his way of life, he loses it, regardless of the outcome of the conflict." This I wrote in 1947.† "When the issue is favorable, the victor usually suffers disillusionment because he sees slipping through his fingers the very way of life he thought to have established with his victory. Our experience in recent years has illustrated once again the functioning of this little known but easily demonstrated law of history."

As I made that statement I was thinking of the wind-up of World War II. Since then a gigantic laboratory experiment has begun to develop, still very clearly observable because until now violence has played only a small part, and destruction, therefore, has been limited. Through the kind of purity only obtainable indeed in laboratory-controlled experiments, this law of history is being proved valid. The field of experimentation is both enormous and at the same time very definite in structure: it is the United States. Conditions

† *Biografía de la Filosofía*, I, 5. (*Obras* II, p. 448.)

for observing are superlative; so much so that the observations all but make themselves, and all we need to do is open our eyes.

During the last few years the United States has felt the threat to the Western world. This expression does not always have the same referent each time it is uttered. For North Americans, however, the meaning is perfectly concrete, though perhaps for that very reason hard to analyze: it is *their* world, the way of life in which they lodge. The curious intellectual may inquire "For how long has that been true?" The average American would tend to answer: "Since the very beginning." And he would not be wrong, because on his "real" historical horizon, not merely that of the world of intellect and information, he discerns only continuity in his way of life, without breaks or fissures; an uninterrupted system of *mores* which vary with the course of history but which tie the American of today to his counterpart in the War of Independence and, indeed, to the Pilgrim Fathers and the origins of colonial life in the United States. All this is what is threatened, what must be defended. There are more than a few reasons for such an attitude, but even if there were only the idea of continuity, this would not be so contemptible as one might tend to think. Besides, the American is aware of being settled in his way of life—in principle, a happy one, and by this I mean that it possesses the necessary social "alveolus" in which individual happiness is normally possible and even relatively easy to achieve. Almost all the contacts he has had with other cultures have led the average American to value his own more highly, and I say "average" because beginning some thirty years ago there was a spread of nonconformism among the "intellectual" minority which attained considerable influence. I am not here about to go into the very subtle question of the extent to which either that evaluation or that nonconformity was justified; both attitudes have points in their favor. What I am interested in remarking is simply that the situation of thirty years ago has altered in such a way that the two attitudes have converged. That is, the disparate viewpoints of the average American and the intellectual *élite* of the 1920s came about largely because they were talking about different things, and as their respective foci have enlarged, their points of view have come close to coinciding. Let me explain myself.

As there are few things harder to "see" than a way of life, Americans have customarily believed that their life consisted of the "things" they possessed, not to mention the resources and facilities on which they could rely: abundant food, autos, gadgets, and excellent plumbing. On the other hand, intellectuals—especially from 1920 to 1940, and indeed even before that—have habitually felt a kind of discontent colored by what they "miss" in the way of a whole series of refinements, preoccupations, and possibilities that Europe normally offers: "literary life," centers of artistic endeavor, the publicity given intellectual life, and the social reverberations therefrom. This gave rise to an intellectual contempt (and if we press the point, not a very intelligent disdain) for the prosperous "vulgarity" of the United States. And when at a certain moment prosperity appeared to evaporate, the contempt began to harden into resolute nonconformity and even hostility. But the situation in recent years is no longer the same. The average American, even the man in the street, has begun to realize that his way of life cannot be reduced to objects, facilities, and resources at hand; above all, because he has come to see that that way of life is neither obvious nor secure enough for him to be able to bank on it. He has realized that his existence is dependent upon a series of problematical conditions that require a persistent fusion of effort. Even though it is commonplace to consider the United States the country of the masses (and in a sense it is true), I believe it is the place in which the phenomenon rigorously described by Ortega as "the revolt of the masses" has least reality. The enormous mass of the American population is quite unrebellious: there are fewer examples than elsewhere in the world of the "spoiled child," the gilded young scion—petulant and self-satisfied—who considers himself capable of discussing and understanding any subject at hand and who uses up the goods of this earth as though they grew on trees. This type is more common to "importer" countries, who receive carefully packaged and as though by magic the most complex products of modern technology, for which of course they must "pay," but which they do not "invent" or "fabricate."

North Americans have somewhat confusedly begun to be aware that they enjoy a well-fashioned and valuable way of life that makes happiness plausible. They do not yet know for certain how that way of life is constituted, and today they tend to identify it with its institutions, for none but the most perspicacious realize that the opposite is true: that the institutions spring from the way of life, and by that I mean that those institutions do serve in an effective and adequate way. But the fact is that the American way of living is gradually being discovered, analyzed, and subscribed to.

On the other hand, partly because they are disillusioned with certain tendencies in European "literary" or "artistic life," and partly stimulated by their own national historic enterprise whose values they have been late in discovering, the intellectual minorities have begun to abandon their posture of contempt and nonconformity. The testimonials gathered a few years ago in the *Partisan Review* demonstrated not only that this was the case, but also that intellectuals were clearly conscious that it was so. It is difficult to ascertain how much this new attitude contains of nationalism, pride, rejoicing over others' misfortunes (such as the decline in prestige of certain European countries) or of "conformism" in the pejorative sense of the term. I suppose that there is a little of all of that involved, but in small doses. Besides, that attitude did not originally germinate in the heart of American society, but was injected into it by a type of European who, ceasing to be European, becomes a "pluperfect American" precisely because he realizes that he can never be "just" an American. Most of these people are ex-Europeans, but in some few but unmistakable cases they are South Americans.

The result today is that masses and minority, thanks to this movement towards convergence, are much closer to each other than they were thirty or even fifteen years ago. And just at this moment, for the first time in American history, there is arising a grave and serious threat to the way of life to which in the United States the whole social structure subscribes. And the problem, naturally, is to organize an effort at defense. Nothing is more justifiable, but we must inquire *how* it is to be organized.

Because if the defense effort is too intense and overenergetic, then the danger is that that effort itself, and the changes it brings about, will accomplish the destruction of the very way of life it seeks to protect. It can be argued that such a defense *must* be sufficient because if it is not, the country is exposed to defeat and ruin. This is true, of course, but the point is that such efforts must not go beyond what is truly "necessary." American life up to now has been based on certain prevailing usages, on certain ways of behaving, on certain underlying assumptions which appear to me to be splendid ones and which I, as an outsider, should tremble to see disintegrate. Above all else, the United States is a country where confidence predominates. Confidence in what? In everything, in reality: the American believes that if the soil is well worked, it will produce good crops; that if he digs in land where there is coal, iron or oil, those products will be brought to the surface; that if he pursues his studies in a good college, he will graduate an educated man with a certain training; that his neighbor is happy to know him, and will, if he can, do him a favor; that the human race has many possibilities; that God is good and tries to give the United States a helping hand from time to time. Confidence does not mean credulity, nor even ingenuousness; but the American, if he has to choose between opposites, tends to favor ingenuousness over distrust. Of course he is aware that every so often someone presents the teller at the bank window with a phony check or a forged signature, but since this happens very rarely, he believes it is cheaper and easier to cash checks immediately instead of wasting millions of work hours—and dollars—in laborious verification and precautionary measures —with the understanding, of course, that some time or other he may have to call the police, and that then some fellow will wind up in Sing-Sing or Alcatraz. For the same reason an American rarely locks his door or registers a package through the mail; he leaves milk deliveries, clean laundry, or the suits returned from the cleaners on his doorstep; he parks his car on the street for hours at a time without even locking it; he does not proctor students who are taking their exams; and he does not spy on his customers in the self-service market. Again for the same reason, he cordially welcomes the person recently introduced to him as a new arrival to the city and indeed to the country; he takes a man's word with respect to almost anything; and he does not believe that an electoral victory for the opposing party means the end of the world, nor that the people who go to the church across the street from his are authentic representatives of Satan.

On these principles, and on many other analogous assumptions, North American life is firmly founded. The immediate consequence is a vital double "plus": a greater return and more efficiency on the one hand; and on the other, greater joy in living. Americans are a rich people, but their wealth has not been handed to them as a gift. It is true that they have tremendous natural resources, but there are countries with excellent resources who are nonetheless poor. Americans work energetically and assiduously, almost all of them and almost every day. Therefore they do not have occasion to lose courage and slacken—as do certain individuals in other countries who really do work, when they realize they make up only a small fraction of the population, when they continually rub shoulders with loafers or "part-time" colleagues. Besides, Americans waste far less time and effort than other people in setting up checks, controls, and other administrative traps, or in other words, in making work for others. When even a small tendency towards that kind of thing (what Americans call "red tape") automatically encourages the growth of bureaucracy, which then tries to justify its existence by creating more obstacles and intervening in every possible way in the business of others, the proliferation of needless precautionary measures can be ruinous.

The other plus factor is that sense of joy in being alive that makes the American air so easily "breatheable." Americans tend to believe that the sense of freedom and ease which impresses the foreigner as he arrives in the United States arises from their political institutions. This is not so, because a visitor customarily has few dealings with such institutions, except in some especially oppressive particulars. The transient, therefore, does not go away impressed with American freedom precisely because he runs up against an entire catalogue of government controls, perhaps inoffensive, but extremely visible, and encounters a network of rigidly organized day-to-day details. The foreigner who does garner an impression of ease is the person who manages to immerse himself in American social life, in its friendliness, in the confidence by which it is permeated and enriched. After a few months such a visitor feels that the social "tension" or pressure under which he lives is indeed benign and easily borne, that he can henceforth abandon a whole collection of inhibitions and reservations, suspicions, and precautions. He feels himself under the influence of the invigorating cross-currents of many benevolent emanations.

His position is not without some risk, of course. But the

point is that American life has always entailed a margin of risk, and it continues to exist under that proviso. In the same way that Social Security leaves a broad area of insecurity, that private investment may lead either to gain or loss, that an occasional tornado may destroy half a city, or that the car one is riding in may crash into another, there is also the danger of being deceived, robbed, or murdered. But those perils are as much a part of life as polio, cancer, and coronary occlusion.

So be it, but can the Communist menace be placed in the same category? This is where the ambiguities begin to arise. No one doubts that if a Communist power were to conquer the United States, this would signify the total destruction of its structures and way of life. In this sense the Communist threat cannot be classed with any of the perils mentioned before, which are partial and internal risks to the existence of American society as such. Nevertheless, we must assess the degree of danger represented by Communism and try above all to indicate accurately what that threat comprises. Naturally, a war with Russia; and the possibility that in such a war the Russians might enjoy an advantage because they would have uncovered certain scientific secrets which bear on military developments or, equally important, because they would have obtained advance knowledge of United States military strategy. Does the menace also include the possibility that the United States itself might turn Communist? I do not believe that anyone should think seriously of such a possibility for more than five minutes. If there is anything which can be said to be humanly impossible, it is that American public opinion should incline towards Communism—not only because of the high standard of living, because there is a minimum of social injustice and because the distance between extremes among social classes is less than anywhere else in the world; but precisely because of that way of life of which I have been speaking: because of the small amount of hostility displayed by the average American, because of his rather tepid enthusiasm for state control, because he tends to be satisfied with himself and his lot, because he loves effort for its own sake, free play, being able to best his neighbor (in a sportive sense) by making more money than he, having a newer car, going farther away on his vacation; but all of this without the slightest desire to send his neighbor to jail or into exile, without hating him, without being obsessed by him in his dreams at night.

It is clearly evident that the United States today needs a tight and clever network of military defense and counterespionage. Also apparent is the strict necessity, as of today, to spend the largest part of the nation's resources in arming the country and the country's allies—or at least those who declare themselves to be friends. But while care has been taken to keep the enormous military expenditures from upsetting the country's economy, I fear that the same precautions have not been taken to prevent the countermeasures taken against the human danger from menacing the moral well-being of the United States; in other words from threatening the forms of living together, the way of life that everyone is fighting to protect. As mistrust becomes more general and as caution spills over the normal level, whether the process begins with a military chief of staff or with the guardian of certain atomic secrets, but eventually comes to influence a dentist or a high school teacher or the owner of a drugstore, there is then and there destroyed, to a degree that the Russians could never hope to achieve short of victorious war, part of the very essence of American life. And that way of life is destroyed because it is altered and channeled in the direction of life in Russia which, according to all reports, is characterized by a lack of initiative and by mutual distrust among all its citizens.

There is nothing more fragile than a social structure, a way of life. Confidence is a tenuous quality, extremely friable and very sensitive; once it disappears, it does not return. If the day comes when Americans truly look with mistrust at each other, what we think of as the United States is finished. Such suspicion assumes two forms, one active and the other passive: there is the danger that each American may fear that his neighbor is going to denounce him, spy on him, persecute him; but there is also the peril that he may come to believe that if his neighbor does not agree with his own way of thinking, then the man is a monster who must be destroyed. Either kind of mutual hostility has equal power to destroy the American way of life. Strategic military and scientific vigilance is indispensable and offers little risk because it is confined to a particular sphere and has little impact on social life. It is unfortunate and significant that the physicist who devotes himself to nuclear research must feel the breath of the F.B.I. on his neck, but in this day and age it is unavoidable. What is *not* necessary, useful, or bearable, however, is that an ordinary man possessing no military secrets, no political or atomic bombshells, one who certainly does not hold the fate of his country in his hands, should feel himself to be under surveillance and investigation. I am convinced that such a change would within five years finish off the climate of American life as we know it, undermine that society just as though a horrible contagious disease had been unleashed—depriving it of all ease, flexibility and joy.

Someone might say that some danger lies in the possibility that some petty employee, some dentist, cook, schoolteacher, or university professor might manage to convince his intimate friends, his clients, or his pupils of the excellence of the Communist philosophy. This is not likely in the United States, but neither is it metaphysically impossible. Well, let us suppose that after a few years of persuasion there are several thousand people who think that Communism is the best possible system. What impact could those few thousand possibly make on American life? On the other hand, the decision to avoid entirely the possibility of that happening brings very shortly, as its consequence, a change in the orientation of the American way which would, of course, be called anti-Communism, but which would very closely resemble Communism itself—a way of life based on mutual mistrust, lack of confidence, and resentment. Last April the Catholic prelate Bernard Sheil, director of the Catholic Youth Movement and auxiliary bishop of the diocese of Chicago, asserted that all "anti-communism" is not effective nor even morally tenable; he went on to say that in the morally-suspect name of anti-communism the United States was losing its sense of humor, of fair play and clean sport, of intelligent analysis, of charity, and of veracity; and he added that to present that negative attitude as a positive value is "a monstrous perversion of morality."

The point is that defense efforts must be bounded; if carried to an extreme, beyond the limit tolerable given the realities, those efforts themselves are mortally dangerous. An organism succumbs if given an overdose of medication; an all-out anti-communist defense can win the enemy a moral victory without any necessity for firing a shot or taking the slightest risk. An extremist effort at defense is exactly equivalent to a surrender of the way of life one wishes to protect. And since this phenomenon is abundantly clear, it may occur even to the least malicious mind to wonder whether these avid and intemperate defenders of "Americanism" really can tolerate American life; whether they do not actually hate the prevailing climate of liberty, ease, confidence, and lively day-to-day enjoyment; whether they would not prefer to substitute for that climate a world of crooked sideglances, resentment, and hostility between "us" and "them"—in a word, a disassociative society.

30 THE PULSE OF NORTH AMERICA

I have arrived in New York City by air, by highway, and by train which suddenly deposits you in the center of Manhattan—from Europe, from South America, and from other parts inside the United States. (I should also add a "false" though flavorful arrival by ferryboat from Richmond, battered by the wind and with the Statue of Liberty to the left, the Brooklyn Bridge to the right, and Manhattan's skyline of skyscrapers dead ahead.)

From a plane at night New York appears to be no more than a swelling in the chain of colored lights—not white lights as in Europe—that stretches almost uninterruptedly along the Atlantic Coast from Massachusetts south to Washington. If New York is a city, what then is a city? This is the doubt that soon assails the mind. When one has arrived among those many lights, from the heart of disorientation, a new and strange security begins to germinate.

However, in order to be completely surprised at New York and then (and only then, of course) to begin to understand the city, one must be permeated with history and alert to its lessons. Because the crucial thing, the root reason for the violent impact of the place, is that there is entailed here what the Greeks call a shift in category. It is not that New York as a city is different from other cities; rather New York is a city in a different sense altogether. Between the Hudson and the East River the word "city" acquires a new meaning no less. And an unexpected result of that fact is that all other cities familiar to us are transformed before our eyes, acquiring now a dimension they did not have before: their difference from New York. Madrid or Salamanca, Cordova or Paris, Athens or Buenos Aires, Jerusalem or Rio de Janeiro,

Tübingen, Cairo, Cuzco—all of them change in aspect. And when you begin to speak of New York it is difficult to know where to start, precisely because of the base that is missing. So I prefer to speak of my arrivals.

Similarly, New York leads us into contradictions when we speak, for example, of its beauty or ugliness. The person who can explain the quality of New York's beauty, of its incomparable and monstrous beauty, will be doing a worthy piece of work. Admittedly, he would have to speak at length on the concept of monstrosity, a very handy expression which everyone uses but which seems to defy rational explanation. But it is precisely the irrational thing which most requires us to exercise reason; rational matters get along very well on their own. As with the burro in the Spanish song, reason is needed more on the upward slopes than in the flatlands of mathematical analysis and Euclidean geometry, or in syllogistic theory.

For another thing, New York is a medieval city, or at best Renaissance in flavor. That means that unlike such modern cities as Buenos Aires or Los Angeles, it has a profile. It is not a surface, not a flat-mosaic of houses and green spots, nor is it two-dimensional: thanks to Manhattan's skyscrapers, New York stands out from the horizon, it stretches forth and comes out to greet us. It has much less affinity with the cities of our modern age than with the walls of Avila, the domes and minarets of Constantinople, or with Heidelberg and its castle and Gothic towers. But New York's profile, its expression, its gesture, are quite distinct; and not so much because of steel and concrete as because there another arrow of human life soars toward a different set of targets.

It is a historic city, but with an accelerated rhythm, like the movies, with another gait. What in other places would be centuries, in New York are decades. In Europe we can distinguish the Gothic quarter from the one built during the Renaissance, the eighteenth from the nineteenth-century neighborhood. In New York one knows without a doubt that this street was built up around 1890 and that one between 1910 and the Versailles Treaty. And these streets differ from each other just as do the *Place Des Vosges* and *l'Étoile*, the *Diagonal* and the *Plaza del Rey* in Barcelona, the *Gran Vía* and the *Plaza Mayor* in Madrid; Wall Street, in the same way, differs from Fifth Avenue. One can see the form that the human soul has taken in New York every few years (probably in each generation, though that is an unconfirmed hypothesis); the soul that has gone on involuntarily expressing its confidences on Third Avenue in the atrocious and thundering shadow of the El, on Fifth—one variety in the Forties and still another in the area near the Frick Museum—and on other downtown streets near soot-blackened Trinity Church, among the strident colors of Greenwich Village, or on Riverside Drive.

I have just said that these are confessions the American soul has made, and yet this is very doubtful. Somewhere I wrote that although New York is America, America is not New York, just as the plant is not identical to the medium from which it springs. In some ways New York is the opposite of the United States: its haste contrasts with habitual American calm; it represents astonishment and lack of stability in a country made up of ordinary, day-by-day "business as usual"; it suggests vertigo in a land where time seems to pool and form a backwater; and it stands for unpredictability in a nation which almost makes a religious cult of the ability to prognosticate.

And yet, regardless of the fact that in so many ways New York is different from the rest of the United States, it is perhaps only in that city that America can be encountered. The human being lives from his eyes: when we look from our eyes into those of a fellow man or woman, then we are in each other's company, together. It would be an exaggeration to say this is true of New York, because reality presents itself to our eyes as a visible presence, and in New York this does not happen. The rest of the United States continues distant and far flung in all its width and breath: while we seek to close our eyes and rest, New York, the centrifugal city, shoots us out toward the enormous country at large. This is the key: we can *sense* the United States in New York, though we cannot *see* what we feel. The country is there, not as a visible presence, but working, living, throbbing like circulating blood which pulses in the temple or at the wrist but does not remain at the pulse, returning incessantly to renew itself within the circulatory system. New York is the pulse of America, and that is the reason why we feel upon arriving that it is like a throbbing hand.

31 THE OPEN WATCH

There is a certain moment when a child's curiosity brings his entire soul, tense and avid, into his eyes: his father or grandfather is going to show him what a watch is like on the inside. He has already seen the round white or gilded face; he has noticed how the second hand advances in nervous jerks; he has proved to his own satisfaction that the minute hand, which seemed fixed, does indeed also slowly move; and he knows that if you come back after a while, you can see that the hour hand somehow or other has changed position. He has listened to the beat of this strange animal which seems half alive and makes him smile in anxious incredulity; he has suspected its mystery when he has seen how it is wound and heard something inside of it working away. But now the back is removed, the watch is open to view; he discovers its works, its how and why, its inner secret.

This is the impression that Chicago produces, the reason behind its strange coarse attraction. In no other American city have I seen the mechanism of the United States functioning so much in the open. Washington is only the lovely face of a very expensive watch on which the hands are scarcely noticeable. New York is the quintessence of the United States, the most original and unmistakably American product there is; but though it is true that New York could only happen in America, the fact remains that the United States is not New York. In other cities (Boston, for example, to speak only of the large towns) you can see the result, the end product of a certain activity: American life backed up, the watch carefully closed, ticking away, indicating the time.

Chicago is not like that. It is an atrocious city: that must be admitted from the very beginning. To start with, the climate: the *average* temperature in January is around 20 degrees, but occasionally the thermometer may drop to 20 degrees below zero. And what wind! I wonder why they don't have taxis with sails running north and south on Michigan Avenue. There are moments when pedestrians simply have to give up and either try to find another street farther from the Lake or recuperate a few degrees of warmth in the first drugstore they come to. (I suspect that the chief mission of such spots is to serve as a refuge for the frozen wayfarer whose ears have lost all feeling, but who revives upon contact with the torrid heating system and can soon continue on his way.) In summer, on the other hand, the temperature can go over 100, in fair reparation for the snows of the past winter. The average temperature, as one can see, is delightful.

Chicago has about four million inhabitants, but if one includes that portion of reality called the "metropolitan area," the total ascends dangerously close to some six million. And all of it clicking away, working under our very eyes. What I mean is that the factories are visible and very close to the luxury hotels; that huge trucks come and go incessantly. In front of Michigan Avenue, a very elegant street housing the largest hotels, the most exclusive shops, the exquisite Art Institute (El Greco, Velázquez, Rembrandt, Tintoretto, all the Impressionists, extraordinary Picassos, and a fabulous Oriental collection); a few steps from all this, and a few feet lower down, are the railroad tracks where snow-covered trains are shifting back and forth, especially those enormous and extremely rapid freight trains which with their hundred cars traverse the American prairies like a flash of lightning. Everything is in motion, agitated; the whole place immodestly exhibits its power, its motors, its pipes, its chains, its mountains of crates, its innumerable lights. Millions upon millions of horses race through Chicago—in the form of horsepower, of course, but in such visible fashion that they seem like real runaways with their manes streaming in the terrible wind from the lake shore, their tails flowing, their hooves pounding as they gallop over the snow.

The United States is an implausible country, and the fact that it exists and is as it is in no way alters that statement. If one looks at results, at the products that have already come into being—wealth, power, monotony, cordiality, innocence—they seem inexplicable, incomprehensible. One must infer and deduce how these things may have become as they are; one must call into practice what the renowned detective Hercule Poirot liked to call the "little grey cells" in order to analyze and understand. But one cannot see all this, one can only figure and conjecture. American life makes itself visible only at certain points: at those junctures it is enough to open one's eyes and look—reality pours in with magic ease. One half of this way of life reveals itself in small towns, in the tranquility of their tall trees, their gardens, and their frame houses: but *only* a half, which itself would be impossible, which could not exist without the other atrocious vehement half (that does not itself lack—if one looks closely—a hard and violent kind of poetry). It is the latter half which one suddenly discovers, almost painfully, when the case of the watch is opened and one peers into Chicago.

32 NEGROES IN THE SNOW

Something must be wrong. What are these Negroes doing in the middle of the snow? In the cold Northeastern cities of the United States a goodly number of Negroes are visible. They are always a small minority, but quite numerous in the big cities. Their presence is normal in the summertime, beneath a blue sky, in the midst of humidity and heat; the white of their smiles flashes among the dusky shadows of their skin, and they cause us to smile too. Negroes in small doses, dappling the white population, incite a kind of tenderness and the use of the Spanish diminutive: "Los negritos." I wonder whether anyone has remarked all that is connoted by an expression of such ancient lineage: condescension, disdain, infantilism, protection. (We must also remember that in English one uses the Spanish word *negro*, and that the term "nigger" is pejorative, a near-insult.) But when the thermometer registers many degrees below zero, when the streets are loaded with snow, or when the snow is falling from leaden skies in great thick flakes, when entire cities turn pale in the glacial winds, then Negroes begin to seem absurdly indigent, displaced and pitiful.

Then it is we can observe how all things have their structure, even though we humans insist on trying to do everything against the grain as though no such forms existed. The Negro suggests and evokes the tropics; he carries them with him wherever he may appear. Heat, palm trees, jungle, lianas, baked sand, cabañas, or whitewashed houses. Indolence, an easy rhythm, light cotton clothing, or bare skin. For that reason, when we see a Negro in a hurry, wrapped up in a heavy woolen coat or in a storm coat with a fur collar, wearing sturdy rubber boots, with his breath frozen on the air of the streets of New York, Buffalo, or Chicago, we always get the feeling that he has gone the wrong way, that he has mistaken the road. It is apparent that he is not native to the place; it seems as though he must feel the cold much more (though this is probably not true) and that something extraordinary is going to happen to him: he will freeze solid, he will dissolve, he will evaporate entirely into his frozen breath, so visible before him. And besides, obviously, he makes a smudge against the snow, appearing to leave behind him as he walks a long track on the whiteness, just as a pencil does when drawn across the paper.

A Negro in the snow is bewildering. He is an intruder, a man from another world—another physical world, I mean, not a different one economically or historically. He seems to be defying the laws of nature, like a fish out of water. The Negro, forever endowed with a certain childlike quality, turns into a lost waif amidst the snow. And when is he a child, truly a "negrito"? When an entire family—father, mother, children with corkscrew curls, and the black blossom of a small baby —cross over the whiteness? One feels then an irrational, biological sense of pity, and one's heart is somehow heavy. The Negro and the snow are opposites, antonyms such as wet and dry, odd and even.

We of the Mediterranean and of the temperate zones of Europe do not know what the seasons are. It is hot or cold, of course, the days lengthen or shorten, planting time is succeeded by the harvest, but we do not experience violent changes in nature: the "closing in" of winter that means many months of snow; the frenzy of spring which is like a resurrection; the long burning stupor of an implacable summer; the joyous festival of a lengthy autumn during which the landscape—at least in New England—exhausts its resources as though, like a woman, it were trying to hold off the cruel sword of winter by the sheer force of its beauty, to hold back the inevitable shroud—a silent swan song, in which the melodious notes are marked by colors.

How greatly the Negroes must regret winter's coming. Because for them it is not just that the world becomes cold, muffled or dull, or that it is a harder or more painful place to live; rather, the world becomes alien to them, incoherent and contradictory. Without budging from where they live they become exiles because their world—their own—has disappeared, has been made to vanish as though by sleight of hand from under the magician's well-known handkerchief. This is why they seem so alone; this is why they evoke irrational pity. When Christmas comes, when the world takes on a more intimate tone for white people, when all footfalls seem to be hushed in a familiar carpet and all voices seem closer to us, the Negroes suddenly become expatriates: dissonant, unarticulated, implausible, lost children who do not need to mark their path with bread crumbs because as they walk they leave their dark traces against the snow, the vestige of their figures, a shadow that persists when all other shadows have disappeared.

33 TELEVISION

For some years two initials have been invading this country (which is so given to the use of capital letters that it even puts its own name into them): they are TV, symbol of the scientific toy, the flowering of technique, the greatest artifice of what the nineteenth century called "recreational physics." Little by little, or rather by leaps and bounds, those two letters have been gaining ground. Three years ago† many hotels offered, for a modest fee, to install a TV set in our room; several days ago when I entered a hotel in Mormon Salt Lake City, in the wilds of Utah, the first thing I saw was a television receiver installed and ready for free use. I turned it on and the face of Groucho Marx appeared on the screen; in a few minutes I turned it off again and went out onto streets covered with snow.

Many millions of Americans were at that moment all watching the same small figures in black and white. In 1948 the United States produced the modest number of 250,000 sets: in the seven succeeding years almost 40 million more were manufactured, but at present only 33 million are actually in operation in the country, one for every five inhabitants. The economic volume represented by the two initials TV surpasses two billion dollars a year. These figures prove that we must take television seriously into consideration; but, above all, they indicate a need to explain the phenomenon.

Because we must concede at once that, in its present state, television is rather dull. It gives the impression of having been born with its wings clipped, or perhaps not so much without feathers as with nothing more than down. It has fallen into the hands of the advertisers, and although advertising exerts

† Written in 1955.

considerable ingenuity in the United States, in this case it seems to exhaust its wit on itself. What I mean to say is that perhaps the most amusing features on television are the commercials and not so much the candy coating in which they are embedded. It is evident that those responsible for television are much too preoccupied with trying to aim it towards a bogus whole ("everybody"), without realizing that their audience necessarily consists of parts, and that the essence of diversion lies in the possibility of emigrating temporarily from oneself into one's fellow.

How can the tremendous growth of television in the United States be explained? Why does almost the entire population follow certain TV programs, switch to their preferred channels, and keep their dates with the same performers? Someone might suggest that the same thing happened all over the world with radio, and that is true, but with a significant difference: radio is heard but frequently not attended to. Television is not simply seen, it is looked at and contemplated. In millions of homes it is common to have the radio on without listening to it: it is background music which we ignore as we work, read, or eat; it is a voice that chatters on in unattended words among conversations that automatically rise in volume to cover the radio's sound. Television is not like this: when it is turned on the children sit on the carpet and the adults on the sofa or in chairs, and everyone peers closely at the comings and goings of the small figures on the screen, the questions and answers in the contests, the sports event, the reconstructed exchanges between Mary Todd and her husband Abraham Lincoln. Because of its very optical character, television is not diffuse; it attracts and holds the eye via a peculiar "suction," analogous to that of the movies, though with some small differences about which I shall add a word later.

I believe that the influence of television in the United States must be explained starting from two dimensions of American life that do not exist in other places or, if they do, present themselves in different forms. One of them is loneliness; the other, the extreme triviality of what is "public knowledge" in the United States.

American solitude expresses itself in many ways. There is the loneliness of uninhabited lands, so well known in South America: there are thousands of miles to cross between the midwest and the Pacific, and shortly after leaving Illinois, through Iowa, Nebraska, Wyoming, Utah, and Nevada, the populated centers grow few and far between. Moreover, such a center is only rarely a city or a town; it is usually a grain storage depot, a gasoline station, an oasis in the world apart of the American highway. Throughout many areas of the country people live in this solitary dispersion, sometimes in a tight family group, occasionally in a small village. Statistics are helpful but always require interpreting: the most recent figures indicate, for example, that 64% of the population is urban in character and only 36% rural, but by "urban" they mean people who live in cities of a population of over 2,500. Therefore a large part of that "urban" population is living a rural life, or at least living in small towns. At least half of the inhabitants of the United States, and probably even more, do not live in what a European would classify as a city, but rather in what he might, after some hesitation, choose to call "the country." I mention the hesitation because in the United States there is a characteristic mixture of both elements: one might say that the majority of the "urban zones" or "metropolitan areas," as they are called here, are *cities in the country*, and their houses, surrounded by greenery, have space to spare between them. The most attractive American cities are parks with houses built inside their borders. But as I have remarked before, the small towns or sections of small cities usually have no plaza, no convivial center where people go to meet each other. Private life is dominant; contact with others, fleeting and exceptional, is from house to house. That is the reason American homes are generally so pleasant, so warm and hospitable: they represent a refuge. Our adopted word *confort* has in Spanish a connotation of considerable triviality; but in English we must understand that *comfort* means consolation, aid, and even hope.

North American life created itself outside the cities: the pioneers were pushing back the frontiers of the country from North to South and towards the West—on farms, in the forest, with the fur trappers, at the placer site where gold was washed, among the cattle herds, in the Conestoga wagons that rolled toward the lands on the shore of the other ocean, at the oil fields. First came the log cabin, if not the shanty; then the small outpost with a church for Sundays and a saloon for Saturday nights; then a railway station, where a small puffing train whistled along between the snow banks or in the heat of the sun; and later the gas station and the drugstore and the movie house, where everyone is alone in the dark with the screen in front of him—unless it is a drive-in, where each spectator watches the film from his car, solidly encased in a rolling urn of steel, chrome, rubber, and glass.

Well and good, but what about the real cities? I said before that they should be called by the title given a certain book of Spanish poetry: *Soledades Juntas.** First, because the American soul was formed out of solitude; second, because the structure of the urban centers does not eliminate loneliness. The big cities—are so big! It is not easy, even in an automobile, to get around in them. The majority of the people who live in big cities inhabit the suburbs, which are, incidentally, delightful; that is to say, they move to the country and they go into the city to work or to attend a performance. In other cities, such as Our Lady Queen of the Angels, Los Angeles, which was founded in 1781 by a small group of Spaniards from San Gabriel, to go from one point to another inside

---

* A book by the Spanish poet Manuel Altolaguirre whose title may be freely translated as *A Cluster of Solitudes*, or *Solitudes Joined* —Trans.

what we might term the urban nucleus requires three-quarters of an hour or an hour by auto, and an hour and a half or two hours by bus or streetcar. Friends rarely live close to each other; the Hispanic *tertulia*, the habitual get-together, is simply not possible.

Nor is that all. In Europe the custom is to live many years in the same city, perhaps in one's home town or, if not, in the city where one established his residence at an early age. Europeans therefore enjoy a large circle of relatives, friends, and acquaintances. In the United States people move frequently from place to place; among other reasons, because American cities are so much alike that the change is not an uprooting. What difference does it make to exchange Providence for Baltimore, Buffalo for Philadelphia, Riverside for Santa Barbara? On the other side of the Atlantic, would the person who lives in Bilbao move easily to Granada? What a turmoil that would mean, what a change in his way of life! How could anyone leave Seville to go to live in Burgos without feeling a tremor in his deepest roots? And, to a slightly lesser degree, we could say the same about someone who left Munich to live in Heidelberg, exchanged Bordeaux for Metz, or Naples for Florence. Therefore, in United States cities there is a good chance that a man is a stranger, surrounded by his solitude. Then add to that fact the number of foreigners who live in the United States: more than 10 million inhabitants of the country were born outside its boundaries. They are uprooted people, only partially at home in a new land, that is, they are to some extent solitaries. Add again the members of the second generation, sons of immigrants who are American-born but not yet firmly planted in American soil, and the total exceeds 23 million. It should not be necessary then to insist that American life can only be understood from the standpoint of its loneliness, that it is made up of the sometimes divine, sometimes dreadful thing called solitude. Television is instant magic. You turn the dial and a human face appears—a face that looks at you, speaks to you, laughs, and sings—and then another and another. Company! The world we have lost is returned to us. Over the deserted plains to the snowbound house in Nebraska, and under an Arizona sun that bakes the dust, fellow men appear before us. What difference does it make what they say? They are there, they are talking for our benefit, we can almost talk back to them. We are no longer alone. They tell us what is happening in the world, they take us to Broadway—three thousand miles distant—to Boston, which is three days and a hundred dollars away by train, to the beaches of Santa Monica when it is below zero where we are, and perhaps to Paris, London, or Rome. Or they transport us to the past which lends body to our lives: Lincoln and his very nervous wife Mary Todd, Gettysburg and the timeworn struggle between North and South which is still moving and painful because the scars have not yet healed. What difference does it make if all this is mixed up with the latest model DeSoto and the new air conditioned Nash whose seats convert into a bed? And by the way, we ought to be thinking about getting a new car, and it wouldn't be bad if we want to go to Maine this summer to———.

TV, TV, TV. A new name in one's inner circle: comforter of the lonely ones; interlocutor of the little old ladies who live alone with their "frigidaire" and their "kitchenette," walking softly over wall-to-wall carpeting, concerned with their daffodils, their morning glories, or perhaps their orchids; friend of the retired professor who no longer hears young voices nor sees the girls' laughter; discreet visitor in the sick room who goes out when the patient is tired.

And where does the triviality of "human interest publicity" come in? That is a serious subject, a different matter, which we must ponder another day.

34 "PUBLIC KNOWLEDGE"
IN THE UNITED STATES

"What is The Public and where does one find it?", asked Mariano José de Larra with tears in his eyes a hundred and twenty years ago. "What is the public domain and where, in each society, can it be discovered?" We might inquire the same today with even greater perplexity than *Fígaro*.* For it would be an error to suppose that "publicness" always maintains the same forms, the same appearances, or identical conditions. There are societies which shudder at the thought of publicity; they flee from it, and yet it penetrates to the marrow of their bones. Others, to the contrary, make a cult of it, and yet that public quality never fails to slip through their fingers.

If there is any country which seems dominated by "publicness," it is the USA. On the pretext that "it's news," the papers go into everything in great detail, often including many things which in other countries would seem to belong strictly to private life. When a citizen is appointed to whatever official position, the information given out about him and his *curriculum vitae* mentions not only his degrees, the books he has published, the awards or decorations he has received, but also that he weighs so many pounds and is five feet nine inches tall, that he plays golf, that he has a very pretty wife named Pat and three children, that his grades in High School were on the low side, that his grandfather was a Polish Jew, that he likes the opera and enjoys drinking beer, but that he cannot stand the movies. It is quite common to read column heads such as these: "Blonde Wife Run Down by Truck"; "Balding Financier to Re-wed"; "Mother of

* *Nom de plume* of Larra (1809–1837), famous essayist and bitterly humorous social critic—Trans.

Four Children to Give Lecture on Oriental Art." Such details as these, which seem to us to belong entirely to private life and which we would never dream of putting into print, all form part of the public domain in news and information. The first time I accepted an appointment at an American university, *The New York Times* and *The Boston Globe* announced to their readers that my wife and sons would soon join me and added all the boys' names—including that of the baby who had been born ten days before and therefore was not yet exactly a "public figure." I choose these inoffensive and trifling examples because they are, strange to say, significant. Sensational material needs no special explanation: no one is surprised if a tabloid tells all—or as much as it can—about the divorces or loves of a movie actor. What *is* of interest is that publicity should be given to normal *details*, features that in other places would seem to have little to do with the case. A European would be of the opinion that it made little difference whether the accident victim was a blonde or a brunette, whether the lecturer was a spinster or a mother with children (unless she were going to speak on a related topic) whether the new Minister of Agriculture was fat or thin, a football fan or a concert-goer. The American does not react that way, he wants to know all about it.

Similarly, many things are done "in public." Everyday I pass by the windows of a beauty shop in Westwood Village, the most elegant district of Los Angeles. In four comfortable pink plastic chairs, under the chromed hoods of the dryers (which in this country inevitably call up a disquieting association with the electric chair) there are usually four ladies patiently sitting and waiting for their coiffures to be finished as they read a magazine, smoke a cigarette, or simply doze. This is one instance among a thousand others.

But the query arises as to whether all this is truly "public" or whether it is not rather an indication of the inability to transcend the sphere of private life. Blonde curls, bald spots, and babies in the news: does this indicate that the press is invading the privacy and intimacy of people's lives, or does it rather signify that individual domestic life assaults the newspaper and imposes itself in the arena of public knowledge? Who is the aggressor, the huge rotary press or the particular content of homes which overflow themselves and expose their intimacy everywhere? That is the real question.

The first thing that caused me to suspect the existence of this structure in American life, the difficulty "publicness" has in making itself felt in society, was my verification of the fact that "intellectual life" is to a minimum degree "public life"; it is only "professional life," which is an entirely different thing. The difficulty in America of attaining fame as an intellectual is simply incredible. When I arrived at the University of California I was well aware that one of the world's foremost and best known logicians was teaching there. Several professors to whom I happened to mention him had no idea at all of his renown; and his office was thirty feet down the same corridor where we stood talking. Naturally, in all the Departments of Philosophy in the country everyone knew all there was to know about the illustrious scholar; outside of those departments, almost no one suspected his existence. The institution's prestige functions automatically and supplements, to some extent, the public reputation of the individual; but this confers a character on American intellectual life which Latins especially find difficult to comprehend.

The most serious aspect of the situation shows up in politics; if anything is public life, it is precisely the *res publica*. Very well, but public life needs a stage; and this is the principal difficulty, because in the United States that setting is only rarely to be found. After all, the United States is composed of *many states*—united, of course, and very energetically so—but there are forty-eight of them and each one has a thousand private concerns. Second, the capital is not comparable to those of Europe or South America. Washington, as I have remarked before, has a minimum of "visibility"; it is a relatively small city, peripheral and artificial, which follows the leader. It is overshadowed, of course, by New York, and to a lesser degree by the social and economic force of Philadelphia and the intellectual splendor of the Boston area. As a "stage," Washington is hardly a contender. (One of the evidences of myopia on the part of many European newspapers is that they station their correspondents in Washington, as though it were a center similar to London, Paris, Madrid, or Buenos Aires.) In the third place, there are almost no *national* newspapers in the United States; people read the local papers, which have a very large circulation even in small cities—relatively small cities, of course. For example, the *Kansas City Star* has a circulation of 350,000, as does the *Milwaukee Journal*; the *St. Louis Post-Dispatch*, more than 400,000—while the *New York Times*, which is one of the few papers read all over the country, scarcely tops 540,000, or very little better than the local news sheets. And we must remember that none of these papers publishes articles of general or literary interest. What is most in the public domain in the United States are the magazines, of which there are sixty-three whose circulation goes over the half-million mark, twenty over two million. Since a magazine is not thrown away until all the members of the family have read it, and since it is sometimes passed on or loaned, the number of people who read the most popular ones is simply fabulous.

And currently television is intervening in the situation. The consequences in American life of the invention and rapid spread of this device are going to be far-reaching, for television has lent "visibility" to many things. It is bringing them out in public—or, if you prefer, in "semi-public," since it is still doubtful whether the phenomenon of TV unequivocally transcends the bounds of private life. The presidential elections of 1952, from the moment when the respective party conventions nominated their candidates, were under the thumb of television; in all succeeding elections, the influence of TV will be even stronger. Washington is being "publicized" over the nation's TV sets which, to a greater degree than anything else has ever done, are conferring effective capital quality upon the city. Thanks to this technological advance, Washington is being converted—*mutatis mutandis*—into a stage much as were once the Courts of Europe and as are at present the capitals of smaller countries, or of top-heavy ones where the influence of the principal city is disproportionately high. This factor, in addition to the essential loneliness of American life, explains the success of TV in the United States. Thanks to television, millions of persons are present while events transpire; they are in attendance at political happenings which may be taking place two or three thousand miles away and which in themselves might scarcely be noteworthy.

But . . . and another doubt continually springs up. Can it be so easy to overcome (if that *is* what is happening) the inveterately private character of United States life? Will a technological artifice, no matter how efficient and marvelous, be able to confer an effectively public character on American political life? I am not at all convinced. The ways of society and history are infinitely complex and delicate. Could it not happen that the super-exposure offered by television might in some way kill itself off, allowing us to return again to the domestic sphere of private life? How? I shall try to explain my suspicion.

I have used the word *stage* several times when I have referred to public life; even more often I have talked about the "representative" character of politics, the phase of politics that seems akin to a stage performance, at least in Europe. Now a stage presupposes two things: an audience which looks at it, and an adequate perspective; in fact, a theatrical perspective. Does television provide for those conditions? Even though eighty million Americans see their President, if they watch him in the half-light of their living rooms, with the children lying in front of them on the rug, with a glass of ginger ale near at hand, do they truly constitute an audience, and does the speech they are listening to and contemplating have a strictly public character? I think that is highly arguable. On the other score, does a theatrical perspective exist? Does the public not see the President *too well*, at too close quarters, in too much detail? The twisted point of his collar, the quality of his tweed suit, his way of moving the corners of his mouth, the wedding ring on his finger, the thinning grey hair—are all these things for public knowledge? Could it not happen that, being so over-exposed in such familiar detail, the President should revert to Mr. Eisenhower, Mamie's husband, the golf enthusiast, a lean man born in Texas but raised in Abilene, Kansas, the father of one son and a grandfather several times over? Television's perspective returns us again to the private view. The King with his crown and his mantle of ermine, imagined rather than observed on his raised and distant throne, or on horseback, or passing rapidly by in his royal carriage, was outside and beyond private life. The true King, let us not forget it, is always a playing-card king: a conventional, ideal figure who does not lower himself to our level.

Political figures in the United States acquire tremendous notoriety in the hands of television, but they are impressed upon the minds of the citizenry with a particular private stamp. Is this an advantage or a disadvantage? Only time will tell; what can be asserted is that this is an innovation. Always before, politics were abstract in character: names, badges, party titles, slogans, and catchwords; and this quality was responsible for their prestige, their sorcery, their excitement (also for their cruelty, since there is nothing crueler than an abstraction), for their implacability and their inhumanity. Enthusiasm and hostility have always responded in politics to conventional stimuli. When a man appeared from behind the inscriptions, countersigns, and invectives, there was always a movement of dazed surprise. Now the irresistibly victorious leader, he of the fiery words and arresting gestures, turns out to be fond of jokes; he is nervous and he puts on his glasses before reading. The monstrous and tyrannical enemy, the demagogue, is discovered to have two small daughters whom he takes to the circus on a Sunday when he does not have to address the masses; he is on a severe diet because his blood pressure—not his political rating—is too high, and he is fondly addicted to chess. All of this is what television reveals, what it indiscreetly uncovers, and because of that much of politics is going to take on another aspect. Isn't it true that already we have insisted a great deal—especially in the United States and, through its agencies, in the world at large—on the fact that Mendès-France drinks quantities of milk and that his attractive wife is a painter?

It is quite possible that the politics of the future may be less rough, less atrocious, less lacking in compassion. At the sight of our political enemy's bald spot, our heart softens; it is difficult to identify as Lucifer that slightly perspiring gentleman who drinks a glass of water with great thirst and then wipes a drop off his chin with his handkerchief. The first real influence television exercised in the field of politics was, I believe, responsible for the decline of Senator McCarthy. In other times his rise or fall would have been dependent upon general, abstract factors, principles, countersigns, and political maneuvers; what actually most influenced the average American TV viewer was that he was so obnoxious in the question periods! He had such a disagreeable way of frowning, of leaning over towards his collaborators, of addressing his adversaries. Many, many people were physically repelled by his particular human makeup. Yes, it is quite possible that politics may cease to be an atrocious, horrible, inhuman activity. What remains to be seen is whether politics, in order to be politics, in order to fulfill its true function, can be anything other than what it is.

35   MASTER OF LOS ANGELES

Walking is the most natural thing in the world, and yet . . . I have an extremely vivid memory dating from three years ago. It was in Washington; I had decided to go to see the Lincoln Memorial and afterwards, since it was such a tempting morning, I continued walking along the Arlington Bridge. I crossed over the Potomac and, entering the State of Virginia, I headed towards Arlington Cemetery. Nothing could have been more innocent, but after a while I began to feel the way one does in a dream when he finds himself out on the street in pajamas, or wearing one black shoe and one of another color. I was walking; that is, doing something no one else does, engaging in an unheard-of activity, something subversive and almost indecent. Automobiles passed me on all sides, and I realized that their occupants were watching me in amazement; my posture was disquieting and suspicious. On the entire horizon (and it was a very broad one) I could discover no other individual on his feet. The situation was growing steadily more anomalous, then finally I made out in the distance, close to the entrance to the cemetery, the figure of a woman dressed in green. A fellow being! Robinson Crusoe must have felt a similar kind of emotion when he came upon the trace of a bare footprint in the sand.

My walk this afternoon afforded me a different emotion—born under a positive sign. The Los Angeles sky, usually so blue, was pearl gray; the air fresh and still. So I walked along

Wilshire Boulevard from Westwood towards the eastern part of the city; of course, I traced only a few miles over a road already familiar to me but which, in all truth, I saw today for the first time. Because I had always covered the route by bus or automobile, and today I walked it, I discovered therein an unhoped-for beauty. On both sides of the very broad avenue are small houses, almost all of them white, some pink, yellow, or green, occasionally with dark beams. Gardens surround them, the greens and yellows blending with magenta and purple flowers. And the sidewalks, thin paths of asphalt or cement in the midst of all that verdure—sidewalks only in a manner of speaking— are part of the endless lawn that extends along the road like a fringe of meadowland. Nothing more is needed. In the pale gray sky the setting sun shone fiery red, and from time to time light clouds hung horizontal bands across it like those that astronomers see surrounding Jupiter; an enormous sun, close, accessible, luxurious. Yes, luxurious as is everything in these surroundings: the houses with their almost Andalusian patios, wherein occasionally one catches a blue-green glimpse of a large swimming pool; the interiors visible through the slits of the Venetian blinds; the multi-colored cars, two opposing streams that flow by each other in the powerful channel of the avenue. And at intervals, tall-topped palm trees with their fronds hanging down like skirts —palm trees that look like women, to invert the literary platitude.

And all this was for my benefit; it was mine without any competition. For I had walked an hour, following the elegant curves of Wilshire Boulevard and its ups and downs, without encountering another soul on foot. Why the other sidewalks? For whom? No one was looking at the delicate beauty of that afternoon. Thousands of men and women were navigating upstream or down toward Westwood, toward Santa Monica, toward the Old Town (as old as the day before yesterday), perhaps toward Hollywood or Beverly Hills, but the surroundings were not for them. Inside their cars, speeding by in tight files with attention fixed on the traffic lights (which change silently) and on their signals to each other, they were receiving only what I had seen before—the reverberations. But one ought to be there, to stand there, not to pass by but to stay; to enjoy the fresh breeze and the light constantly sifting itself into even finer particles; to appreciate the transparency of the air and the smooth power of the automobiles themselves, with lacquer finishes expressly made to shine there amidst the green grass and the light-colored houses. Houses which seem unreal because they represent both the prize and the memory lost of so many victories won in other places over a brutal, violent, and hostile nature: ice, winds, forests, open country, mines, the vertical shafts of the oil wells, pistons and wheels—all forgotten now in this feminine city founded by Spaniards.

No one at all on the sidewalks, on either side of the street; they are all mine. Every once in a while a gentleman with a package in his hand, having parked his car, goes into his house; or a lady leaves hers and gets into her cherry-colored auto; or another in a blouse and slacks picks up the evening paper which has been thrown on her lawn and goes back into the house; finally, now almost in the business district, there is an elderly lady strolling slowly along; but she is not taking a walk either, for she is carrying a letter with an airmail stamp and is heading toward the mailbox on the corner.

The strategists say that automatic weapons are not adequate, that only infantry can occupy, hold, and dominate terrain. And being of the infantry, walking slowly, peering and looking again, all this had made me, between five and six this afternoon, master of Los Angeles.

36 MORTUARIES

I have not yet wanted to visit the cemeteries of Los Angeles, despite the pleas of so many friends. Why not? I am not sure: perhaps because of a horror of the cliché as when a foreigner in Madrid senses that he should not rush to the bull ring, that he might do better to postpone watching those taurine rites. Perhaps the fault lies with that ingenious but disagreeable book of Evelyn Waugh's, *The Loved One*, a book very impiously written, very misleading in its probably deliberate omission of all perspective. Perhaps I have felt a certain shame in having to submit to such a well-known "initiation," as Aldous Huxley did reluctantly in *After Many a Summer Dies the Swan*. If you "go after" things you displace them, you take them out of their accustomed niche (as, for instance, when you go to pay a visit to an illustrious figure); you misuse them and you lose the potential fruition or, in any case, the authentic quality of an encounter. It is better to wait and let the thing come to you.

But all these reasons which have combined to make me flee the cemeteries, even as a temporary visitor, now oblige me to deal with the mortuaries of California. Because these establishments assault the eye of the passer-by—of the relatively few pedestrians, and of the many who go by bus, frequent the parks, or riffle through the "yellow pages" of the telephone directory, of the innumerable directories in this city which alone has more telephones than exist in all of Spain and almost half as many as the whole of South America. Funeral homes are generally discreet; at most, in Spanish cities, they have some marvelous name such as El Ocaso,* and almost

* The Twilight, or Declining Hours—Trans.

always the generic subhead "Pompas Fúnebres"* which means that the word "pomp" (a term in Spanish that has come to have a slightly comic connotation far removed from its Greek meaning of deputation or following) marks our lives from the moment of baptism, when our godfather renounces in our name the pomps of Satan, to the final moment when we "enjoy" the luxuries-at-a-price offered by private enterprise, or the services of the municipality. In the United States the mortuaries come out to meet you; they literally catch you by the eye in various ways, some quite enticing. There is one ad especially: an enormous billboard in the most delicate of colors pursues you throughout the entire city. On it, seated with her back to us, there is a lady with an attractively veiled hat that reveals a magnificent knot of blonde hair done in what, since the American cannot bring himself to use the vulgar word "bun," he prefers to call, in a more suggestive and distinguished manner, a *chignon*. A gentleman is laying his hand upon the lady's shoulder and murmuring (at least we assume that he murmurs it) a line printed in large letters: "It is such a comfort to know that X Cemetery costs no more." (And since accuracy is never superfluous, it adds in smaller print: "Only $70.")

There is another ad that becomes an obsession during the interval of a bus ride, interminable rides of from an hour to an hour and a half over cheerful avenues: a gentleman of middle age, with an expression of moderate suffering—eyes half-closed, and between the lids the suspicion of a "furtive tear" —and the legend "At a moment when only the P Brothers satisfy *completely*——." And there are so many others: some with an impressive bust of Moses promise the most solemn Jewish rites; others advertise approval by Catholic or Episcopal clerical authorities; in some cases they offer a wide range of denominational possibilities.

* Funeral ceremonies—Trans.

But this is not all. At the bus and trolley stops there are usually wooden benches, put there for those who are waiting —evidence of a delicate sense of civility. Sometimes one reads on the bench "Courtesy of the city of Beverly Hills," or of a hotel or a department store. At other times what is on the bench is an ad for a funeral home. The tired wayfarer starts to sit down, and right away he is reminded that he is going to die, perhaps even before the bus arrives. Occasionally it works out even more appropriately: at the intersection of two busy streets, instead of one bench there are two placed alongside each other. On the back panel of the first is the ad for a product that guarantees a lithe and graceful body, and you can see the silhouette of a slender young girl doing gymnastics. On the next bench a funeral parlor offers its most austere services. Valdés Leal* could not have done it better. (However, Valdés Leal has possibilities that he himself never suspected which go beyond his paintings. I recall that the municipal government of Córdoba gave his name to one of the city's streets. To which one? The city fathers carried out their intention with amazing intuition: on the sign the name of the painter appears in large letters "VALDES LEAL"— with no indications afterwards, since they do things so elegantly in that city, but underneath one can read "Formerly Abrazamozas."**)

Still and all, none of what I have had to say so far is what truly surprises me about the mortuaries of Los Angeles. What really defeats my powers of conjecture is why so many ads, especially those in the telephone directory, include a portrait of the man in charge. To what purpose? The portrait of an actress on a theatre program is comprehensible, even that of the bullfighter on a poster or of an author on the dust jacket of his book, but . . . the director of the funeral home? Right

---

* Juan de Valdés Leal (1622–1690) Painter from Seville, contemporary and follower of Murillo—Trans.
** "Embracer of Women"—Trans.

next to the praises of the incomparable service offered, the circumspect face of a gentleman with a small mustache, and underneath him the lettering: Mr. Richard Fletcher, Manager. Can it be that his responsible appearance calms the client and lends him assurance that Mr. Fletcher would never be capable of mixing up the cadaver of a hardened general of the Russian Czar's army and that of a gentle Swedish student, as happened, we are told, in *The Story of St. Michel*. But not even this guess serves to quiet my doubts, because one of the funeral homes belongs to the A Family, and on its ads are the portraits of three blood relations and one in-law, and among so many hands. . . .

37 UNAMUNO IN FOREST LAWN

If there is anything anywhere that is far distant from the tragic sense of life, it is the cemetery in California named Forest Lawn, which looks out over Los Angeles from the hills of Glendale and Hollywood. It is also far afield from the comic sense of life, which Unamuno recognized as akin to the tragic. That is the explanation for the errors of those who, with greater or lesser genius, have launched out from there in a comic vein, especially the British writers—Evelyn Waugh in *The Loved One* and Aldous Huxley in *After Many a Summer Dies the Swan*. As I traversed Forest Lawn, I thought ceaselessly about Unamuno. What would he have said? What would he have kept unsaid? What would he have done? I am not sure that he would have been able to look at everything there is to see, to cross through the shining mausoleums replete with statues, flowers, and stained glass, or to pass over the flowering turf where, half-hidden by the well-cut grass, small bronze plaques which glint in the sun mark the resting place of each one of the dead. Dead? That is assuming a great deal. Are the residents of Forest Lawn dead? Doesn't that word sound inexact there, doesn't it have an almost indecent ring of violence? Promenades, avenues, small old-world churches, perhaps from Scotland (Wee Kirk o' the Heather), where young couples come to be married; "exact" reproductions of the *Sistine Madonna* or *The Last Supper* of Leonardo da Vinci, the *David* of Michelangelo or his *Moses*, and an immense, incredibly sumptuous auditorium for the sole purpose of contemplating a painting of the Crucifixion whose size brings it closer to geography than to art; and birds and music and swans with lakes to go with them, and a museum and the green and white garden where an uplifting sculptural group called "The Mystery of Life" is exhibited.

Forest Lawn is without a doubt the gayest cemetery in the world, and the most luxurious, and the most amusing. Wrapped in the clear light and bland atmosphere of California, gentle, kindly, and pleasurable, Forest Lawn is for the living. Colors, perfumes, music, placid forms tuned to the eye. And what about the dead? It seems as though here the dead too may "live." The illusion is so powerful that next to the two doors with the signs LADIES and GENTLEMEN, one's imagination can easily conjure up a third marked GHOSTS. After all, why shouldn't there be a place for the phantoms, the revenants, the real owners of this realm of facile delights?

> "Corral de muertos, entre pobres tapias,
>   hechas también de barro,
> pobre corral donde la hoz no siega,
> sólo una cruz en el desierto camp
>   señala tu destino."

So wrote Unamuno in "En un cementerio de lugar castellano" (A Cemetery in a Place in Castile).*

> "Cavan tan sólo en tu maleza brava,
>   corral sagrado,
> para de un alma que sufrió en el mundo
>   sembrar el grano;
>   luego sobre esa siembra
>   ¡barbecho largo!"
> "la cruz, cual perro fiel, ampara el sueño
>   de los muertos al cielo acorralados."

Could anything be farther apart? Unamuno would have been distressed and upset amidst the amiable peacefulness of Forest Lawn; he might even have been frightened. I can imagine him fleeing in long strides down the avenues with head lowered, refusing to look at anything. He would not have been inclined to make jokes, as was Huxley, nor to unleash impious sarcasm, as did Waugh. Because Forest Lawn is not funny nor is it impious, but rather devout in its own peculiar manner. The point is precisely that—its manner. The

---

* A well-known poem by Miguel de Unamuno, written in Salamanca in 1913 and first published in the collection entitled *Andanzas y visiones españolas* in 1922, which has been compared to Paul Valéry's "*Le Cimetière marin*" (1920). A literal rendering of the excerpts quoted might read:

> Corral for the dead, between poor walls
> Also made of clay,
> Barren corral where the sickle reaps no more,
> Only a cross in the deserted field
> Marks your destiny.

> They only dig in your wild underbrush,
> Sacred corral,
> To sow the seed
> Of a soul that suffered long in the world.
> And later over that planting—
> How long the ground will lie fallow!

> The cross, like a faithful dog, guards the sleep
> Of the dead corralled in heaven.—Trans.

founder, one Dr. Hubert Eaton who planned it in 1917, has left his credo chiseled on a stone. In what does Dr. Eaton believe? In many things: "in a happy afterlife in eternity," into which those who have left us have already entered; "above all, in a smiling Christ who loves you and me"; in the beneficent educational influence of his cemetery, to be frequented by children and lovers and in which artists will display their works; in the practice of not dipping into capital (three million dollars worth of it), but of living on the interest and on new income—and in many other things.

The only thing in which he apparently did not believe was death. And that is the key. Forest Lawn is a cemetery where there is no death, a place which would have chilled Don Miguel de Unamuno to the core. Those who are buried there —with or without cremation—"passed away." Without doubt (and what doubt could there be?) they entered into another happier life of which Forest Lawn gives an inkling. Their bodies remain here, of course, bodies which must be dealt with in some manner, somehow preserved after being beautified by the mortician's techniques, as does the memory of them among the living, sweetened by birdsong and the splashing of fountains, by the contemplation of statues and stained glass. All of which leads to the conclusion that "the loved ones" (*not* "the deceased," nor much less "the souls," the blessed souls in Purgatory so much alive in Spanish popular piety) are having a fine time of it somewhere and that they are as happy as the founder assures us.

Forest Lawn is not a comic place, it is not ridiculous; it is horrifying and overwhelming. Its significance is very simple: here the effort is to make death disappear, evaporate, by sleight of hand—and in a cemetery at that. This life and the afterlife—let us not forget eternity—but without death in between. This is neither more nor less than the myth of Paradise. Forest Lawn could only have come into existence in California.

38   CALIFORNIA AS PARADISE

The usual word for California, the one that first rises to the lips, is that it is a paradise. And that is true. Arriving in California from the East, you gain the impression of entering into the land of Paradise. And not only if you arrive in winter: for the contrast between the ice, snow, glacial winds, and bare trees of the rest of the country and California's warm air, blue sky, greenery, and lazy ocean is too obvious and therefore not particularly significant. It is the same impression as that induced by a move from one hemisphere to another when a plane takes us in a few hours from winter to summer. No, an arrival in California takes on more interest when the circumstances are more equal; when, for instance, the sun shines forth with as great intensity in the East and Middle West and in the Rocky Mountains as on the shores of the Pacific; when the whole land is covered with green and the entire sky is heavenly blue; when all that beauty is absolutely true. Then one still feels (and this time without tricks or playing false with the seasons) that one has entered Paradise.

What is Paradise? A garden, as was the Garden of Eden. Few places in the United States are garden spots. There are wild, untrammelled, and rugged forest lands in the North Atlantic states and along the Canadian border; there is utilitarian land, good for growing wheat and corn, on the endless plains of Illinois and Ohio; bleak prairies and wastelands in Wyoming or Utah; deserts in Arizona and New Mexico. California is another matter, truly an oasis—especially Southern California—a colossal oasis nourished by irrigation and the Pacific Ocean, where the hand of man is felt close by. And even in the wildest areas, where nature has taken charge of everything, there is a strange kind of carefulness, a peculiar composition of forms, a kind of order—*kósmos*—that is reminiscent of a garden. Thus it is even in the redwood forests, among the sequoias that border the city of San Francisco, trees two thousand years old, straight and tall and all nicely arranged. A whole family of deer may start up from among them, and at dusk there is an air of mystery that descends; but it is a literary mystery, out of a child's book, that has to do with a gigantic garden, a paradise from *Gulliver's Travels*, the wonders of Alice, and the magic world of Bambi and Falina.

And the cities? They too belong in Paradise. White stucco houses, often capriciously incongruous, that look like toys or, better, like a stage setting. And gardens that in some places, such as Pasadena, dominate the whole scene. And an air of constant fiesta or vacation; nowhere else in the world is effort less visible, less apparent, less exhibited. Thus Adam cultivated the Garden of Eden—without painful effort, without toiling, without suffering. Even in the least prosperous or well-to-do sections which are, if one looks carefully, very sordid and depressingly ugly (East Los Angeles, for example) the ever-present ghastly billboards with enormous letters of all colors, the paper or plastic streamers surrounding the lots where hundreds of used automobiles are stockpiled for sale, the transient air of the flimsy frame houses, almost shanties, all lend an atmosphere of fair or carnival, a party disguise, to those shoddy remnants of Paradise. (Where there is no Paradise at all is in the old town, the downtown center of Los Angeles, today mostly a Mexican quarter, because there the city is decaying under the sordidness that crept over it; it has "fallen away"—quite the opposite description from Paradise; Paradise Lost, if you prefer.)

This paradisaical character of California makes all the more surprising the discovery, only a few miles from Los Angeles, of enormous oil fields, of refineries working around the clock, of Navy Arsenals where colossal pyramids of underwater mines are stockpiled. This presents a brusquely unexpected transition from Paradise to the City of Enoch, but the first stage remains so "natural," so alive and so powerful that perhaps the oil wells therefore spring up from a foreground of blazing flowers. And nearby is a cemetery for dogs, with small monuments and even a Conestoga wagon: again we get the impression of a plaything, a child's tale, a fable, unreality.

Paradise is the absence of limitation, the lack of difficulty. The first condition may be found in many places, in all lands with space to spare where history is scarce; the second condition is more improbable. It cannot obtain where nature is rugged, violent, or immoderate, where heat and cold are oppressors, where there is an everyday battle against inclemency; nor can it flourish where man is inferior to his environment, where he is in need of everything or of many things—nor even where he lacks superfluous but vital luxury.

For this reason many gentle lands are not Paradise, and for the same reason California is; for that is the place where a well-nigh miraculous technology, an unprecedented amount of wealth, and the perfect structuring of man's cities have together achieved the height of pure implausibility.

Certainly, California is a paradise. The complimentary cliché is right. But even as I admit that, I am inclined to turn the statement into a reproach. In a sense, together with all its joys, that is the defect that California presents; because Paradise is an impossibility for men to construct on earth, and the Californian is no exception to the rule. Furthermore, the excellences of Paradise are in the long run deficiencies in the "real world," which is of necessity constituted of possibilities and limitations, facilities and difficulties, urgency and constraint. To live in the world means to be always between the swordpoint and the wall, to have to make the right choice with every moment, to have infinite resources at one's disposition but a counted number of days, to be born and to die.

Yes, also to die, of course; the world is a place where death does exist. And California (especially the most indubitably Californian part of the state, Los Angeles) tries to make death disintegrate and vanish. Not by denying death—that would be too naive— but quite to the contrary, by infusing its presence everywhere, making it part of everyday trivia, removing its sting, despoiling death thus of its inevitability. This is why ads for funeral homes and cemeteries are as common as those praising automobiles, beer, or perfume—and similar in tone. This is why one "manages" with such complete naturalness everything "that has to do with" death, an ingenious manner of eliminating death itself. This is also why, finally, Forest Lawn Cemetery, one of California's most representative creations, is established on the basis of two kinds of life: that of those who stroll through the gates, bathed by the sun and caressed by the breezes of the Pacific only a short distance from Hollywood; and the happy afterlife of those with property rights therein, whether lying horizontally or encased in an urn of ashes. This avoids the elementary fact that the latter are *dead*, that in order to enter Forest Lawn and that blessed life thereafter, they had to cross through the narrow door we call death—the one thing that is missing in any paradise, the thing that appears on the horizon when one leaves Paradise and enters irrevocably into the human world.

39 THE INVERTEBRATE CITY

Several months ago (not without excitement) I read in a showcase of the Archives of the Indies in Seville a letter which announced that in 1781 a group of Spaniards from San Gabriel and their captain had founded a town in California and called it Our Lady, Queen of the Angels. A couple of days ago I was in a Constellation flying for many long minutes over the mass of lights which is today the city of Los Angeles. The plane took quite a while at something like 350 miles per hour to cross over the largest urban area in the world. It is not a city that fits the traditional image engendered by that word—little more than a dot either on the map or when seen from the air; it is a form of landscape, a piece of territory that through some extraordinary prodigy has transformed itself into a polychrome glare, into a reverberation of gemstones, into an inverted firmament of innumerable stars. The stars, of course, differ in magnitude. Some are pale and spaced relatively far apart—these are the lights of the small houses in the residential districts, set off from each other by their gardens; some, intensely brilliant and cone-shaped, appear in ordered series—these are the streetlights of the great boulevards or of the compact built-up areas downtown; last but not least, since they are incredibly numerous, some are "shooting stars" which flash rapidly like twin comets across space—these are the headlights of millions of automobiles.

Seventy-five years ago Los Angeles had eleven thousand inhabitants; today it has two million (or five million, if we include the entire metropolitan area, Los Angeles County). There are over a million telephones in service: that is more than in all of Spain or Argentina and not many fewer than on the continent of Australia. Statistics concerning Los Angeles seem destined to produce stupefaction. But the "how many" is not so important; the "how"—in what way—is the decisive factor. If I remember correctly, on a page of an early edition of Ortega's *El Espectador*, there appeared this dialogue:

"Papa, what is the world?"
"Son, it's a very large thing, filled to the brim with trifles."

I don't know whether that is a good definition of the world or not, but it certainly fits Los Angeles. In this enormous city everything is tiny: except in a very concentrated area there are no large structures, skyscrapers or office buildings; everywhere you find small houses of one or at most two storys which are separated from each other by their compact gardens and even more so by the width of the broad streets. Even in the business districts the buildings seem minimal, unsubstantial, fragile. The strongest and most persistent impression one receives is that of a stage set. I have trouble avoiding the suspicion that all this is the work of Hollywood, which has secreted around itself this monstruous studio; and I go to bed each night with some anxiety, lest when I awake I find that they've taken everything else away and I shall be left only with the California earth so similar to the lands of the Levant in Spain.

Underneath the structures of most American cities there is usually the feel of the campground, but this city wears an inexplicable air of fictional unreality. Perhaps that is the reason the whole city appears in a festival mood, on vacation, so to speak—an atmosphere difficult to explain. Is it perhaps because of the gentle and perpetually summery climate? Maybe because there are so many beaches close at hand, so many hills and mountains to be seen towering over the small white, pink, and pale green houses? Or the habit so many people have here of dressing in a picturesque fashion, which they call "casual," very different from that of more proper San Franciscans or Easterners? Ever since I arrived in Los Angeles, this "vacation mood" has pursued and irritated me, because this is a hardworking city, highly industrialized, very active, extremely rich, and surrounded by enormous factories and even by oil fields.

Finally, I believe I have found an explanation, a reason inherent in the very structure of the city and in the way its processes function. Los Angeles is a far-flung city composed entirely of breadth and width. It is the exact opposite of New York: I find it incredible that Americans could have built two such diametrically opposed cities. It is an urban film of very, very little thickness spread over a tremendous amount of natural expanse. The city covers everything: hills, valleys, ports, beaches. It dilates without constraint, limitlessly; the story of the prankster who put up a sign in the middle of the Arizona desert reading "Los Angeles City Limits" makes profound good sense, because through its exaggeration it shows with true insight what the city is like. Naturally, since physics has its exacting laws, the freedom Los Angeles has taken with regard to space has imposed two other kinds of slavery: speed and time. Los Angeles is possible thanks only to the automobile. In a strict sense, there is no other way of getting about; the means of public transportation (buses and trolleys) are few in number, slow because of the innumerable stops to be made, and they appear infrequently. Despite the fact that the broad boulevards—Sunset, Pico, Wilshire, Westwood, Sepulveda, Santa Monica—and the "freeways" permit driving at hair-raising speeds, it takes easily three quarters of an hour or an hour to get from one point in the city to another, without ever touching on its outer borders; by bus, it takes an hour, an hour and a half, or two hours to go any distance at all.

This situation leads to unexpected consequences. First, nobody walks in Los Angeles. I have already described how I strolled for a couple of hours and several miles along Wilshire Boulevard with both sidewalks all to myself. But scarcely have I written that sentence "Nobody walks" when I must rectify it: nobody walks in order to go anywhere; that is, no one hurries eagerly to "get somewhere," as in all other large cities. The person who is walking (and he does so only in certain parts of the city, mostly in the business districts) has just parked his car; that it, he has already *arrived* and there-

fore is not *going* somewhere. He walks along slowly, therefore, windowshopping, choosing an attraction to see, buying
this and that. He does not have an "employed" look about
him; he is not just "passing through"; he has rather an air of
unconcern, a "vacation mood," I repeat. And it is not just a
question of having that "air"; he is in effect resting from the
"continual and virtuous" occupation common to all Angele-
nos—driving. A pedestrian is simply someone who has left his
steering wheel for a few moments: shortly he will get back
into his enamel and chrome urn and drive for hours and hours
through the immensity of the city.

In what direction? That brings us to the second point. Los
Angeles is an acephalic city if ever there was one. A downtown center does indeed exist, but its importance is negligible.
The "Old Town," the old Plaza, Mexican-flavored Olvera
Street, the touching Church of Our Lady of the Angels,
where novenas are said in Spanish; all this is in a state of decay.
The streets of the downtown districts have been superseded
by other more lively and prosperous quarters, and they can go
weeks and even months unvisited. Everyone goes to work and
returns to his home in one of the numberless residential areas
by the way of a route *he has selected*. This factor is a decisive
one; the relative scarcity of public transportation makes for
the establishment of individual human trajectories, which are
optional and often hazardous. There are no guidelines, no
predetermined pattern; there is no nervous system, no spinal
column. Los Angeles is the invertebrate city, *par excellence*.

Almost everywhere else the metropolitan structure, and
especially the various means of public transportation, channel
the movements of individuals into a configuration. In Los
Angeles this is not the case: each man and each woman, in his
or her car, is an autonomous unit in free circulation. At best
there are vague stress lines of the great traffic arteries, but
they indicate only the most probable routes. And since there
is open space on all sides, the driver knows his own favorite

way to avoid dense traffic and get there faster; and once he arrives at his destination he feels like the discoverer of the Northwest Passage.

All this explains why in Los Angeles there are no places where "everybody" goes, where one can count on meeting one's friends. There is no place here for what I call "lending a helping hand to coincidence," because here coincidence is as regulated a phenomenon as the movement of electrons. This is doubtless the reason why, in an enormously wealthy agglomeration of almost five million inhabitants, there are no permanent legitimate theatres, but only short-lived sporadic performances given by various theatrical companies. Theatre requires an audience of *habitués*, and this requirement can be fulfilled only when there is a structure to a city and a "center." It is a well-known fact in European cities, and in many North and South American ones, that theatres prosper only in certain zones; outside of such areas they are doomed to failure because people do not "go" except to certain districts. In Los Angeles no such districts exist. The movies, typically with films that can be shown simultaneously in many different houses, represent the only spectacle appropriate to Los Angeles. In actual fact the repertory of possibilities is very much limited because the tremendous distances impede one from making a habit of going to a movie at any other than the three or four neighborhood film houses. And even the movies require too much effort. They are rapidly being replaced by television. (In Los Angeles County there are over a million and a half TV sets.) The citizen of Los Angeles gets up in the morning and goes to the place where he works; he interrupts his labors only to have a brief lunch; when he finishes his work day, around five in the afternoon, he takes steering wheel in hand and drives an hour or sometimes two to reach the district where he lives. There he finds himself on broad, empty streets which curve and slope amid carefully watered green lawns (don't forget that we are in the most colossal oasis in the world), multicolored flowers, trim shrubs, and trees which lack the rough vigor of those in Atlantic seaboard cities and grow close to small houses or in diminutive gardens. The Angeleno puts the car away and goes into his home. He has driven two or maybe three or four hours that day; he has braked innumerable times in front of the white pedestrian lanes; he has watched the red and green traffic signals; ten or twelve times he has found some solution to the parking problem. Now inside his comfortable and cheerful home he lets down and relaxes; he has dinner with his family. And now what? He could go out, go to the movies, visit a friend. But that would mean getting the car out, driving again for a long space of time, watching again for flashes of red and green, looking again for a parking space. Urban cities—if you will permit me that phrase—are always small, relatively small; at least they have a nucleus which can be encompassed. Park cities—such as are almost all American towns—are diffuse, but they are composed of finished units; in one outlying area everything is to be found: a church, movie houses, markets, a shopping center, friends. When one is in a residential area in Los Angeles, for miles around there is nothing other than *homes*, one-family residences closed in upon themselves, minuscule islands of private life with only neighborly relations —*good* neighborly relations, it must be conceded. In these delightful districts no one walks along the street. Everyone is in the house, arriving in the early evening and staying there. The huge city is thus fragmented into millions of isolated units, solitary and uncommunicative entities. Los Angeles is a city that ought to have been founded byLeibnitz: the lights, those uncounted stars in the metropolitan sky that a plane reveals, are windowless monads, united, coordinated, and linked by that form of preordained harmony called television.

40   BUREAUCRACY AS A FORM OF SATANISM

Two entirely different items happen to have fallen into my hands almost at the same time, and I believe I have discovered a recondite connection between them. One is an administrative report on the federal government of the USA, and the other is an old Spanish engraving of a religious nature. The report, published in the daily press, offers some data worth remembering. Administrative paperwork costs the U.S. Government—the taxpayers, that is—four billion dollars a year. The Government puts out four million letters every day; and since each letter involves considerable work (copies, filing, etc.) and labor is highly paid, it is estimated that each letter costs one dollar. The report offers many other pieces of information, but it is not necessary to run it into the ground. Perhaps one more fact might be enlightening, however: in the United States there are 750,000 employees handling government paperwork.

Naturally, we are dealing here only with employees of the federal government: if we were to add on state and municipal employees and office workers in private enterprise, the figures would be much more terrifying. The problem of storing all this paperwork is beginning to be a very serious one; the country is threatened with obliteration by a flood of manila folders and three-drawer files. It should not be supposed that the United States is an exceptional case in all this, except in one particular: that of keeping detailed statistics and releasing them, for the phenomenon is a universal one from which no country is entirely free. In some places the problem is more crucial than in others, but it exists everywhere. What is worse, it is spiraling dizzily into an ever larger dilemma: in North America the average number of official letters put out

per employee was 55 in 1912; in 1954, it was 522. It is horrifying to think of what the figure may be by the end of the
century, if the piles of paper do not keep us from reaching
that date.

The engraving which I mentioned is rather moving. I
found it in a place which also has a touching quality about it,
the church of Our Lady of the Angels in the Old Plaza, which
used to be the center of this city of Los Angeles, and which
gave it its name. The plaza is decayed, fallen upon hard times,
discarded along with its Mexican-flavored neighbor Olvera
Street, and today no more than a vestige remains. In this
melancholy plaza spent men sit upon the benches, men with
olive skin and black hair who have doubtless never found
their way. The only splendid things about the place are some
enormous, century-old fig trees about whose impressively
furrowed and contorted roots one might write a chilling
chapter of existential philosophy. And in the restored yet
ever old church, filled with gilded objects and lit by candles,
with its white patio and its awning, beaten men and resigned
women come on a Sunday afternoon to listen sadly and hopefully to a novena said in Spanish, while a short distance away
innumerable automobiles speeding at sixty or seventy miles
per hour flash along the freeways which interweave nearby
at four different levels.

The engraving is very old, probably dating from the Romantic period. Its legend reads: "The Omnipresence of God."
At the top appears the head of God the Father with curling
hair, a rosy face, and a long whitish beard. In His right hand
(His arms appear from among the clouds swathed in a purple
fabric) there is a cross; close to His left hand are streaks of
descending lightning: and on the two sides it says "Either
the Cross in This World—Or Hell in the Next." Underneath
the divine figure to the left there is an ear; in the middle, an
eye; and to the right, an open book being written in by a hand
that comes out of the clouds. There are three inscriptions:

"God hears everything"; God sees everything"; God knows everything." Lower down, supported by the earth's sphere, a hand holds a balancing scale: on one of the pans a white figure is kneeling next to a cross with an angel at its side, and the inscription reads "A Moment"; on the other pan there is a black devil with bats' wings and the lettering "An Eternity." Even lower there are four scenes, each in an oval inset with its own caption: "The Just Man"; "The Death of the Just Man"; "The Death of the Sinner"; "The Sinner." Finally, at the very bottom, a skull and cross-bones and one last inscription: "In this mirror you may see—What you too will come to be."

What does the report of the Hoover Commission have to do with this naive and horrendous Spanish engraving which still figures in the grimy devotionaries of the Mexican women who come to hear the novena at the Los Angeles church? It seems to me that here we have the ultimate aim of contemporary bureaucracy: to achieve on earth the omnipresence of God. God hears all, sees all, knows all; yes, but only God can do all this. And that has been man's greatest consolation throughout his Christian history. Man has known that he was living under the eye of God, but God is infinitely good. Except for Him, no one knows so much, One could still live without leaving a trace; our steps, our words, our gestures being gradually erased from this world as the swimmer's wake disappears in the water. One could feel fresh, free, light of foot. But the day came when bureaucracy began to want to investigate everything and to make a record of it: first, with quill pens, as in the book in the old religious engraving; then on perforated IBM cards in complicated electronic archives; with X-rays, analysis, finger-prints, affidavits—perhaps even with serums that uncover one's most carefully hidden thoughts. If a man travels, the trip is never over: it remains on the register. If he changes address, the entire series of all the addresses of his lifetime is still assigned to him. Everything we do is noted and indelibly recorded: it is known by someone, retained, remembered unto perpetuity. By whom? By whomever it may be; by the State, the Administration, by the Bureaucracy which is trying to supplant God and achieve (minus charity) His reign on earth, by which I mean His power—and His control.

And the encroachment is ever greater. Like all mechanical things, Bureaucracy is insatiable and implacable. Always it asks for more information and wants to know more things, and it needs more copies of all this to be recorded in more places and there related to additional further data. Though we may feel that there is some fragment of our life which should remain hidden or at least overlooked, simply because it is of no interest to anyone; lo and behold, Bureaucracy is interested in that part also. Therefore, I say that Bureaucracy is a form of Satanism, an attempt to usurp the prerogatives and point of view of God. Those who referred to Philip II as the "Demonio del Mediodía"* (playing on Spanish geographical designations and the Psalm's reference to that disquieting and bothersome "Destruction that wasteth at noonday") did not realize that they were right only with regard to one trait: the obsession with clerical detail, the bureaucratic mania of the Escorial's king.

Bureaucracy with a capital B, the kind that today rules the world, is then a manifestation of Satanism. If one looks closely at its deepest motivations, its aims are revealed: desertion of God, replacement of Him by the temporal power of the organization, retraction of vital faith in an everlasting life. But this does not mean, naturally, that the individuals who accomplish the tasks I have been discussing participate personally in that Satanism. The instruments of all forms of Satanism, in whatever era, have always been just poor devils.

---

* The pun here is based on the word *mediodía* which, in Spanish, means "noon" but is also used to designate the southern part of the country—Trans.

41   POINTS OF VIEW

Two letters prompted by my article "Bureaucracy as a Form of Satanism" have come into my hands at the same time. Both are from Spain, and both were written by government employees, one of whom is from La Coruña and the other (Registrar of Deeds, to be exact) from Madrid. I received these letters in the state of Minnesota, not far from Canada, by the banks of the powerful Mississippi river among the eleven thousand lakes of the region, a few steps from the falls of Minnehaha with its memories of the Indian youth Hiawatha —a world in which nature and legend join to carry us far off towards a rudimentary, child-like, and primitive state; a world, that is, in which one finds it hard to remember that bureaucracy exists.

My two Spanish correspondents, whom I should like to thank for their interest, disagree entirely—and I was going to add, as good Spaniards always do. The one from Madrid congratulates me on my article and encourages me to keep on demanding that things be simplified. The gentleman from La Coruña, on the other hand, is upset by my article and feels offended by it—to my not inconsiderable surprise. Of course he cites only one small part of the article, the last two sentences, in which, trying precisely not to involve individuals in what I was saying about Bureaucracy as a phenomenon in history, I concluded by writing: "But this does not mean, naturally, that the individuals who accomplish the tasks I have been discussing participate personally in that Satanism. The instruments of all forms of Satanism, in whatever era, have always been just poor devils." These are the sentences that wounded the sensibilities of the government functionary in La Coruña, and my first reaction was to ponder the degree to which we have lost our sense of humor, and what is more serious, our sense of the exigencies of literary style. How could anyone possibly be hurt by such innocent sentences, intended specifically to exonerate from all Satanic associations the excellent people most government employees are? My chief occupation is Philosophy, and often I have said that all Philosophy is a matter of four cats closed up in the same small corner; without fearing that for that reason Plato, Aristotle, or Kant would turn over in their graves, or that living philosophers would become angry with me. Could such a completely general sentence as mine—"all forms of Satanism in whatever era"—indicate an indiscreet and treacherous intention to "offend an honorable, hardworking group" among which are numbered "many persons with degrees, advanced studies, experience and personality?" To the extent that we are victims of the blind powers that weigh down upon humanity, we are all "poor devils," playthings of our masters. It is the same for the man sitting behind the counter as for the one standing in front of it. Both are in a world which often closely resembles that of Kafka.

Because it is not a question of anything less than a nightmare. Let me tell you a small story about what happened to me three years ago. The problem was to obtain exemption from obligatory social service for my wife. In order to get that, we needed a marriage certificate and my life certificate* for, of course, it could be that I had died and left her a widow a short time after marriage. I went to apply for my life certificate in the proper district. The clerk consulted an enormous ledger similar to the one St. Peter must keep—or, no, perhaps the really large ones are kept in another place. He looked for my address and said to me solemnly: "Building under construction." I explained to him that the building had

---

* In Spain, in addition to a birth certificate, there is also a document called a *fe de vida* (a life certificate) which is somewhat like a domestic passport—Trans.

been entirely finished and that I had been living in it for several months; then I inquired as to the date of his records and he told me they dated from 1940. I reminded him that we were in the year 1942 and that the apartment house had been finished in 1941. All to no purpose: he suggested that I go to the district where I had lived in 1940 and apply there for my document. (The passing thought occurred to me that if I did base my appeal on that information it would prove at best that I was alive in 1940, but I carefully refrained from saying so.) In the other district my name and address was on record, but before handing me the paper the clerk asked me what I wanted it for. I was not convinced that the query was necessary and justifiable, but since there was no mystery about my reason, I explained.

"Well, then," he said to me, "I cannot give you your life certificate."

"Why not," I asked?

"Because it seems that you are married, but it says in my register that you are a bachelor."

"Naturally," I answered, "in 1940 I *was* a bachelor; I got married in 1941."

"But I can't put down 'married' because my register reads 'bachelor'."

So I said, "Well, go ahead and write down 'bachelor,' because I'm going to present a marriage certificate together with this document."

"I can't put down 'bachelor' because you are married."

This was Kafka in the purest possible form, as well you can see. There was no way out. The clerk suggested that the only thing I could do would be to go to the main Statistics Office, re-register there with my present address and civil status, and then apply there for a life certificate. I asked someone a little less busy than I to take care of the necessary steps for me; at the end of a week, he appeared with the desired document. I read it over avidly: the space under Civil Status was blank.

Since I have traveled a great deal, I can remember such instances in a dozen countries. But take, for a moment, the Spanish requirement of a document certifying that one has no police record. It seems simple enough: this person does not have a criminal record and that is that. But no, you also have to specify in the document for what purpose it is to be used— for example, to obtain a passport. Simple soul that I am, I can't help exclaiming to myself, "But, Sir, is it possible *not* to have a police record when one wants a passport, but yet to have one when it is a question of applying for competitive state examinations? Either you have a criminal record or you don't!" But apparently that's not the way it works, and if you are required to present "the same evidence" but "for another purpose," you have to start all over again and obtain another document. The same problem arises when you consider the general supposition that every Spaniard, until he can prove the contrary, has been repatriated at the expense of the government. Good heavens, how many among 28 million Spaniards could possibly have received that benefit? And in a Latin American country, with a transit visa that "obliged" me to leave the country within a week, I found I would not be "permitted" to leave without obtaining police authorization—all of which left me exposed to remaining forever in a state like that of Garibay's soul.*

In these frequently recurring situations we individuals on both sides of the counter, though involved in them, are innocent. A mocking destiny, reminiscent of Descartes' "malign spirit," is laughing at us. This is the reason that Bureaucracy —with its essential capital B—frightens me. Its gears are usually inoffensive and harmless, but the moment someone slips

* Esteban de Garibay y Zamalloa (1525–1599) an erudite humanist who was Librarian to Philip II—Trans.

a few grains of real evil or madness into them (and recent examples are numerous) they can bring about hell on earth. This is the reason that when I spoke of the men involved in bureaucratic affairs, especially of those who are permanently and professionally bound to its wheels, I use the expression "poor devils." And I thought that the cordiality of my smile would be visible even in La Coruña.

42   YES AND NO

The picaresque rogue knows—as Cortadillo is witness—that heaven has given the bold man a tongue that may save his life. "As though," Cervantes adds through Cortadillo's lips, "there were more letters in 'No' than in 'Yes'!" True, at times a "yes" or a "no" is not really a matter of life or death nor, upon occasion, a question of dignity or cowardice nor, in the long run, of salvation or perdition. Still, the word "no" has been out of fashion for some time. People say "yes" to everything, and the consequences are dangerous. When a good history of the contemporary era is written, it may become apparent how much better our history might have been had there been a couple of dozen negatives placed strategically throughout the last twenty-five or thirty years. When "no" falls into disuse, when we forget that man has the elementary capacity not to accept, to refuse a benefit, a position, a title, or a proposition, then "anything goes," and the few are in a position to do whatever they may like to all the others.

I was reminded of this by a minor happening in the United States that was taken up by the newspapers and that may be a sign of a comeback for the word "no." A couple of months ago,† the President of the University of Washington in Seattle, a university with thirteen thousand students, vetoed a series of scientific lectures that the physicist J. Robert Oppenheimer had agreed to give. Shortly thereafter, three well-known university men, a sociologist, a historian, and a physicist, all belonging to the faculties of respected institutions, refused one after the other to give lectures at the University of Washington. A few days later it was announced that seven first-rate scientists were not going to attend a meeting there on an important problem in biochemistry; the reason given was that the President's veto "had placed the University of Washington outside the pale of the intellectual community." Consequently, the head of Washington's Department of Biochemistry stated unhappily that the meeting would have to be indefinitely postponed.

Notice of course that here it is a question of conflicting negatives. I am not the one to moderate the debate, nor would this in any case be the time and place to do so. The situation interests me simply as an instance of the use of "no" on the part of all those who intervened in the matter: the veto of the President and the refusals of those invited. If the president of the University has a legitimate right to veto lectures and believes that he should exercise that right, he is not stepping out of his role in prohibiting a speech. But as he does so, he is also placing his university in a posture which other American intellectuals, in their turn, will judge and evaluate according to their own criteria. If their evaluation is negative they will, in accordance with their judgment, decline invitations and refuse to collaborate with that University. A simple introduction of the negative factor restores the figures on the balance sheets: besides the sum, there is also the remainder. The calculation was apparently based on the supposition that it was possible to add a veto on one scientist to the cooperation of

† Written in 1955.

ten others. It turns out this cannot be done because of the intrusion of the minus sign: unexpectedly, it is necessary to subtract ten units, ten for the moment, because the most interesting aspect is that we are dealing with successive but independent subtractors which may not yet have finished appearing.

Despite its being such an unspectacular and unmelodramatic instance, occurring as it did in a place so remote as the extreme north of the Pacific Coast, this happening caused a wave of feeling to arise amidst intellectual circles all over the country. It has been commented upon on college campuses with a certain astonishment and an involuntary tendency to speak in a lower-than-normal tone of voice: with a mixture of respect, concern, and hope, as when people are discussing awe-inspiring discoveries of nuclear physics that bear in them the germ of life and death. This event too deals with a rather mysterious and subtle something whose name resembles that of an element and is, in effect, an elementary force: the word "No."

43 THE STATE OF HEALTH OF AMERICAN SOCIETY

As a consequence of reading American newspapers and magazines for the last two years, I had built up a considerable concern over the social sanity of the United States. The impression projected by a large part of the American and world press, and especially by certain foreign correspondents in Washington, contradicted my own previous direct experience. But since history moves very swiftly these days, the possibility of a significant change could not be ruled out.

Besides, even in 1951 and 1952 certain slight, but not for that less alarming, symptoms of a dangerous shift were making themselves noticeable. Such a shift could lead heaven knows where: to a tendency towards interventionism, an over-sensitivity to the political aspect of individuals and events, flashes of intolerance, threats to liberty or to what people here call "academic freedom." Nothing at the time was serious; everything was explicable; but the good European—"once bitten, twice shy"—cannot observe these phenomena without anxiety because he thinks that there must be a reason for this kind of thing to begin.

And there is no doubt that American society did run a risk, though not to such an extent as has been suggested, and is still being reported because of the understandable journalistic tendency towards arbitrary selection of details, towards magnifying and slanting them, lending them interest at home by the use of such time-honored sayings as "history repeats itself," and "it's the same story everywhere," and other platitudes of notorious utility. But even taking into account these qualifying factors, there was still a considerable risk. I occupied myself with its description in the article entitled "Defense and Surrender of a Way of Life."

The reader may have noticed that I have been using the past tense; I said that American society "was" in danger. Has that danger now evaporated? I must admit that I returned to the United States at the beginning of 1955 with a certain trepidation: what would I be likely to encounter? Perhaps it would be a "politicized" society, irritable, restless, nervous, perhaps hysterical, full of suspicion, divided by hostility. Could the magnificent harmony of American life have disappeared, and that sense of mutual confidence, the habit of considering one's fellow at least a friend if not a brother? Could the American's focus on private life have been replaced by an obsessive political orientation? Scarcely had I arrived in the United States when my fears began to dissolve: American society was the same as when I had left the country in 1952. The same? Perhaps somewhat better in two senses: first, more prosperous and secure; second, "back at home" cured of a slight case of the measles and immunized against further possible infection. I believe sincerely that Americans did catch a glimpse of the wolf's ears (luckily, of no more than his ears) but, without tearing themselves apart, with an energetic but good-humored stance, without playing up to the wolf, without becoming wolverine in tone themselves, but also without turning into lambs, they have frightened him off—I hope for a long time to come.

And American life continues to be, as I have before described it, "tough but gentle," because although everyone works and works hard, although the climate is frequently punishing, although enormous wealth is gained only at the cost of strenuous daily effort, the human psychological environment is a consoling one. This is a country in which one does not have to be always on the lookout for enviousness: it exists, of course, as such things do in all parts of the world, but here on such a small scale that one is not obliged to be wary of it. This is a country in which the first reaction of one's fellow man is pre-disposed to be favorable even though we may not have met; a country in which there are rules of the road and people believe that it is well to follow them; in which the good fortune of another does frequently bring joy; in which, eight times out of ten, the stranger is not questioned about the political regime dominating his country, but asked rather whether he has children and, if so, how many boys and how many girls.

As I have been writing this, I came across two opinions— one American and one English, one that of columnist Joseph Alsop, and the other of René MacColl—which energetically emphasize the improvement brought about in the United States in 1955. MacColl asserts that the temper of North America has changed completely since the month of February. Alsop believes that in 1955 the Eisenhower administration found itself and that the American political process got back on the track; and he adds that to return to the United States after a six-month's absence is like discovering a new country which is embarking on "an era of good feeling." The two attitudes expressed here seem true to me but exaggerated; I believe that that past illness was something much more minor, rather venial and perfectly explicable. How so?

I conclude that what has happened in the United States in recent years could be described using an electrical metaphor as "induced radicalization." What does that mean? Something very simple. When certain exterior phenomena gain unexpected strength outside, everything inside a country that has any relation to or affinity for them changes along with them in aspect and significance. What before looked perfectly harmless—and was—and therefore seemed quite legitimate and acceptable, suddenly becomes disturbing and menacing. What was moderate before now converts itself into an extreme, simply because its connections within a general pattern have been altered. Gestures that were considered normal as of a certain date cease to be so, independent of the will of those who make them. This is what I call "induced radicalization": the electric charge outside electrifies the interior without any necessity for spontaneous internal changes to take place.

This is a process which has repeated itself a hundred times over in history. Skirting events too close at hand, let us remember the significance acquired by "enlightened" Spaniards of the eighteenth century (from Jovellanos to Moratín) under the electric impact of the French Revolution. And we may consider the situation in which—involuntarily and unjustifiedly—they then found themselves, and the consequences in Spanish history for the last hundred and fifty years. This is precisely what American society is managing to avoid and, I am confident, in a permanent fashion. Its inherent health, at equal distance from spasm and from paralysis, is automatically rectifying the abnormal condition, reestablishing what we might call an electrical balance of pressure. And since the enormous power of the United States affects and acts on all the world, imagine the risks we non-Americans have run. Think of the disturbances that might have been "induced" in the rest of the world by a violent, stupid, intolerant, and insecure American society in a state of disorder.

Since I am not a professional pessimist (though that office is enjoying quite a vogue) I believe that health too is "catching." And I hope that the irradiations of the American section of humanity, restored once more to health, may in the near future prevent or cure in other areas some ugly skin eruptions or even hidden visceral tumors.

44   FRIENDSHIP IN NORTH AMERICA

No one in the world is friendlier than a North American, man or woman. The bus driver looks at you amicably as you get on, and if it is not rush hour, he says "Goodbye" to you as you get off. (A few months ago an important corporation with an eye to publicity offered to finance the long-suppressed, secret desire of a handful of lucky individuals. One winner in the contest was a bus driver. His desire was to invite his passengers to dinner and the theatre, so all those who had the time went with him to a restaurant and to the performance. Few things seem to me so typical of the United States.) The telephone repairman who is going to fix your phone offers you a cigarette and chats cordially with you. Even the implacable policeman who gives you a ticket for speeding smiles as he does so and helps you get the guilty car back into traffic. ("Courtesy does not detract from valor.") The preacher in church smiles at you from the pulpit or the altar and finds you truly worthy of love. When you are at the beginning of a friendly person-to-person relationship, the American from the very start is at ease and puts you at ease; in ten minutes you are communicating with each other in truly cordial terms. It has been said, and not without reason, that the United States is a paradise for friendship.

And yet.... Contrary to what we might expect, Americans have very few friends. If you take the trouble to investigate, each person has a very small circle of friends; besides that, these friendships are not frequently brought into play, and very few are truly intimate relationships. How can this be possible? How can it be that a race so excellently endowed for friendship, so inherently friendly, cultivates such relationships in a sparing or deficient fashion? Friends (and, I reiterate, a small number of them) see each other only infrequently; college friendships (close ones, even those between roommates) are allowed to drop. Friends do not correspond: they send each other a Christmas card, they visit each other when one passes through the city where the other lives, but that is all. There may be as many exceptions as you like, but statistically that is the rule and the form that friendship, taken as a general phenomenon, adopts.

The reasons underlying this situation are not easy to ascertain. When you ask Americans about it, they are first surprised (it had not occurred to them that that was the way it is, or that the situation is anomalous), then they admit that indeed the thing does work that way, and third, they seek to explain it in terms of isolation and lack of time. But these are secondary factors. I believe that the chief explanation lies in the fact that the United States suffers a shortage of one single element: imagination. When they first meet a person, Americans react positively, because the United States is one of the very few places on the globe where one does love his neighbor. (A little less than oneself, perhaps, but even so, how miraculous!) They enjoy contact, the presence of an individual who often seems to them a fine person; they leave each other full of cordiality and good will. And afterwards? Probably nothing. On another occasion, perhaps at a party, they will again encounter that same person, be delighted to see him, and again enjoy each other's company. Between such encounters a vacuum reigns. And that is not friendship, because, like all human concoctions, it must have a dramatic structure—it requires a narrative thread, a plot. And to invent a story line for a friendship requires imagination. When I meet a pleasing person I imagine another, future encounter perhaps under different circumstances; for example, alone, or maybe to discuss some topic of particular interest, or perhaps together with other, older friends. And when that second meeting occurs, I imagine a third and a fourth, all different, all signifying steps along a path. What path? That of our lives which thus begin in some sense to be "ours" and intertwined. I have the feeling that the trajectory of my life is interwoven at different intervals with other strands, those of my friends. And all these friendships have their own intermingled plot threads that weave in and out, or criss-cross, or go off on a tangent, as in the novels of Galdós.

In the United States "occasions" for friendship multiply rapidly; sociability is encouraged and social gatherings are frequently planned. The churches are centers of conviviality with clubs, teas, parties, lectures, and dances (yes, of course, even in the Catholic churches). In the universities the fraternities and sororities are legion (each one identified by a combination of three Greek letters); and people generally belong to all kinds of associations: professional, athletic, literary, acquisitional, charitable, commercial. On the pretext of stimulating business (a pretext necessary to salve the puritan conscience) but actually to enjoy a bit of leisure, all kinds of conventions are organized. The first time I was in Chicago, when I came from my room into the lobby of the immense Conrad Hilton Hotel, I saw the place was full of gentlemen, ladies, and young girls all with a badge on their lapels that read in large letters: NADA (in Spanish, the word for "nothing.") Was it a congress of existentialists, or of nihilists? But they all exuded well-being, cheerfulness, and affirmation. It was a convention of the National Automobile Dealers Association, and to judge by the traffic jams and the difficulty of finding a place to park, they had ample reason to be content.

But all this implies that society has to provide the impulse, that individual initiative and imagination is not up to arranging for the proliferation and intensification of purely personal friendship. Friendship in the United States is usually discontinuous, like a rosary of isolated identical moments, with no progression, no plot, no dramatic route to follow. Friendship for the majority of North Americans has no biography: it lacks a biography because no one invents a program for his friendship, a more or less imaginative narrative thread.

Yet when someone does bring a little imagination to bear, friendship flourishes miraculously. An American responds with unanticipated eagerness; he throws himself into the proposed enterprise, lends to it his entire wealth of demonstrativeness, likableness, affection, and lack of vices. When the tap of imagination is turned on, the American soul gives forth the same fantastic crops as the dry soil of California when cultivated under irrigation.

45 THE BALLAD OF THE DRUGSTORE

I remember my arrival in Salt Lake City on a sparkling train that had crossed the interminable prairies of Illinois, Iowa, Nebraska, and Wyoming and now had come in to Utah, land of the Mormons. A few hours before, we had passed the Great Divide in the Rocky Mountains and through Green River, which recorded that very day the lowest temperature in all the United States.

When I got off the train and started to walk along the long broad avenue, swept by glacial winds, that goes from the station to the Mormon Temple, alone amidst the lovely snow that reflected the gleaming lights, I asked myself what on earth had brought me to lose myself in Utah, where I didn't know the name of a single soul. Jules Verne was at fault—in this as in so many other things. Do you remember *Around the World in Eighty Days*, Phileas Fogg, the phlegmatic gentleman, and his roguish servant Passepartout? In their company, and in my far-distant childhood, I had made my first acquaintance with Utah and her Mormons. But let us not deceive ourselves: childhood endures, and for ten years I had had a rendezvous with Salt Lake City. Now I was coming to keep my date, step by step over the snow, along the deserted boulevard toward the Mormon Temple which shone in the distance.

Could there be anything stranger than that religion founded a century and a quarter ago by a man named Joseph Smith, with his Angel Moroni who blows a trumpet from the spire of each temple, his tablets of revelation, the Book of Mormon (which you will find in your hotel room in Salt Lake City), and his policy of polygamy (until that was prohibited by law)? The Church of the Latter-day Saints, which elicited violent hostility, was continuously persecuted and forced to flee toward the West: from New York State to Ohio, then to Missouri, next to Illinois, where Smith and his brother suffered violent deaths, and finally to the deserted wastes of Utah, where among mountains and lakes the Mormons settled, relaxed, and prospered. And now more than a million members pay their tithes, and there is a Tabernacle where exquisite organ music is played and a Temple open only to the faithful.

The mammoth illuminated Temple appeared to orient and explicate the city. At the intersection of the two main streets there was a snowy statue of Joseph Smith; and like a belt around the city, very close, the ever-present mountains which offer to the heart of the city an image of the rugged west. Frozen streets, almost deserted. And then suddenly, a drug-store! Here in Salt Lake City at last I fathomed and understood what a drugstore represents. Always open, night and day, no matter what the weather; gleaming with the brightest lights imaginable, like a beacon in the middle of the city; sheltered and hospitable as a harbor; as full of things as—as a drugstore, because nowhere else are there so many. Twenty-five cent books on revolving wire racks, children's story-books, magazines and newspapers, cigarettes, cameras, candy, suitcases, electrical gadgets, chairs, pens, toys, eyeglasses, perfumes, stationery, fishing equipment—everythink you can possibly imagine. And since the American drugstore has "everything," it even sells drugs and medicines. There is also, and most important, a long counter flanked by plastic-covered stools where for a few cents at any hour of the day or night you can order a couple of fried eggs, coffee, a milk-shake, a hamburger, or that variant so delightfully called a cheeseburger.

If you have to buy something in the United States, don't ponder over it. An alarm clock? Don't go looking for a watchmaker, because you may not find one; and if you do, he probably won't have an alarm-clock. Go to the corner drugstore. Do you need a pipe, a reel for your camera, a stove, a life-preserver, some airmail stamps, a bath sponge, a sandwich grill, an atlas, a salmon filet, some aspirin, some chocolate or strawberry ice cream, or a Davy Crockett coonskin cap? Do you want to use the telephone to call Miami, Chicago, Columbus, or the last outpost in Minnesota or Arizona? Lean confidently against the glass door of the drugstore and "Push." Do you wish to defrost yourself and get the blood back in circulation toward your ears? Are you dying for a breath of fresh air rather than a furnace blast when the sun outside is softening the asphalt? The drugstore will return you to a habitable world.

And especially if you need company, if you are feeling lonely and strange and on the outside of everything, if it seems to you that you are the only one left in the world, that humanity has melted away from you, you will find people once again at the drugstore. Each store is alike, always the same, your drugstore—whether you find it in Niagara Falls, on the Canadian border, in California, by the shores of the Pacific, in one of the intimate small towns of Connecticut or Massachusetts, at the edge of Wisconsin's meadows, amid the thunder of Chicago, or next door to the gardens which insulate the millionaires in Pasadena. Whenever you cross the threshold of a drugstore, you enter the same well-known world; you are "at home." The same smile that you left behind in a familiar city waits for you back of the counter. From the counter stools, a complex sampling of humanity looks at you with benevolent good will. A pair of students are drinking a shake and staring into each other's eyes as she smoothes back a few locks of blonde hair. A nurse is having a hot cup of coffee to break up the trip to the hospital; there is a solitary night-owl who doesn't know where else to go, and a truck driver who is gobbling down some bacon and eggs while his gas tank is being filled outside. A lady who has been shopping sits surrounded by packages having a hasty luncheon. Sometimes the counter is circular or forms three sides of a rectangle; faces smile at the other faces across from them, the aroma of coffee spreads, cigarettes send up wisps of smoke, a few words are exchanged, there is the sound of young laughter, and an old man cleans his glasses so that he can better observe the three generations gathered there.

The drugstore is a refuge providing relief for the wayfarer, amusement for the curious and the contemplative of spirit, solace for the lonely and afflicted. In an enormous city, its lights beckon and call; in a tiny town where respectability reigns, it welcomes the stranger who finds himself lost there when everyone is asleep. How many charitable works the American drugstore performs without knowing it! It feeds the hungry, gives drink to the thirsty, even occasionally clothes the naked; it entertains those sick with nostalgia, comforts many who are sad, teaches through its books those who are ignorant, and gives good advice to all who need it! How many people on their way to doing an evil deed—perhaps to perform a murder or to commit suicide—must have found a drugstore en route and decided not to do it! In this statistics-conscious country that set of figures is missing: all would-be suicides who repented in a drugstore and were there reconciled to life should send a colored postcard to the appropriate authorities.

46 ENGLISH FROM THE INSIDE

"Tantos millones de hombres, ¿hablaremos inglés?"*

Rubén Darío was thinking of North American imperialism, of the eagles sent flying southward by rugged Theodore Roosevelt. The thing that surprises me is that so many millions do speak English as though it were indeed their own language. If it were just a case of a small group of human beings living somewhere among the brusque defiles of the Caucasian Mountains, the thing might be more easily understandable; but hundreds of millions of people on every continent? And thanks to their influence, many millions more of us are speaking in English from time to time, for better or for worse. This spread, this effectiveness, the tremendous circulation of English as a written language, the splendid literature that exists in that tongue, all of this leads us to accept as the most natural thing in the world something that is anything but natural. Because English is something very peculiar, and we should not forget that.

When one considers English from the outside, as a written language, it appears to be similar to many others, certainly to the other Indoeuropean tongues. But the first point that suggests itself is that the expression "written language" is extremely problematical in English. In the strictest sense, English cannot be written because its sounds have very little to do with its letters. And the thing is all the more surprising since English *comes* from those letters; that is, from the Indo-

---

* "Will so many millions of us have to speak English?" Quoted from a poem by Rubén Darío (1867–1916), eminent Nicaraguan poet and major figure in the Modernist movement, whose voice was one of the many warning of the danger to Hispanic American culture from the then-threatening "Colossus of the North," the United States—Trans.

european roots common to various other western languages. When Turkish was written in Arabic characters, that was a completely incongruous condition for which Islam was to blame, because Turkish has no connection with Arabic or the Arabic system of written symbols. Now that Turkish is written in Roman letters—by decision of Mustapha Kemal or Kemal Attaturk, as you prefer—it is a question again of a similar incongruity for which the pressure of Western culture *en bloc* is responsible. But in English we have a different case; English is an Indoeuropean language capable therefore of being written down through the same symbols which serve so well in representing the other languages of the same family. However, as is well known, English uses completely different letters to represent the identical sounds; and, inversely, the same symbol or group of symbols may have entirely distinct sounds corresponding to them, depending upon the words in question. To cap the problem, the sounds exceed the symbols and their combinations in number, and the variations, in symbol and in sound respectively, have only a very remote interconnection. What does all this imply?

I have just said that English is an Indoeuropean language and immediately regret having said so. Not because I have any doubt that it is Indoeuropean, but because the doubtful thing is whether it is, in fact, only *one* language. Take any page written in English: you will notice that it is composed of words completely different from each other: half are Latin, half Germanic. The foreign reader, when he reads English, is constantly traveling back and forth between Latin and Germanic lands: written English seems like the River Rhine.

Is English then a composite language? Two half-languages put together? Could that be the reason for its appearing often—especially British English—to be an "infantile semi-language"? I believe, to the contrary, that English is the most unitarian language I am familiar with. But understand me, I mean the tongue itself, the speaking of it, the spoken language. English is a system of phonetics. Other languages are morphological systems which are pronounced—according to a given syntax, of course, but that does not interest us here. Heard and spoken English, lived with on and from the inside, turns out to be an extremely homogeneous and unitarian system of phonetics which makes use of certain forms (and, I should say, in principle of any forms whatever) in order to express itself articulately. In spoken English one does not perceive, of course, the slightest difference between words whose roots are German and those from Latin. Moreover, words derived from Greek, which always sound strange in any language (even in the Latin ones which are phonetically very close to the Greek), are incorporated into the backbone of English and completely "naturalized." The same thing happens with all kinds of importations and borrowings —from Spanish, French, German, and the Indian tongues— with all neologisms, and even with the most artificial and conventional of set terms. The all-engulfing English system of phonetics makes vassals of all these forms and is served by them in perfect naturalness and indifference. It is enough to cite the geographical nomenclature of the United States: the names of cities and typographical features come from all imaginable linguistic sources, yet all sound alike, all sound "like English," without the slightest dash of foreign flavoring.

When one speaks of the difficulties of English "pronunciation," the expression is not accurate because it derives from what is true of other languages in which, given a certain form, one can pronounce it. (For this reason, ordinary "pronunciation" difficulties usually remain attached to certain specific sounds or groups of sounds. The person who tries to speak English, on the other hand, has to plunge into another phonetic system in which *all* sounds differ, even in the degree to which they are sounds, or better, in the manner they are sounded; and he has *constantly* to make movements with his mouth that he has *never* made before—that is, he has to *speak in a different fashion*.) For the same reason, when we look at the matter from another angle, taking speech as a point of departure, English-speakers do not often talk about orthography or proper writing, but rather of spelling. Only in the United States do boys and girls engage in horrifying and overwhelming spelling bees, in which the participants use up all their strength trying to remember (or guess) which are the letters used, according to custom and Webster's Dictionary, to fix certain words on paper. (And please note that to determine whether or not a given word is good English, no linguistic criterion is sought beyond its inclusion in Webster's—no matter what the word's origin.)

At this point we seem to be completely lost. The language is a tongue, above all; speech, not writing. Moreover, English forms are related to written symbols, not to sounds. Nevertheless, the English phonetic system engulfs, embraces, and impregnates every linguistic form tossed in its direction: it melts it, assimilates it, and makes it over definitively into "spoken English." English phonetics are the true "melting pot," the term customarily applied to the United States as a whole. As a result, while linguistic forms and written symbols—that is, words and writing—are perfectly coherent, the phonetic system has very little to do with either. It seems almost as though English phonetics had gone off on its own, had escaped as a system of forms from the language as a whole, had set up its own operations. Could anything be stranger? Do we need a detective to investigate linguistics in English?

I believe that it is very important to follow up, capture, and study this paradoxical situation. In my opinion, it reveals that underlying both writing and the *language* as such, there is a more radical basic phenomenon, which is the "saying" itself. Here is a vital, primary, decisive reality which more than anything else resembles the quality we call "temper" in a blade, or perhaps the distinctive "voice" of a particular group of blended instruments.

And that is what, in my belief, characterizes English as seen from the inside—honest-to-goodness English. Given this vital "temper," from the starting point of that unique "voice" people speak, listen, and understand. The essential, basic interplay is transmitted, not through writing or literature, of course, but via the tongue itself; an accidental coincidence, if you will. (Please accept this statement with a whole fistful of salt, since the evident exaggeration has no other purpose than to render this strange phenomenon more comprehensible.) What I mean is that if we were to stretch things a bit, it would be possible to *speak English* . . . in other languages. In Latin or Greek the idea could be better expressed: the Romans did not say "to speak *in* Latin" or "*in* Greek," but rather to speak Latin*ly* or Greek*ly* (*Latine, Graece*). Therefore, they also said *Hispane loqui*, which it would be ridiculous to translate as "speak *in* Spanish" since Spanish did not then exist as a language; rather, it was a question of speaking *Hispanically*, in a Spanish mode—not speaking *in* Spanish, but *à la* Spanish, with Spanish temper or tone, but *in Latin*, of course.

For this reason there are significant differences between British and American English, even though they are not linguistic (or pronunciation) differences, properly speaking, but instead differences in temper and tone. English may be spoken "Britishly" or "Americanly"; and since this temper or tone quality represents a "mode" or way of being, the effects of which are felt on the very deepest human level, investigation here might lead us through an unsuspected secret entrance to discover very significant secrets with regard to American and English society, and with respect to the English or American soul.

47 THE ARCHERS AND THE TARGET

We are, said Aristotle, like archers who are aiming at a target. The image has enjoyed the good fortune its simple elegance deserves—its elegance and, in all fairness, its insight. Each one of us takes aim at a bull's eye and shoots his vital arrow, risking his happiness and, if not his life itself, then the potential plenitude of that life. Each man has his own target (that is what we call his "vocation"); each race has a particular style of bending the bow. (And what about women? Someday someone must write an essay on the Amazons.) But before asking ourselves toward what targets our own eyes are turned, we should consider a simpler, preliminary question: at what range or distance from the target do we stand? When we bend the bow and release the arrow, what is the figure of its curved flight, from quivering cord to the last tremor of the shaft as the point goes deep into the target? Because in large part this comprises what we might call the form of life of the archer in question.

When one is engaged in experiencing in depth the life of a foreign people, there comes a day when one realizes that the thing which separates that nation most profoundly from his own is just that way of drawing the bow of life, that response in the arm, that manner of raising an eye automatically to gauge a certain distance—which is of a different range from our own. Life programs, ambitions, expectancies fall short or overshoot. Another optical system is in play, another kind of kinesthetic sensitivity: in other words, a different temper.

North Americans cause a Spaniard to lose his bearings as soon as he comes to realize what the problem is. He feels, with annoyance, that they are both undershooting and overshooting. How so? Whereas with respect to everyday details the Spaniard uses a very close focus, the American maintains a certain distance. An unanticipated visit paid to a friend, right now, simply because it seems like a good idea; a spur-of-the-moment invitation for the very same evening or, at latest, the next day; a sudden trip improvised, perhaps because of an old memory briefly revived—all of these things are customarily avoided in the United States, where forethought and preparedness are the twin regulators of a daily life which is, for that very reason, less intense and neither so chaotic nor so flavorful as our own. But when, on the other hand, it is a matter of the overall lines of that vital trajectory, the myopic Spaniard shows surprising symptoms of farsightedness: he chooses a wife once and for always, a life-long occupation or profession, a permanent position (if possible a civil service job with a pension) which offers an unlimited horizon for inactive retirement; and, almost always, a city in which he definitely fixes his residence for the indefinite future. (When he does not so establish himself it is because he has already settled in his mind on Madrid—or perhaps Barcelona—and he is wherever he is only in the sense that he is there waiting for the occasion to establish himself once and for all in the spot of his choice.)

In the United States, to the contrary, people do not look that far ahead. Almost always an American is booked up for a considerable period of time—a year or two, at least—and any other condition would seem to him intolerably unstable; but a truly long-range commitment would make him feel chained down. Jobs are frequently abandoned in search of better openings; a change in profession is not at all uncommon; a change in city of residence is a constant possibility; a change of spouse, a plausibility—and those instances suffice for my purpose here. What it boils down to is that the American aims at the middle distance, the foreground and the long-range aim both being unfamiliar to him, while the Spaniard constantly swings like a pendulum between the two extremes of close and far range.

Why is this so? It is difficult to be sure; yet, though I may be wrong, I should like to venture an interpretation: the Spaniard takes aim from a fixed upright position; the American shoots as he moves along. When one stands still, attention can be concentrated on the immediate surroundings or shifted to the far-off distance; in movement, one does not tend to look right in front of his feet (except when he is unsure of his footing) but rather a few yards ahead, and as one moves forward, his gaze advances to the same degree so that the focus of his attention shifts constantly farther ahead, leaving little leisure for looking up to contemplate the far horizon.

This situation leads to serious consequences in the lives of those concerned. The Spanish posture entails obvious risks: the propensity to inertia, to petrifying an attitude that once was authentic but has ceased to be so; monotony; persistence in a profession which once made sense, perhaps, or was expedient, but from which one should have switched in good time; fossilization of many structures; historic lack of flexibility. On the other hand, it brings the advantages of a wealth of detail, a fullness both of the moment and of the nuance, that only close vision can offer—an image than can be encountered still only in a very few places.

The greatest risk for individual life in the United States is this: an American concentrates on the middle range, as I have said; he projects into a future which, though extended, is clearly foreseeable—one, two, or perhaps even five years. On that limited horizon he sees various possibilities and he chooses the one among them which he believes to be the best. Let us suppose he chose well. In a few years another constellation of opportunities presents itself to him, and again he selects and chooses accurately, and so on through successive decades. But perhaps the life pattern formed by the total number of those choices, I mean the complete figure, the entire trajectory, is not the most preferable: in any case it is not the one preferred because it was never elected in its totality but only fragmentarily. The American professional who is offered a better position (involving more money or greater prestige) tends to accept the offer; what is more, it seems to him that he is constrained to accept it, for if he does not, he has a sense of frustration and, in some way, of wrongdoing. Perhaps the transfer will oblige him to move from his home to another city. He will no longer see as he shaves in the morning the old elm tree for which he has developed a certain fondness; as he starts out in his car, he will no longer turn the corner where the azaleas blaze in brilliant color; he will no longer meet with the group of friends with whom he is accustomed to spend occasional leisure hours. And at the end of a couple of years another fresh opportunity will take him, perfectly reasonably and expediently, to still another new scene. When he stops to take the measure of his life or when, in his declining years, he begins to think about it, he will discover— perhaps to his surprise—that he has not directed his own life; that others, assuming his consent in the matter, have been shaping it for him through the play of chance. If he had looked farther ahead, if he had pre-examined the question of his possible biography in its total configuration, perhaps he would have made other decisions. For it is not the same thing to select among the possibilities that life offers me for the next year, as to choose for the first year of thirty to come the link that represents the beginning of a long chain. The apparently unreasonable decision which I have just made, the choice of the seemingly most disadvantageous of all possibilities available for next year, may make very good sense indeed when the year in question falls into place in the long trajectory that arches toward death or the hereafter.

All of this may explain a fact which has always troubled me. American society is incredibly solid and stable, much more so than any other with which I am familiar. It is self-regulating in an astonishingly efficient manner, it corrects its own errors, it asserts itself with smooth, sure energy, it expands with singular facility, it transforms itself calmly, rhythmically, without serious blunders, without any apparent loss of coherence or continuity. Spanish society—no need to insist on it—has for centuries been the very model of instability, permanent insecurity, or blundering as a way of life. (When I choose to contrast American and Spanish society, I do not mean to imply that the characteristics I mention are only to be found associated with those countries. I select the two since they are especially clear examples of two different general tendencies.) In Spanish collective life it is difficult to make plans, one never knows which cards to hold and which to discard; the weaving and ripping out process is constant, as are improvisation and the wanton destruction of what has scarcely been begun.

However, if, on the other hand, we disregard society and look at individual lives, we are amazed at the solidarity, the sense of security, the "normalness" of Spaniards and the frequent instability and maladjustment of North Americans. Take as an example the experience of the Spanish Civil War; it was not only atrocious as wars go, but it was complicated as well by all possible forms of insecurity, suffering, and crisis. Nevertheless it is awesome to note the vital resiliency with which Spaniards assimilated into normality such a tremendous accumulation of hideous happenings. Whereas in other lands, military service, the sufferings of those behind the lines, or even isolated cases of persecution sufficed to unleash epidemics of suicides, innumerable instances of psychic disturbances, and even occasional annihilation of personality, such reactions were unbelievably scarce in Spain. I cannot cite comparable statistics. However, it is not a question of figures but of the evidence offered in actual Spanish reality. I will not aver that certain negative factors did not also contribute to that portentous result—among them a certain insensitivity, a tendency towards over-simplifying, a reliance on routine habit—but I doubt that these traits account for more than part of the situation I am trying to describe.

Spanish marriages are rarely broken. A man and his wife may come almost to blows three times a day, yet they need each other and they need that outlet; even if they could, it would not occur to them to seek a divorce. The doctor who every day of his life curses the hour he enrolled in medical school, the professor who sighs to himself at the beginning of every class, the military officer who has dragged along through the monotony of years and years of garrison duty, the housewife who thinks of domestic chores as an earthly version of Purgatory: none for a moment seriously considers going off to set up a farm or an industry, becoming an engineer, a business man, or an actress.

In American society—placid, prosperous, secure, and rich in possibilities though it may be—cases of individual maladjustment are numerically significant: those who must seek compensation in alcohol are a rising problem. And it is no rarity for a person to become unhinged, whereas in Spain too many lives are firmly hinged onto structures that threaten to fall into ruin, and that the technologists regularly denounce at least three times a month.

I believe the explanation is that the American aims at a middle distance which represents precisely the range of collective life, of society as a whole. At that range it is possible to foresee, to anticipate, to think ahead in concrete terms, to rely on one another; this is the structure which makes co-operation possible—a quality known in Spain only by name. On the other hand certain small, subtle details of the immediate foreground are overlooked. An excellent new project ahead, a most pleasant home, a new car in the fall, a well thought-out change in political affiliation in the coming elections, and, in a few years, a son at Yale and a daughter at Wellesley—well and good, but what about this very afternoon? No one has taken the trouble to provide a café where a couple of hours can be whiled away in the company of good friends whose presence is urgently needed at times as a tonic for the spirit. And a life program, the entire trajectory of an individual life: if it is blurred, composed of fragments, never prefigured in its totality—what reflection will we see when with our whole soul we look at ourselves in the mirror?

Someday someone should inquire seriously into what contrasting elements make livable, sometimes intoxicatingly so, that often bankrupted reality, that impossible medium on which no one can rely, that nonsensical enigma which oscillates between weird distortion and utter delight—collective life in Spain.

48   REFLECTIONS ON
THE UNITED STATES

The thing that is wrong with talking about the United States is that one is not sure just *what* one is talking about. They are lumped together as an entity, yet there is a disturbing plural in the country's name. Moreover, in that name the word "state" appears, and it is doubtful that the state is what most concerns us. We speak of "an American" or "Americans" but it is questionable whether we are referring to individuals or to something else. Reading Henry Steele Commager's book *The American Mind* has acted as a stimulant for me and precipitated several reflections which more than anything else represent questions that I want to ask myself in not too loud a voice. Commager's book, published by Yale University Press in 1950, is one of the major contributions of recent years towards an understanding of the United States. The author, a professor of history, manages a copious amount of material interestingly and with great skill. He has an amazing familiarity with everything that has happened in his country, with all that has been thought and said. If perhaps by any chance, like the good American he is, he errs on the side of excessive wealth of detail, nevertheless, again like a good American, he generously offers many riches to the reader, sharing with him his mother-lode, an excellent bibliography which is exciting both to the erudite investigator and to the explorer.

European that I am, and Spaniard to boot, so much wealth frightens me a little. I am fearful of not handling it properly, of letting it run through my fingers. Even more than that, I am at a loss as to where to put it, where to deposit that fortune, the many varied and complex pieces of knowledge which he entrusts to us. And I wonder whether this perplexity may not represent the expression of a decisive, critical problem, the formulation of a question which must be clarified. When one speaks of the United States, what is one talking about? Yes, to my mind, this should be the first point to investigate, perhaps the most difficult point.

One of the first things that surprises every observer of American society is the relative but evident uniformity of the whole country despite its tremendous size and the variety of its inhabitants' origins. "Who unites the United States?" is a question I asked myself shortly after arriving in the country for the first time. Commager undertakes to consider this problem from the very first page of his book. For him, inheritance and environment are the two factors responsible for producing the American character. Both are complex and diverse, thinks Commager. The inheritance, he emphasizes, is not only British but also European; it cannot be confined to the seventeenth and eighteenth centuries but goes back two thousand years because, although the United States sprang from England, its culture and its institutions are rooted in Greece, Rome, and Palestine. In a sense, all of this is correct and evident, but if one tries to grapple with the problem at closer range, several difficulties arise. Commager notes immediately that despite the similarity in institutions, an American has a hard time feeling socially "at home" in England; and, further, that second generation immigrant Americans—from so many other racial stocks—feel themselves to be complete foreigners in Italy, France, or Germany. Since therefore the inheritance was so heterogeneous and the product so homogeneous, Commager affirms that we must consider the environment as the decisive factor. He adds—perhaps pressing his point a trifle—that the environment also is varied, that the American continent is as multiform as Europe, but that in spite of this, the environment has never represented a serious barrier to uniformity. He concludes that it has not been the "particular environments" which have determined American character and personality but rather "the whole of the American environment." He hastens to explain the latter in terms of a sense of spaciousness, an invitation to mobility, an atmosphere of independence, a kind of incitement towards optimism and enterprise.

Let us meditate for a moment on what these ideas imply. It is slightly dangerous to attempt to derive "character" from heredity and environment; in the first place, because we are obliged to pose the problem with respect to *individuals* (for there is no other direct referent possible when we speak of the effects of heredity and environment) and because when we start to consider *social* realities, we are consequently obliged to reduce the phenomena in the last instance to a multiplicity of individuals, running the evident risk of overlooking their essential peculiarity and uniqueness. In the second place, it is dangerous because we thus omit consideration of other factors which could be even more significant, perhaps for people as individuals and certainly for collective forms of life. Difficulties do indeed pile up as soon as we try to avail ourselves of this conceptual scheme. When the statement is made that the United States' inheritance is not limited to England and the centuries of colonialism, but rather that it includes all of Europe and goes back two millenia to Greece, Rome, and Israel, is the word "inheritance" not being used in two senses? Clearly, the first colonizers of the United States came from England, that is to say from an English *society*. Does the fact that England contained within itself the intellectual, artistic, political, and religious heritage of Greece, Rome, and the Orient authorize the establishment of an analogous relationship between American society and that of the Greeks, Romans, or Jews? If we are analyzing the heredity of an individual, we shall doubtless find in him traces of the entire past from which he springs. But if we are speaking of the implantation of a heritage in a given society, this is a very different matter, and we should distinguish meticulously among: the society of which that given society is an off-shoot; that from which the mother society derives; and other societies from which the given society has absorbed certain abstract *elements* that have been passed along from one to another in the chain.

On the other hand, when particular environments (or circumstances) are set in opposition to the whole of the American environment (or what we might call the totality of American circumstances), very diverse things are lumped together—some of them extremely hard to reduce to environmental or circumstantial factors. If it is true that there are physical (or semi-physical) elements, such as the sense of spaciousness, others are clearly social, such as the atmosphere of independence; and still others, such as the invitation to mobility or the incitement to optimism and enterprise, though they may be considered as circumstantial or ambient for each individual (in the sense that he finds them in the social climate surrounding him), when viewed from the standpoint of society itself they appear rather as collective *goals*, as guidelines for human vocations.

I believe that the first thing to be made clearer is the collective *who* that we recognize as bearing the name of the United States. Put in other words, who or what is the subject of the collective life which represents the country's history? But scarcely is this sentence written when fresh doubts assail us. Of which country are we speaking? The one that stretches from the Atlantic to the Pacific, from the Great Lakes to the Caribbean? But all this territory has not been part of the country for very long: is today's nation the same country that less than two centuries ago declared itself independent of England and took the name of the United States? Do the sparse four million inhabitants of the seventeen eastern states which made up the Union in 1790 represent the same country as the hundred and sixty million of the present forty-eight states? It is not a question of territory, of course. It is not a matter of borders. Nor has it to do with that original population in terms of the component individuals and their genealogical descendants, because since the Revolution more than forty million foreigners—from all over the world—have entered the United States, and during long periods in its history population upsurge has been much more the result of immigration than of what is called "vegetative growth." Well, what is it then we are dealing with?

Literally, we are discussing a society (that is, a unit of historic coexistence) not defined by a territory nor by a population in the sense of a particular grouping of individuals, but rather by a *system of common sanctions*—the usages, beliefs, ideas, value judgments, and aims that each individual encounters and has to deal with—that form a certain configuration which can justly be called a *social structure*.† The United

† See my book *La estructura social*, Madrid, 1955, (Second edition, Buenos Aires, 1958) Obras, VI.

States has constituted a society which has had the *same* social structure (though subject to historic change, as is natural) since the days of Independence and probably considerably before. That society has been the subject of American history: not a variable and ever-enlarging territory, nor a mere "totality" of individuals who are as individuals completely different, each one literally the child of his parents and only partially British in origin.

In my opinion, the singular homogeneity of the United States may be explained in this way: the system of common sanctions characteristic of American society has been imposed upon each and all of the people who have entered that society; it has converted them into members *of that society*, regardless of what they may have been before they belonged to it. How was this possible? How has the United States managed to be the melting pot for so many men of different races, religions, languages, and customs? And why has nothing similar occurred in other lands—to take the most compelling example, in Spanish America?

I have always felt that the United States is a country defined by a mysterious and tremendous force: solitude. "The American soul is composed of loneliness," I wrote, shortly after my first arrival in the country and as soon as I had had some direct experience with American life. I myself was not then aware that that insight was of so basic a nature, nor that it would explain so many other things. But in order to use that key, it is necessary first to explain the concept itself, to analyze the components of North America's multi-faceted solitude. We have to begin at the beginning because that is the foundation of the whole process: the first American colonists were loners; they were men who had been left alone, set apart. Alone, apart from what? Apart from their mother society, from England in general. The large majority of the seventeenth-century colonists—at least those who influenced events—were dissenters, objectors, often fugitives. They intended to preserve a tie, an allegiance to England and particularly to the Crown, but they were leaving to fashion a *new* life, alone, on their own. They expected to remain as colonists: not to conquer, perhaps become rich or at least enjoy adventure, and return. No, they were going to live far from Europe, alone—I reiterate—accompanied only by the nostalgia that led them to give old country names to the new lands and recently founded towns. The Spanish conquistadors, first and foremost (and note the emphasis) were men going to the Indies (the customary expression was "passing" to the Indies), probably to return thereafter to Trujillo, Cáceres, Seville, or Avila; at least they dreamed of returning, and many actually did. The English colonists *departed* for America, with the firm intention of establishing themselves there. Once arrived in New England, Pennsylvania, or Virginia, they looked around and thought "we - us - ours." That "us" did not take in England; it meant "we alone," never "we English" as Cortés, Pizarro, Balboa, Ponce de León, or Almagro would have said "we Spaniards."

They were alone in yet another more radical way: in addition to being cut off from England, the colonists were alone in America. The Spaniards were not: they were together with the Indians, surrounded by them, coexisting with them in all kinds of relationships—criminal acts and evangelization, looting and the *encomienda*, exploitation and the universities. In North America there were few Indians: those there were did not mix with the colonists; the two groups almost always fought each other—and even then from a distance. The Spaniards, united by a previous bond as they confronted the Indians, and precisely because they lived with and among them, attempted to incorporate them into the Spanish social structure with its religion, language, customs, and values. Moreover, in the more developed countries, especially Mexico and Peru, they encountered other types of social structures which they had to confront with their own *previous* pattern, the

Spanish mold. Only in the countries at the extreme southern part of the continent, where there were relatively few Indians, did a situation prevail that was analogous to that of the North American colonies. For that reason, Argentina, Uruguay, and Chile are the only Hispanic-American countries that *somewhat* resemble the United States.

In the third place, whereas the Spanish conquest spread out towards many very different points all over the American continent, from the Mississippi to the La Plata River and even farther south, the lands held by the northern colonists were for long years confined to a relatively small and close-bound territory which was to stretch and expand cautiously and slowly, that is, step by step from its own base. When the Spaniards arrived at a place some three to five thousand kilometers distant from their starting point, they entered *as Spaniards*, virtually enlarging and extending Spanish society so as to include that spot. That is why they founded cities in the image and likeness of those of Castile, Extremadura, or Andalusia, with their Plaza Mayor; why they immediately began to stroll through those cities, conversing, living in company with others, and talking—probably about Spain. For the same reasons, the courts of the Viceroys attempted to imitate the Court of Valladolid or of Madrid, and colonial court life was principally concerned with Lope de Vega's plays, Góngora's metaphors, la Calderona's dramatic interpretations, Villamediana's latest barbs and witticisms, the decisions of Count de Aranda, and the new ideas circulating among the young gentlemen of Azcoitia.* Could anyone imagine the passengers on the Mayflower, William Penn, or Benjamin Franklin in a

---

* Luis de Argote y Góngora (1561–1627), eminent Spanish Baroque poet who created a new style (Gongorism) similar to Euphuism in England, rich in imagery, conceits, and poetic imagination.

la Calderona—see previous note.

Villamediana—see previous note.

Pedro Abarca de Bolea, Count of Aranda, (1718–1799), Prime Minister under Charles III, author of a number of reforms; greatly influenced by the French Enlightenment—Trans.

similar frame of mind? In North America *a society* was constituted, in isolation both from Europe and from the natives (and the emphasis here lies equally upon the word "society" and upon the fact that it was one, united); a society which then expanded, grew, and in good time incorporated other small groups representing the nuclei of Spanish, French, and Dutch colonial settlements that formed the minority elements in the American body social.

The Declaration of Independence of 1776 is fraught with meaning if it is carefully read. "When in the course of human events," it begins, "it becomes necessary for one people to dissolve the political bonds . . . ." Note that the English says *one* people, using the number instead of the article, emphasizing unity. And then it goes on to speak of "our British brethren" whom it reproaches with being "deaf to the voice of justice and of *consanguinity*."

American solitude manifests itself in a fourth decisive fashion: once that unitarian society has been constituted, with its system of usages, beliefs, ideas, values, and aims, only then does immigration begin to assume importance. From Independence to 1840, that is in more than sixty years, the total number of immigrants did not amount to 400,000; whereas, from 1850 to 1930, *every year* several hundred thousand foreigners entered the United States—and in some years the figure rose well over a million. What does this mean? It means that while American society was in the process of formation, individual members of that society could continue to say "we alone." The social structure of the United States originated in an isolated, limited, and homogeneous world; and here is where that famous quality of homogeneity comes in. When the "others" arrived, immigrants from abroad, they entered *alone*—and I mean as individuals, each looking out for himself —*into American society* and were initiated one by one into the system of sanctions which constitutes that society.

Why not start with the principal component of that system, the most obvious and yet most problematical of all: language. The United States is uniformly an English-speaking country: the remains of Spanish, French, and Dutch in some regions are just that—vestigial remains penetrated and dominated by the absolute power of English. How can we explain the fact that English is the only tongue in a country made up of individuals who in such enormous proportions have spoken other languages before? And we must not forget the tremendous difficulty of English, which as a spoken language often presents an insuperable barrier—to the point where there are many immigrants who never manage to master it to a passably proper degree and for whom it becomes a lifelong obsession. American society was originally English in character, linguistically English; any individual upon entering that society ran up against that vigorous primary demand. The number of newcomers is not important: it means nothing that millions of Americans were originally speakers of Italian, German, or Spanish. In each instance, it was a case of an individual confronting an established society, and naturally the latter imposed its authority. If immigration of non-Anglo-Saxons had taken place in the seventeenth or eighteenth centuries, other linguistically distinct societies would have been constituted, with individuals grouping together according to their language communities. But widespread immigration occurred only after the coming into existence of American society, of what we call the United States. The social structure, in this area as in all other matters, gradually transformed the individual who became part of it. But could they not have gathered together somehow, seeking the warmth of a common language and kindred customs? To some extent, this did happen. In the poorer sections of New York, in the slums, communities of Italians, Puerto Ricans, Polish Jews, and Armenians did form and still continue to form. Along those streets the respective languages are spoken, national dishes are prepared and eaten, the old abandoned society is revived and relived. But what do these manifestations signify with respect to the entire social body of the United States? They are more or less parallel to the first stomachs of the ruminants; the "foreign" quarters are organs for the digestion of immigrants before they are incorporated into the American organism. After a few years the foreigner passes (as an individual) into American society in the strictest sense: he abides by its code, he speaks English or near-English, he uproots himself from his past and its picturesque appurtenances. For example, he often changes his name from a Slavic surname to Watson, or transforms a Cohen into an O'Brien, or takes off the final "i" in a name that revealingly terminates in "elli." In almost every case, and this usually happens in the second generation, which has grown up speaking English, he forgets the language of his forefathers and he inserts himself into the social structure of the United States.

Nor does the role of solitude in the gestation of United States society end there. American life has offered and offers now a minimum of conviviality. For decades Americans lived in isolation, in tiny urban settlements, on farms or ranches, amid forests, near mines or trading posts, plotting roads and railways, fighting the Indians, pushing back the frontier despite those Indians and a hostile nature. They have not been accustomed to talking a great deal, they have been limited to the family circle or other small groups—the team and the family, two great forces in present day American society. They have experienced the sense of solidarity felt by lonely men who are gladdened by the presence of a fellow being (at some out of the ordinary festivity) and they have given each other a helping hand. They have also supported society because it meant company, solace, and strength. Power also: on one hand, cooperation and the development of techniques; on the other, the struggle against unsocial behavior, excesses, crime. Americans have had to support society, or better, its code, and they have become accustomed to referring to that

code—accurately but imperfectly—as the Law. The Law, that
is, that does actually prevail, the Law with a capital L with
all its strength, vigor, and sway, not a legal text nor a piece of
juridical theory. The capital L of the American Law comprehended the Colt revolver—the "Peacemaker"—and the
Winchester rifle; therefore American law has had little to do
with jurisprudence. As the frontiers of the United States were
pushed back toward the west, the north, or the south, the
Law followed just behind: in other words, behind individual
Americans came American society with all its demands. Individuals constituted the reconnaissance patrols, the ad-
vancers, the pioneers of society. Figuring significantly among
the accusations made by the Declaration of Independence
against George III of England was this one: ". . . and [he]
has endeavoured to bring on the inhabitants of our frontiers,
the merciless Indian Savages, whose known rule of warfare,
is an undistinguished destruction of all ages, sexes and conditions." This was an alien act because it was beyond the pale
according to all existing codes. Afterwards, Americans reacted very similarly to the outlaw, the man who lives outside
the Law, or, more precisely, the man who refuses to acknowledge the existence of society as a whole.

All this may help us understand the hotly debated issue of
conformism vs. nonconformity in America. Americans are
entrenched conformists, so the saying goes; yet on the other
hand, they have always wanted to be independent, dissenting,
singular. Malicious spirits may suggest that they are tolerant
about matters which do not greatly concern them, and rigidly
authoritarian when their interests are at stake. I believe that
the problem is both simpler and more complex. Among the
forces that constitute American society, one is the right to
dissent, to nonconformity, to independence of choice; when
an American dissents, he is acting in accord with one of the
principal substantive forces within his social structure. But if
his dissent involves a negation of his society as such, when he

fails to conform not to this or to that but to the dictates of the code supported by *American society* in all its solidarity, then that society falls upon him with all its weight, not excluding the Colt or its modern equivalent. In other words, an American dissents *from within*, seeking the support of society in order to oppose some segment of its structure. From that standpoint, there is almost nothing immune to dissent.

Using this perspective, it seems as though we should be able to clarify many aspects of American life; for example, the rhythm of its history. No one doubts that the rhythm is a fast one, but why it is so rapid is a clouded question. Usually people refer vaguely to American dynamism, to individuals' activity and energy, to their progressivism, their lack of a sense of history, to the fact that—unlike Europeans who live so much in the past—they are decidedly oriented toward the future. It does not seem to me that these explanations are sufficiently precise. These characteristics or psychic qualities have appeared before and appear presently in other societies, and they are lacking in many individual Americans, some of whom are, for instance, fairly phlegmatic. Progressivism, after all, was a European invention, and Europe has lived on the capital of that myth for some two hundred years. With regard to futurism, there is scarcely another quality which so defines Europe, a continent that throughout its long history has employed much more imagination than America and has erred in the direction of utopianism and a fondness for the Greek Kalends—that is, for detaching itself from the present and resolutely installing itself in the future. It is precisely for that reason that Europe has needed its past, for only by availing oneself of the past is it possible to project ahead; only a long memory enables one to imagine ahead into a distant future. And now that the United States is beginning to try long-range projections, Americans realize that they need more substance to their past and they are seeking at a lively clip to flesh it out. Insofar as a sense of history is concerned, they have it and very vividly, even though they bring it to bear only on their *own* past which is, of course, of short duration. Commager, in order to substantiate the American's lack of historical sense, asserts that sons of the men who heard Indian war cries and saw the herds of buffalo used to play at "Cowboy-and-Indian" as English children did at being knights of King Arthur's Round Table. But this instance seems to me to demonstrate instead a very sharp sense of history, a feeling for the tenuousness and instability of the present, a tendency towards the "Historization" of life, the attitude that whatever is not part of the actual present is remote past history; whereas the truly a-historic mentality considers lengthy periods of many decades and even centuries past as the stuff of "present day" affairs.†

I believe that the accelerated rhythm of American history must be accounted for in another way. Specifically, it would be well to start by studying the dynamics of the generations in the United States. The situation there with respect to generations is, however, extremely peculiar: on one hand there is a society in the strictest sense, with a system of well-defined rules and values, a social body which should be subject to the rhythm of the generations and the succession of the customary fifteen-year time periods. On the other hand, especially between 1850 and 1930, there is also the constant influx of adult male foreigners emigrating from other societies and bringing along with them the "level" of their respective generational scales. What happens then? That is the problem that only an exacting investigation can resolve. Do individuals adapt themselves to the American code from the very beginning and lodge themselves within a given generation? Or do these numerous individual impacts modify the rhythm of

† See in this regard the first chapter of my book *El método histórico de las generaciones*, Madrid, 1949 (*Obras*, VI). [Published in the United States as *Generations: A Historical Method*, trans. Harold C. Raley (University of Alabama Press, 1970)—Ed.]

certain generations in America? It would be risky and difficult to take a position without benefit of a meticulous, empirical investigation, particularly since people in the United States talk a great deal about generations (in Commager's book there are constant references) without anyone, to my knowledge, having written a line about the theory of generations, of their whys and wherefores, or of what they are. It seems to me, therefore, that we are far from being able to give a satisfactory answer to these questions.

But however it may work out, whether the generations operate on one scale or another, the thing that is abundantly clear is why the change from one generation to another is much greater than in Europe—at least it has been up to the two last generations; why, in short, the rate of change is more rapid even though the steps taken are of the same measure—the long giant-steps that cover a great deal of space. The reason seems to me to be the following: the individuals who make up a normal generation in a country are first children, then young people, next mature folk, and finally old people. However, in the United States an enormous proportion of those making up each generation have been adults who were incorporated at the stage of full historic effectiveness, men who in their countries of origin had lived through the passive stages of development and formation, who had left their inertia behind them, carrying to the New World their dynamic energies and their historically operative strengths. Someone may remark that then the same thing would happen in all countries affected by immigration, formed by successive waves of adults arriving at their coasts. And indeed that is so, providing always that the other all-important condition also is fulfilled: that of the preexistence of a *society*, of a preformed social structure into which each individual is incorporated. Because if there is no such society, if the social structure is in the process of being created, struggling with tendencies toward separatism, unsociability, disorientation, then this battle absorbs so much energy that its drain compensates for and even exceeds the strength brought in by the numbers of adult immigrants. Each time, however, that both conditions exist in a given place, an extremely accelerated historical rhythm is demonstrable.

This suffices to show how delicate a topic the United States represents. The American social structure (in the sense in which I have explained it) would not be too difficult to study, but there has been no such investigation. The enormous efforts of American sociology have concentrated precisely on *everything else*, on social content of all kinds, leaving us fairly well in the dark on the structure itself, the context in which such content becomes meaningful. Few projects would be so absorbing as a thorough investigation into the United States' social structure: into its historic "who"; the dynamics of its generations, in the sense that I have just outlined; the codification and evolution of its system of reigning values and sanctions; the function and the content of beliefs, ideas, and opinions—three very different things which are often confused, at least when taken in pairs; the forms assumed by its individual and collective aspirations; the state of happiness in the United States—as much with respect to aspirations as to actual reality; the role of the government and the other power organisms; the order of social classes, the principle behind them and their resistance to change; the actual state of human relations, beginning with the concrete figures of a man and a woman, considering interindividual relations (love, marriage, family, friendship) and arriving finally at the external forms through which the orientation of a way of life expresses itself —houses, cities; the deepest sensibilities of an American confronting his life, his vital equilibrium between happiness and ill fortune, his hopes and his despair.

Much is already known about all these things; Commager's book gives ample proof of that. Perhaps more is known than is necessary, but less than would be truly sufficient, because what is known is not fully and sufficiently known. What I mean is that the deficiency is not so much a matter of what is or is not known but has to do rather with the mode or category of that knowledge. Human reality is historic and it is systematic: it has a structure which is intrinsically an historical one; besides, it is, on one hand, universal and accessible to analysis, but on the other, empiric and open to cognition only via specific, concrete considerations. When speaking of ideas in the United States, when tracing American history, the question must be posed: "What is the function of these ideas —and of ideas in general—in American life and in each generation?" Might it not turn out that the answer is very different from what we supposed, and that the function that ideas have is far from that they serve in Europe, for example? Are what are called "ideas" really that, and do they function as such? How does religion fit into the United States' way of life? So long as all that is not clear, statistics are useless. What good does it do us to know the margin of sexual "liberty" in the United States so long as we do not know whether, for example, liberty really enters into it; so long as we are not certain to what extent other factors intervene—elements such as loneliness and the desire for company, the friendly reaction towards a fellow human being, the promiscuity of adolescents in families with no domestic servants, the lack of conversation in American life—all aspects evidently quite different from each other?

Nothing human is intelligible except in the context of life as a whole in all its dimensions. And human life is not only individual but also collective, social and socio-historical. In addition to noting the analytic structure of human life and its empirical framework, it is necessary to formulate clearly the social structure of each of the units of history. In Europe we have a more or less accurate idea of our structures. When a European arrives in the United States and observes a society at once so different and so similar, the problem is a serious one. For in one sense American society greatly resembles society in Europe: it is made up of Europeans, its "inheritance" in fact is the same as ours as far back as memory serves. But in another sense it is radically different, because it has a different structure which the resemblances tend to disguise. This is the reason that it is so difficult when one is speaking of the United States to know truly what one is talking about. Yet it is certainly worth the trouble. I mean both things are: speaking of the United States, and, of course, knowing what one is talking about.

PART TWO

THE SIXTIES

Translated from the Spanish* by
Harold C. Raley

* First published as *Analisis de los Estados Unidos* (Madrid: Guadarrama, 1968).

It was exactly sixteen years ago today that I came to live for the first time in this country where I am now writing. It was the same time of day, mid-afternoon. There were masses of greenery about me, thick trees like those I see now. I wondered with some uneasiness what "living" in that new setting was going to mean. It was the twenty-first of September, 1951. Harry Truman was President; there was war in Korea, but there was a deep peace all about me.

There are places and countries that compel me to write about them. There are cities or nations I often visit and which are very dear to me that do not move me to say anything, or if they do, it is only years and years later. This is not a question of my interest, nor even of the difficulty of interpretation. It is something else, or better, several things. The United States moved me to take my pen (to be exact, my typewriter) from the very first weeks. I was perfectly aware that I could not know what the United States was at that time, but I had no doubt that what I was seeing and experiencing was something unique, and that if I did not communicate that sensation then, it would never again be the same, never again fully as real. "The first impression is the one that counts," we say in Spanish, which is a language of extremes. I prefer to say with more moderation: "The first impression counts."

The method I used then was this: *impressionism and analysis.* It was to tell what I was seeing as I saw it, but without forgetting that one sees not only—nor even primarily—with his eyes. Does one see through thought then? It is also true that one does not think with the mind alone. One thinks and sees with his life. And I was living in a unique and inimitable way: as a newcomer. I was seeing the United States through

Spain, through Spanish eyes; but I was living a life that was beginning to probe toward the inner character of the country. Everything I found, every word I heard, every human gesture that concerned me, seemed to appear against the backdrop of American life. All this had to be placed within this background in order to avoid the greatest untruth: truth that is merely factual. Within this background of American life had to be placed each look, each conversation, each hope, each rejection, each emotion, each unhappiness, each illusion. All these things had to be made to "live" also in the United States. If possible, this total reality had to be reconstructed almost in every sentence I wrote; or if not, at least it had to be pointed out so that the reader might find it.

All these impressions came together in a book, *Los Estados Unidos en escorzo*.‡ Written in separate chunks without any deliberate aim, it turned out to be one of my best organized books, probably because it was based on the strongest of systems: that of life itself. I wrote it almost entirely in a year, delaying the ending until, back in Spain, I might look at the United States from afar. In 1955 from California other notions were added which complemented the initial impression without changing it. Since that time I have never taken up the theme again. I have not continued my series of writings on this country, although it often appears in those of my works not connected with it.

Many years have passed: the space of an entire generation. My eyes are no longer those of that earlier time. I have done and experienced many things—and one of those experiences has been the United States. I have seen countries, cities, and people I did not know. I have had experiences that were unknown to me then. The horizon of my life is now quite different. And above all, the plane from which I view life has changed.

Moreover, where does the world stand now? Where is the

‡ "The Fifties," Part I of the present volume—Ed.

United States today? So many men have died; so many have appeared on the stage of history; so many fond hopes have fled; so many things have happened. The books everybody was talking about in those days have perhaps been forgotten, and others are the current topic. The girls who were my first pupils have daughters who could almost be my students. When I first came to the United States there was no television, no rockets or artificial satellites. Eisenhower was only a general; nobody talked of Kennedy and Johnson. Computers were in their infancy. There was some timid talk of integration, and the Negroes themselves did not dream of what would have seemed incredible to them at the time. Faulkner, a "Southern Gentleman," was asking the North to have patience.

Year after year I have returned to the United States; to the North, the South, the East, and the West. I have been in the big cities and in the small, remote towns. I have talked at length with eminent men—Adlai Stevenson, to name one who has since passed on—and with workers repairing my telephone or the heating, with professors and doctors, with newspapermen and directors of foundations, with countless cab drivers, with boys and girls, with Jesuit and Protestant theologians. I have seen the ramshackle airports of La Guardia and Newark transformed into splendid magnificent structures. Propeller-driven planes have been replaced by jets. I have seen great buildings demolished with enormous iron balls; and from one trip to another, new avenues have appeared.

Is it not perhaps time to look again at the United States and to write more about it? If an entire generation has passed, for the United States and for me, is it not time to ask what has happened? Tacitus said that, "Fifteen years is a long time in human life." If this was true in the calm, untechnical world of Rome, when men wrote with gravers and spoke slowly with Latin hyperbaton in the Senate and Forum, while the Legions marched step by step over the Imperial roadways, what has happened in the accelerated rhythm of our world? What has taken place here where everything changes with incredible speed? Are these United States where I am writing and where I seem to be, the same country to which I came in a Constellation (by comparison, one could almost say I arrived by stagecoach) one afternoon sixteen years ago?

Everything is different. At first glance, there is more of everything, and everything has grown. There are more and more Americans; they produce more, spend more, save more. They travel more and more miles across the face of the earth and through the air. More and more travelers cross the Atlantic. The numbers of those traveling around the world are almost legion. The number of university students is now approaching five million. And there are more accidents, more Negro unrest, and more whites involved in the movement; there are more automobiles on the highways and more airplanes in the sky—and what is worse, more on the ground. I crossed the Atlantic in seven hours and a half, but after landing the plane had to wait forty-five minutes before getting to the terminal, making its way painfully through the jets blocking gigantic Kennedy Airport. It was like trying to get through the crowd after a show. It took longer to get to the terminal after landing than it does to fly from Madrid to the Portuguese coast.

Electronic computers are transforming the world more than any other technical device. Many more than half of all these are in the United States, and the rest are scattered throughout the world. This means that North America is changing from a country run "by hand" to a reality disturbingly organized by perforated cards that mysteriously manipulate, order, identify, and mobilize everything.

If it is true that human reality is a reality in expansion, this is literally true and obvious from the outset in the United

States. There are possibly more and greater changes here in a year than in a decade elsewhere. If the sixteen years of my experience in this country are placed one after another in a sequence, the result is somewhat chilling.

Yet it happens that when I arrive in the United States, when I begin to look around me, when I begin to get settled and collected and start to examine the outer world about me (life is an inwardness that creates an outwardness for itself), I begin to feel again and anew the same pulsation, the same rhythmic beat, the same familiar voices, the same flavor of life. Why this feeling? Is it the trees? Is it the squirrels climbing their trunks, jumping from branch to branch, seeking and calmly gnawing a nut, or asking passersby for one but cutely rubbing their paws or frolicking in the grass? Is it this surge of nature, quickly reappearing with its great rivers, its forests, its endless plains, and which before all the technical contrivances—airports, highways, bridges, dams, blast furnaces, factories, skyscrapers, cranes with arched necks, endless trains loaded with goods, great piping—seems to say: "Do not believe it"? Is it this five o'clock flight homeward, to the company (and solitude) of the family in their isolated house, to the lawn to be mowed or snow to be shoveled? Can it be the unchanging businessmen, dressed in dark suits and small hats, with their briefcases or attaché cases, who with the same gestures rush year after year to their suburban trains, or who gather with the same good will in hotel lobbies every time a convention or a college class reunion calls them? Is it the churches that bring an inexorable pause on Sunday mornings, holding everything in abeyance so that people may dress calmly, gather frugally, hear Mass or the service, sing hymns, and silently slip envelopes with checks into the collection plates? Is it the young girls who go out smilingly toward life every morning, sure in their hope, without that deceiving feeling, the disillusioning mirage, of having seen it all?

I do not know. I cannot say. I only see that in the midst of the enormous and innumerable changes, the same *flavor of life* reappears. The United States, although quite different, has the same "savor of life" for me as in 1951. At times I think that *everything* changes so much in order that the *country itself not change*, that nothing is "the same" so that the United States can go on being "the same." For if only a certain thing were to change, if only a few elements of the whole were to vary, this would cause a *disfiguration*. The living organism, the human body, the face, for example, retains its "sameness" for a long time. We can recognize a person because almost everything is changed in that person, because the cells are no longer the same, because that person's metabolism continually replaces certain elements with others, and in doing so, remakes the same fabric and rebuilds the same structure.

None of the countries I know in Europe has experienced in ten or in fifteen years so much change. Yet none seems so unchanged in its inner substance. Spain, which makes a profession of not changing and which has even claimed at times to have anticipated and captured the future, as one would cage a bird, is a country incomparably different from what it was a decade ago. It is disturbingly different, because so many things do *not* change with the others that there is a danger of losing and altering the total appearance, of letting whatever gives it form and personality slip away.

The United States has a rare ability for organization. It has made "Americans" of the human materials that Europe and other continents poured into its territories. Now it is incorporating all the gigantic historical change of these last decades, all the unlikely technical transformation, into a simple and yet complex plan, a plan endued with an inner life and which is capable of bringing the diverse elements together in a historical project so original it conceals its very uniqueness.

This capacity which life has for internal organization has always amazed me. We take an egg that happens to be a crocodile egg. This seemingly inert reality lying motionless before us has within it a fabulous ability and power to organize and transform this bit of matter of which it is made and to convert itself into that powerful and horrendous thing we call a crocodile. We could crush it; we could violently interrupt at any time the process of its transformation. But unless we do, the egg inexorably will be a crocodile. As long as it lives, an unstoppable power causes it to impose this particular pattern.

Human matters are different, but they still contain this same organizing power. Yet this power does not come primarily from the past, but rather is aimed toward what is yet to be; it is not impelled by a genetic current, but drawn by some ideal aim, by a calling, by an individual and historical vocation. Human reality is stirred and moved toward its destiny by some nameless love.

This is what astonishes me most about the United States. Its youth, its power, the speed of its development—or if you prefer, the rapidity of its projection toward a future image which is being drawn over the map of its vast territories—all permit us to see this project and to read the program of organization it is following. Although it seems incredible, almost no one sees this (although a catalog could be made of the incredible things that are happening).

The trouble is that when we try to read these things, the letters are different; all the elements and usual signs uncovered in our scrutiny have changed. With new signs, with new elements, with a different alphabet, the United States is writing its own secret message. It is trying to express that impulse that moves it toward what at some moment of its history it felt it was destined to become.

50 WHITE AND BLACK

THE BLACK ELEMENT AND
THE NEGRO PROBLEM

Among the more visible changes in the United States in the last fifteen years is undoubtedly the one affecting the Negro population of the country—some twenty million people, a little more than ten per cent of two hundred million Americans. What is being said of Negroes today cannot be compared with what was said in 1950. Neither is there any comparison between the way Negroes felt then and their situation today. Many people suppose, in Europe and other countries—even in the United States—that the Negro problem has "worsened." I am not sure this is the most accurate expression. I would say rather that the problem has "ripened," that it really has become a problem.

So as not to lose ourselves, not to err dangerously, we should speak first of other things. During the nineteenth century, timidly in the first third, insistently after 1848; and overwhelmingly in recent years, people have talked about the "social question," a topic mockingly echoed even in *La verbena de la Paloma* in Madrid.* Does this mean that earlier there were no social problems, that the situation of workers and farmers was comfortable, decent, dignified, and acceptable? Not at all; in many ways they had always been worse off, at least for long periods of time. What happened during the nineteenth century was that the condition and situation of the working and farming classes of European society came

---

* A popular late-nineteenth century *zarzuela*, or Spanish operetta—Trans.

to the fore, rose to the social surface, and became the object of theoretical consideration and practical action, including direct action. A problem is not simply something we do not know, a matter of which we are unaware, but rather something *of which we must be aware*. A practical problem is not something that is merely going badly, but something that *must be remedied*. When there is insufficient motivation to do this, or if it is not urgent, or simply impossible, then *it is not a problem*. It is something else: a misfortune perhaps, a calamity, a curse. Poverty and sickness are problems. Death as such (and of course it matters to us!) is not.

The Negro element within American society has been an important factor since colonial times. In one of its dimensions —slavery—it became a problem over a hundred years ago, and the way it presented itself along with other closely linked problems, and the way it was "resolved"—as far as real problems can be resolved—was the War of Secession; the Civil War between the Union, representing North *and South*, and the Confederacy, which claimed to be only the South. After the war and its phase of the problem, there was a readjustment in American society that allowed the Negro at least two ways of living in this society.* Then other problems came to occupy the foreground: the expansion of the country to its full boundaries, its economic development, its industrialization, its cultural growth, the formation of a national character, the assimilation of millions upon millions of immigrants, its participation in two world wars, its entrance into world affairs, and the opening of the United States to the outer world.

Negroes were an ingredient in the makeup of the country; they were an annoyance, a difficulty, an injustice, a remorse, a form of art, a religious nuance, a complaint. But they were

* Segrated or integrated is intended—Trans.

not yet a problem, because a problem only becomes so when it is posed.

This is what has begun to change in recent years. In large measure, this has been because Negroes are acquiring a better economic position, more education and unity, and a greater capability for action and influence. To a great degree also this has been because a sizable white minority has assumed a progressive conscience concerning the difficulties and injustices, and they share the American attitude that the things of this world have a solution. Let us not forget that it is the whites who talk most about the Negro problem. Nor must we forget that everything that happens in this field is made known to us, even exaggerated for us, by the country's press, radio, and television; by countless books and articles; and by governmental and private committee reports. This is not hidden information; one need not look to the outside for news of what is happening. All the world news about the United States comes from this country, from strictly public American sources.

In principle at least, the Negro problem begins to appear solvable. And this is precisely when it becomes a *problem*. An unsolvable problem, such as squaring a circle, is not a problem. Progressively and with an accelerated tempo during the last fifteen years, the Negro problem has taken on increasingly important proportions in the practical and mental horizon of the United States. Negroes themselves expect a solution; the majority of whites hope for it. A considerable number of the latter— principally in some Southern areas: Mississippi, Alabama, Arkansas, Georgia, Louisiana—are afraid that a solution would upset their way of life, bring disturbances and uneasiness to the cities, and lead to a country-wide decline. One must not think of these people as "anti-Negro." In some cases they are, of course. Others are what could be called "anti-Negrist," that is, opponents of pro-Negro whites whom they scornfully call "nigger lovers." A similar situation is implied in the European term "anticlerical." Does it mean an enemy of the clergy, or of the pro-clerical? Does it mean opposition to clergymen, or to clericalism? Many Southern whites are opposed to the means used *in the name of the Negro* to change the status of Negroes. And even if we discount the hypocrisy and insincerity this attitude may conceal, there still remain many whites who believe that in the long run the Negro will come out the loser. Nor is there any doubt that some Negroes, especially among older groups, share this opinion.

How should this problem be approached? The way in which a problem is stated is all important. Philosophers know that a stated problem is already half-solved and that the terms in which a problem is presented form the primary elements of theory and solution. They also know that a problem poorly posed and formulated may remain inert and unsolvable. The history of philosophy consists in large measure of new ways of viewing and formulating philosophical problems. There have been times when an accurate approach that avoided false postulates has led to a solution of some problem with almost magical ease. Consider, for example, the problem of freedom or that of the existence of the external world.

Three concepts have been apparent in the formulation of the Negro problem in the United States: discrimination, segregation, and integration. Discrimination consists of the distinction made according to whether a person is black or white. This means that skin color and other racial features influence the job and salary one may seek, just as they determine who is to be protected and who persecuted, oppressed, and restrained in the exercise of freedom or other rights. We should remember that the list of "discriminations" for other reasons is endless throughout the world: for reasons of sex, age, social class, religion, political beliefs, language, region, education, personality, beauty or ugliness, and profession. Think of the objections based on similar criteria made every day by people around us.

Everybody agrees that discrimination is unjust. It is practiced, but rarely affirmed (there are exceptions, of course). What is affirmed are the two solutions vaguely represented by North and South: integration and segregation. The latter is the belief that whites and blacks should have "separate but equal facilities," that each have schools, universities, hospitals, hotels, restaurants, buses (or at least the back of the bus). These facilities are to be independent and equally good. Even in theory this idea is questionable; in reality it becomes much more so. What happened, and still happens, was that the facilities were separate and unequal. There were more and better white than Negro facilities; at times the latter amounted to nothing but hindrances.

Discounting the artificiality and repugnance of the segregation principle, its injustice and failure to fulfill what the formula promised were notorious. It is a fact that Negroes statistically are more poorly paid; their schools and universities rarely reach the level of excellence of white schools. The same thing happens with other services. Voting requirements and the steps necessary to exercise other rights were changed through stratagems into mere roadblocks designed to exclude a considerable number of Negroes.

Over against this system, some fifteen years ago there began to be imposed, by public opinion first and later by law, the other formula: integration, the abolition of all separation, the common use of all institutions, resources, and rights of the country. In other words, this meant the forced (including legal force) mingling of whites and Negroes in the same neighborhoods, hospitals, schools, hotels, etc. Is this a workable solution? What I mean first of all is: can it be carried out? And second, does it solve the problem? As integration has progressed, as legislation and practice have taken incredibly rapid steps regarding society, there are growing reports of unrest, protests, and disturbances. What are the real dimensions of the problem? And above all, is the final problem really what it was first thought to be?

INTEGRATION

Since 1954 the die has been cast: the United States has decided to integrate Negroes into the whole society. The great majority of white Americans want this; some like it, others do not, but they are convinced that it is either just or inevitable—or perhaps both. A considerable minority, not exclusively Southern but concentrated there, view integration with fear and distaste. Some believe it is a mistake, others simply that it is an annoyance. We must add that the segregationists have very little confidence. They are convinced that nothing can stop the tide of history, and the extremism and virulence of some of them only prove this: they are defending a cause they know is lost.

When William Faulkner, the great writer who knew both the South and the human condition so well, asked the North to have "patience," his position at the time was very intelligent and I would say very American. A characteristic of the United States is the patience it has with the ills and troubles of this life. It will accept the poor state of many things before intervening surgically, as it were, to correct them. It trusts in what we could call *vis medicatrix societatis*, the ability of society to cure its illnesses, and it even believes that the latter have some justification, or at least some reason for being. If things are to be done in truth rather than merely so appearing, they require time.

Set against this position was the impatience of the Negroes, and *above all* that of the white integrationists. When people urge calm, is this not a ruse to avoid decisions? Has not the Negro been free from slavery for more than a hundred years without being able to exercise his civil rights, unable to vote in many localities because of technical pretexts, living under conditions that clearly show his inferior status, exposed to dangers and abuses, and obliged to be a second-class citizen? We want equality and we want it *now*, has been the Negro's reply.

Here the process begins to speed up. Negro pressure—I insist that it is motivated mainly by whites—has become more and more insistent. Integration has been imposed on many schools, busses, restaurants, hotels, hospitals, and universities. Sometimes this has even gone beyond the Negro's convenience, and he finds himself having to attend a school farther from his home in order to be with whites rather than blacks. At the same time, resistance by segregationists has intensified, in some cases because they believe themselves still strong locally. Others on the contrary, show a Numantine spirit,* a strength born of hopelessness. The result can be summed up in a single word: tension.

But we ought to ask, how much tension? Newspapers, beginning with the American ones, always exaggerate everything that is "news." If a Negro is beaten in Alabama, if a civil rights worker is shot at in Mississippi, if Negroes burn and loot in Newark, Detroit, New Haven, or Watts, headlines around the world tell us about it. On the other hand, they say nothing of the millions of negroes who live peacefully side by side with whites throughout the country, North and South, who increase their earnings and who attend high schools and universities, who are doctors, engineers, ministers, professors, businessmen, generals, Supreme Court Justices, millionaires. The newspapers do not say that these Negroes have white subordinates, that there are blond Anglo-Saxon colonels who stand at attention before their Negro generals. And these men are not exceptions, although they may be a

* A reference to Numantia, an ancient Iberian city whose inhabitants chose death rather than surrender to the Romans in 133 B.C.—Trans.

minority. It is certain, for example, that the proportion of Negroes who go to college is less than the national average. The difference, of course, is not as great if the South is considered, because these poorer states have a smaller number of whites in college. In any case, there are more than 250,000 black college students out of a population of twenty million. Spain has a population of thirty-one million and the number of college students barely exceeds 100,000. This means that it is much easier for an American Negro to attend college than for the "whitest" Spaniard (and this is leaving out the difficulty a Spanish, French, or Italian *worker's son* would encounter).

These considerations lead us to make an important distinction: the juridical and legal aspect must not be confused with the *social* and more truly "real" side of the problem. Legal integration means the full force of the law for all Americans and the practical equality of rights. It is essential that Negroes be able legally to do exactly the same things as whites, that there be no prohibition affecting them, that the exercise of recognized rights be unhindered. This still has not come about, but it is coming with incredible swiftness. Everybody knows that it is going to happen, and only a small minority is opposed to it.

But the word "integration" does not mean this alone. It really implies two things: (1) the real "equality" of blacks and whites, and (2) the mixing of both groups in a single society. We must ask whether these two things are possible, and if they are, how they can be achieved.

It is a fact that the standard of living for Negroes is statistically lower than for whites (although many whites are economically inferior to many Negroes). It is also a fact that the number of Negroes with a higher education or special training is proportionally less than among whites. And since American society demands more and more specialized work, the difficulty of finding it inevitably affects Negroes more. Although many Negroes live under the same conditions as their white compatriots, anyone acquainted with North America knows that in many cities there are Negro sections poorer, dirtier, shabbier, and more abandoned than the rest, and that in some places they are stinking and filthy. Many years ago I said that American society has no "ground floor"; it begins with the mezzanine. But I added that it does have "shafts" deeply sunk. Now, a goodly portion of these "shafts" are Negro (or recent arrivals, for example, Puerto Ricans, who often are also Negro or mulatto).

Today the United States is fully aware of this, and has a guilt complex about it besides. There is an incredible moral malaise, the kind that is so rare elsewhere, about the inferior way of life of part of the population. And there is a budding determination that this must be corrected, and soon. How? This is the question.

The United States is not a totalitarian country. The state has limited powers. It is charged solely with certain specific functions and interferes only modestly in the lives of individuals and the activities of the society as such. Individual and collective (but private) initiative is responsible for carrying out most things. This system is consistent and does not easily tolerate exceptions. It has proven to be extraordinarily effective. It has brought about an impressive accumulation of wealth, and a distribution of the latter that comes incredibly close to being just; it has led to a very high minimum standard of living, great social mobility, and an individual responsibility to which the American clings tenaciously and which he refuses to give up. He dislikes being a "minor," a child cared for by the benevolent (or perhaps not so benevolent) authority of the State. This means that things have *to be done* and not merely decreed. Here the margin of freedom is quite broad. Americans themselves must raise the level of life in all areas; it cannot be given them from without. The function of the State is to remove obstacles and perhaps lend some aid, but nothing else. Anything else would destroy the system of freedom and weaken the vitality and initiative of society. This is what nearly all Americans believe.

The transformation of groups living this lowly existence must come from their own efforts, and it depends therefore on their will, determination, and perseverance. Equality of *possibilities* may be derived from the society as a whole, but not the realization of those possibilities. Consequently it will take *time* (some time, but not much, given the present tempo of life) and an active ethical attitude. Equality of whites and blacks cannot happen by magic, from one day to the next. It is necessary that Negroes be *able* to achieve it, that they not run into hindrances, obstacles, barriers, and delays. But it is also necessary for them to want equality, and this means that they must *want* the conditions, too: willingness to work full-time, cleanliness, meticulousness, self-discipline, and a capacity for sacrifice. These are qualities that American society has been accumulating for nearly two centuries, and which are the only explanation for its present prosperity.

It must be said that many Negro groups have adopted this attitude and have long since been on a par with whites. In many places Negroes are as distinguished, competent, educated, and efficient as whites. And they are held in the same esteem. In first-rate colleges and universities that even socially are quite distinguished—for example, in girls' schools attended by the most prominent groups—Negroes study and teach, they share the same dormitories with whites, and they form friendships with them. And this occurs not only in the North or West, but also in the South. Last year I spent over a month in a small city in Virginia. I witnessed not a single act, not a single gesture that would imply contempt for the Negro. Naturally, no newspaper reports this. It may seem that only the other exists, while the truth is that mainly we find what I found in Virginia.

CONDITION AND SITUATION

Those who do not understand the Negro problem always say that it is something superficial. This is what is serious: that it is something superficial, that is, on the surface. Let me explain. If someone is a Catholic, Jew, Presbyterian, Methodist, or atheist; if he is a liberal, fascist, communist, or Republican; if he lies or tells the truth; if he is faithful or unfaithful to his wife; these are things I *may* learn in time and after contact with that person. But if he is a Negro I shall know it at once, precisely because the telling pigment is on the surface, on that quite external and quite important thing we call skin. In my judgment, it is a mistake to call Americans worried about Negroes, "racists." "Racism" is a theory represented by Gobineau, H. S. Chamberlain, and their National Socialist disciples in Germany, who spoke of such questionable and invisible things as "Semites," "Alpines," and "Pure Aryans," that probably did not exist. What has this to do with the elemental and quite simple difference between white and black?

One may respond that there are also American racists, and this is true. They are the ones who theorize or believe that whites are, for example, superior to Negroes (or there are some Negroes who think themselves superior to whites and destined for sublime enterprises). But the normal American, white or black, who merely notices the difference and takes it into consideration, is not a racist. For the difference is there and readily visible. Moreover, and precisely for this reason, it influences our contact, not exactly in a negative manner, but indeed in an apparent way. But for that matter, is not our attitude toward a beautiful woman influenced merely by the immediate fact of her beauty?

My reservations about the idea of integration stem from these considerations. Of course, the differences between white and black are, from many points of view, irrelevant. In juridical, legal, economic, religious, and professional terms, they should have no bearing. In all these dimensions, any type of "segregation" is unjust, unjustified, and above all, stupid. But there is more to it than this.

Whenever I attempt to formulate a social theory, I distinguish between "condition" and "situation." Situation has to do with how one is. A man may be very unhappy with his situation, but delighted with his condition. The man who is told "no" by his lady love is quite unhappy at what is happening to him, but not unhappy that he is a man. The writer whose books do not sell bemoans the fact, but not his profession as a writer. Most of us are dissatisfied with our situation—this is the ferment behind improvement and progress, the impulse toward perfection—but not necessarily unhappy with what we are. When a human group is unhappy with what it is, with its condition, then I think we can speak of "proletarization." The proletariat was formed by workers who, around the beginning of the Industrial Age, felt deeply dissatisfied with being workers. The *manolos* and *chisperos**
of the eighteenth century (and their counterparts outside of Spain) were justly unhappy with a situation that in general was much worse than that of industrial workers of the nineteenth century. Yet they were proud and delighted to be what they were, and under no circumstances would they have

---

* *Manolos* were from the lower classes and were characterized by gaudy dress and picturesque speech; the *Chisperos* were so called because of the many blacksmiths in the Maravillas district of Madrid (*Chispero* from *Chispa*, "spark")—Trans.

changed places with the aristocrats and "Your Lordships," although certainly they would have traded their respective situations.

Now then, the only sizeable American group that feels "proletarian" is the Negro. If you tell an American worker that he is a proletarian, undoubtedly he will not know what you are talking about. If you explain it to him, he will probably laugh. In general, American workers have reason to be satisfied with their situation, but they are not completely happy and they struggle trying to improve it. But the fact that they are workers in no way seems a misfortune to them; in no sense is it a humiliating condition or degradation.

Negroes, on the other hand, are not happy (how can they be?) with many things that happen to them, and especially with things that have happened. But neither are they happy "to be Negroes." And this is the serious point. For the only real solution to the problem, besides justice and equal rights, besides comparable opportunities, would be for Negroes to accept fully and comfortably their differential condition, as one more group within the complex American society.

The coexistence and cooperation of whites and blacks are imperative; they can and must be reached. Yet the mixing of the two groups, omitting the very fact of difference as if it did not exist, is a blind alley. Because the difference *does* exist, and it is visible and immediate precisely because it is superficial.

It is not surprising that efforts to achieve integration, the astonishing advances made, have brought about an increase of tensions. On the one hand, this is because the very nearness of success, the closeness of the aim, causes haste and impatience. Negroes and those who want integration are hastening toward an end that appears in sight. Hence they forget caution and stir the anger of their adversaries. But there is something more important: proximity, constant contact, accentuates the difference, makes it more noticeable, and aggravates it. In other times it was something "taken for granted," and it allowed for a certain distance between both groups. Today for good or ill, this separation is no more, and the result is uncomfortable.

Negro sympathizers, defenders of civil rights, and extremist integrationists (often admirable examples of generosity, integrity, and courage) contribute a great deal toward intensifying the condition of both races, and by mixing them, they cause their differences to be painfully acute.

Perhaps it would have been better to approach the problem from a different angle. It is possible that Negroes, in general, and in certain situations of close proximity, feel more comfortable by themselves than with whites. The same could be said for whites. It would not seem necessary for them to be "together" everywhere. In countries where there are no racial differences there are cafes or restaurants frequented by bankers and businessmen, and others by painters and writers. It is essential that no one be forbidden to enter these places, so that the poet *could* go to the bankers' cafe and vice versa. But probably both groups feel more at ease with their own kind. It is imperative that the Negro raise his economic, health, and cultural levels. But once this is done, I see no harm in Negroes living together as a primary social unit with normal contact with the rest of the population. The important thing is for the Negro to find himself within his condition, for him to accept naturally and with satisfaction the fact that he is a Negro, without feeling that it is ill fortune or a mishap.

Today riots are quite frequent. These tumults unleashed in Negro districts, at times very violent, are often directed principally against Negroes. In some cases they can be explained by conditions that really are grievous and unjust; in others, they are brought on by the inflammatory mood of these social groups, by the exasperating heat of the summer, or by any grievance that spreads like wildfire. The timing and doubtful justification of riots (at times, they break out where there would seem to be the fewest causes) lead one to think of planning on a broad scale and of their manipulation for other ends that are easy to guess.

In contrast to moderate and reasonable leaders in these movements, others have arisen who are frenetic and extremist. Some are agents of foreign interests; others, agitated to the point of abnormality; others, ambitious. These are the ones who talk of burning the country and of doing away with whites (if things were to come to this, imagine what would happen to the Negroes); these are the leaders who demand "Black Power." The majority of Negroes watch these outbursts of extremism with consternation, and they make it plain that it has nothing to do with them. Many believe that this approach will set the Negro cause back, and they suspect that this is really the aim behind it. Some Negroes, especially the very young, are enthusiastic, excited, and entertained by it.

Many times I think that "It's an ill wind that blows nobody good." I have very little sympathy for extremists and demagogues, who usually destroy the most noble and interesting causes while claiming to support them. Crude approaches to questions rarely persuade me. Yet I think that some good will succeed this exasperation. If these movements rid themselves of aggressiveness and senselessness, they may unwittingly contribute to a solution of the problem by reinstilling in the Negro an awareness of belonging to a particular group, but without the implication that this group is better or worse than any other. The Negro may come to feel that it is normal to be a Negro, that it is *one* of many things which one may be in the world and, specifically, in the United States. In this way, hand in hand with legal integration and economic, intellectual, and educational improvement of the black minority, a satisfactory status of Negroes could be reached in this country, and this would allow the last stronghold of that form of unhappiness called proletarization to be conquered.

51 NORTH AND SOUTH

POLARITY

The United States are, as the name implies, *united*. Many years ago, in my earlier book, I asked the question: what or who unites them? Today I am interested in something else: in underscoring the fact that they are not a "unity" but a "union" (from the latter has resulted, or will result some day, a unity).

This union has a dynamic structure, as does all living reality. It is a system of tensions. The critical fact is that the structure of the union does not correspond to the present makeup of the United States, but to the original structure of the country. Let me explain.

The United States came into being as a polarity between North and South. Each of the two nuclei looked at the other in admiration at times, and with jaundiced eye and envy at others. Each pulled the nascent country in a certain direction, each proposed a future based on its own aim. This priceless duality, this rivalry, gave the country a "plot" or "argument." Unless I am mistaken, this is what made the United States a *historical* country (something a new country colonized from without achieves only with great difficulty).

But if we try to apply this scheme without further ado to the United States of today, it leads to confusion. If we attempt to interpret large portions of the country as "South" or "North," we immediately see that it makes little if any sense. Besides the original North and South, there are many other things: the Midwest, the real geographical north—Minnesota, Oregon, Washington, Montana—California, Texas, and the entire Southwest, and so forth. These are new modes of life, later inspirations that came on the scene in the second half of the nineteenth century, and which have been incorporated into the original system, somewhat like outsiders who take sides in an argument. The fact that what is called the Midwest or Middle West is a group of states found in the eastern half of the country—Illinois, Wisconsin, Ohio, Indiana, and so forth—is a kind of geological "proof" of an earlier situation when the United States was only a small area of what it is today.

The society of today was basically formed from the older one, the one arising from the original polarity between North and South. Massachusetts, Pennsylvania, and New York, on the one hand and, on the other, Virginia especially, Georgia, and under slightly different circumstances, Louisiana; these were the key points. Corresponding to these were several cities: Boston, Philadelphia, and New York in the North, and of lesser importance (and this is crucial), Richmond, Atlanta, Charleston, and New Orleans in the South. This alone is enough to show that the culture of the North was more urban; as for that of the South, I would not say it was more rural, but rather that it was based on towns, small cities, and plantations more akin to Spanish haciendas than to the open wheat country. And of course one must add that the South was slavery territory, while the North had either few slaves or none at all.

The march of history since the dawn of the Industrial Age was to condemn the South to an inevitable crisis. The establishment of a real democracy made the perpetuation of slavery impossible, for a new historical conscience would not permit it. Did this necessarily mean a break between the North and South? Would not a gradual transformation of the South, an adaptation to new conditions, have been possible? I believe a gradual change could have occurred. Perhaps I am mistaken, but I think I detect in the North a little over a century ago the creation of an attitude of "success," the slightly petulant psychology of the triumphant, joined with a great faith in its own destiny and disdain for everything else. This aroused a sorrow in the South, a proud introversion, a different kind of scorn for Northern insensitivity that could not perceive Southern graces and values. It seems to me that if the South had felt "understood" by the North, had it felt that the latter "regretted" the transformation or destruction of certain ways of life, then it would have accepted the course of history. Instead it saw, or thought it saw, a vulgar pleasure taken at the disappearance of certain superior features and charms which existed in the South, but which the North had been unable to attain. One could say, as did the North, that these charms existed for the few and that those who enjoyed them did so to the full. They did not think that life for other people was so bitter, either because in fact it was not, or because of a smug hypocrisy on the part of the privileged.

The South came to the Civil War exasperated, resentful, and hurt because the common, equalitarian, and triumphant men of the North had not bothered to notice the beauty, charms, and refinements of the South. They had not paused to sympathize with the South's sad destiny. The North did not "understand" them. It appears to me that this attitude still has not entirely disappeared.

On the other side of the coin, the American Civil War is called the War of Secession. Opposing the United States of America (USA) were the Confederate States of America (CSA), that is, the South *only*. While the North spoke and fought for the entirety—North *and* South—the South wanted to break away from the rest of the country. This fact alone was enough to decide the fate of the struggle. The historical reason for the United States was too strong not to win out.

But once I asked the question before an audience in the South, in the old and illustrious state of Virginia: did the

South really want victory? Did it wish what is claimed: separation, the Confederacy? Had it triumphed militarily, would not it have viewed tearfully and with unconsolable pain, the destruction of the United States? Was its rivalry with the North, its hatred, strong enough for it not to have looked on separation as an unexpected defeat? What would have been the situation of the Southern states *alone?*

I had the feeling that a breath of apprehension and concern went through the six hundred people listening to me. Few of them were certain that the South in the final analysis really wanted what it thought it did a century ago.

The South was beaten; slavery was abolished and a large part of the white population was subjected to pressures and abuses. For their part, Southern whites, in control of the balance of political power (especially on the local level), most of the wealth, and higher culture (the contrast between this culture and other segments of the population did not exist in the North), took it on themselves to see that the old way of life did not entirely disappear. If slavery could not survive, then social servitude of Negroes and white supremacy could continue. But the most serious fact was that after its defeat, the South lost weight and power in national life; the political scales were tipped in favor of the North. We might say that at this point the South "went out of style." There were other more pressing, interesting, and promising topics: the exploration of central and western territories, the creation of great industry, railroads, and the growth of the population with millions of immigrants from all the European countries to be assimilated. These were people who did not originate in the older American society, the ones who, after 1870, did not really have any idea of the South. There were several reasons for this: first, the South no longer was what it had been; second, the image these newcomers received was the one the North imposed; and, third, they settled mostly in the North and the new territories. In a sense quite apart from secession, it was at this point that the South really found itself alone.

After a century, the South is only one element in a country that has several. But its original character, the fact that it is a part of the very *root* of the country, that it is a *radical* ingredient of what we could call the country's social makeup, the fact that the South is mainly a "style" or way of life, all this gives it a special relevance. While other Americans think of themselves as "Americans" of such and such a region or state, those of the South think of themselves as *Southerners* first and *therefore* Americans. (Unless I am wrong, something similar could be said of the Catalans in Spain, making all the allowances that one must for the differences involved.)

It seems to me a great loss for the United States during the past century not to have retained the North-South tension and the meaning of the South as a living element in the American scene. There is something lacking in all the new generations of Americans whose roots are not planted in the original society and who, therefore, are not so strongly imbued with the Southern spirit as with the Northern. I doubt that the vast majority of Americans today have ever thought about this problem, and probably it is hard for them to realize it. Nothing would surprise me less than to see the South rediscovered and to witness the reincorporation in a different form of a way of life that flourished, and which has endured in relative isolation, in the southern lands of the United States. My own personal experience would permit me to understand this process, which I consider probable. I began my experiences here under the Northern way of life; I first lived in New England and along the North Atlantic coast. Then new lands were included in my horizons all the way to California, but with only references to the South. Only in recent years has the South come to form a real part of "my" United States. What I mean is, it has come to be something real enough for me to take into considerations of this kind. This is why it has appeared here, and why it must keep on appearing as I continue this new look at the United States.

FRAGRANCE OF THE SOUTH

When one enters the South of the United States from another part of the country, he becomes aware of what Valle-Inclán would have called "a delicate and ancient fragrance." Nearly everywhere one goes, things are "modern," up-to-date, sometimes excessively so. I once said that Los Angeles gave me the impression of a recently erected stage decoration. When I lived there I would go to bed with the vague fear that it would be taken down some night and nothing would remain the next day. In some places there are many old things—for instance, Boston is an older city than Madrid, and the *average* age of its buildings is greater. But old things in the United States are like "relics"; they are what "remains" of the past, what "has come down" to us (and sometimes the antiquing is deliberate, as is the case with the gothic structures of universities and colleges).

In the South old things do not seem to "remain" but rather to "continue." They are not isolated from new things, but rather they preserve an up-to-date appearance; and new things either are not so new, or they do not appear to be. The past comes down to us naturally. It continues to happen, and the new blends in with it harmoniously. The old lordly mansions of the eighteenth century or the first half of the nineteenth, in Virginia, Tennessee, or Louisiana, are "fresh" in the midst of their antiquity. They are ancient but not old or out of date. This is why they exude that fragrance that we never find in things belonging only to another time.

I believe this impression of the cities and houses could be extended to all dimensions of life in the South. The South is not as hurried as the North. This has always been said, but I would add something else: the South is not as calm as the North. The isolation, the secluded life of the small New England town, or the limited activities apart from economic life in the Midwest, reach extremes that I have never seen in the South, where a certain amount of activity is associated with rest and leisure hours.

The fact that the task of organizing the United States was largely an economic undertaking (exploration and exploitation of the territory, development of agriculture, industry, administration, roads, and means of transportation), has given rise to the economic point of view in American Life. Americans believe themselves to be "utilitarian." They think, above all, that they ought to be so. In my opinion, they are one of the least utilitarian peoples on the earth. They are effective, which is something else entirely. Nevertheless, they believe they ought to justify economically what they have done for "lyric reasons," to use Ortega's admirable expression. It would be impossible to say how much confusion this has caused in the United States, and more so outside of it. In the South this "economism" is less active. I do not mean by this that the South is any less utilitarian than the rest of the country, but certainly Southerners think this of themselves. And this leaves more time for the manifestation of this "lyricism" behind their reasons. This is why the Southern man or woman enters more easily into conversation and contact with others, and why it seems less sinful "to lose time" (or if it does seem sinful, at least they enjoy a certain voluptuousness in doing it).

This fragrance of the South is also due to a feeling of seclusion. The United States is "open," sometimes too open. In this enormous plain of the Midwest where I am writing now, after having spent a few days in Virginia, at times one has the impression that the towns have been placed there and do not naturally belong. They are like structures that cross highways or roads, or buildings that have grown up around an airport. In the South there are many "hidden" places that suggest roots in the land, as a man (and especially a woman) suggests ancestors, and as a woman gives an impression of many hours of solitude and silence and long minutes spent before a mirror. This is a delightful quality, but it has a drawback. In the South one does not have so strong an impression as elsewhere (in New York especially) that he is at the center of world history. The future is less vibrant in the South and its expectations are more modest. Growth is not automatically anticipated; everything seems at once more stable and uncertain (for the South is a land of paradoxes).

One of the most serious paradoxes is the following. There is nothing more American than the South. If you look in the telephone book of a Southern city, the great majority of names are Anglo-Saxon: English, Scottish, Irish; in Louisiana there are some French and Spanish, but these also hark back to an old tradition. In the rest of the country, German, Scandinavian, Italian, Spanish, Greek, Slavic, Japanese, and Jewish names are uncountable. The millions and millions of immigrants who came to this country, a million or so a year for decades between the Civil War and the First World War, brought with them a variety of elements to a predominantly English society, a society resting largely on British customs, laws, and traditions (including the language, the most important heritage of all). These later changes affected the Southern states much less than the rest of the country. The South remained relatively intact and much truer to the old Anglo-Saxon line. In this sense one can say that the South is more American than other regions. But it happens that while remaining closer to the older America, the South is less "American" in another sense. I mean by this that the South did not experience the historical synthesis of disparate and heterogeneous elements. American unity is forward looking, keyed on the future. It is not based only on a common past, but rather principally on similar aims and on common hopes for the future. And if this is so, then the South is less American than the rest of the country.

As if this were not enough, we find a still more noticeable paradox. This supposedly homogeneous society of the South, almost without aliens, without new arrivals, made up of Americans whose families go back several generations, represents the extreme in heterogeneity. For the society is composed of whites and blacks in comparable numbers; that is, in numbers that may vary, but which are of the same approximate magnitude everywhere. The changes occasioned by immigration in other parts of the country are much less in comparison. They are only variations within the same pattern. However, the variations are many and recent. On the other hand, Negroes and whites are very different—and, especially, the differences are felt in the South. Yet both have been there from the beginning; they "belong" to the South, and for all intents and purposes, they have been in the United States forever. The South, then, is *uniformly heterogeneous*. The same pattern of marked heterogeneity is repeated uniformly everywhere, in contrast to the gamut of variations in other places. It is like the black and white chess board compared to the greens, ochres, yellows, and reds of a map. Despite the abrupt contrast, a chess board is much more of a whole than a map, even though the transitions in the latter are smooth and almost imperceptible.

In correctly stressing the plurality of the South, the geographical, economic, and cultural diversity of its regions, one must not fail to stress also its unity, its deep sense of identity, which tends to be emphasized with the definite article: *the* South. There are at least two reasons for this. One I have just explained: the persistence of the same uniform pattern of heterogeneity. The other is its relative isolation that leads to a sometimes polemic affirmation of its total personality. I have always been surprised that, notwithstanding that a century is a completely artificial, temporal unit, each century nevertheless has a personality and exhibits a marked life style. The sixteenth, seventeenth, eighteenth, nineteenth, and twentieth centuries are rather homogeneous in themselves and distinct from one another. "Awareness of one's century" is a powerful factor of unification; it creates a strange kind of "temporal patriotism" that accentuates traits common and peculiar to a century. Something similar happens, I think, in the South. The fact that Southerners *feel* united makes them more a part of what they are physically, ethnically, and economically. As always, it is history that makes countries (fashioning them from the raw materials supplied by geography).

The South, which has remained a little off the beaten path and outside the mainstream of American history for the past century, seems to me to be a storehouse of enormous value. Many things seemingly lost elsewhere are preserved there intact as though in a reservoir. I am reminded of what Andalusia means in Spain. Above all, what the South has maintained is the most precious of human things: possibilities. The *real* backwardness of the South seems to me undeniable. In statistical and measurable things the South *is* behind the rest of the country. But man is not only real; he is also and at least equally unreal and unrealized; he is *possibility*. Now that the United States is "made," now that there is less urgency, less haste, now that the time has come to stop in order to think and select, when abundance and with it what is inappropriately called "idle time" ("leisure" would be a better word) have become widespread, we realize that the poorest part of the country may be unexpectedly rich in merchandise hitherto rarely noticed. It offers unrealized possibilities, potential life styles, a deepening of the American temperament. Has not the hour come for the South to open its doors and spread its fragrance over the multicolored map of the United States?

52 SATISFACTION AND CRITICISM

When I first came to the United States, a mood of self-satisfaction prevailed in the country. Criticism of everything was frequent, but it was made against a backdrop of general approval of conditions and a comfortable acceptance of society. Today, after a generation, the criticism raised by the United States about itself is so frequent, intense, broad, and publicized as to be unimaginable in other places. I am not referring to countries where criticism is forbidden, but rather to those where in principle it is tolerated. I mean by this that there are countries where the "right" to criticize exists, but this right is exercised with extreme moderation. If one is attentive and has a sensitive ear, he can hear above the critical voices a breeze of complacency. Nevertheless, criticism invades and dominates everything. Compared to the United States, *all* European and Latin American countries are incredibly "conformist."

Why this change? Does this mean that things are going badly? Has the United States failed in its undertakings? Has the well-being of fifteen years ago vanished?

During this time the cost of living has increased approximately one-third, a little over thirty per cent (this means that it has increased in fifteen years what takes five in other countries, and in some, one year, and in even others where a similar increase occurs monthly). At any rate, what cost a dollar in 1951 costs a dollar and thirty cents in 1967. For the sake of accuracy, it should be pointed out that the price rise is not uniform. Services (doctors, hospitals, transportation, postal services, and so forth) have increased more, perhaps by as much as fifty per cent. Goods have gone up less; countless things cost exactly what they did then; a few cost more, and a few, less. One should add that many things are better than they were. Machines and appliances, automobiles, refrigerators, heating, television, all continue to improve in capacity, comfort, and efficiency. The stability of prices and money impresses foreigners of all countries.

Furthermore, Americans earn approximately twice as much as in 1951, and this is true at all levels and in all professions. In some areas salaries have tripled. But taxes increase at a similar rate and this reduces the advantages of very high economic levels, so that the differences are more of prestige than of real economic superiority. In other words, the American who earned twenty dollars per day and paid ten out in taxes, now must pay at least thirteen in taxes. But since he now earns forty, he has twenty-seven instead of ten dollars left. Everybody knows the consequence of this: the number of travelers is strikingly greater; almost twice as many people attend colleges; before, families had one car, but now the majority have two or more. Houses are better; savings and investments have increased prodigiously.

Poverty pockets undoubtedly exist, and it is not comfortable to be poor in the United States because it is not expected or frequent. Everything costs something; the country functions economically. One rarely finds those cheap poor-quality items found in other places. Fifteen years ago I said that American society has no "ground floor"; it begins with the mezzanine, yet there are "shafts" penetrating its depths. Today these "shafts" are smaller and not so deep, but they are more noticed and people find them intolerable. Two decades ago they still seemed "natural." Michael Harrington's book, *The Other America*, has contributed—not without some demagoguery—to arousing this conscience. It has been translated in Mexico with the title, *La cultura de la pobreza* (The Culture of Poverty), and has received much attention in Spanish America, where, as elsewhere, the ills of the United States are looked on with some glee. But many fail to realize that what here and in Harrington's book is called "poverty," would be called "being well-off" elsewhere. Today Americans are greatly concerned about poverty, and it is a cause of some unhappiness and criticism. In the midst of general affluence—the "affluent society"—Americans are in anguish over the poor and they mobilize themselves to awaken the conscience of the country in order to end these poverty pockets. The phrase, "invisible poor," has been coined and has caught on. I can only envy a country where the poor are invisible and where one must sharpen his sight to find them.

The Negro problem is another element of criticism, and one of the country's most serious matters. The situation of the Negro has improved a great deal since 1951. This is true at all levels of life. Yet the awareness of the problem and the urgency in trying to solve it lend the topic a conspicuousness which I have elsewhere tried to show. It is precisely the improvement of the situation that inspires the constant criticism.

From the military and technological point of view, the beginnings of astronautics led to distress in American public opinion. From the first *sputnik*, the Russians tenaciously kept the initiative. They seemed to do everything a bit better and sooner until three or four years ago, when the advantage disappeared and finally swung to the American side. Then people stopped talking of the matter. As long as the imbalance was against the United States, it was a topic of talk; when it became favorable, it ceased being an item of public debate and commentary.

One may say that today the United States is waging—and suffering—a war: that of Vietnam. One may also observe that this war is the principal cause of uneasiness and criticism. It is curious that in a country committed to a war, one hardly hears anything except voices raised against it and against those who conduct the war and affirm the need for it. In this university building where I am now writing (and in a state rather than private university), the students gather names and money for a campaign against the war. Peacefully, every day and throughout the day this goes on, with no one doing or saying anything to the contrary. Posters are nailed to the trees of the campus inviting people to join forces to negotiate peace. This very morning a petition was received signed by a group of professors proposing "to organize opposition to the war in Vietnam." In other words, criticism is possible and so possible that it is constant and listened to much more than the Government. Yet on the other hand, we must remember that in 1951 there was another war in Asia, a not very different war in Korea. Their reasons for criticism and unhappiness were similar. Nevertheless, the demonstrations were incomparably milder in that war.

The question of the Vietnam war is quite serious and must be dealt with in detail. What I am interested in here is pointing out that a similar war did not unleash the same criticism; it hardly disturbed the general complacency. The temperament of the United States is what has changed, the *propensity* to criticism is what has been developed. The causes come later. There were similar or even greater causes before and there was less criticism. Now criticism has become widespread, even regarding matters where some general satisfaction would be in order.

What accounts for this new attitude? Later I shall attempt to answer this question. But first I must do something else: examine the attitude itself. For this attitude of criticism—whatever its causes—*is not something new*. Rather it has been a constant in American life. Criticism, disagreement, dissent, have been at the very heart of American life. The only notable exception to this was the South. As a partial national unit the South exhibited no inner disagreements, but rather as a bloc showed its criticism of the North and the way things were going in the most energetic way possible: the Civil War. It seems to me that the War of Secession cannot be understood if it is not seen as a colossal outburst of impatience by Southern citizens with the style, aims, and politics of the North, that is, with the entire Union. A great deal of the bellicose Southern attitude was in the form of a "challenge" to what it considered an intolerable situation. The expression that would best sum up the state of mind leading to the war would be: "We are fed up." We must not forget that it was the South that wanted war; it celebrated its coming with joy, and threw itself into the conflict with all its strength. It reacted like someone who, after a long, angry argument, says: "Let's step outside!" It would not be erroneous to interpret the American Civil War as a colossal exaggeration (all civil wars are, moreover, horrendous exaggerations) of the tendency to criticism that one finds in the United States.

Speaking of things nearer at hand, disagreement has been the usual attitude of the American intellectual, from the beginning to the "Lost Generation." Fifteen or twenty years ago, for the first time in history, American intellectuals began to feel reasonably at ease in their country. They began to compare themselves with others, to break away from their particular perspective, and to look at the whole of things; they began to admire, to forge ties, and to feel a satisfaction. This latest inundating wave of widespread and immoderate criticism has only restablished the older tradition.

And now we must ask why. What has happened to that feeling of self-satisfaction? Was it unjustified to start with? Does it no longer exist? And this new or renewed criticism: is it the same as before? Moreover, we should ask, unless we have posed too many questions already, what this criticism feeds on, or, if you prefer, what name does it assume as it stirs like the rustling of leaves in autumn throughout the broad land of America, from one coast to the other, "from sea to shining sea"?

After the Second World War, the United States, which was now fully formed, suddenly found itself *in the world* and not simply withdrawn into itself. For the first time in

their history, Americans could really compare their country
to others. Always before the comparison had been drawn by
immigrants, those who were still not Americans. The advantages the United States had over other countries were so
impressive that satisfaction was justified—not only militarily
or economically, not only concerning importance in world
affairs, but intellectually and morally. The disdain of the cul-
tured American toward his own country, over against his
admiration for Europe, especially England, France, Germany,
and Italy, now seemed erroneous and perhaps even frivolous.
This feeling was based not only on the war itself, but also
on the wave of stupidity and evil that since 1933 had been
unleashed over Europe. The unity, freedom, efficiency, moderation, and will to improve in the United States seemed now
only too evident. This is when the "reconciliation" of intellectuals with their country occurs, following their irreparable disappointment with things European.

During this situation is produced what we would call figu-
ratively the "freezing" of the Cold War. After the war,
while the United States was pouring over a hundred billion
dollars over the whole world, and especially Europe, in economic aid to rebuild and get both old enemies and friends
back on their feet, permanent antagonism grew up between
the West and the Soviet Union, the latter having become a
threat, a rival, and a potential enemy. What I call the
"freezing" of the Cold War is the automatic hardening of
an attitude. It is what was called almost from the beginning
"anticommunism," which reached its extreme form in Senator McCarthy.

I do not think the United States has ever gone through
a more dangerous period in its history. What was called
McCarthyism was on the verge of endangering American
life even more than the War of Secession. For it brought with
it distrust, fear, hostility, and suspicion; that is, the contrary
of what makes up the very substance of the United States:

trust, cordiality, and the acceptance of dissent and disagreement. I know of nothing more *un-American* than the McCarthy attitude.

It was so un-American that American society reacted with alarm and consternation as soon as it realized what was involved. McCarthy received the sanction that demagogues deserve: not death or prison, but indifference. American society turned its back on him in boredom and disgust.

I would say that in the long run McCarthy's action was beneficial. It was a *vaccine* against extremism and intolerance. Since that time the United States has had "antibodies" to resist any infection. In 1961, when many Americans were worried about the rise of the John Birch Society, or in 1964, when reactionaries dominated the Republican Party, I was not gravely disturbed. I was sure that these tendencies would not last, as others of different kinds do not.

But those excesses of fifteen years ago left a mark, the most serious mistake the United States has committed in recent times: "Anticommunism." "Anti-isms" are always deadly; for they are negative and parasitical. One may become enthusiastic about many things, but not about an "anti-thing." Besides, anticommunism, like antifascism, needs communism or fascism in order to exist. It depends on them, thereby leaving the initiative, creativity, and planning to them.

By its very nature, one may certainly assume that the United States is not communist, and because of this, perhaps, may be opposed to communism. But the United States cannot postulate its entire existence on such opposition; rather it must be based on what the country wants and ought to be. Likewise, the antifascism of thirty or so years ago deprived democrats and liberals the world over of their creative inspiration, and this assured the triumph of fascism in a good portion of the globe.

Besides, this "anticommunism" adopted as a negative label has caused the United States to feel "allied" with anyone else who may be also "anticommunist," although something even more hostile to the United States could be implicated, for instance, the unrepentant heirs and perpetuators of German national socialism.

This outcropping of reaction in the early fifties (it lasted only a few years in fact; in 1954 McCarthy was censured by the Senate and his popularity vanished) vitiated the attitude of satisfaction which Americans had felt for a decade concerning their country. It had been a free, spontaneous, and sincere contentment; now it seemed a duty. It became a thing of value because it could be denied. Now disagreement was looked on with suspicion. It was no wonder, then, that as soon as the tombstone that for a moment lay on the country was lifted, Americans avidly renewed their tradition of dissent and criticism.

Add to this the fact that Europe, after its initial surprise at seeing that the United States was rebuilding it and raising it to a level where it might continue its historical position, began to feel a curious resentment. Some countries that had had an exalted idea of themselves, and rightly so, but which had not fought well and were unable to rebuild alone, felt obliged to forget the American efforts and to downgrade those who had liberated them from German domination, who had restored their economy, and who had made possible the continuation of their historical position without a long period of impotence and misery. The countries that had been enemies and had received similar aid also felt uneasy. Evident American mistakes furnished a pretext for critical attitudes based not on the mistakes, but on the bitterness and unhappiness of Europeans and many other peoples. All this, of course, was systematically exploited by the enemies of American policy in the Cold War.

Americans have always been disposed to listen to others. Their predisposition to self-criticism causes them to think that other people do the same thing. American negative statistics are published to the four winds, and they assume that others do the same with theirs. If they do not hear others speak of their blights, vices, mistakes, and crimes, they think they do not exist because nothing is said of them. If others are scandalized that a Negro is beaten in Alabama, it must be because nobody is being beaten in London, Madrid, Algiers, or Bogota; if other people are so concerned about poverty in Harlem, it must be because it does not exist in Buenos Aires, Naples, Caracas, or Brussels.

More and more, Americans—tourists, students, professors, members of the Peace Corps, businessmen—are subjected to the negative picture the world has of them. It seems wrong to them not to accept it, at least in large part (out of courtesy and in the belief that if they are being portrayed this way, there must be a reason). To a certain degree, the criticism Americans make of themselves is fed by massive doses of foreign criticism.

Despite all this, Americans like their country very much. Now and then they rub their hands in their eyes and wonder whether they are dreaming. They begin to compare again, to look around them, and they feel a wave of contentment. It is a curious thing to see how an American, on returning to his country, feels a rush of enthusiasm, how he is "relieved" as though awakening from a nightmare. But this mood is short lived. He sees many problems, many shortcomings, many errors; his ever alert moral conscience is disturbed for reasons that in other places would not interfere with digestion or sleep: the erosion of freedom, social injustice toward a certain group, the poverty of some segments of the population, the duplicity in certain political activities, the poor quality of intellectual or artistic efforts, or the immorality of certain social groups. He is unhappy and feels the urge to dissent, disagree, and criticize.

For what reason? Certainly not because of any image in a distorting foreign mirror, nor simply because evils exist in the world. Above all, the American acts because of the future. If he believes anything, it is in the possibility of improvement. Satisfaction has the drawback of slowing the pace of things; it smacks of leisure and Saturday inactivity. The United States has always looked on itself as an enterprise, an unfinished task, a far off goal hard to reach. It does not come from the past, but goes rather toward the future. Its unity is a convergence on a target aimed at from many angles.

The current criticism raised by the United States of itself —and everything American—is not very intelligent. Often what is their own and superior is criticized in the name of inferior foreign things. Sometimes the criticism is right but elementary. But undoubtedly all this criticism does reveal one thing: a strong urge toward correction, rectification, and perfection. Americans are prone to believe they are wrong— even when they are right. They persist in correcting, even when they are correct. The real cause of this is not uncertainty, as might be supposed, but rather that the United States, like Cervantes, prefers the journey to the destination, the road to the inn.

53 THE EVILS OF THIS WORLD

Throughout history the two most frequent attitudes regarding the evils that weigh upon us, especially in collective life, attitudes today found nearly everywhere, are these: the first consists of accepting these evils as something that "is there" and *inevitable*; the second attitude looks on them as *intolerable* and strives to eliminate them at all costs, at any price and without second thoughts.

Poverty and disorder, for instance, have respectively thus

been considered. In many European societies it has been thought that poverty was something disagreeable (especially for the poor, not so much for others), but the attitude was: "What is there to do? This is the way things are." On the other hand, if public order is upset, the state machinery moves inexorably to restore it. Examples could be multiplied if one wished.

The attitude of Americans is entirely different, and if it is not clearly understood, hardly anything about the United States is either. This attitude arises from the assumption that amounts to a deep faith on the part of the United States that things can be worked out. American faith in man—and by extension in all reality—is deeply rooted. The American does not believe that things are "unsolvable," and when something does turn out to be so, he feels deeply uneasy and disconcerted. This explains, I think, the difficulty American society has in facing death. For death is, in fact, one of the things that cannot be remedied. Other men are more prepared to accept this unpleasant reality and to look upon it as something that cannot be changed.

Americans cannot resign themselves to the fact that things may go badly, or not at all, or imperfectly, or that they may be morally unsightly. If, for example, the plumbing is poor, it must be fixed. The resignation in some countries (in Spain, for instance) to poor plumbing, as if it were man's adverse destiny, is something the American does not understand. If there is poverty, it must be eliminated; if there are many pregnant schoolgirls, if there is alcoholism, if there are accidents, epidemics, air pollution, tree blights, graft, if the aged cannot afford good medical services, or if children cannot learn to spell, something must be done to remedy these things.

And since they live *in the world*—and not merely within their country—since they are informed and interested in what is happening all over the world, they carry this attitude over to international relations and try to get the world on the right footing so that it will correct and overcome its problems (or in any case, what seem to be problems to Americans). By not understanding this attitude, and almost no one does, a gross element of error is introduced into what the world thinks of the United States. Nobody believes that Americans really want to improve the lot of others. Everybody presumes that if Americans are concerned about conditions elsewhere, it is because they "have a stake" there. Sometimes they are unable to see what that stake might be; they fail to see any benefit the United States could derive from many undertakings requiring great effort and huge sums of money. Nevertheless, they assume that "there must be" some monied interest, and the more invisible it is, the more important it must be. Furthermore, there is always someone who "takes advantage" of any situation for his own good, and such examples are easy to spot. But no one stops to think that the one taking advantage is not the one doing the work, or that any personal gain is infinitely less than the effort and money expended; that is, looked on as a whole and in terms of business, these undertakings would represent very poor risks for the United States.

But this is only one side of the question. The other, in contrast, is an odd "patience" with the world's ills. For example, they are convinced that integration must be carried out, but integration proceeds slowly. Once integration has been decided upon, it cannot be realized overnight. Americans are concerned about juvenile delinquency, about the frequency with which teenagers steal cars, drink illegally, have sexual relations, take drugs, loiter, form gangs, and occasionally commit serious, even bloody, crimes. People keep on talking about the problem; they spend great sums of money and set up commissions to do studies, and still juvenile delinquency continues. Many think that strengthening the police and ordering it to act boldly (as it usually does elsewhere) would solve the problem. Were this the case, very probably news-papers would stop printing what they now tell. It is known that some unions are run by real gangsters who have enor-mous funds which they use partly to commit various abuses and to coerce others, and partly to allow union officials to live luxuriously. Yet public authority is unable to remedy this situation, and year after year we witness the largely un-successful efforts by authorities to condemn such officials legally and to break up their organizations.

Why should this be so? Why this passivity or ineptness? I believe that Americans are deeply convinced that social evils have *some* justification; that if they occur it is *for some reason*. This justification may be vastly insufficient, while the problems caused are of a much more serious order and hence unacceptable. Yet there is an ultimate feeling of respect for reality that leads the American to see a measure of reason in someone who evidently is unreasonable. The drunk who is disorderly and may kill someone with his automobile may have some real—and in a sense, respectable—reason for getting drunk. The young who misbehave perhaps come from fami-lies or social circumstances that impel them to their behavior. And besides, their misconduct is perhaps born of a worth-while spirit of adventure and initiative, but which has not had the proper channel for expression. In any case, they have their whole life before them. Must we think of remedying every-thing with rubber hoses and imprisonment?

In addition, there is this thing called *law*, and something else called *freedom*. There are some who abuse one or the other, and the authorities cannot do whatever they might wish. Rather, they must obey the rules of the game and perhaps even leave certain crimes unpunished. This is the price that must be paid so that the innocent may live secure and safe from arbitrary authority. If everybody's hands are tied behind their backs and gags applied to their mouths, no one will make an indecent gesture or say a bad word. But is it worth paying this price? Many think it is; Americans do not.

I would say that the United States has a fear of surgery, and hesitates to perform it except in extreme cases. Surgery is usually quite effective; but it is dangerous, it causes pain, it leaves scars, and, what is worse, it lessens the organism's ability to react. Rather than resort to it, think Americans, it is better to stimulate the social body so that it may *really* overcome its ills; so that it may rectify, correct, and transform the undesirable manifestations of something that is fundamentally good, legitimate, or at least inevitable.

This explains the strange "patience" of a people so active and enterprising, so ready to cure all ills. Rather than covering everything with a semblance of perfection formed of equal parts of coercion and concealment, they prefer to air their sores and blights, to concern themselves with them, to give them time, and to trust in that *vis medicatrix societatis*, that healing power of society, to effect a *real* cure of their ailments.

Part of this therapeutic technique is what we could call isolation. With certain ills, for example, extremisms and all kinds of demagoguery, American society generally reacts through indifference and avoidance. "Not this way," it has said more than once and in various situations. In other places, extremist groups, irresponsible—at times simply frivolous—sometimes evil, are able to lead large segments of the social body in different directions, so that society is divided, separated, and in disagreement. The extreme consequence of this is civil war or the oppression of a social group by another stronger, quicker, or larger.

The United States, where extremism always flourishes, is able to keep such groups reduced to what is called "the lunatic fringe," which is tolerated because it is not overly dangerous. And this is not because society will not allow itself to be drawn or divided, but rather because it remains united in unstated agreement. And it offers its scorn to those who propose its destruction or the loss of those things without which life might not be worth living.

54 THE ART OF LYING

Americans do not know how to lie. I am not saying they do not lie (would they be human if they did not?), but rather that they are not very adept at doing so. In other words, they lie poorly. And the upshot of this is that they lie little; because in order for a lie to be practicable, it must have verisimilitude, similarity to, or giving the appearance of, truth. When Americans begin to lie, they immediately lose heart and change their mind. Here more than anywhere else it is certainly true that lying is not a prevalent trait.

This statement could be carefully documented with a wealth of experience even with regard to private and personal lying in this country. I would venture to say that the American, notwithstanding his first intention, always ends up by telling the truth. After some experiences, he does not have the heart to go on lying and prefers to tell the truth from the start.

But all this is much clearer and much more meaningful when it is a question of public lying. We may recall a very painful memory for Spaniards: the blowing up of the *Maine* in Havana Harbor in 1898, which was the immediate cause of the war between Spain and the United States. It was said at the time that the cause of the disaster was an external explosion, probably a Spanish mine. The commission named came up with nothing concrete. The Spaniards always maintained that the cause was an on-board explosion, an accident instead of a deliberate mishap. No doubt there was lying on the American side, since in any case there was no proof that the explosion was external. Feeding on the supposed aggression, popular sentiments soon led to war. How long did this story last? Not very long. The episode of the *Maine* has weighed heavily on the conscience of many Americans. "Remember the *Maine!*" Indeed, many did remember it as that time when they lied, and for many years now no one holds to the story of a Spanish mine. One might say it is time it was forgotten. This is true, yet look at the history of other countries and you will see lies that are still lively and unchanged after a thousand or two thousand years.

But to speak of more recent things, in 1960 the Russians shot down a U-2 reconnaissance plane which the Americans had used for spy flights over the Soviet Union. The American Government said that the flights were for meteorological observations; but a few days later it was ashamed of having lied and almost absolved itself of any guilt for having done so, guilt not for having spied as the Soviet Government claimed, but for having lied. "Yes, you know," they admitted, "that we really are carrying on espionage. We regret having momentarily denied it. It was a temporary lapse, a momentary weakness." At this moment, I can recall no country in the world ever having admitted to espionage. Every country has spied, is spying, and, I fear, will continue to spy. This is known, but it is not talked about.

Do we need more examples? There was the American intervention in the uprising in Guatemala that overthrew Arbenz fifteen years ago; the part they played in the attack by Cuban refugees at the Bay of Pigs in Cuba; or even the CIA financing of certain activities of the Congress of Cultural Freedom. In all these cases, participation was at first denied, then admitted almost immediately thereafter. First, it was discovered and announced by Americans themselves, and then admitted by the parties involved.

Diplomacy and foreign policy have been founded traditionally on lying, as are some businesses and certain forms of love. They belong to what we might call the "culture of lying," as we now talk of the "culture of poverty." Lying is not the forte of Americans, who are unskilled in the delicate art of lying. Is this ineptness due to dullness and lack of refinement? Or to faulty imagination? I am not sure. Antonio Machado, elaborating on an idea of Ortega, said in verse:

> Se miente más de la cuenta
> por falta de fantasía:
> También la verdad se inventa.*

Taken as a whole, Americans almost always tell the truth. If at first they do not, wait a bit and they will. But it happens that, since this has never been done, nobody believes it and nobody accepts what the United States says as the truth. This leads to something quite odd: everybody believes *something else* about this country, something that naturally is false. And a cloud of lies and untruths envelops to an incredible extreme everything about this country.

The whole world spends its time "translating" what the United States says into what it thinks must be the truth. Since in a high percentage of cases what is told is the truth, the "translation" turns out to be an almost unending error, much greater than with the traditional forms of politics and diplomacy.

This seems quite serious to me. I think telling the truth is a wonderful innovation and I am personally fascinated by the idea. Marvelous, yes, but still an innovation. Hence, it is something that should not be done ingenuously as though it

---

* The poorer their imagination,
  The more men lie:
  For Truth is also creation.—Trans.

were something normal. It is something new, daring, inventive, and original. It should be done with the same feeling of launching oneself into space. In this way it is prodigious and can be a gigantic American contribution to history. If done any other way, it may simply turn out to be a bit of stupidity.

Telling the truth means modifying all the ordinary structures; it means anticipating reactions that may not arbitrarily be taken for granted. It entails creating behavioral patterns based on what has already been stated, and not on contrary and different things. In a word, it requires a great deal of imagination. Does the United States have this imagination?

I would say yes, but I would not be so bold as to state that it is always found where it is needed. Certain bodies, groups, and sections of the United States, on which heavy responsibilities rest, are evidently not up to the task. Other sectors of American society exhibit more adequate and outstanding qualities, but they are not in a position to apply them. The presence of "experts" in nearly everything, and their acknowledgment by the public, has certain undeniable advantages (for instance, the rarity of the "mass-man"), but the risks are also great. Possibly these experts are not really very "expert" after all, or they are "self-appointed experts," or they are experts in a field seemingly related, but which is really something different (as one might think himself an expert on Spain because he had been in South America, or another might think a General was needed because someone mentioned the word "bases"). Those who think they "know it all already" are a hindrance to creating and understanding the new, and in large measure they stymie this marvelous innovation by the United States.

I would add to all this that in the present world at least, we find a certain resistance to truth. The truth annoys many men of our time. One of the causes of the anti-American atmosphere (for it is an "atmosphere") is the irritation generated by the customary veracity of the United States. Try an experiment (which almost no one is willing to do): compare what has been said in other countries with what has happened; make a similar comparison for the United States during a comparable twenty-year period of its history. And this can range from statistics to general goals, taking in the reliability of the people involved. It would seem natural after a period of experience to believe what is usually the truth and to reject what has time and again turned out to be deceit. But this is not what happens; all this is automatically forgotten; and instead what contradicted yesterday's official truth, and will in turn be contradicted by tomorrow's, is affirmed. Meanwhile, the probable American truths are scorned, and, of course, those from the past that can be verified are never remembered.

Here lies one of the deepest and most troublesome features of our time. But this explanation does not entirely satisfy me. By this I mean that the United States must be responsible in some way for this attitude. There must be something wrong with the way it "expresses" itself even though what it says may be the truth. For in any case, telling the truth is a matter of communication; it is telling the truth to someone so that it will have its effect on him. When one speaks, he must consider how it is received by the listener (or by someone who refuses to listen). Americans do not know the art of lying. I shall be completely happy about this the day they learn a more subtle and delicate art: *the art of telling the truth.*

The literary tradition of the United States is not very old. For a long time it was blended with the English, since it was expressed in the "English" language ("traduit de l'Américain" is a stupidity found in French books, but which does not exist in the United States). Occasional literary geniuses (Poe) and some great figures (Hawthorne, Henry James, Emerson, Mark Twain) gradually were making a reality of a possible American literature that became an imminent promise in Walt Whitman. Only in our century has American literature become a reality to be reckoned with: so real in fact that, unless I am wrong, it has probably become the foremost world literature since 1900 (and I say "probably" because I wonder what effect Spanish literature will have, especially that of the "Generation of 1898" and the following generation, if some day it becomes a "world" literature and not just of the Spanish language).

Yet for many years literature was just literature, and it has not had very much influence on American society as such, and even less on American public life. The high regard for "action," for "facts," and for "workability" was, with reason, very evident in the nineteenth century and even in the twentieth. The United States would have gladly repeated the line in the old *Poema del Cid* (Poem of the Cid): *Lengua sin manos, ¿cuemo osas fablar?** (Oddly enough, they would not have noticed that this is a beautiful rhetorical invective, a feat of the tongue and not of arms.)

There are moments in American political life when rhetorical fires appear: often in the time of Independence (Franklin, Jefferson); and later, from time to time (the Gettysburg Address); at times with unseeming modesty (*Manifest Destiny*; Wilson concerning international relations). From 1921 to 1933 (Harding, Coolidge, and Hoover), businessmen came to the fore and rhetoric disappeared. The United States was rescued from this situation by the writers of the "Lost Generation," Hollywood, jazz, and perhaps also by the "Charleston."

Things changed during the presidency of Franklin D. Roosevelt (1933–45). During these years the United States had a voice that expressed its aims and programs for the

* "Tongue without hands, how dare you speak?"—Trans.

future in two words: *New Deal.* Unfortunately, this was the
period of antifascism, which means that the initiative was
left to fascism, and all the United States did was react to
Mussolini and Hitler. As if this were not enough, the last
years of Roosevelt were dominated by war, which, besides
destroying, always confuses things. Moreover, and within the
English language itself, Roosevelt could not compete with the
great political orator and true creative genius of our time:
Winston Churchill (the other, the nonpolitical orator—or
who at least was not primarily political—was our Ortega).

Roosevelt's death coincides almost exactly with the end of
the world war and the beginning of the "Cold War" and the
"Iron Curtain" (the two metaphors on which all policy has
been based for the last two decades, and which are rhetorical
devices as we may observe). Unhappily for the rest of the
world, the English hastened to replace Churchill with one of
the most unappealing realities of the century: Clement Atlee.
I hope someday men will find this surprising, and if I am still
living when this happens, my faith in humanity will be renewed. As for the United States, the long years of Truman
and Eisenhower (1945–61) represented the consummation of
the process.* I have great respect for both presidents, but not
for their rhetorical and literary talents. The great mistake of
Adlai Stevenson (or rather of the Democratic Party) was in
presenting his candidacy in 1952 when he could not win, nor
historically should he have, after twenty years of Democratic
government. This deprived the United States of an interesting
president and American policy of a voice able to say what
must be said in our time.

This condition seemed to right itself in 1961 with the advent of Kennedy. Kennedy represented a new policy because
he brought with him a new rhetoric, a new style: Robert
Frost in his inauguration, the slogans, the undertakings, *The
New Frontier.* But we all know that this only lasted a thou-

---

* That is, the decline of rhetoric—Trans.

sand days; evil, stupidity, and chance worked together to snuff out a great American possibility.

Was it only an American hope? Kennedy's supreme talent was his oratorical ability to make the rest of the world feel affected by the problems of the United States. Everywhere they became "our" problems. But is it correct to attribute this to "oratorical ability"? Rather is it not true that these problems really are universal? Indeed they are, and Kennedy's greatest success was in presenting them in this way, as they *really* are. Yet the proof that his was an oratorical triumph is that now, so soon after his death, when the problems besetting the United States are more universal than ever, when they affect others more directly, *nobody believes it* (or at least they can act as though they do not believe it).

The present American administration may have all the same talents except one: that of persuading others—beginning with Americans—to become a part of what is being said and done. With an attitude of "I know best," American policy has withdrawn to itself and remained mute—with the surprising consequence that it also appears deaf. We are dealing here with an *attitude*, because we see the same thing happen when the Administration offers explanations, even lengthy and true explanations of its policies. For the attitude with which it acts is one of "giving" explanations, not of sharing with others events and *common* history as they happen. I never saw Kennedy, but once I saw and heard him on television speaking from Washington. The occasion was one of the incidents arising when Negro students tried to attend a Southern university. Rarely have I felt more "involved," more "inside" a public affair, despite the fact that the matter was relatively minor, an internal problem of the United States, and limited to a racial incident. What I witnessed was Kennedy's "dramatization" of history that changed the minute affair into a universal event. *De te fabula narratur.* ("The story is about you"). This is what the spectator felt. And the most serious fact of the matter is that today, in discussing what is happening, we are really talking about ourselves, about each of us. Good rhetoric is always *true*.

On the other hand, what is stated badly *is not true*. "How can you say this?" the reader might protest. If he will pardon a professional intrusion, truth is discovery, manifestation, uncovering, laying bare; it is what the Greeks, who were great rhetoricians, called *alétheia*. Long ago I showed that the words "to argue," "argument," come from the same Latin root as silver (*argentum*), that white, brilliant, and shiny metal. To argue is to cause things to glisten and shine. That which does not shine or glisten is not "truth," for it is not uncovered, revealed, and made clear. I am afraid this is what is happening today with American policy.

Of course it happens elsewhere as well. One of the great fallacies being committed all the time is to state certain things about the United States without stopping to think whether the same things might not be happening everywhere else. For if indeed they are world-wide happenings, it is erroneous to attribute them exclusively to the United States.

With the advent of Kennedy, the succession of presidents "jumped" a generation. By chance this anomaly was corrected, and with Lyndon Johnson the generation threatened with being "left out" is now represented. Possibly there is sound historical sense in this and it may have rectified an anomaly. But it is apparent that the distance between Eisenhower and Kennedy strengthened the impression of innovation. After Kennedy, Johnson represents literally a step backward. I do not mean by this anything inferior, but rather a historical step backward, an older "style" (this is what a generation is primarily).

This is a serious matter, for history has no reverse. If Johnson had had a literary feeling (and *perhaps* this means a sense of history), or more astute advisers, he would have tried to preserve as a priceless heritage the Kennedy rhetoric and style; not so that he might remain in them personally—this cannot and should not be asked of anyone—but to absorb them and go on from there. It is a little late for this administration to change this situation. As for me, I have no doubt that this is the basic political problem of the United States.

Naturally this means also that it is the basic political problem of the world. It is us they are talking about here. And it happens that what we need above everything else is, as Antonio Machado said, "a few true words." And to be true, they must be brilliant.

55 VIETNAM

The clearest example of a lack or failure of rhetoric is the Vietnamese war. If there is any topic that disturbs and divides American society, if any produces concern, moral uneasiness, and unrest, it is the war. The United States is spending enormous sums on the Vietnamese campaign; every day American boys are dying, others return crippled, mutilated, and sick; families grieve for those in hospitals, in the jungle, in the training camps readying for the front, and for those who are going to be called. They think they are losing a great deal without any visible gain. Besides, the threat of atomic war, of total war, hangs over them. In movie houses a sober, chilling English film is being shown, *War Games*. The title is excellent; I have always believed that war is possible because essentially it consists of "playing soldier" and appeals to man's childish and irresponsible nature. The film deals with what a nuclear attack would do to the British Isles.

But it would be a mistake to think that Americans are anguished over the suffering, ills, dangers, and risks of the

Vietnamese war. They are, of course, but this is not the most important concern. American concern is intellectual and especially moral in nature. The anguish they feel is primarily over whether what they are doing *is wrong*.

Nearly everybody thinks it is. Some feel that a military solution is necessary, using all resources needed and nothing less. They believe that a war cannot be fought with halfway measures, that anything less is insufficient. Others believe that any war is too much, and that none should be waged. They believe all wars to be unjustified and wrong. Both positions are oversimplifications. The first group does not stop to think that perhaps we have reached a point where full-scale war cannot be waged and that it can no longer claim to be what once was to some degree its justification: *ultima ratio*, a last resort. It may well be that today war is only a penultimate resort, which means that war is meaningless and no longer possible, although it may still be waged. The second group forgets that the other side is also carrying on a war. They do not look on the other side's activities as war, and apparently think that only the Americans are firing. Moreover, after repudiating war they do not for an instant stop to think what would happen tomorrow if the war were to end today with a total withdrawal of American troops.

But aside from both these oversimplified positions, the great majority of American people are convinced, or at least suspect, that they are making a mistake. I believe that if Americans thought they were doing *what has to be done*, they would willingly resign themselves to all inconveniences and dangers. Yet they are by no means sure of themselves. Why is this so?

This war in Vietnam is strangely like the Korean War I experienced when I first came to this country. It is an Asian conflict, in a territory formerly held by a foreign power and artificially divided into two halves (north and south) as part of a compromise recognizing differences of opinion and spheres of influence in the Cold War. In both cases, the northern half, the Communist half, threatens and attacks the southern half, called without much conviction "democratic." Pacts with various countries exist, but for all practical purposes only the United States intervenes to dislodge the Northern forces from Southern territories, while the rest of the world watches the spectacle. On the other hand, the North is backed up by China and, in a less evident way, by the Soviet Union. The fear that the war may spill over the boundaries of the divided Asiatic countries and become a general conflict increases its importance.

There are too many analogies. Why, then, is the American attitude toward both wars completely different? The wars themselves are somewhat different, and shortly I shall point out some of the differences; but it seems apparent to me that it is the Americans who are different. Between the Korean War and Vietnam a generation has elapsed, and here is where we find the principal difference.

A generation is not simply a temporal interval of some fifteen years; it represents a step in history with a precise content and certain experiences. This means that from one generation to another a different group of people is "in power"; specifically, they are the ones who formerly were trying to impose their viewpoints on a different world. The generation now in power is the one that began appearing around 1950, but which then lacked a historical voice. The youngest members of the present generation, those who are leading the combat today, the students who agitate, protest, march, and hold rallies, were children in 1950 and completely off the historical stage.

The Korean War was (and above all had the appearance of being) a "continuation" of the Second World War. It is of little consequence that the enemy was after all a former ally. The impression was that this represented simply a "defection" of a marginal ally whom one could not trust in any case. The proof of this was that before becoming an ally, it had been the enemy of democratic countries, an ally of National Socialism, and the invader of Poland, as a result of the Soviet-German Pact. The combatants in Korea (especially the leaders and officers) were veterans of the world war. Once peace had been reestablished and the machinery for international coexistence set up, a policy imposed by violence could not be tolerated. This is the way the United States saw the Korean War.

Now it is a question of *another* war, a "new" war. Those fighting it are not veterans; those leading and planning it had little or no responsibility in the other war. Great numbers of the American populace have not lived through the world war; they have only heard it spoken of, and they cannot really imagine what it was like. They are like a great many Spaniards who have no clear and vigorous idea of their Civil War (in the latter case, they have a greater need to know about it, and this increases their disorientation). The Vietnamese war has come about at a time when the "appearance" (at least) of the Soviet Union has greatly changed, and Russia is no longer looked on to the same degree as a threat and imminent danger. Nor do China and Russia appear as a monolithic bloc, but rather as rivals sharing certain common assumptions.

Furthermore, "anticommunism" has run its course. Americans are literally tired of seeing that for many years it took only an "anticommunist" pose—sometimes it was only a gesture—to receive Washington's support, although it might involve people who were wholly undesirable and far removed from everything the United States stood for. The automatic use of this negative label has produced the foreseeable consequences. The knowledge that Senator McCarthy represented in truth the most un-American things possible, a position that really was anti-American, has caused a pair of generations to feel inclined to reject pat phrases and commonplaces and to indulge in the delights of dissent and disagreement. (People outside the United States have no idea to what extremes this disagreement reaches, nor of the violent, heated, and even vulgar criticism to which Johnson, Rusk, McNamara, and the Pentagon are subjected.)

The spirit of self-criticism of Americans causes them to accept eagerly everything said against them. This is why for decades they have been absorbing the criticism and even defamation that Russia, China, Europe, and Spanish America have been heaping upon them (accepting it without very much criticism, and this is a paradox). They easily believe what affects them adversely; they automatically distrust what seems favorable or flattering to them.

In great detail Americans point out the differences between Vietnam and Korea or the incongruous policies of the Government in Washington. In practice they forget all the enormous analogies I enumerated before. That the Vietnamese war is also a civil war seems undeniable; that the United States is not only defending South Vietnam against North Vietnam, but also certain Vietnamese against others, is evident. But Americans only heed the second fact. No one doubts that the bombing of the North is extremely painful and cruel. Yet it is almost certain that war is being waged by both sides. Listening to Americans, one would think it is a one-way war, being waged only by them; although on the other hand—another paradox—they assume that the United States cannot win and that North Vietnam will continue unharmed and undaunted as if nothing had happened. Many Americans take for granted that their country is defending in Vietnam the interests of the military-industrial complex against which Eisenhower so strongly warned (Eisenhower was a conservative general, so the paradoxes continue to mount). Americans do not stop to consider whether any benefit could compensate for the huge losses of the war, which far outstrip any gain.

Amid so much confusion and paradox one thing is clear:

the Government of the United States has lost the battle for public opinion *within the country*. It has not been able to make its reasons stand up, nor to involve Americans in them. Although the Government talks of all this a great deal, the impression the people have is that it would prefer not to, and that it would rather do things alone with its political and military advisers. Only then and reluctantly, since the system will not allow anything else, would they "communicate" the things that have been decided and done. This is, literally, the contrary of good rhetoric, which is the only possible policy for free peoples.

The main difference I see between the Korean war and that of Vietnam is that the first was decided by politics, while the second is being decided by military techniques.

When General Douglas MacArthur, a hero of the world war and an uncommon man of genius, wanted to bombard Chinese territory north of the Yalu River, clearly he was right *militarily*. But it happens that the commander of the armed forces of the United States is never a military man, but rather a civilian; and Harry Truman, former shirt salesman and experienced politician, decided that the bombing would not be opportune. Political reasons prevailed over the military and MacArthur lost command of the troops in Korea.

For some years things have been happening in a different way. The problem of aid to South Vietnam has been presented more and more as a military matter: technicians, instructors, and specialists first; naval and air support units later; troop contingents to "take part" in the fight, when none of the previous things were enough; finally, half a million Americans fighting almost alone. Finally? This is what American society is anxiously asking itself.

In order to fit into place this military apparatus, which has grown for *technical reasons*, a political organization was needed in South Vietnam. It was necessary to have a "State" although it was not very clear what its relationship to the society would be. Whether it was Diem, or Thieu and Ky, it had to be an administration that "represented" the country and could make it function. The military needs someone at the head so that they can deal with him and reach an understanding. We cannot blame the military for this: it is the practice of their profession. A military man always asks who is the one who stands out as the most responsible. When an official dies or is incapacitated, another takes command. The seriousness of this is that a country as absolutely *civilian* as the United States has routinely accepted this professional and parochial point of view.

The result is that today there is uncertainty in deciding *what Vietnam is.* To what degree is it a country? Is it represented by its government? What is the status of the military pursuing the war? The United States knows quite well *against whom* it is fighting in Vietnam; what it does not know is *for whom* it is at war. The war is a gigantic mistake. Many Americans realize this and feel perplexed and anguished.

Of course most of these same people make the same assumption as the military administration about the North. They assume that it is a country, that it is represented by its government, that its people "want" to make these efforts and sacrifices, and that it has a policy. This notion seems to me absolutely gratuitous and irresponsible; either it is fallacious or it points to naiveté.

Everywhere these days, especially in Asia and Africa, there is much talk of "self-determination." But people forget that the uncertain element in all this is the "self." What is the "self" or essence of these supposed social realities so blithely and lightly called "nations," four or five or which are born every year and which take their place in the United Nations where each of them (few can name and identify them all) has as much a voice in that organization as the United States, Russia, England, France, or India?

The defenders of the war, and they are not few in number, reproach their adversaries for their shortsightedness. The "leftists" (to use an expression that has little meaning, and still less in the United States) were those who thirty years ago maintained that fascism must be "stopped," and they believed it should be done before Danzig. Over against those who claimed that "Danzig had no importance," they maintained that it was not a question of Danzig, but of saying "no" somewhere or else surrender. The defenders of the war believe that now the situation is being repeated, and that if they do not fight in Vietnam, they will have to fight somewhere down the line.

There is much truth in this argument. I cannot believe that those who propose a withdrawal of American troops do not have some concern or suspicion that if they do so, within a few months we would hear of "small" wars, infiltration movements, and finally full-scale combat in Cambodia, Thailand, or India. Here lies the real strength of the Pentagon and the present American administration. Critics have to bury their heads in the sand when they try to simplify things and remain unconcerned.

But in turn, these defenders of the war, those who make comparisons with the world war and fascism, slip another fallacy into their reasoning. And I feel a repugnance for all fallacies, as for all crimes, and not just for half of them.

Certainly it was necessary to "stop" fascism and the series of aggressions carried out by Germany, Japan, and (as a childish bit of mischief done on tiptoes, as it were) Italy and other smaller countries. Then, England, France, and the United States were ready to stop it by doing what they had to; which turned out to be nothing less than the Second World War. The fallacy lies in whether the present situation is the same. Perhaps it is, but this is not apparent. For it turns out that war is *impossible* in the sense that it is no longer a political instrument. It is "impracticable" and *cannot be waged* (despite the fact that it may be waged in isolated instances). What happens, then, is that no one seriously thinks of war as a means of stopping a threat or aggression. Hence it is entirely unjustifiable to carry on a "small war," a "pseudo-war" which, regardless of how atrocious it may be, is essentially false. For it can decide nothing; it is no longer the *ultima ratio*, the last resort, when it cannot be carried to its final consequences as it was between 1939 and 1945.

When military aid to Vietnam was begun, probably no one thought it would lead to where it has. Technical thought tends to be inertial and concerned only with means. Whenever a group of technicians is not enough, more are brought in until finally a huge army is built up and a real war is at hand. Fraudulently, it leads from one thing to another quite different. Politics is quite the contrary; it consists in being alert, in seeing when the situation changes, and in changing paths when the one followed, for any reason whatever, does not lead where we want to go, or when it leads nowhere.

The United States is a civil and free country founded on discussion, assent, and dissent. All this continues, but Americans have the disturbing impression that the political actions of their government have only marginal effects on them. Of course, next year there will be elections, and the present unrest will have the last word. But between elections four years pass. And even though this may seem a short time to the Spanish mind, Americans feel it is too long for them not to bring what they are thinking to bear on public life, not to inject their questions and make known their wishes that certain things be done.

It is very difficult to stop a military machine once it is put in motion. It is hard to watch it go its way like an avalanche, growing as it gathers more snow. How far will it go? It is possible that the price that must be paid in all areas, from the economic to the strictly moral, to avert a real evil, may be exorbitant.

American criticism is noble and appealing, but I fear that it is not very intelligent. It says: "No war." But it does not add what would be necessary: "Instead of war, this." It lacks imagination and intellectual force. This is true in large measure because this criticism is decisively influenced by anti-American propaganda, one of the filthiest and most stupid things of our time. Propaganda is necessarily lies, for it is the technique of using men by abusing them. The only effective weapon against it is good rhetoric, which can move men and imbue them with enthusiasm without the need of lying. This can be done with a mere breath of air that becomes a beautiful and true word, a word that gives a name to things as they are being born, to a new world, to politics, or to love.

56 LITERATURE

If we consider the whole of American or North American literature from the end of the nineteenth century until today, the period when it has become truly "dense," if we look at it so as to see it "physiognomically" and in perspective, we are surprised to find two apparently opposing features along with yet a third that is probably the explanation for the first two.

This literature has a strong personality and a national style that immediately distinguishes it from the British and marks it as unmistakably American. First, there is the language, and I do not mean the use of words or expressions in an American manner, but rather the way the general language is used. To begin with, the manner is more direct, lacking the interpola-

tions that British English places between the "I" who speaks
and what is said. The American writer energetically trims
these ramifications without entirely dispensing with them.
For if this were done, then it would no longer be English.
But when we go from the British to the American, we have
the impression produced when two people in the midst of a
conversation bring their chairs closer together. It is a literature
with an "elemental" flavor about it. It seems less elaborate,
more primitive than the English—much less the French. Not
infrequently a certain coarseness pervades even the greatest
names.

Despite these factors of uniformity and simplicity, American literature is highly diverse. It gives the impression of
springing from different sources and at different levels, and
its tastes, despite being so "American," are infinitely varied.
I would compare it to fruit. In Spanish we wisely use the
word in the singular: fruit is always fruit, something that
is unmistakable and irreducible, always the same and different from everything else. Yet this singular term diverges
into an inexhaustible variety: melons, oranges, apples, straw-
berries, bananas, pears, cherries, grapes, peaches, mangoes,
papayas, cherimoyas; without considering all kinds of dried
fruit. Each of these fruits has its own taste, its own consistency and aroma. Manufactured products which at first are
quite diverse, on the final scale of sensitivity all seem somewhat the same. Compare American literature with French,
for example.

The third characteristic (which perhaps clarifies the differences between the other two) is that American literature
seems less *literary*. French literature is what the *hommes de
lettres* set apart for themselves. This is the only way to explain
why French literature is so uniformly excellent, without
periods of decadence, without droughts and languor. It is a
manufactured product, or—if you prefer to use a word that
Ortega invented partly in jest, for only in jest can one invent

a word—a "mentefacture."* American literature displays a certain "rusticity" because it is the fruit of the land. It arises from levels that are more *terre à terre*, closer to the land, but for that same reason closer to the roots. The American writer has never been an *homme de lettres*. It is laughable to apply this expression to Hemingway, or to Faulkner, to Steinbeck, to Mark Twain, or Carl Sandburg. Perhaps it might apply to T. S. Eliot, who hastened to England and became a British subject. When Hemingway received the Nobel Prize and later visited Pio Baroja, to whom he gave a bottle of whisky and some wool socks, he said that Baroja should have received the prize, because he was his teacher and the teacher of others. And he added: "I am only an adventurer." Actually this seems to be the truth and not just a mark of appealing modesty on the part of Hemingway. For Hemingway can only be understood as an adventurer, and one of his adventures, his most daring adventure, was literature. In this sense the first "American" writer was Cervantes.

This is why the American writer has usually done many things; to be brief, he has lived, and he has usually failed as a writer, sometimes at the beginning, but at other times—and this is more interesting—in the middle of his career. Such has seemed to him to be in the natural order of things. Usually he has not made the claim of having "arrived," or that he has been consecrated by the public. Failure is an eventuality in all dimensions of life, and the life that does not count it among its possibilities is the poorer for it. Allow me a personal reminiscence. Some years ago in Paris my friend, the poet Pierre Emmanuel, paused during a conversation and said to me: "Your strength lies in the fact that you are not interested in popularity."

We shall not say that the American writer has not been interested in success, for this would be unlikely. I would say

* A play on "manu-" from *manus* (Latin for "hand") and "mente-" from *mentis* ("mind")—Trans.

that for him failure has never been a true obstacle. This is why this unliterary literature has become the most interesting in the world.

Strictly speaking, is this the truth? I mean, is what I have just written true *today*? I am not sure. Intellectual life, in the United States as elsewhere, is much easier now. There are countless publishing houses, magazines, and newspapers. Many more copies of books are printed, and the pay is better. Legions of publications exist to comment on what is written. And as a consequence, between the reader and writer stand administrators and technicians: editors, directors, and critics. They are the writer's first consideration, the first to whom he refers. His success or failure depends in large part on them; they largely determine whether he will really become a writer.

Here is where my fears begin. Pedantry, European in origin but easily acclimated to other parts, is quite noticeable amongst these agencies. I should like to know how many of the men controlling criticism and the publishing industry in the United States are European by birth. But the most interesting statistics are never available, or at least I am unable to find them. In recent years there has been a reaction against the "elemental" that is so appealing in this literature, and instead a tendency to "elaborate" it as one would age a wine (forgetting, of course, the exceedingly complicated chemical process necessary for producing fruit flavors). This explains why American literature has veered more and more toward what we might call extreme situations and marginal types. The homosexual, alcoholic, or demented person seems more interesting than the "ordinary" man or woman. This, of course, is not true; on the contrary, anyone can talk of anomalous or eccentric kinds of life, but the writer who can recreate daily life is not "ordinary" but extraordinary. When I read Tennessee Williams, or Albee, or several others, I wonder whether it is a weakness on their part to avoid the habitual forms of life. Certainly it is not a lack of talent. Perhaps there is too much interest in being successful and too much fear of being considered "square"; or perhaps writers are afraid that critics might look on their work with condescension or say that they represent middle class culture, as it is said of Thornton Wilder by some who would never be able to write anything as good as one of his pages.

The literary consequences of this can be quite serious, but this is not what I am concerned about. Literature has a human function that is most delicate, that of *interpreting and projecting* life. It is apparent that Petrarchism conditioned the *reality* or quality of love for over two hundred years in the lives of countless men and women who had never read a poem or heard the name of Petrarch. It disturbs me that American literature does not lead the way in imagining, recreating, enriching, exalting, and expanding the limits of real life with a view to the unreal and unrealized. It seems to me to be a sign of literary impotence, a lack of true ambition on the part of the writers.

In some of their works, J. D. Salinger and John Cheever seem capable of attempting today what the great writers of past generations did for their time. But I see them beset by dangers that appear here and there in their writings. One can never be sure.

When the American looks ahead, when he explores the horizon, when with bow in hand, as Aristotle put it, he looks for the target of his life, what does he find? In the immediate past, he would have encountered the recreation of everyday life and also, certainly, the stirring of life's deepest strata (Faulkner, O'Neill). Yet these elements would have had a creative function with a lyricism that allowed one to surpass the depressing reality at hand. But we must look at things from the present moment. I am afraid that the boredom that insidiously is beginning to pervade American life and which, as happened to the first-born princes of Egypt, exterminates

an's best possibilities, is due in large part to the
ken by literature.

less, there are many hopeful signs. For example,
novel by Thornton Wilder, *The Eighth Day*, has
ne best-seller list for I do not know how many
months. The critics have spoken respectfully of it, but in
general without much enthusiasm. It is a mild, serene book,
devoid of extremisms and without thunderbolts to hurl. In
contrast to so many books of late, it does not appear original.
It is. There are no faddish or ulterior reasons for reading this
admirable book. And yet, the American public continues to
read it month after month without tiring. Perhaps they feel
that in the midst of the factories of the literary industry, a
fruit has appeared, a fruit that is theirs.

57 EVERYDAY LIFE

THE HIPPIES

We see them, in small doses, everywhere. In some places they
are concentrated in considerable masses: in certain districts
of San Francisco or in Greenwich Village of New York City.
They are also represented, although only symbolically, perhaps, in the smaller university towns, while on the campus
itself they are less noticeable. They cluster in some more
or less darkened "joint" or gather on the sidewalk in front of
a music store (we must not forget that besides serving as an
instrument, the guitar is also a symbol to them). The boys
usually wear their hair very long and often have beards too.
They dress in blue jeans or tight pants, shirts or turtleneck
sweaters, and perhaps sandals. The girls wear miniskirts or

pants and sometimes shorts, and are often barefoot. They have an air of dirtiness, camaraderie, and gentleness about them. When there are four or more of them, there is nearly always a guitar. They are opposed to almost everything: they favor minority causes, preferably those that are lost. They are for the underdog, although he may turn out later to be the top dog. These are the *hippies*. The term itself is of doubtful etymology and meaning, and it might be best not to go into them. I would say that the real meaning of the term is being formed now. At first glance it seems they are successors to the *beatniks*, and that this is merely a new term for them; but I believe the *hippies* are a new and different reality.

Many of them lead wretched lives. They suffer financial hardships, they eat little and drink more, they do not bathe often, they smoke marihuana and sometimes take drugs like LSD or others even more dangerous. Sometimes they mingle with underworld elements and habitual delinquents, and it is not at all rare to find one of them dead in some squalid room or in a basement, as happened recently to an eighteen-year-old girl from a respectable and wealthy family from Connecticut. And we must add further that for the most part, hippies come from well-off or even wealthy families. They are well-educated and have been reared with the utmost refinement. Furthermore, in spite of their disheveled hair, bare feet, and sleepless look, often they are quite likable.

What are the hippies? Why do they abandon the comforts of home and family to live in hovels or in the open, in want and danger, in unending instability, exposed to vice and often within its clutches? How does it happen that many young men and women can roam about without knowing where they are going, with what little money they have soon gone, living on the run? Their parents look for them, publish their pictures, and there are agencies that undertake to locate their whereabouts. In some cases they return footsore and disillusioned to the family hearth. Often they run away again after a few months; sometimes they refuse to come home, or do so under protest if they are minors.

These questions were answered three and a half centuries ago. The theory of the hippies was written in marvelous Spanish at the beginning of the seventeenth century. The author? Cervantes. Read the opening paragraphs of *La ilustre fregona*:*

> Carriazo was probably about thirteen years old, maybe a little older, when, stirred by a picaresque whim, and without any ill treatment by his parents to cause him to do it, but following his own wish and caprice, he tore himself away from his parents' home, as boys say, and went out into the world. He was so happy with his free life that in the midst of discomforts and miseries that are part of this life, he did not miss the abundance of his father's house. Neither walking tired him, nor the cold bothered him, nor the heat troubled him. For him all the seasons of the year were like sweet and temperate spring. He slept as well in haystacks as on mattresses; he was as happy hiding away in a pile of straw in an inn as he would have been between Holland linens. He went through all the grades of the *picaro* and then was graduated as a master in the fishmarkets of Zahara, which is the *finibusterrae* of the picaresque art . . . .
>
> Here, here is where wretchedness is at home with sloth! Here abound clean filth, sturdy obesity, quick hunger, abundant satiety, vice undisguised, unceased gambling, disputes and deaths at any moment, obscenities at every step, dancing as at weddings, poetry worthy of print, rhyming ballads, free verse. Here is singing; there, cursing; beyond, arguments and gambling; and everywhere theft. Here freedom dwells and misery sparkles. Here many notable families come in person or send others in search of their offspring. And here they find them. And they bewail being taken out of that life as much as if being taken to their death.

---

* "The Illustrious Kitchenmaid," the title of one of Cervantes' *Exemplary Novels*—Trans.

This is the text. With singular insight, Cervantes sought the motives of those who would be derelicts by choice, vagabonds without need, choosing of their own accord and not for financial reasons this shabby life of uncertainty and danger. They did it especially to flee from excessive pampering, from monotony and boredom. The parents cannot understand why their children run away and hide in this disorderly life that borders on misery. Partly, it is the contagious spirit, the spirit of imitation and novelty. Undoubtedly there are hippies everywhere who play at it, who are really conservative and seek adventure supported by the family budget paid by the parents. But in the United States there is a nucleus of these young men and women who represent something authentic that responds to a justifiable unrest.

Moved by the death of the girl from Connecticut, the newspapers have commented at length on the matter; they have talked about the anguish of the parents who, like those described by Cervantes, look for and find their children in American Zaharas, and they are not always able to make them return with them. Moving and revealing letters have been published. Nearly all the parents are surprised and insist that their families are decent, moral, and virtuous. The mother of a girl hippie wrote some days ago in the *New York Times*: "We believed that example was better than preaching. My husband and I took part in community and church activities. We do not drink or smoke . . . . We are 'humdrum' parents, hardworking, and responsible. We did everything as a family."

Is it not just possible that what surprises such people is the very reason why the children run away? Is it not perhaps possible that this respectability, the sober, conscientious discipline, the boredom, and the reasons for the tedium that dominates so many worthy, decent, fine families, repel the young and cause them to look for *something else*? Can it be that morality is confused with lack of imagination, dignity with monotony, kindness with conformity? Are not many social usages being accepted that are not even common to American society as a whole? Are they not rather the exclusive property of certain groups and merely mistaken for norms that ought to regulate life?

The United States moves between opposing impulses. On the one hand, it is a country full of inventiveness, initiative, and effort; it is enough to read a newspaper or an American magazine to see the number of things being attempted at all levels, from scientific research to charity, from religious activities to sports, from the techniques of teaching to artistic creations. Taken collectively, the United States today exceeds in imagination any other country. Yet, on the other hand, mechanization, uniformity, the belief that many things simply "should be done this way," the loneliness of many people who either live alone or are isolated with their families, all show the power of uniformity and restriction that in a certain sense, invalidate the creative impulses.

If it is true that the United States is the country where more things happen or are done, if it is the most creative and enjoyable, it is no less true that boredom insidiously pervades many levels of life and corrodes what would otherwise be the most exciting patterns that humanity has attempted up to now.

Hippies are an extravagance, a grotesque fad, a social sore, a source of worry for educators and legislators, and a nightmare for many families. They also represent an attempt to escape certain subtle ills of American society. They are a defense, an antidote against boredom, a stimulus for overcoming inertia. As young extremists spring from the most reactionary Spanish homes, those where complacency is supreme and all independent action has been stifled, so the hippies are the reply to the deadly boredom of American families that distrust imagination, that accept no inventiveness, surprises or improvisation, families that do not allow in their lives the saving spice of a grain of folly.

TOWN AND SUBURB

"Tell me where you live and I'll tell you who you are"; this could be a variant of the Spanish saying.* Cities shape our lives; to a great degree, our form of life depends on their structure. To be born in a Mediterranean city, or a South American one, in a town in India, in a Galician village, or in a great European city, at once influences what we are going to be, how and with whom we shall come into contact, how we divide our work and leisure, solitude and association, conversation and silence, and what form the presence of others will assume in our lives.

Americans have been abandoning the large cities, and now the majority do not live in them. For many years the great urban centers have been for business, entertainment, trade, and offices. After work or pleasure Americans go home, and home is not in the city. Where is home then?

Two urban forms have been competing with each other for the last few decades as the home of Americans: the small city or town, and that form of urbanization linked to the city, different from but dependent on it, called the *suburb*. The latter term has connotations that are exactly the contrary of the Spanish word *suburbio* (what is meant here by this term would be something referred to in English as a *slum*).

Originally, towns were small population centers that had not reached the status of cities. Because of their size, they have been at times improperly called "villages." Improperly, because "village" has a rural ring to it, and towns are not rural. Should they be called urban, then? Neither is this term very

---

* *Dime con quién andas, direte quien eres* ("Tell me with whom you associate and I'll tell you who you are")—Trans.

correct. The structure of the big city with its suburbs adjoining is copied with some modifications by each tiny town. A town is composed of two quite unequal parts: a purely urban center that is quite small, in fact consisting at times of only one principal street, "Main Street," with its various lateral intersections, sometimes a plaza or square which is the crossroads of this nucleus, and a limited number of streets with stores, movie houses, churches, and public buildings; and a group of residential areas that are quite extensive, with homes amid green grass and huge trees, of a style depending on the terrain. This means that the towns are urban only in a very minimal sense. But neither are they rural. They are neither cities nor villages. In Spanish they might be called *villas*, were it not that this word is no longer used in colloquial speech and has been reduced to official nomenclature and toponymy.

Towns are delightful; they belong to the most enjoyable and appealing forms of collective life. They are usually pretty, unspoiled, and traditional despite frequent new things, clothed in splendid vegetation, as Melibea's hands were "by sweet flesh accompanied."* Most of the people know each other; they see each other in church, in the movies, in restaurants, in the market, before store windows, in the bank, or in Howard Johnson's (which is a replica of all the others across the country), where they eat and enjoy the forty-two flavors of ice cream. The only thing bad about the town is that the residential sections are far from downtown and from each other, and that the town as a whole, despite its smallness, is not very small. Its inhabitants do not live "together," but rather only do certain things together. Neighborhood relationships are reduced to only those inhabitants whose houses are close by, that is, relatively close. The others are far away, and instead of knowing exactly where they are, people know

* A reference to the tragic heroine in *La Celestina* by Fernando de Rojas—Trans.

rather how "to get there" (by car, of course). Highways are the circulatory system not only of the entire country, but also of the towns. The automobile is the antiurban element *par excellence*. Properly speaking, where the car starts, there the city stops. This is why American cities have within them a germ of dissolution (and a worm has slipped insidiously into European cities also and is destroying them).

The suburb is something else. People do not "live" in the suburb, if we mean by that term to experience all the activities of man. Of course people do not work there; in general, they sleep there, go shopping, go to the grocery store—usually in a shopping center that may not necessarily be in the suburb, but which is accessible to several and is well situated on a highway and has parking facilities. The key to the suburb is its distance from the city, good communications, the social prestige of the location, and its facilities. Its inhabitants are commuters; that is, daily travelers by car, train, or bus to the big city in the morning and back again after the day's work. The wives (and I shall speak of them at greater length later on) stay at home all day; the children go to school, or, if they are small, are in the care of the mother in the house or yard.

The reason for residing in a certain suburb is professional convenience. Nobody is *from* there originally, nor do its inhabitants have their most recent roots in the place. When someone rents or buys a house in a suburb, it is usually not for a very long period, for the mobility of American society soon leads him to a better job and an adequate residence in another place. The kind of life found in the town once was more complete, although it no longer is. But the suburb is decidedly a fragment of life. The risks of this kind of life seem innumerable to me.

Properly speaking, the suburb does not offer one a place to "live," a place to establish oneself and be a part of something. The Americans' insistence on a house, a home, their desire for it to be beautiful, attractive, and pleasant, is excellent in principle. Yet in fact, it often restricts the possibilities of a satisfactory life exclusively to the home, and it dangerously ignores the demands of public contacts and associations outside the family circle. Solitude or tangential contact (which is almost the same thing), the greatest obstacles in American life, are intensified in this suburban urbanization. If you want a literary example of what this means, read John Cheever, especially the fine volume of stories called *The Brigadier and the Golf Widow*.

This is quite serious, so serious that it is beginning to worry the most alert and sensitive minds in the United States. The big city is being rediscovered. People are beginning to realize that it is wonderful to get out of the house and see the real city: streets with sidewalks, stores, people, restaurants or dives, cafes, and movies. One of the reasons why Spanish cities are safer than American cities and why you can go nearly everywhere at any time without any danger whatever (something that is not possible in many American cities), is that they are much more "urban" and, therefore, more populated and crowded; while the American city, especially after six in the evening when people are at home, is almost empty in many quarters. People are beginning to realize that living in the city, in the big cities, holds many charms.

But the American finds it hard to part with his family home and be happy in an apartment. He quickly feels nostalgia for his lawn, flowers, trees and nature. Without them he feels deprived and almost as though he were in prison. Whenever this attitude prevails, he tries something else: the revitalization of what I called "villas," that is, the small city or town. Industries and branches of large companies are diversified. Colleges are multiplied. Instead of the large universities concentrating in a single campus, they are spread over several and situated in small cities. More and more people work either in the town where they live or in nearby incorporated areas.

In some cases towns are created. A short time ago I visited what was really a suburb of Washington, Reston, in Virginia, a few miles from the Capital. Everything in Reston is new, but the spirit that guided the construction was that of establishing a structural unity. There is a large pond like a canal, where the houses look across at each other. It has a modern, up-to-date plaza with a daring fountain which is the present day version of a town square. All the conveniences, harmonious forms, and even the picturesque elements, have been added with visible good taste.

It is quite clear what Reston means. It is a cry of alarm, the awareness of a peril; it is the will to bring back to life within the new suburb the old town that was so appealing, so full of poetry, so inspiring in daily life. For like the condition of European cities destroyed by growth and technical innovations that they have been unable to assimilate, suburban life can go very far; what I mean is it can go very far downward.

SPACE AND TIME IN AMERICAN LIFE

In order to go by plane from Bloomington, in Indiana, to South Bend, in the same state, you go through Indianapolis. But if a flight is canceled or a connection is missed, things become more complicated. A few days ago in making this trip, I had to choose between going through Chicago, in Illinois, or through Detroit, in Michigan. Both ways meant a much longer trip. I had to leave Indiana in order to enter it again. But this did not matter; the only thing that counted was that there were flights between Indianapolis and South Bend by going another way. What would have been an "itinerary" was changed into a combination of abstract routes of the airlines.

This led me to think that it was not a matter of geographical or even geometric space, but of functional space. The shortest route between two points is not a straight line, it has nothing to do with geography; instead it has something to do with that enormous, frightful book in which the flights of all airlines are registered. In other words, the shortest distance is a social and technical reality.

This is not peculiar to the United States, but rather is a characteristic of today's world. What happens is that new things usually start in the United States and are more intense and outstanding here. This is why things that often simply belong to the twentieth century seem "American" to us, as in other times certain things were thought of as Gallicisms and of French influence, when really they were merely part of the eighteenth century. It is true that in the United States we find the full development of things that elsewhere are only unsurely and timidly begun. This is why we can learn so much by observing the United States, and this is why almost nothing of what is happening in the world (and especially what is going to happen) can be understood without watching the United States. This is why I am constantly astonished at seeing those who claim to be interested in current problems ignore the United States and look in other directions.

American society is marked by a great amount of mobility. Everybody moves constantly. Not only do they come and go, travel by car, train, or airplane over the whole country, but also they are hardly ever very long in one place. College students rarely study in the city where their parents live, not even in cities with universities and colleges. In part, this is because they are not admitted: each student makes application to several institutions of greater or lesser prestige and waits, anxiously sometimes, until he knows whether he has been accepted by one or the other. Also this is due in part to the fact that students want to attend a college of their choosing, regardless of where it is. Finally, it is because in principle and according to tradition, they believe it is better to study in some other part of the country. This means that as early as seventeen or eighteen, Americans begin to cut their ties with their paternal homes and go to live elsewhere. Quite often they spend their junior year abroad, and if not, they go for graduate study overseas. Many join the Peace Corps and spend a couple of years in an exotic country. Immediately upon completing their studies, at least the first level, they accept work, nearly always in some distant place. And they usually change jobs several times in order to improve themselves and to assume other positions of greater responsibility and salary.

Consequently, those of us who have American friends frequently have to change their addresses. After a few years, under their names we find we have listed in our address books the names of different American cities and perhaps of foreign countries. We could say that countless Americans have the look of "having just arrived," and this means that they are quite alone. They move about alone if they are unmarried; with their wives and children if they have families. The nuclear family is at the center of American life; the rest are quite remote from the center: the larger family of grandparents and collateral relatives, friends, acquaintances who are not "close" but who have been known for a long time, all those who in small cities in other countries would be "everybody."

The economic abundance of the country permits this mobility to increase. I have spent many hours awaiting flights in countless American airports. Few spectacles are more interesting than the humanity that passes through them. If one knows what to look for, if one is able to identify the different types of people and the probable reasons for their trips, the inner workings of American life immediately become apparent: businessmen on their way to see clients in person or else on their way home; students on their way to college or to a weekend at home or with friends; men and women attending conventions in distant cities; intellectual gatherings and meetings; gatherings of salesmen or industrialists; political meetings; college reunions. The nation's airlines, which blanket the country to an incredible degree, spread over the map a considerable portion of the most representative inhabitants, who in principle might be found anywhere. Good or bad, this mobility seems to be the decisive factor in the nature of American life. For this wonderful possibility of being everywhere is bought at the price of not really being anywhere; or, if you prefer, the verb "to be" loses a degree of meaning in this country.

As for time, the prodigious productivity of the United States has allowed the time spent "on the job" to decrease considerably. The American of any profession, with a short working day of generally less than forty hours per week, achieves a standard of living higher than that of any other country; and with it not only greater economic, but also human possibilities. But there is a drawback: the time the American loses, the "no man's time," that spent moving, waiting for public vehicles, parking his own automobile, waiting for a green light, is a considerable portion of the day. Nearly all Americans are commuters; they practice what the French call *faire la navette* and in Spain is sometimes called *guadalajarismo*. It is impossible to say how much this reduces the amount of free time, personal time, the leisure time seemingly assured by the marvelous way in which work is organized.

On the other hand, the American schedule leads to consequences that are more serious than might be expected of such an apparently trivial matter. The Spaniard stands at the other extreme. It has been pointed out, as I myself did some years ago, that the Spanish timetable, so unbelievably late in everything, with a lunch at two-thirty or three in the afternoon and dinner between ten and eleven or later (those that are prolonged always end the next day), has several inherent drawbacks. Among them is the working day which, with its long interruptions, lasts almost the whole day, leaving none of the "free" time which is available in the United States, where the working day usually ends at five in the afternoon.

Yet, this long Spanish "morning" that may last until two o'clock, and the endless "afternoon" lasting until ten at night, seem more and more interesting to me and more conducive to the happiness of daily life. They leave time for so much more conversation and other pleasant pursuits.

Unless I am mistaken, there is a fallacy in the American timetable. In theory, work ends at five and dinner is at six or six-thirty. This means that the day is not over, but rather that now "free" or "personal" time begins. After the meal one does what one wishes, not what has to be done. But in fact, this is not the way it happens. After work, the American has to walk to where his car is parked, he drives for a long time on highways with heavy traffic, and he finally reaches his house. Or he goes to the station, takes the suburban train, travels many miles, finds his automobile in the town or suburb where he lives—or perhaps his wife waiting for him in the car—and finally gets home. He has a whisky or a cocktail, has dinner and . . . discovers that he is tired. He finds it incredibly hard to go back to his car, drive again for a long time on the highway to a play, concert, or to the home of friends. And he ends up by turning on the television and staying at home. In theory the day does not end with dinner, but in fact it does. The difference is that instead of ending, as it does with us, at ten or ten-thirty, it ends for the American at six. If we look closely, we see that the absurd, unlikely Spanish timetable is unexpectedly realistic and wisely takes into consideration human weaknesses. The experience of life makes me shudder when I think that in Spain we may decide to become "reasonable" and to "Europeanize" or "Americanize" our timetable.

58 THE EARTH'S WEALTH

WORK

American attitudes toward work are the result of both old traditions and recent conditions of society. The United States is the product of an incalculable amount of work accumulated without interruption for over three hundred years. Only through unending, well-directed, and cooperative efforts has this gigantic, hard, and difficult country with its immense hot and frigid territories, with as many obstacles as resources, been able to get under way. The proof is apparent throughout the country, and Americans shelter this attitude in the recesses of their being.

This is why their first morality was based on work, reinforced by religious considerations. The need to do *everything* in a land where nothing had been done, the awareness that nothing could be left out and that, save for the South, there was no "lower class" to take over certain kinds of work, led to one of the deepest convictions of American society: a belief in the fundamental equality of work and jobs. Work is good, and since everything must get done, any work is good. This is, more or less, the mental process of the United States, and it is quite different from what has frequently been the outlook in Europe. But the Americans go one step further, and this is when I begin to have my doubts.

When you ask an American what he does, he will tell you about his present job, and often he surprises us. The great demand for qualified people causes Americans to begin working quite early and at a good salary. The American feels, moreover, a moral haste to take a job with an organization as soon as he reaches twenty-one and in many cases as soon as he is graduated. He does this to be independent of his parents and not be a financial burden to them. The Spaniard has no qualms about accepting support from his family for several years, at least as long as he is single. The expression "to live on the check" is often used to refer to students or job-seekers perilously close to thirty. In similar conditions the American would feel both humiliated and remorseful. This causes him to accept a position right away when it is offered him, having barely finished his studies. Generally, when asked about his job, he says that he is delighted and that it is very interesting. We cannot understand very well how a person of outstanding intellectual education, with refined tastes, capable of understanding difficult books and of appreciating painting, who understands Plato, Milton, Cervantes, Descartes, Ortega, Goethe, and Machado, can be happy in an industrial office, in the personnel department of a big department store, in a fabric store, a hospital, airline, or perhaps in a cafeteria.

The American carries his good will to extremes. He respects work and all kinds of jobs. He is grateful for his job because he is well paid, and he feels an obligation to be "loyal." It seems immoral or inconsiderate to speak ill (or even to think ill) of his work. Unlike the Spaniard, who usually is critical of what he is doing, even though his may be a very important position (and he is more disparaging if his work is unimportant), the American goes to incredible lengths to try to like his work, and in any case he acts as though he likes it. In many ways this is admirable and it is the reason that most work is well done. Besides, it gives the worker a splendid awareness of "dignity," prevents unhappiness with one's lot in life, the kind of unhappiness that undermines so many other societies.

The only bad thing about this is . . . that it cannot be. For not all tasks are equal. They are equally worthy and in the United States, within certain limits, they are relatively equally remunerated (and taxes tend to make them more so). Furthermore, many so-called "inferior," unpleasant, and laborious jobs, for instance, many manual jobs, pay extremely well. And this seems just to me, because their unattractiveness must be compensated for economically. But this means that they are no longer equally interesting. Neither are they of course equally adequate for different people. This attitude toward jobs leads Americans, with disturbing frequency, to accept a job that is completely inadequate and which amounts to a mistake.

Of course the extreme American mobility includes the working force. One may easily change jobs, and not only in location but also in kind and profession. The Spaniard remains permanently with an occupation that he may never have liked, and which he meaningfully refers to as a "destiny" (*destino*). The latter term is impressive because, come what may, the Spaniard never changes jobs, and he dies doing what perhaps he would never have liked to do. The American is always ready to begin again. One of my colleagues at Indiana University told me that he started out as a bookkeeper; then he was an engineer for Bell, the fabulous telephone company of America. At thirty-five he discovered that this was not his vocation, and so decided to specialize in Spanish. Now he is preparing for his doctorate. This seems admirable to me: that at any point in life one is ready to rectify, to start anew, and to come closer to one's authentic vocation.

The biographies of all Americans present a surprising list of professions, and besides they are true. Spanish writers and artists also make such lists, as if in imitation. But sometimes they say they have been actors because they had a role in an amateur play, or druggists because they once helped a friend prepare a medication at a party in the back room of a pharmacy. Americans, though, have done many things and done them seriously, and they have earned their livings doing them professionally. This has allowed them to acquire skills and experiences, to know many different kinds of people, to put their aptitudes and abilities to the test, and to see what is behind the facade or show window of many things. This is no small gain. But like everything else in life, it has its price. They have had to pay for it not with the efforts of an apprenticeship, but with time, the very substance of life. While doing one thing, they are not able to do something else; while straying about, they reach no goal; and as long as they spend time in an occupation that does not develop the personality, their life is partially empty and lacking in quality. Human time is limited, and this is why it imposes on us the most painful of all obligations: that of finding our place.

When an American youth is told that he should not have accepted an unsatisfactory job that holds no interest for him, he generally justifies his decision with secondary reasons. And especially does he assuage his own concern with the idea that it will not last very long. It is a provisional job; soon he will leave it and do something really interesting. But one must ask, will he be able to? At the very least, will he not have lost something in the meantime? When first out of the university, with his wits and sensitivities sharpened, with the habit of intellectual work and a feeling and appreciation for beauty, with the polish from associating with teachers and classmates, he is ready to shape his life in an original and personal way. After several years of letdown, of less tension, of routine tasks carried out in the company of less stimulating and more common people, will he be the same? Will he still have the drive, the enthusiasm, the fine perception, and critical sense to do what he wants?

Fortunately, the growth of American society is so fabulous that the opportunities for qualified young people are unlimited. It becomes truer all the time that an American can be *what he wants to be*. Before he is through college, employers begin offering him interesting positions. Naturally, these are in different places, and here is where his wandering begins that will last a lifetime. If Americans were a little calmer, if they were able to wait, if they did not feel this almost pathological urgency to have a job as soon as they are graduated, if they would accept their parents' help for a few months or a year more (most parents would be happy to do it, but sometimes they do not even dare to make the offer), if they were able to wait, if they knew how to say "no" to a tempting and convenient proposition, but which holds no lasting satisfaction because it is not what attracts them, or because it means leaving cherished places, if they would learn the small arts of private life, then the incredible resources that the society has to offer, the habitual integrity in selecting, the normal appreciation of merit, all this together would permit their work (since work is a portion of man's condition) to be the expression of their perfection and fulfillment, and the certain companion of their happiness.

CAPITALISM

Without doubt, the symbol of capitalism is the socioeconomic system of the United States. When the word "capitalism" is used in Europe or in Latin America, and probably also in Asia and Africa (and of course in the Communist countries), people think of American society above anything else. And in this country itself, people usually admit that it is capitalist. And if we consider the general factors that are thought of as characteristic of capitalism, no doubt this is so: private ownership of the means of production, private profit as a stimulus to economic activity, free enterprise, an economy regulated primarily by supply and demand, bank credit—all exist in the United States.

But is this what is really understood when people talk of capitalism? When they speak of "private ownership," do they not think of "privileged ownership"; I mean belonging only to a few individuals? Do they not understand also by this that profit goes to a small minority of "entrepreneurs" or "capitalists," to the exclusion of the vast majority of people? In the *Vocabulaire philosophique* of Lelande I find this revealing definition: "A social system in which capital does not belong to those who make it productive through their work." This is a curious negative definition in which capital is explained in terms of those to whom it does *not* belong.

It is no wonder that it has been so understood, for this was more or less the situation in fact when modern capitalism came into being, especially in the first century of the Industrial Revolution: when Adam Smith rightly protested that workers could not reach an agreement in order to claim their rights, while the owners, who were few, could, and were in fact in tacit agreement; when Karl Marx declared in his *Communist Manifesto* that, "The proletariat has no country," because they possess nothing in it and do not share in its wealth, it might be thought that this is what capitalism was. Few denied its benefits, and of course neither did Marx, who was persuaded of capitalism's economic efficiency and its power to create wealth. Its harshness, oppression, and injustice were evident to all those who did not have their eyes closed.

The question is whether the capitalism of today in the United States is very similar to what was called capitalism eighty, a hundred, or a hundred and twenty years ago; or to what existed in the United States itself around the turn of the century. It is generally presupposed that the alternative to ownership by a few individuals of the means of production is ownership by the State. If we admit this, certainly the United States is still capitalistic. But is this the only alternative? Who possesses American wealth, this incredible American wealth? Not the State; *Americans* themselves own it, that is, American society owns it.

Nearly all companies have more shareholders than workers . . . for the workers are also shareholders. If not directly, they are shareholders through their deposits in the Savings and Loan Associations or through mutual funds that abound throughout the country. Women (and especially widows) possess an enormous amount of the country's wealth. This means that the capital belongs "to those who make it productive by means of their labor," or to be more truthful, it belongs to nearly all those so defined. This would mean that the United States is not a capitalistic country according to the definition of Lelande.

More than half of all American families own their homes. Practically all of them have at least one automobile. Within the home there are many valuable items, and in the bank they have sizable savings or securities. The Gross National Product grew to 800 billion dollars by the end of 1967. This sum is so vast that it outstrips our imagination, like astronomical measurements. And we must not fail to note that the most costly item is labor, especially skilled workers, either intellectual or manual, who are incredibly well paid. According to the terms of the last agreement by Ford and the labor unions, workers in the automobile industry will receive, counting wages and fringe benefits, $5.30 per hour of work, exactly 371 Spanish pesetas.

But I have already stated that nearly all Americans share in this wealth. Nevertheless, there is poverty in the country, and people talk about it constantly. The "war on poverty" is carried on in many ways, through the criticisms offered back and forth by different groups. In the United States people are technically considered "poor" who have an annual family income not exceeding three thousand dollars (210,000 pesetas, more than the recently reached *average* income in Spain). In this case this amounts to fifteen per cent of the population (thirty million out of a total population of over two hundred million). Who are these people? Above all, they are blacks from the Southern states and the ghettos of the large cities of the country. A smaller percentage is made up of recent immigrants, mainly Puerto Ricans. The latter are American citizens and can go wherever they like. They have come to this country by the hundreds of thousands, nearly always without an education and speaking no English, and they spend a difficult period of adaptation and incorporation. Then there are the old and invalid, some small farmers, and people from mining areas who are impoverished or at minimum operating levels. In other words, those lacking the education for a skilled job are included, for jobs requiring only physical strength are steadily becoming more scarce. It includes also those who lack perseverance, the unstable who leave any job or apprenticeship after a few weeks or months and slip rapidly down the scale thereafter.

This can also explain the unemployment and jobless percentages in the country. At this writing unemployment stands at four per cent, compared to seven per cent six years ago. But I have always distrusted figures that were not explained concretely. What does it mean to be unemployed in the United States? How are these statistics compiled? In the following way: a person is asked whether he or she has worked in the last two weeks. If he answers no, he is asked whether he is seeking work; if he answers yes, he is put down as "unemployed." Is this what those of us from other latitudes understand by this term? Not at all: in American statistics those who have lost their jobs are included with those who did not have them, but who think it would be nice to work. This group includes adolescents or teenagers who want to begin working; women who have not worked while their children were small, but now that the children go to school, the mothers think it would be nice to have another salary in the family; and those who have left their jobs to look for better ones, perhaps in another field, another profession, or in another part of the country.

In a society with an exceptionally high educational level, where nearly everybody has professional skills and knowledge, the person without such preparation is in a difficult situation. And poverty is particularly painful in the United States, which is organized on a foundation of abundance. The poverty zones, the poverty "pits" of which I spoke before, are much gloomier than those in Naples, Malaga, or Extremadura, which have compensations not found in the United States. This is why such urgency is felt to eliminate these zones and to liquidate what residual poverty still remains in the country. This fifteen per cent weighs on the moral conscience of Americans with an intensity unknown elsewhere, despite the fact that except for very small nuclei, the American poor have an economic level higher than that of great masses of the population of some countries, and of the great majority in others.

It may be thought from outside the United States that to raise the standard of living of fifteen per cent of the population in the midst of such prodigious wealth would be no great problem. It may be felt that if the United States wished, it would quickly heal this blight on the country. I would agree with this opinion with the exception of the adverb: not so "quickly," for the United States is not a dictatorship in which what the Government wants is done, and in which the inhabitants—not citizens—passively obey willy nilly. Nor is it a welfare state where a certain social situation is received from a benevolent state. It is, rather, a country centered on the concept of "opportunities," that is, on human possibilities, each of which is to be realized. Poverty and wealth, prosperity and decline, are risks that depend on initiative, effort, and tenacity of each man and woman. Intervention by the State must be limited to correcting the consequences of bad luck, to mitigate inequality, and to make available opportunities to the young, so that they may begin approximately at the same level as others. The rest is up to each person. These are the consequences of life under freedom.

CAPRICE AND THE MARKET

The usual image of capitalism is associated with caprice and arbitrariness. One thinks of the all-powerful head of a company making decisions and doing what he wants. In America such a person would be called a tycoon, the great shark on whose will depends the economic destiny of the multitudes.

Just how true is this image? As for relations between companies and workers, the situation in the United States is that, first of all, workers are organized in unions wielding enormous economic and social power, able to bring great pressure to bear on any sector of the country. The conditions that troubled Adam Smith, if not entirely reversed, have greatly shifted in the opposite direction. Agreement between workers is much easier, more constant and workable, than among owners. It may be argued that the large companies are extremely powerful. This is quite apparent, and they have an influence that often is pernicious and used in an undue manner. But compared to the labor organization, they amount to little; and the proof of this is that the great majority of strikes end with the victory of labor demands, even in those cases in which even the labor leaders admit their demands are excessive. On the other hand, antitrust laws limit the power of the companies and combat monopolies; and even though on occasion these laws are flouted with legal loopholes, and monopolistic conditions do exist here and there, on the whole they do not flourish.

Furthermore, we must keep in mind that the economic interests of owners and workers only very seldom clash. Not that there is any intrinsic kindness on the part of either, but because the workers share in one way or another in the profits of companies of which they too are owners.

But even this is not the most important factor. The key is that the basic instrument for regulating and rationalizing economic life is the market. By this I mean the free market. The economy of a country as developed and complex as the United States is a system of rigorous precision, and any modification that affects any part affects the whole. Production cannot be increased or decreased, nor can the price of a product be raised or lowered, without this having wide economic consequences. Caprice is excluded by the very nature of economic relations. The company that tries to "do what it takes a notion to do" would quickly fail and drag others down in its collapse.

Arbitrary attitudes are only possible in economies in which the decisive element is not the market, but rather the will of the government or its technocrats. They may tranquilly decide on the production of something they want, regardless of need, and sell it at a fixed price, because consumers must be content with what is offered them by the administration and because losses are of no concern, since the State—that is, the economy of the inhabitants of the country—pays for everything. The ministers and technocrats of State-operated countries are the only heirs of the tycoon of old capitalism who, behind his office desk, did as he pleased.

This explains the great sensitivity of the American economy to any rise in prices and, therefore, in the cost of living. If the latter increases more than two or three per cent in a year, economic circles become concerned and measures are taken to reduce it. In other countries, an increase of this size would not even be noticed, nor, of course, would we know the exact amount of increase. We find after four or five years, without knowing why, that everything costs fifty or a hundred per cent more (in some countries, for instance in Latin America, this may be as much as two hundred, three hundred, or five hundred per cent more), so that salary raises are really fictitious. Price stability is a key element in the social and even moral stability of a society.

The situation is different in the case of very specialized products handled only by a few companies. Strictly speaking, in these cases there is no completely free market, but rather a more or less attenuated kind of oligopoly; for example, in the manufacture of computers, certain complicated electrical equipment, airplanes, and especially the space industry. Yet even in such cases, a considerable restriction should be placed on what I have just stated. These delicate and highly specialized industries are not "basic." What I mean is that they do not use raw materials, but rather the products of other complex industries: metallurgical, chemical, electrical, and optical companies, among others. These industries depend, then, on the whole of American industry and are subject to the regulation of that industry by the market. Oligarchistic or monopolistic tendencies only affect the top echelons of production, and therefore their importance in the total volume of the economy is minimal. Besides, the Government is the best customer of these industries, and the Government has at its disposal means of applying pressure greater than any the companies might wield. The final consequence of this is that a residue of the American economy is not subject to regulation by a free market.

Who, then, makes the economic decisions in the United States? We should have to answer: products. Products themselves, with their systematic connections and their fine balance, are what decide. Industry does not manufacture what someone wants, but *what has to be made*. If anything else is produced, it turns out to be bad business and a financial loss. And private industry, unlike state-run businesses, cannot lose money. The state always loses someone else's money, that belonging to all the citizens. Since businesses are the property of American society, the entire social body has an interest in them.

This is why Americans have a deep-seated aversion to the Government assuming the role of business, to its possessing wealth, and to its having the decisive voice in economic life. Probably they see in this the decline of economic prosperity and the decrease or loss of political freedom besides. The term "socialism" awakens mixed feelings in the United States. For this word may mean two quite different things. If we mean by it the ownership of wealth and production by the state, the great majority of Americans radically distrust this kind of socialism. But if we mean the protection of individuals against oppression or abuse, misfortune, sickness, or accident, if we mean social security, the establishment of minimum wage, medical insurance, retirement, and pensions, then a growing majority of Americans are more or less in favor of this kind of socialism. Those who are called "liberals" in the United States (a term subject to misinterpretation) are generally referred to pejoratively as "socialists" by others who consider themselves more truly liberal, while the liberals look on the latter as "reactionaries."

How does this misunderstanding come about? Who is right? Although to be exact, we would have to admit many reservations and restrictions regarding these observations, we can in general say that the Democratic Party, which considers itself more liberal, is accused of being "socialistic" by the Republicans, who look on themselves as the guardians of true liberalism. Republicans instinctively distrust the government. It is with some fear that they watch the growth of the federal administration and its bureaucracy, its budget and powers: big government seems dangerous, anti-American, and destructive to national vitality. The Democrats, on the other hand, consider big government necessary and believe that the position of their opponents amounts to a tenacious defense of the privileges of big business.

If the present situation is compared to that prevailing in the United States when I came for the first time in 1951, it is apparent that the government has grown enormously. With the aid of television, Washington now weighs incredibly more on the life of the country. The federal authorities now deal with much larger budgets (even discounting the large sums for defense), and they have many more duties than before. The fear of the Republicans seems justified. Yet, on the other hand, there is a constant complaint that the federal government is not doing enough, and that it is too subservient to social forces. For some it is almost "socialistic"; for others it is too "liberal." ‡ What does this mean? Is there not a misuse of these economic, social, and political terms? Do they not mean different things in Europe and the United States, and even among Americans themselves?

UTILITARIANISM

Every time there is evidence of American generosity, it is thought that the United States acts this way because it stands to gain something from it. Others try to uncover some selfish motive in this seemingly altruistic and generous behavior, and usually they do. As a matter of fact, the situation resulting from their generosity is to the advantage of Americans. The best example of this is that of Europe after the Second World War. It is evident that without the Marshall Plan, European countries would have lived in a precarious state for the rest of the twentieth century, huddled in destroyed cities, in unhealthful conditions, industries razed and ruined by the war and difficult to rebuild, and with a shortage of raw materials. With this would have come as a consequence a very low standard of living with its attendant political instability and immorality. The population would have been reduced to occupations based on a bare subsistence; activities having to do

‡ In the classic, European sense, essentially meaning nonintervention of government in economic affairs and maximum personal and political freedom from an overweening state—Ed.

with luxuries or with higher intellectual and artistic things would have been scorned. Such would have been the situation of Europe today and for a long time to come, if the United States had followed the traditional policy of oppression of the vanquished and indifference to the fate of others.

But it can be seen that a Europe in ruin and decadence was not the best thing for the United States. It was better for America to have a strong and prosperous Europe able to block the expansionistic path of Russia and not be at her mercy; a Europe with a market able to absorb American products and contribute to the development of American industry; Europe as a stable political body, rather than as a focal point of disturbance. All this is certainly true: the rebuilding and development of Europe did benefit the United States. And herein lies the greatest originality: for the first time in history a great country, a leading country and to a degree a ruling country, has come to believe that in order for things to go well for it, *they must go well for other countries.*

From private to historical life, and throughout the intermediate areas, this is one of the most deep-seated of American convictions. This is the principle behind the economic innovation of Henry Ford, who was convinced that it was to the industry's benefit to enrich the workers so that they could buy the automobiles they were building. This is the attitude that holds that it is not good to be surrounded by the poor, ignorant, sick, or weak, but by their opposite numbers. It is the reverse of the popular Spanish saying: *En tierra de ciegos, el tuerto es rey.** The United States believes that it is highly uncomfortable to be one-eyed, and that the prospect of ruling over the blind is not very attractive.

The strange thing is that the correct consequences of this consideration are not drawn. What I mean is, despite the evidence, people still think that the United States is concerned exclusively with *its* own advantage. The key is that it seeks its

* "In the land of the blind, the one-eyed man is king"—Trans.

own benefit through the benefit of others, in connection with, and inseparably linked to, the good of others. American *utilitarianism*, which is quite strong, is tied to *idealism*, which constitutes one of the abiding features of society and individual life in the United States. The two tendencies have contended with one another in private lives, in politics, industry, economic attitudes, and in international conduct. They have alternated in predominance at times within the same biography; and of course they are visible in the vicissitudes of the country's history. Finally, and this is one of the great facts of our time, they have made peace with each other. Americans of today are convinced that utilitarianism and idealism do not clash, but rather that they are mutually enhancing and necessary. Are the Americans right or wrong? This is another matter altogether. The harvest of ingratitude and defamation Americans have reaped in the Europe that—for whatever motives you may wish—they rebuilt and saved from ruin, is not exactly encouraging. Nearly all the countries of Europe are using the wealth obtained through American aid in trying to harm the economy of the United States. They use their military power derived from that economy to hinder American affairs, including among the latter the defense of Europe. They take advantage of their outstanding success in many fields in order to launch anti-American campaigns. All this has reached such a volume that Americans might ask whether it is really to their benefit to help others, and whether a healthy, strong, and rich Europe is preferable to Europe impoverished and decadent.

For the most part, Americans still think they were right in what they did, and their attitude is unchanged. Although they feel and weigh the drawbacks of the present situation, they believe the other alternative would have presented more problems. They realize that to a large extent these attitudes can be explained by resentment. Some countries have on their conscience collective guilt, and they console themselves by creating—or at least exaggerating—the guilt of others, such as comparing the elimination of six million Jews to the unjust treatment of some Negro groups. Others were until a short time ago leading countries, but no longer are; they have a glorious military history, but in the last war they fought little and badly. It weighs on their conscience to be indebted for their independence and prosperity to the sacrifice and help of others, and they refuse to be grateful. They have seen their stature shrink in world culture and even the international use of their language decrease. They observe all this with regret and try to remove "the thorn in their sides" with hostility and pretended disdain toward those who have succeeded them in the vanguard of history. When General De Gaulle went from Paris to Mexico, he flew in an American plane to the French Antilles; there he took a Caravelle because he wanted to arrive in a plane from his country, and it so happens that one cannot cross the Atlantic in a French plane. It was an extremely puerile gesture (but one of the most revealing).

It is still thought in the United States that this is a passing and understandable phenomenon, and that it will not last. Americans believe that beneath the spite, ill humor, or vanity, there are stronger and more sensible feelings. They think that after a certain time Europeans will become convinced that prosperity cannot flourish in an attitude of seclusion, but rather that it requires a general system in which the whole world definitely can and should be included.

A real and outstanding example of this belief is the Peace Corps. Young graduates of American universities, many of them the more brilliant students, some of them intelligent and refined young women, go to countries that are largely under-developed and agree to live there for two years or more amid conditions of the lowest social classes, with minimal pay, much lower than what they could easily earn on any job in the United States. They undergo arduous training and then work very hard, exposing themselves to considerable risks to help the people of some far-off land, teaching them the necessary skills and techniques to reach what is accepted as the present standards. These young people have interesting experiences: they see the world, they put their capacity for endurance and action to the test, and they take the human measure of themselves. The ends they pursue are utilitarian if you like, but of a kind of utilitarianism that is significant and seldom found. But they also go into this service with a moral purpose, because they feel more at peace with themselves when they have shared in the most dramatic way possible: through giving of themselves, that is, through contributing in fact and not just in word to the sharing of these American privileges, so that in a sense they are privileges no longer.

American utilitarianism is very real, but let us not forget that it was originally defined as "the greatest happiness for the greatest number." In reality, it is based on a respect for benefit. The American generally accepts what he thinks benefits him, although it may benefit others as well, and it is better if it works for the good of everybody. This attitude is not so normal as might be supposed. Sayings like *quedarse tuerto por dejar ciego a otro** are incomprehensible to the American. He believes that it is very bad business to lose an eye, and he sees no good in blinding others. He prefers that all see well and not bump into street corners (the corners against which, in other places, people want to crush their fellow man).

The negative side of all this is that at times there is confusion between the moral and technical aspects of problems. Sometimes Americans have a moral view of questions that need strict, technical straightforwardness. I do not mean to imply that politics does not have a moral dimension, but simply that in such matters moral concerns should, as it were, decide, but not interfere. Considerations about whether or not a surgical operation should be performed are of the utmost importance, since the operation itself depends on them,

* "To lose an eye in order to blind somebody else"—Trans.

but they should have not the slightest influence on *how* the operation and the surgical technique ought to be performed. This is why American foreign policy, which is almost always noble and well-intended, is sometimes not very intelligent. And we should not forget that intelligence is a form of nobility.

FLESH AND BLOOD

The growth of the federal government is probably the most apparent, and for many Americans the most disturbing, change in the last fifteen or twenty years. The specter of governmental intervention, planning, and socialization, perturbs many who adhere to the traditional forms of American life, in which individual initiative prevailed, where everyone was responsible for his life, and where the state in the background regulated in a simple way the general form of collective life. Since this system was exceptionally effective, it is understandable that any substantial change may appear dangerous. There are many Americans who are alarmed at what they consider the hypertrophy of the machinery of government. Barry Goldwater's appeal to many in the 1964 elections was because of his "reactionary" significance; but to others of his followers he symbolized true liberalism and was looked on as a safeguard against socialistic and governmental tendencies that were threatening individual freedom.

But we must question whether such hypertrophy really exists. It is undeniable that the machinery of government has been multiplied several times over. But is this not a particularly clear case of changing so as to remain the same, an example of the changes made by the United States so as to remain true to itself and to its essential and original structure? Government is only a relatively abstract fragment of the social body. We could say that it is its skeleton, on which are implanted the muscles, vessels, and nerves that make up the organism. Now the skeleton is much larger than it was a generation ago, and its osseous mass is impressive. But what about the flesh? Has not the *total* growth of the United States demanded the development of the governmental skeletal structure in order not to lose its equilibrium?

American society has expanded prodigiously. If the government had remained the same, would we not now have an adult body on the skeleton of a child? Could this immense American complex be moved with the governmental structure of fifteen or twenty years ago? It is hard to express human changes quantitatively, and statistics, which only give figures dealing with abstract amounts, are usually misleading. Nevertheless, my impression is that society has grown *more* than has the Government. This means that the *ratio* or proportion is even more favorable to society than it was when I first came to this country. The population of the United States has gone from 160 million to over 200 million. But this growth does not reflect that of society itself, because each individual today represents many more social actions in every area than fifteen years ago. The gross national product has more than doubled; the number of books published and read has increased several times over; the number of students has increased enormously, out of all proportion to the increase of the population. Last year more than 650,000 academic titles at the university level were conferred. This is fifteen times more than fifty years ago, when the population was half as great. The use of energy, the number of telephones, cars, appliances of all kinds, shareholders (twenty-two million; in other words, counting the members of each family involved, this amounts to at least a third of the population), travelers within the country and abroad (two million passports either new or renewed in 1967 alone), have all increased tremendously. And to these figures must be added all kinds of new associations, initiatives, actions, pressures, inventions, displacements in every order of life, and countless letters and packages that the mails transport from one point to another. American society as a concrete reality, that is, as an active and living structure, has crossed over into a new order of magnitude.

In order for the United States to remain the same, its government has had to convert itself into something else. This is what men of traditional and inflexible minds do not see. In longing for the past (the recent past, for everything flies by), they do not realize that if their desires could be fulfilled, they would find themselves suddenly living in a country entirely different from the one they long for and recall with nostalgia. If the federal government and the entire administration had not grown and changed, if they had not increased their effectiveness, especially by means of mechanization and computers, the United States would be so deformed as to be unrecognizable.

Is there, then, no grounds for the concern and worry of these liberals? Is there no socialism in the country, of the kind that seems a dangerous tendency to them? We must not forget that on the one hand, the innovators, the advocates of governmental growth and its functions and, therefore, of a certain amount of governmental intervention, are called "liberals" in the United States. Is there a distinction between political liberalism and economic liberalism? Are the Democrats the advocates of the former especially, and the Republicans of the latter?

Undoubtedly something of the kind does occur. But I believe, besides, that these concepts are not very clear in the United States as elsewhere. The inspirations of liberalism and democracy, which are different although they converge and complement each other, are confused with each other. And even more misleading, liberalism is mistaken for *one* of its forms that originally was identified with it, but which has contributed greatly to distorting it: individualism.

The United States is too big and complex a country for individual action on the public to be easy. In the sector of private life, the United States is still an individualistic country. The rights of the individual are defended against the intrusions of power. Year after year the Supreme Court, one of the most alert, advanced, independent, innovative, and incorruptible bodies in the world today, hands down rulings affirming the independence of the individual and limiting (many think too much) the powers of the federal government, the states, local authorities, the police, the army, company owners, and the press, while vigorously defending the freedom of the latter. But when it comes to an individual exercising effective influence on the country as a whole, then it is a different matter.

The very size of the territory makes this quite difficult; its largely decentralized structure; the lack of a capital that is, in other than an administrative sense, the "head" of the country; the lack of national newspapers (most of them are local, and the few read nationally, like the *New York Times*, reach a relatively small minority); the enormous cost of any action broad enough to reach everywhere—all are obstacles to action by a single individual. Although he may be successful in publishing his opinions in a newspaper or magazine, multitudes of Americans will never be aware of it. If someone wishes to sell a product, he must distribute and announce it to the huge national market, and this requires a large volume of production and a great financial outlay. Often a product will be shown in a store window with a caption saying: "Advertised in *Life*"; that is, they are advertising that the product is advertised in *Life*, or, if you like, they advertise in *Life* so as to be able to say they do. This means that the product is important, produced in quantity, and widely distributed. It is advertising raised to the second power.

Yet as soon as Americans join together, the difficulties disappear. Everything then becomes possible, any social action, backed by law, is a technique and is really quite easy and effective. Political parties, unions, fraternities and sororities, the alumni of any university, student groups, religious groups, ethnic minorities, the countless cultural, political, sport, and benefit organizations of all kinds and for all purposes that fill the country, including the ephemeral and temporal groups brought together for a specific and passing purpose, have the economic and bureaucratic means to impose their points of view, their opinions, and their wills in any zone, stratum, or aspect of American life.

American liberalism is not individualistic in the sense that isolated actions are easy and effective. It is individualistic in the sense that the individual is defended not only by the State, but also by society. But he is defended in an active and politically efficient way that is *social* liberalism. It is a liberalism that primarily affects *society* against abusive and undue intervention by the State as well as *social groups* of any type, not only for their protection, but also for the possibility of their influence and historical projection.

Only lately has it become clear that the identification of liberalism with individualism was a mistake of the nineteenth century; it was a general error of a way of thinking that set the individual apart from the State, while ignoring entirely the reality of society itself in its entirety and its several manifestations. This error has in fact been corrected in the United States, although this has not been duly noted intellectually. If the word "socialism" were used precisely and in its true meaning, the United States would be the most socialistic country on earth. In this country neither the State nor the individual are overly strong; *rather the power lies with society and its social ingredients.* The countries that call themselves socialist are those where society has neither voice nor the means to act, to influence, or to express itself. All this is done in the name of society by the state. They are "statist," not socialist countries, and for this reason, they are not liberal. In the United States the bone structure, the inert skeleton with its rigid parts, is neither the end nor the key factor. It merely serves to lend consistency, continuity, and force to the elastic, sensitive, living, and changing flesh that makes up the social body.

MONEY

The symbol of the United States seems to be the dollar. When political cartoonists and even famous painters want to show an American, they draw a dollar sign on his stomach. It is true that the United States has produced the greatest accumulation of wealth that has ever existed on the planet. It is also true that Americans are in proportion richer than the inhabitants of other countries of the world. Besides, they talk a lot about money and have no hesitation in agreeing on what they are going to pay or charge for something. Money is not a confidential matter talked about in hushed tones, as it is in other places. Besides, everybody knows that in talking of a person, they say: "So and so is worth a hundred thousand dollars, or a million."

Leandro Fernández de Moratin,* who was in England at the end of the eighteenth century, relates that this is what the English said—in pounds, naturally. So, it turns out that this expression is not original with the United States, but rather comes from old, spiritual Europe. Among Spaniards and in many other places of the world, it is fashionable and in good taste to speak ill of money (while looking for it, naturally). The traditional expression used in talking of money has been *bienes* [wealth], but it is seldom used nowadays. People in the United States still believe, and make no effort to hide it, that wealth is a good thing. Moreover, money is a unit of measure; many things can be measured in dollars, and many things can be bought with them. They are, then, the equivalent of many possibilities. Americans are idealistic about money and try to accumulate it. They work to earn more and they respect the

* Spanish neo-Classical dramatist (1760–1828)—Trans.

man who is able to do so. Why? Because this man has it at his disposal and can do many things with it, and because having made it is an indication of his effectiveness, ability, capacity for work, and as if this were not enough, his good luck. Someone worth a million dollars, especially if he has earned it himself, is unquestionably a worthy person (this is the way an American usually reasons).

This attitude is what invariably is interpreted as "materialism." But things are not so simple. In the first place, it cannot be seen that in the rest of the world people seek money any less. Everywhere things must be paid for, those who work charge, and people want to make more money. In other countries I have visited tipping is more prevalent than in the United States, and in some the demands are ferocious. But above all, the relationship to money is "looser" in the United States. Let me explain.

Once an American has earned or possesses money in some way, he feels relatively few ties to it. There is little avarice of the sordid kind in American society. The American spends with largesse, he repairs his home or buys another, gets rid of his old clothes and appliances and buys new ones, he travels, he entertains others, and hoards relatively little money. Furthermore, this money is donated in amounts that are absolutely incredible and incomparable to anything found in any other society. Privately and publicly, it is given in small amounts and astronomical figures for many purposes.

The United States has countless orchestras, one of the costliest things imaginable, supported by contributions and donations by citizens of the cities and states that organize them. Museums, which are excellent even in small cities, count especially on private donations to continue, to construct new buildings, and to buy new items. The universities are financed largely through donations by alumni and people completely unassociated with the schools. When I was teaching in Harvard, a gentleman *still living* made a single endowment to that university of thirty million dollars. In nearly all universities there are splendid buildings, laboratories, and libraries bearing the names of endowers; many chairs are privately endowed with enough money to give the holder a splendid salary year after year. Of course, churches are supported by the faithful —and occasionally by those who do not belong to them, but who admire them for some reason. Hospitals are supported with donations that reach hundreds of millions of dollars. Countless prizes and scholarships are offered by private citizens.

Often a fortune, especially if it is a sizable one, is not left to the family. Part of it, perhaps the major portion, may be set aside for religious, charitable, or educational purposes. The American father feels obligated to give his children a good education, although it may be quite expensive. In other words, he wants to leave them with the *means* for earning money, but not money itself. In other countries this would be incomprehensible. There the fortune is perhaps left to the Church if there are no close heirs. A visit to the great American museums will reveal that they are built mainly with private contributions amounting to vast sums that have been left by wealthy patrons. And all this is normal and frequent. It is in no way the exception but the American *way*.

Furthermore, Americans lend financial support to a wide range of "causes," including the most unlikely and absurd. The only provision is that the cause must seem generous. Any group that is more or less persecuted anywhere on earth, any minority, any need, any project, is supported with sums that continue to surprise me. The readiness of the middle class American to take out his checkbook and donate a check of a considerable amount is completely improbable.

This does not take into consideration what we find when we go from the individual to the large social organizations or the government. The large foundations—there are hundreds of smaller ones—lend financial support in incalculable amounts to almost every area of research, teaching, and charitable work over two-thirds of the globe. The Ford Foundation on a single occasion in 1956 gave four million dollars to American universities and colleges, and since then has continued to make very important donations. The Rockefeller, Carnegie, and other foundations have made similar donations according to their size.

Finally, the United States as such, as the American nation represented by its government, has invested in foreign aid not just tremendous amounts, but sums amounting to another order of magnitude without parallel in history. The rebuilding of Europe—friends, foes, winners, and losers—since 1945 has changed the meaning of foreign policy and the course of history in the second half of the twentieth century. Imagine what the world today would have been had the United States followed the age-old tradition which it daringly cast aside at that time. Europe, which is today prosperous and powerful, with the highest standard of living in history, a political rival of the United States, would have been sunk in bitter poverty, in total powerlessness for decades. And it is impossible to see what Europe would have been after such a period. To a lesser extent, aid to Latin America, Asia, and Africa has been considerable, and it is an important factor in the present situation of these continents.

It would be interesting to pinpoint precisely how many things, how many projects and businesses are supported by American money. If better accounts were kept, we should find that American money is being used to support the anti-Americanism sweeping over the world. Professional anti-Americans, those who write and speak and are actively trying to show that the United States is "evil" or at least a despicable and annoying reality, usually enjoy scholarships, pensions, invitations, and trips sponsored by America. They may be well paid professors in American universities with publications in reviews financed by one of the foundations or by private individuals. I have read fiery attacks against the United States and all it represents in publications sponsored, as can be verified in the publication itself sometimes, by the government or society of this very country. Those who enthusiastically supported National Socialism and all the forms of fascism, the same ones who later shifted their enthusiasm to other varieties of totalitarianism and who feel hostility and disdain for American life and its culture, hasten to find positions in American institutions of learning as soon as life in their own countries becomes uncomfortable or when they simply wish to better their intellectual or financial horizon.

Does this mean that such people change and alter their views? Not at all. Then one might think this can only happen once. In the future the United States will have no truck with such people. But this is not so either. Although it seems strange, the attitude of these people arouses no adverse consequences. Of all the attributes of American money, this is the strangest.

59 THE AFTER-DINNER HOUR

My experience in the United States has been that when you dine with Americans, after dinner the talk turns to religion.

This is always somewhat unexpected. It is supposed to be a topic not to be discussed (somebody has said that it is indiscreet to speak either of the body or the soul). It is an intimate, personal, and controversial theme that can lead to differences. This is why people prefer to ignore it. When it does come up, it is almost always by chance and seems the exception to the rule. But the exceptions are undoubtedly quite frequent.

Religiously, the United States is a pluralistic country. It is mainly made up of groups that are more or less fugitives from their original countries, and who sought in America that freedom of religion that today is beginning to seem a real right, but which has been won at the cost of so many tears, so much suffering and blood, so much smoke of burned human flesh—and so much religion. This does not mean that there was very much religious freedom in the beginning within each community in North America. The first inhabitants of New England, Pennsylvania, Maryland, or Virginia were often strict, intolerant, and even fanatic. But since it was a case of *several* kinds of intolerances and not of any single monolithic view, they were doomed to failure and to mutual cancellation. And this opened the way to tolerance and coexistence. The different religious denominations soon learned to live together and later to cooperate with each other. Now they are beginning to show mutual understanding; perhaps someday they will come to love each other.

A key factor has been that no church has been politicized; there has never been an *establishment*, never an official religion, no alliance between Church and State. For this reason religion has never been linked to a dominant class or to public power. And this is why the well-known "apostasy of the masses," primarily of the working classes, has never happened in the United States. Here anticlericalism does not exist, for neither does clericalism. In America one adheres to this or that religion, or to none, for personal or family reasons, or because of background; but not because one belongs to a certain social class. American workers are as religious—or unreligious—as the other groups within American society.

There are more than two hundred fifty religious bodies in this country, but it would be a serious mistake to say that each is a different religion. In the first place, the great majority of these are small, marginal groups representing particular forms of worship. The large denominations come to only a few today. The largest group is the Catholic, which comprises almost a fourth of the country. But if the large Protestant denominations are added together—Episcopalians, Presbyterians, Methodists, Congregationalists, Lutherans, and Baptists—they make up the majority. To these must be added more or less five million Jews and small groups of other religions. The different Protestant denominations cannot be considered as different religions. Rather they are different forms of the same religion, and although the differences are greater, they are similar to the Catholic religious orders: Jesuits, Dominicans, Franciscans, Carmelites, and so forth.

But just as linguistically American society is English, since the original nucleus of the country was British, so the religious *social form* is Protestant. I mean by this that the social traits of a religious nature are colored by the temperament, or temperaments, that historically have characterized Protestantism. Against this background appear the different attitudes and content that define each denomination. For example, American Catholicism, which was influenced by forms originating in Ireland and Italy, the two most dominant influences, undoubtedly contains elements from Protestant sources. This means an enrichment of Catholicism not found in other countries. Today these elements are quite influential, and this can be seen after the Ecumenical Council aimed at overcoming the narrowness and provincialism of a style that is not "Catholic"—universal—but rather peculiar to certain regions and a reflection of certain nationalistic traits.

I have known quite well Americans of different religious views: Jesuits, theologians, and Protestant ministers; many Jews, some of whom were Orthodox. I have seen from within Catholic universities and several colleges connected to the Presbyterian Church or to nondenominational Protestantism. I have been in contact with people belonging to marginal sects, such as Christian Science and Mormonism. The differences are great; in some cases, it is hard to understand the content of some beliefs that to the European seem somewhat "eccentric," and it is even harder to reconcile them with the undeniable intelligence, good sense, level-headedness, and sense of reality of those who profess these beliefs.

Leaving aside these extreme forms, there is a trait or two that seems to appear throughout the American attitude on religion. Many years ago I observed that in Europe the traditional insistence has been on an element of *belief*—and this accounts for the obsession with "error," heresy, and disagreement. In the United States the emphasis is on *worship*. To this degree, then, the stress is on what is common to the different groups, on what unites them; for the religious differences deal first of all with the forms of worship, and in theory these forms do not exclude or oppose each other.

Furthermore, Christianity has left a very deep mark on this country and has shaped its mode of being in the world. To the American a neighbor is immediately someone who is close, someone "nigh," the man of flesh and blood who lives close by. And while, of course, the American does not love this person as himself, he does love him, and this is apparent. This is what one *feels* when he enters American society: a friendly, benevolent way of viewing one's fellow man that is previous to any contact. Naturally, Americans have all the shortcomings of other people, and they commit all the sins of others. But their *starting point* is for the most part an initial attitude of understanding, trust, good wishes—in short, love. And the degree to which these feelings are maintained in dealing with others is quite high, regardless of the deceit, disloyalty, cheating, or violence that may arise from such contacts and which are always part of the total life of any country. This is why I once said that the United States is *the next thing to a Christian Country*. This is also what Maritain nobly and astutely saw and said in his *Reflections on America*.

And there is still one other trait: Americans feel guilt as do few others, and they are capable of repentance. The confession is a prominent literary genre. American self-criticism does not come in the form of grumbling, denying, or detracting; it is confession with a desire for penitence. The strong and effective expression, "I am sorry," is not only a formula for courtesy and apology; when someone uses it, it means a heartfelt desire to amend what he has done, and he hopes for pardon and a rebirth of friendship and good feeling.

Still, one might observe, all this is human, too human. What about things specifically religious? What about the supernatural? What about the matter of God and the strictly religious life? What of the awareness, not of guilt, but of sin, and of the hope of immortality and resurrection? This would carry us far afield. Undoubtedly there are many Americans who are uprooted, of uncertain moral ideas, entirely secularized, interested only in this world and rarely aware of the next. No doubt in many cases belonging to a church is more a social activity than anything else, a custom, a family tradition, or a sign of distinction. In many forms of Protestantism the kernel of faith preserved is so delicate and imprecise that it becomes problematic as to whether these people can be called Christians. There are orgiastic forms of religion, the revivals of some marginal denominations that produce discomfort, although I would not dare deny them some religious value. Along with all this are frequently found pure and intense forms of religiosity without the socio-political ties so annoying in other countries. Here we find examples of brotherly love—toward Negroes, toward the persecuted, those under attack, the needy, the dissolute and delinquent—that arouse admiration and almost envy.

Above all, I believe that even those Americans like the biblical Martha, who are concerned and burdened with the things of this world, loving their neighbor, whom they have seen, but, perhaps, not remembering God, whom they have not seen, may love Him without knowing it. Perhaps this is why, after dinner, with a foreigner alongside who sometimes talks about philosophy, they unexpectedly start talking about religion.

60   THE UNIVERSITY

In the last sixteen years I have taught in seven universities in the United States, in five programs of other American universities in Madrid, and I have lectured in fifty more in the East, the South, the Midwest, California, and Texas. I have been in private universities, men's colleges, state universities (there are no federal universities), coeducational and women's colleges, colleges without religious ties, Catholic and Protestant schools, huge universities of fifty thousand students and others of only a few hundred. My experience has touched on most varieties of university life in the United States.

In *Los Estados Unidos en escorzo*‡ I examined the American university in some detail. I do not wish to repeat what I said then, but I would like to point out both some changes that have occurred or have become noticeable in the last decade and some aspects that have become more relevant.

The first factor we must take into consideration is growth. Unlike European and Latin American universities, American universities were designed for great numbers of students. But in addition, in the last fifteen years the number of students has doubled and now stands at about five million. This means that of every forty Americans, one of them is studying in an institution of higher learning (as opposed to one Frenchman out of

‡ Part I of the present volume—Ed.

every hundred or one Spaniard out of three hundred). This means that in the very near future the entire American population, the only limitation being intellectual ability, will at some time attend a university or similar school. Most of these students take only the four years of college and obtain the first college degree, the B.A. or Bachelor of Arts, or the equivalent in science, pre-law, and so forth. Fewer than a fourth of the total continue graduate studies for the degrees of Master of Arts (M.A.), Doctor of Philosophy (Ph.D.), or higher professional degrees. In other words, only a million students, approximately, choose careers that are specifically intellectual. The rest take up different professions in all fields where a college education is considered more and more necessary. And in these fields, having a higher degree assures one of easily obtaining a position with the best salary. We may observe in passing that this proves the prestige of the university and the confidence the country has in its graduates.

Yet this presents many problems and necessitates changes that have been occurring in the last few years. The growing number of students forces the universities to expand constantly. Since it is thought that large classes are of little value and are only permitted in beginning and very general courses, and since a very high number of disciplines and specialized courses are taught, many professors are needed. A university is thought to be well staffed when there is a ratio of one professor for every ten or fewer students. One for every fifteen students would be the top limit. But this means that the number of college teachers needed varies between 300,000 and 500,000. Professors' salaries, while perhaps still lower than those in other professions requiring similar preparation, are quite high. Rarely are they lower than six thousand dollars for young instructors, and for full professors they generally range from fifteen to twenty-five thousand dollars. The teaching faculty represents, then, an enormous cost; but the greatest problem lies in finding such a high number of people with sufficient intellectual education and teaching ability. Furthermore, university expenses are immense: administration, classroom buildings, laboratories, housing, and libraries. A small college of some five hundred students may have a library with thirty, fifty, or a hundred thousand books housed in a fine building. Large schools with two thousand or more students have libraries with three or four hundred thousand volumes. University libraries with over a million books now number over forty, and there are several that have between two and seven million. The costs involved in buying, cataloguing, binding, and even disposing of unusable books are tremendous. The American university is a very expensive operation.

And who pays for it? Above all, the students (or better, their parents). Private universities, which make up the majority, charge their students for tuition and housing. The cost of a year's schooling varies between $1500 and $2500. This means that American families set aside a considerable amount of their income for the education of their children, which they consider a duty and an investment—the one bringing the best return—for the rest of their lives. But this is not enough. Education costs much more than what is paid for it. The rest is paid by American society in general: alumni with their regular and sizable gifts, private citizens, foundations, and the properties and wealth owned by the large universities.

On the other hand, there are the state universities—state and not federal. There are not many of these, one in nearly every state, in some two or three, but they are usually quite large. Nevertheless, their students are in the minority. They are cheaper than private schools, although housing is more expensive. In many of them located in big cities, the students do not live on campus. Tuition is only a half or a third as much as in private colleges, and in some it is free. These state universities are supported by all the citizens of a state through taxes. This means they are supported by those who use them and those who do not.

There is still another source of income. Private industry and some federal agencies are deeply interested in scientific research. They set up and finance admirable laboratories and research centers attracting the best scientists to do research in physics, chemistry, biology, and related technical areas. These centers are concerned with pure research which in theory has nothing to do with activities of the sponsoring corporation. But they lead to invention and discovery that may bring to light some new medicine, alloy, radiation, virus, or atomic particle with tremendous consequences for the technical world. In the last few years, these corporations have shown a preference for helping the universities through private contracts so that certain types of research can be carried on. Thus, the resources of industry or of the Government contribute heavily to financing the universities, especially those in the forefront of scientific studies. Nor should it be overlooked, moreover, that this does not mean a technical overspecialization of research. On the contrary. Not only the universities, but also the technical institutes such as the famous MIT (Massachusetts Institute of Technology), Caltech (California Institute of Technology), or that of Illinois, and others, dedicate approximately a third of their teaching efforts to the humanities—philosophy, literature, history, art, and languages—a little over a third to pure science, and only thirty per cent to applied science.

Since today the problems of war are so closely tied to science, and the discoveries made can equally affect medicine, the technical problems of construction, the preservation of food, or intercontinental missiles and space ships, these connections of the universities to industry and the government have given rise to a moral and political problem. Many intellectuals contest the legality or suitability of these associations, especially because of the secrecy demanded of the researchers in certain programs and because of the influence that their discoveries may have on warfare, such as the Vietnamese conflict, to which many of them have raised objections. In general terms, it is the professors in the area of the humanities who are most disturbed by this (although not personally affected), while scientists tend to consider these resources as a means for making prodigious advances in research and for finding solutions to the pressing problems of mankind that will save millions of lives and improve the quality of life in general. Nor do they think that the military use of their scientific discoveries is anything new or avoidable, but rather something that has happened as long as science has existed in the West. This is an open question, and it is being discussed today in American universities and publications. It is interesting to see how moral problems overlap those that are seemingly technical matters. In the ivory tower of the laboratories stirs a breeze fanned by human, all too human, passions.

And this brings us to the question of what these universities are like on the inside.

Nobody in the United States would think that a university is an institution owned by the professors and attended by the students. Of course professors are necessary, and without them there would be no university. But the university is *for* the students, and this overriding aim seems decisive.

The students' relationship to the university is defined by freedom in a good many aspects, and since this freedom is real, it seems limited by the limitations of reality. What I mean is that it is not an abstract freedom that is merely undefined and general. In the first place, students *choose* the university or college where they go to study. They are not limited to only one, nor even to those nearby. Frequently they choose to study in a distant part of the country. The universities fight for prestige and try to secure the best professors, to improve their facilities, libraries, and laboratories, and to stay at the top in research and ideas. But on the other hand, forty-three out of every hundred young Americans—men and women—go to college. This means that the pressure on the best universities is enormous. There are many more students applying for admission than they can handle. Consequently, the universities also *select* their students. Each person who wants to be admitted sends applications to several attractive universities, and these either accept or reject his application depending on the merits and character of the student and according to his potential. Economic considerations are of little consequence, since there are many scholarships that permit a bright youngster of limited personal means to attend an expensive university. Furthermore, many students work for the university and earn their tuition and board. Federal programs of aid to students in higher education has reached fifteen million dollars, more than a billion Spanish pesetas, and this is only a fraction of the total aid granted. If we add to this the fact that the great majority of American workers and farmers can send their children to college without outside help, because their income is enough to permit it, it can be understood why the American university is in no sense the exclusive property of certain classes.

To this "competitive freedom" enjoyed by students in the universities must also be added another kind of academic freedom, or better, two kinds of freedom. Professors have complete freedom to teach according to their convictions and training, and any interference with this academic freedom unleashes protests that ultimately prevail. On the other hand, the universities are free to employ professors, depending on their teaching and intellectual abilities, for a limited time, and they have the freedom of whether or not to renew their contracts. If at the end of two or three years a professor has not performed satisfactorily in his teaching assignments, or has not earned the degrees considered necessary, or does not do research or publish, then the university does not offer him a new contract. The professor who has achieved prestige in his field, in turn, is sought by other universities offering him intellectual or economic advantages. Only after several years is a professor granted tenure, that is, a permanent post; he is then, in theory, permanently associated with that university.

As for the students, they enjoy the counterpart of this academic freedom in two senses. First, they are not required to submit to a rigid plan of studies, but rather, except for certain requirements, are free to choose their own courses of study. They take the courses they find interesting with only a minimum of required courses. In the second place, nearly all universities offer a wide range of courses in each discipline, and the students have an ample program from which to choose. The hiring of professors depends to a large extent on the preferences, esteem, and lack of interest by the students.

It must be said that the relationship between students and professors is usually very cordial in the United States. The student withholds his judgment and gives the professor the benefit of the doubt at first. He listens and notes what he says. Only then does he react, either approving of him or not by questioning and judging. In other countries classes or lecture audiences tend to believe they already know what is being said to them. They translate all they hear into terms they know already. If by chance what is said is something new, they do not understand because they were not expecting it. This is why it is so stimulating to teach American students, with whom the professor carries on a constant dialogue beginning with a trusting and open acceptance of what has been expressed in the classroom. And these conversations, begun in the classroom, continue during office hours, the time the professor is in his office available to students who may wish to consult him or simply talk to him about some topic. They continue also in the hallways or in the cafeteria, in the residence halls where the professor is often invited to come, or in the professor's home where students visit individually or in small groups. Friendships between professors and students are frequent and may be lasting.

Young American students tend to be generous and rebellious. They disagree with everything they think is wrong, freely offer their opinions, and protest. And this does not seem at all unusual to them because it is not. The use of freedom is not a disturbance, not something simply discussed in vain. Only at certain times and places does agitation (probably in such cases manipulated) depart from the rules of the game and become an abusive or scornful attitude towards the freedom of other groups. The reaction of the students themselves to these violations is usually immediate and energetic, and justly so because they have a deep sense of freedom and of the conditions necessary for its exercise.

My latest experience in teaching in America at a time of particularly high tension confirms what I have just said. The ease with which students react to the ideas they receive, the freedom with which they express opinions about them, the naturalness and freedom with which they emphasize their own points of view before those of other groups—professors, school officials, or the Government of the United States—are all part of the system under which they live. Far from being an anomaly, this is the very essence of academic life. Nobody feels hurt by the exercise of these freedoms, but rather by any attempt to suppress them. Students and professors take part in the march on Washington to protest against the policy in Vietnam, and nobody would doubt their right to do so, although they might question the reason or the appropriateness of their action. The same could be said of those who urge an intensification of the effort to achieve a military victory. When it was announced that the Secretary of State, Dean Rusk, was going to speak at Indiana University, the students pointed out to the university officials that six speakers favoring the continuation of the war had already spoken, while only one opposed to it had been invited. They thought this ratio was unfair and for this reason asked that other speakers opposing the war be invited. The university relented and the students announced that in view of this they would not prevent Rusk from speaking, and would limit their opposition to the policy he represented to a silent protest. This small episode, which I witnessed, seems to me to have a meaning that interests little concerned with the truth have sought to obscure. Countries in which freedom is conspicuous by its absence—and unhappily they are many and of all colors—have a curious ineptness in understanding what freedom consists of and an understasdable interest in distorting it wherever they find it.

In this same Indiana University a few days ago I had an interesting personal experience. I spoke before a group of over a hundred students and professors about the United States. I spoke with complete freedom, not in strong criticism of the country, but, what is more unusual, in praise of certain aspects of American life that are customarily abused within the United States. My audience understood admirably well my line of thought. They took it for granted that I had a perfect right to think this way. They expressed their differing opinions—differing in several ways. They demonstrated in the course of their discussion that they were not in agreement, but they did not deplore the fact. Another professor, born in Europe but of recent American nationality, proclaimed his right to disagree, his rejection of the government's policies, and his conviction that in doing so he was showing true loyalty to his adopted country. It all ended in an atmosphere of deep cordiality, of mutual appreciation, with a feeling not only that a step had been taken toward understanding reality, but also that there was a need to modify opinions in view of what others thought and in light of the aspects of problems brought out in other points of view. Unless I am mistaken, the very heart of the American university lies in this process.

61 THE AMERICAN WOMAN

THE COLLEGE GIRL

In the United States there are close to two hundred women's colleges, some of which could be called female universities and some not, because they are small college-level institutions. The great majority of them are liberal arts colleges offering four years of college work in letters or sciences. Only a very few have a graduate school where studies for the M.A. or Ph.D. may be followed. In general they prefer not to offer such complex and costly courses, which students may pursue in a coeducational institution. Some of these colleges are very small, with only a few hundred students; others have a thousand or two thousand. Several are associated with male universities and share professors with them: Radcliffe with Harvard, Pembroke with Brown, Newcomb with Tulane, Barnard with Columbia, Saint Mary's with Notre Dame. In other cases the association is more vague and unofficial, occasioned by proximity and frequent relationships between the men of one university and the women from a nearby college.

Women's colleges were founded at the beginning and middle of the nineteenth century, when women did not attend universities anywhere. They represent the greatest advancement of higher education for women. Now, when more than a third of all students attending universities everywhere are women, this separation seems unwarranted. The general trend is toward coeducation. Nevertheless, there are many of these colleges, and a corresponding number of male schools, that are vigorous and enjoy great prestige. In addition, there are many coeducational schools that are similar in size and character. Private colleges, both small and medium in size, are in no way traditional holdovers, but an active part of American education accounting for at least a third of the students in this country.

Why is this so? Undoubtedly, women's colleges and small colleges in general have fewer facilities than the great state or private universities. They have less money, modest laboratories and museums, small libraries (although they would seem large in other countries) of between tens of thousands and a half-million books. Neither do they often have the most famous professors on their staffs; rarely can they afford a Nobel Prize winner, although sometimes they do have outstanding teachers. Yet these shortcomings have their compensations also. Are marvelous laboratories and libraries of four to six million books really necessary for the undergraduate level before a student begins to do personal research? Are fifty or a hundred thousand well chosen and available books, together with other books and materials available through inter-library loans not enough? Some large universities have two or three Nobel Prize holders on their faculties, and others have ten or fifteen men of international fame. But these men usually do not teach undergraduates. Those called on to do the real teaching of these students are the several thousand professors of all ranks. And these are perhaps no better or worse than those in a distinguished college. The ratio between students and teachers in small institutions may be more favorable: perhaps one professor for every six or eight or even fewer students. There is more closeness between them, with more chance of discussion and personal attention. The student body as a whole can attend lectures by visiting notables or more easily participate in artistic activities. All these things are more accessible in the smaller colleges as yet unencumbered by administrative complexities. Finally, cordial relationships between professors and students are more easily and often established on small campuses, where everybody knows everybody else after a short time.

The alumnae of women's colleges tend to be quite critical

of them. They criticize them for being out of touch with reality and for being a little world apart having little in common with the real world. They reproach the narrow-mindedness that comes from gossip, curiosity, and chatter. They disapprove of the lack of companionship and friendly associations with boys, which leads to an excessive preoccupation with them and an obsession with weekend dates. The attitude of the girls is more erotic than might be desirable, and this sometimes leads to disturbances and frequently to disappointments.

All this is true. Yet without doubt the college girl who studies in one of these institutions has qualities and perfections hard to find elsewhere. These colleges are generally excellent finishing schools. They teach certain human values and certain feminine charms that seem highly important to me. The courtesy, polish, poise, ease of expression, the ability to travel and adjust to any situation, the tact for dealing with different people, with other women, with mature men, children, and infants, are absolutely surprising in girls of eighteen to twenty. What in other countries is found only in the highest classes of society, is found in a wide social range in the United States. Moreover, these qualities are blended with the spontaneity, imagination, flexibility, creativity, and audacity generally associated with students, and are rarely found in narrow and privileged circles.

Two dangers beset American girls attending women's colleges. The first is the abnormal concern with boys with whom they normally are not associated in the college or in town. This can become an obsession and lead to an excessive sexual interest culminating in a hasty and premature marriage. The second risk is of a reverse order in girls of a strong and not very feminine personality. In this environment it may develop into a selfish concern with oneself, into self-sufficiency and a worship of efficiency. These dangers are very real for the mediocre girl, as a person and especially as a woman. For these girls I believe the university and coeducation are much better.

For the girl of personal quality, able to make demands of herself, keenly sensitive and with a sense of value about human things, the women's college is a fine institution of learning. Its very appearance of "unreality" is a virtue. In this magic world, almost always beautiful of buildings and landscape, somewhat isolated with a campus (the very term means "country" in Latin) covered with huge trees and green grass, close to a sleepy, monotonous town, with free time and languid hours, with intellectual stimulation laced with periods of calm, a girl gradually develops and matures for four years. It is like a process of crystallization; she allows the recesses of her soul to be filled with certain essences, something impossible to do with more agitated and tumultuous vessels. This very concern for man who is habitually distant from her, which in the common girl is a negative note, in the superior girl is translated into a more acute and intense awareness of her femininity and into a deeper commitment to womanhood. This seems to me to be one of the most priceless things in the world. Nowhere else have I found the perfection seen in the best examples of these girls. Girls from coeducational universities, generally very pleasant, of excellent character, intelligent and alert, rarely match the feminine quality and intensity found quite frequently among the more delicate and demanding girls from women's colleges.

The characteristic traits of the college girl are the same as those generally found in the American girl everywhere. Of all the types of women I know, she represents the utmost in naturalness, spontaneity, openness, in that amiable and cordial disposition called *friendliness*, in trust—an excessive trust because it does not always evoke the best response—and in human generosity. Impulsiveness, lightness, a lack of caution, haste, a tendency to confuse people and things; these are the defects and dangers that generally accompany these qualities. The college girl represents the intensification of these generic qualities. I would venture to say that she is the most American of all American girls. In some cases the risks are too great and the product turns out defective and above all unstable. But when this does not happen, when a natural refinement or a firm discipline prevents the worst of these pitfalls, her positive qualities shine. When this occurs she is one of the most polished, intense, and attractive women of our time.

TWO GENERATIONS OF GIRLS

My first American female graduate student was born in 1928. The youngest of my present students were born in 1948. Twenty years is a lot of years. These girls could almost be the daughters of the other. My American students undoubtedly belong to two different historical generations, and genealogically the same thing could almost be true. In speaking of my students, which ones do I mean? Are there not enormous differences between them? Has not a profound change occurred in a period of sixteen years in a country as changing as the United States?

No doubt there are differences. I only have to look at them or remember them to see the differences between the two generations. There are the very important differences that can be seen in the face, in the way they walk, in the way their hair falls on the neck or down the back or is gathered on top, in the way of dressing and using makeup, and in their gestures. Fashions affect women, and women affect fashions. Women alter them according to personal or group tastes, and the result, if one looks closely, is an understandable image: a certain way of being a woman. My experience as a professor, the daily dialogue in class, the work coming at the end of the semester, as well as my experience as a friend, reveal very noticeable changes. My students of 1951 are not the same as those of 1967; several perceptible transitions have occurred between the two dates.

But . . . when I try to formulate these changes, I hesitate. If I attempt to take an opposing view, I cannot bring myself to it. What does this mean? Something surprising and very important: beneath the countless differences I perceive a strong continuity, a fundamental similarity. Both generations with all their variations and differences represent *the same type of woman*. American girls I have known over a period of sixteen years, leaving aside individual differences and stressing generic traits, seem the same to me; they manifest the same way of being a woman, of living in the world as seen through feminine eyes.

This is even more interesting if we think of the women of an earlier period, those who were no longer "girls" in 1951, although they may have been still quite young. These women were deeply different. The women who were fully mature when I began to know this country, those who, to pick a safe age, were over thirty at the time, were something else entirely. If this impression itself is true, then at a time before 1951 that I cannot precisely pinpoint, an important change took place in feminine life in the United States, a way of life that still continues. At that time a new feminine variety commenced which continues in the very young of today.

It is hard to justify a global impression of this type, and even harder to document it, for it is a very complex phenomenon. But its subjective evidence is quite convincing. Above all there is a change of tone, of feminine appearance, of outlook on the world. I shall try to describe this impression more concretely (with the awareness that I am somewhat falsifying and distorting it with concepts that are schematic and which taken literally would be misleading).

I would say that the earlier type of woman was brisker and that the younger one is more sure of herself. A certain aggressiveness characterized the mature American woman; she had a tendency to impose herself, and she deliberately tried to be —and to seem to be—"efficient." This is why she had a rather obvious professional air about her. And in those cases where she was not a professional or did not wish to be a woman with professional duties, for instance, when she was busy being a woman, perhaps a *grande dame*, she still displayed her attractiveness and elegance in an equally positive way. She was the refined lady, polished, impeccable, tense, who actively showed off her charms. This is why she inevitably seemed to be in a hurry. But at least this was invigorating for her skin, because it was firm from all her inner tension.

Today the younger American girl seems to represent a relaxation of this tension. She seems more "comfortable," more serene, and more jovial. She gives the impression of being naturally more at ease. She is probably more professional, at least statistics bear this out, but she is less aware of it; she does not stress it, but rather plays it down if not actually hiding it. A woman who can be an excellent professional person in many fields does not become "professionalized" to the same absorbing degree as men, and if she does it is only through a violent effort. The young American woman practices her profession with dispatch and effectiveness, but it remains somewhat distant from her in a vital sense. In contrast to the "toughness" that was so frequent in earlier generations, younger American women display more "tenderness." This is why instead of "showing off" her charms, she simply "lets" them come forth.

I do not know exactly when this change occurred. Possibly it happened around the end of the war, although I am not sure. In any case, one thing is clear: the older woman had to defend herself, claim certain rights, regain a place for herself in society, and create a certain feminine profile that still was not accepted and which met opposition that was more or less open, but at the same time more or less insidious. This explains her appearance of tension and alertness. What these women won, the younger ones found already waiting for them. For the latter it was something they did not have even to think about. They have been able to move into a place carved out with great effort for them by others. This is why they seem more natural and more at ease.

The essential point is that this affects their independence. Women twenty or thirty years ago still had to win or defend their independence. It was their obsession, their mission. Women today have that independence without further ado, and they have more of it. But it no longer obsesses them as much. Rather they are beginning to see its limitations, and to become aware that it can, in a very fundamental way, diminish them or be a handicap. They begin to suspect, above all, that it can be a deceiving mirage.

This is why younger American women have accepted their womanhood naturally and gladly. The women of earlier generations, unless I am mistaken—it is a delicate matter and the chances of error are great—sometimes felt that their femininity was a misfortune. On the other hand, when they were able to overcome this feeling, they announced it "triumphantly." Both these attitudes may be seen in many women born before 1920; they are rarely found in women who came into the world a few years later.

Naturally, these differences have a decided effect on their relationships with men. The element of "rivalry" apparent before has been replaced by an attitude of partnership in everything. The earlier attitude contained an element, however slight, of "hostility," while the present type of relationship is normally warm, friendly, well-disposed, and benevolent. The latter attitude is more pleasant and undoubtedly on the whole a better one. But since everything is bought at some price, it is undeniable that the older women, moved by a critical bent, were more demanding of the older man than their daughters of today are. The latter's benevolence and friendliness lead them to see the positive and to be lenient with the negative (or with the lack of certain qualities which later turn out to be essential).

A confirmation of this impression of mine concerning the two varieties of American women may be found in the famous novel by Mary McCarthy, *The Group*, which shows the lives of a group of girls after their graduation from Vassar College in 1933. It is precisely Mary McCarthy's own group. She was born in 1912 and that year was twenty-one. Mary McCarthy is personally an excellent illustration of the type of woman of the more refined sort that I have been writing about. Her book, although fiction, is written with real traits interpreted and used freely and literally. Now then, I have asked many friends of mine, mature women far into life, married with children, and graduated some twenty years after the time of the novel, whether they recognized themselves in the feminine types and attitudes skillfully portrayed in *The Group*. Invariably all answered no. They have the impression that earlier women were or could have been like that, but they themselves were entirely different. They do not share the reactions, the values, desires, and problems of that generation of girls. They feel that they are living at a different level and under a different feminine sign.

I believe that once again, and within the period of my direct experience, the United States is changing so as not to change fundamentally. The changes experienced by American girls between 1951 and 1967 are minor compared to earlier ones and seem to be aimed at preserving, in different circumstances, the same profile of femininity that appeared in America sometime between 1940 and 1950.

AFTER COMMENCEMENT

One day around the first of June, students of American colleges and universities, and the girls from the women's colleges, having completed four years of study, put on their academic robes, the cap and gown, which they had first worn (with the tassel on the right) as they were beginning their college career, and receive their degrees of Bachelor of Arts or Bachelor of Science. They symbolize this by moving the tassel to the left side of the mortar board. Now they are graduates. This ceremony marks the end of their studies. It is attended by parents and sometimes sweethearts, and it is called commencement, that is, the beginning. What is it that "commences" after college? Real life, of course.

What happens then? I have tried to answer this question in many pages already written, some many years ago, others quite recently. But now I should like to ask a more limited and exact question: what happens to American girls after commencement, when they leave the "magic world" as girls still, and especially what happens to them when they are no longer girls,

One cannot really generalize. When we speak of "Spaniards," or "Greeks." or "Americans," we always run the risk of uttering some stupidity. Yet it is a risk that cannot be avoided. What I mean is that we must generalize, knowing full well that as we do we commit an injustice against exactitude, and that each affirmation should be rectified. When I say "American girls," am I thinking of them all? Obviously not. I have seen thousands of girls, but there are millions more. I have met hundreds and made friends with a few dozen. And what differences there are even among these few! But at the same time it is apparent that there are certain traits that are peculiar to them and which set them apart from girls in other countries. When I say that these traits are peculiar to them, I do not mean that they all necessarily must have them, but rather that *they have them or they lack them.* In the latter case they are deviations from a norm and only approximations of the reality suggested by these traits which they do not fully exemplify and possess. On the other hand, these traits simply are not present in other types of women. This does not imply any lack on their part: these are not traits belonging to their kind of existence, and they have no reason to manifest them.

There are outstanding women everywhere, women whose femininity is distilled and refined until it reaches a particularly high level of intensity and splendor. In our time, unfortunately, people are not very inclined to heed this; rather the dominant trend is to pretend disdain for the whole idea. Only the cinema maintains the social custom of portraying a few exemplary types of women who feed the indispensable ability to create myths, without which life would cease to be human. The problem is how often are these pure and intense forms of womanhood found in each society or in each period. When the Spaniard, man or woman, fulfills the classic mold, he or she displays a kind of reality, a presence, and an appearance very hard to match in other places. But how many are there like this? For a long time the Spaniard has been almost always less than himself. And this is even truer of the Spanish woman. The best types are incredibly fine examples of womanhood, but it must be admitted that many are limited, timid, mediocre, and dull. In spite of their appearance, which is often attractive, there is often no desire to begin any human relationship with them. They arouse no curiosity to know them better. Why is this so? Who is to blame, if blame there be? And what can be done to overcome it? These are interesting questions, but we cannot go into them now.

I would say that American women statistically "begin well." In other words, American girls, especially the many college girls, often have excellent qualities. There is an adjective found, as one might expect, by a great poet, that is rarely applied to women but which fits. Antonio Machado in a self-portrait recalls: "I loved in them all hospitable qualities." This is the essential quality that I would point to as a characterization of the American girl. I can imagine the surprise of those who only know this girl through references. Would this not be rather a quality of the Spanish girl? It depends; the Spanish girl is indeed often quite hospitable, but hers is a maternal hospitality. As a woman *per se*, this quality is much less noticeable. In the name of certain virtues, more than because of them, as a woman, especially as a young woman, she takes on a certain brusqueness and sullenness that have a marked influence on Spanish life. I am not saying that the hospitable attitude is not exposed to deviations that are much more frequent in the United States and which also may mean some damage to the state of womanhood. The forms of sexual freedom that today are found the world over may arise in its most noble aspect from this attitude of hospitality. But this is not necessarily its source, and in any case I think it is possible to have the attitude of hospitality, and to a fuller and more intense degree, without the question of sexual freedom.

This quality of the American girl is born of the blending of three or four traits: trust, generosity, imagination, and benevolence. We saw them before in our study of the characteristics of American society. Openmindedness toward reality, a spirited vision of the future, trust in one's neighbor: these are the essential dimensions of this way of life. They are the qualities of youth. No wonder, then, that we find them in the United States and especially in American girls.

But if now we ask how these girls mature, and how they come to be women and project the entire path of their lives, some important reservations about what has been said are in order. Quite often the American woman manifests in an attenuated and residual form some of the worthier qualities of her girlhood. One might say that this always happens and happens everywhere. But this is not so. In going from adolescence to maturity, obviously something is lost, but also something is gained. Some qualities disappear with the years, but others grow stronger. In many cases the American woman has lost some or much of her spontaneous affection, imagination, intellectual curiosity, and her idealistic attitude toward life. We have proof of this in that a considerable group of American women who are no longer very young preserve their girlhood qualities almost undiminished. Why should it not be so in so many other cases?

We may talk about the harshness of life, of the disillusion and pain that it always brings with it even in the happiest of cases. Or we can mention the frequent examples of misfortune in all its variations. But I am not satisfied with these explanations, for they do not cover many cases, or they are too generalized and applicable to all conditions of life. I believe there are personal and social elements that weigh heavily on the destiny of the American woman.

First of all, the friendliness and benevolence that American girls feel toward men, the way they intimately share their desires, the spirit of rivalry and wishes for success, their enterprising nature, along with the ease and abundance of American life, and social customs, all lead to early marriage immediately after graduation or even before it. The universities are full of married students. For the country as a whole and for people of ordinary qualities, probably early marriage has more advantages than drawbacks. For gifted people of some complexity and ambition, it seems an enormous danger. In many cases, an American girl will marry the first "nice" boy she knows to whom she is attracted and for whom she has any feeling. Partly this is because she likes him and partly because she is in a hurry. But above all and in a very feminine way, she wants to know "whom she is going to marry."

These marriages are quite often mistakes and nothing but mistakes. Quite frequently also they end in divorce. Aside from other considerations, divorce leaves a woman hurt and diminished. But in other cases, in the majority of cases, this does not happen. The boy is a fine man, a hard worker, honorable, kind, and respectful to his wife. She loves him, as she loves her children, only she is a little bored. Too late she realizes that the likable boy was not the person with whom she could talk for fifty years without becoming satiated and tired. Whole areas of her life are then left abandoned and almost barren. She sees that there are other possibilities in the world, more complex and imaginative men for whom life is not a pre-established pattern, and with whom one could be creative. And this realization leaves in a woman a residue of sorrow, resentment, and at times callousness.

Furthermore, a girl who has lived for a few years, four to six, in a college or university, in full and constant communication with others, with long hours of conversation with friends and professors (without counting the many hours of classroom "conversation"), in an intellectually stimulating, imaginative, critical, rebellious, and enthusiastic environment, suddenly in so many cases goes to live in a suburb, in an isolated house with its lawn and flowers that looks out at its neighbors from a distance. Her neighbors are almost always housewives burdened with household chores with whom she exchanges smiles and small talk. For all practical purposes she is restricted to talking to her husband and a few years later to her children, who are a long time in providing her with any real companionship. From time to time at a party, with a drink in hand and her feet tired, she exchanges short sentences with people who do not interest her and whom she may not even be able to identify very well. Is it any wonder that often the sweet and generous creature, who a few years earlier, vivacious and fresh, was beginning her life on some campus, now begins to fade and decline or withdraw into an unfeeling shell?

The day that American girls learn, like Machado, to distinguish "voices from echoes," when they are no longer so hurried and happy with so little, then I shall believe that the American horizon has been opened to the full.

62 THE FRONTIERS OF INSPIRATION

In dealing with Americans, as in assiduously and attentively following the course of public affairs in the United States, I am constantly surprised. I am surprised by the American's hospitality. He will go to some expense, and what is more, give a lot of his time and effort to welcoming some friend, waiting for his arrival, and after taking him to his home (perhaps after several hours at the wheel), he will extend his hospitality to him, shower him with attention, plan an attractive stay for him, accompany him, and introduce him to interesting people. I am surprised by the insight of a young professor who, having listened to a lecture modestly and innocently, perhaps looking like a sportsman or a cowboy, after the lecture is over asks some pertinent questions. Possibly he is not clear about a fragment of some theory which should have been discussed but could not be in the allotted sixty minutes. Or perhaps I am surprised by the capacity for understanding in some adolescent student who has never had a course in philosophy, but who unexpectedly grasps the problem and correctly understands what men of some intellectual claim have stumbled over. I am surprised, of course, by the financial generosity of the American, which always surpasses what might be expected. His dependability surprises me, his unusual aptitude for trusting and being at ease with people, and for getting on close terms with people in so little time. Finally, I am surprised by his ability to understand another person separated by distance, differences, and barriers.

But along with all these surprises, there are others of a negative nature. On occasion, the American can be strangely cold, distant, and unapproachable. He does things for motives we do not understand very well and which do not seem to us to be typical of him. With an attitude of resignation he foregoes something he likes and which seems to us quite accessible. He may devote his time and attention to something he does not like that in our opinion he could very well avoid. After becoming deeply interested in a project and just when we think he is going to carry it out, he abandons it; or for reasons that are not clear, he rejects it. At times he is unexpectedly severe in judging a person or an act, despite being a warm, affectionate, and normally benevolent person. While the American people invent more things in every area than anyone else today, not infrequently Americans accept standards and behavior that are clearly mediocre and routine.

This odd duality is true also when we go from private and personal life to collective and public affairs. Many years ago a gadget that I had recently bought fell to the floor and the motor broke. I went to the department store to see if it could be repaired or whether I should have to buy another. The young lady who helped me took the gadget and disappeared. She returned with a new one, murmuring timidly that "they could not do this again." A couple of months ago in Washington, they repaired an electrical appliance for me in a shop in just a few minutes and for free, a half-hour before closing time for the weekend. And just a few weeks ago, a lady in charge of one of the Offices of Internal Revenue in Indiana spent a long time in talking and studying documents, including a call to the State of Virginia, trying to keep me from having to pay certain taxes which, according to the wording of the rule, I should pay, but which, basically and according to the spirit of the law, it would be more just not to pay. She made true mental efforts and underwent moral anguish until she finally found the legal justification to do what she thought was right. With great satisfaction she exempted me from paying the taxes (unfortunately, I had already punctually paid others that amounted to a great deal). In contrast to these examples, one sometimes runs into a stone wall if he tries to change some tiny detail, like the order in which two petty operations are to be carried out or the way a place setting is arranged in a cafeteria.

Going on to graver matters, we see that the United States, a country that creates and carries out costly and difficult programs to help socially disadvantaged groups or foreign countries, in order to preserve some vestige of freedom in a distant land where they have lost nothing and have nothing to gain, at the same time, and under the label of "anticommunism," tolerates or supports unpleasant dictators who are almost always inept and as opposed as any enemy to all that the United States stands for. And while hundreds of professors and thousands of students study with unbelievable astuteness and love foreign cultures which they come to possess almost as if they were their own, in official circles there is no understanding of what a given foreign country means in terms of attitude and way of life. And of course officialdom does not make much distinction in the caliber of the people it finds there. If a careful study were made of the lists of official, invited guests of the Government, if an analysis were made of the people in other countries in whom the administration of American generosity puts its trust, in the form of scholarships, aid, travel money, and subsidies, then we could see how wrong this practice is and to what extremes routine can reach.

What does all this mean? Whence these negative surprises which belie what we have clearly found in individuals, institutions, and the country as a whole? I always have the impression that an invisible hand, from some unseen source, is intervening and disturbing or concealing the sources of inspiration. At times the people who begin to act seem totally different. Projects under way end up in unexpected places, and the whole country turns over its historical purpose to some strange force that is not its real being. For the real essence is what inspires and strengthens the whole spectrum of life; it is what everywhere gives the country a heartbeat in things both great and small; and it is what we might define as the American style or the American attitude toward life.

This intervention is, I believe, the result of certain social mechanisms, certain strong pressures that bear on the individual American and on his collective enterprises. They are subtle and often insidious, hardly visible to Americans. People come under their influence from their earliest years, and foreigners cannot see them because they do not apply where one would expect them to, and they are not to be found where one would tend to look for them. These pressures are in reality certain expressions of good manners and upbringing corresponding to a former way of life. They are conventional customs accepted out of a tendency toward conformity and which have a profound influence on the deepest portions of life. Let me give an example for clarity. Relationships between young people usually take the form of dates. The word "date" has a literal meaning of "fixed time," that is, a time agreed on by a boy and girl to go out together. A "date" is part of a social ritual: introduction of the boy to the girl's parents, flowers, going out to dine, to a show or to dance, and sometimes a long goodbye in a car. They are not in love, of course, but convention demands that the date conform to an amorous style, what we might call an "ardent" attitude. They know that it is not love that is involved, but rather a mutual like, affection, fun, and normal attraction. But it is assumed that their activities must resemble love. This means that there is an emptiness in them, that the activities are done inauthentically, and in many cases, although probably not in the majority, quite expressively. There is no telling how much this hinders the proper course of things. Many times I have seen a girl return from a date disillusioned and displeased, bored and aware that she has wasted both her time and the chance for any real human enrichment the relationship might have promised. Yet this kind of dating is a social custom that is hard to avoid or change.

The interesting projects that are given up or rejected are usually left in the hands of so-called "experts" who think they understand and are almost always backward and unable to appreciate originality or new things. These might include editorial boards, editors of journals, and governmental committees. In other cases the mere size of an organization delays decisions until opportunity has passed, or it does not capitalize on initiative or does so at the wrong time when opportunity and authenticity has been lost. These are examples of institutional petrification of certain pragmatic positions. And these continue to influence the country year after year. Official "anticommunism" is one of these. Started during the time of Foster Dulles, it continues inertially to hold sway over certain sections of American life: the Pentagon, diplomacy, certain opinion-shaping bodies. It blocks the way to active, positive, forceful, and current positions. The enormous social machinery of the United States, the gigantic costs of projects, the custom of doing everything conscientiously and thoroughly, and the cancerous growth of bureaucracy throughout the world—all these contribute to stifling the deepest tendencies of American life that are immediate, concrete, open, trusting, generous, and eager for reality. These are the boundaries, the frontiers, that limit and hinder and sometimes annul inspiration.

63 THE PROW

If we were to make a catalogue of things we do not understand and if we would reflect a little on what they are and the significance of the fact that we do not understand them, I think our knowledge of reality would be fabulously increased. To bring this study on the United States to a close, I am going to note one of the things that I am unable to understand.

The United States is a power of the first order in the world today. Because of its size, population, and material resources, it is counted among the "great countries": the Soviet Union, China, India—and for geographical size only, Canada, Brazil, and Australia. No single European country compares to it, although Western Europe as a whole does. Now then, if instead of taking a static and relatively abstract point of view, we see things in operation; if we take into consideration production and consumption, the amount of energy used; in short, if we consider *actions*—individual and collective—that are done and the *human reality*, the size of the United States is much greater and far above that of any other human grouping in our time. And since in turn the magnitude of today's world is incredibly greater than that of any other time, consequently, the United States is the greatest "human magnitude" of all recorded history, apart from any judgment of its value.

The Gross National Product in the United States in 1967 has reached 800 billion dollars, while the population stands at 200,000,000 exactly (this means $4,000 per person). The Soviet Union has 230,000,000 people, but its Gross National Product is not half that of the United States. In the production of many natural products and especially in industrial manufacturing, the United States matches approximately the entire output of the rest of the world. Overall, it accounts for between twenty and thirty-five per cent of world production.

But if we look closer at the human side of the question, if we observe what is done with these products, the difference is much greater. We shall not consider the automobile and its use, nor of aviation, since the United States manufactures the great majority of planes used in the entire Western World. American airlines are larger than absolutely all the rest put together. Just one fact: Air France, the largest foreign airline, is smaller than any one of five American airlines, and several of the latter are twice or three times as big. Telephones and the communication they permit, the postal service, television, teaching, inventions and patents—all these are of an absolutely incomparable size. In his recent book, *Le Défi Americain* (The American Challenge), Servan-Schreiber, who is concerned about American industrial penetration of Europe, is careful to point out that primarily it is not a matter of dollars and equipment (Europeans furnish ninety per cent of the capital), but rather of initiative, organization, imagination, patents, and technical knowledge.

The reason for this is found, more than in anything else, in the fact that the United States believes the most valuable item is man. In an admirable study on waste, it was demonstrated that it was perfectly sensible to discard a multiplicity of products and gadgets in order to save human time and energy in exchange. This is why man cannot be permitted to remain below his potential—for instance, through lack of an adequate education. The almost total use made of human resources is, needless to say, the outstanding innovation of our time. It began first in this country, and here is where it has reached its greatest development.

As a consequence of this, the stream of specifically human actions is colossal in this country: invention, tests and trials, experiments, and new techniques. The United States tirelessly tries out new things in all fields. The problems of our time, which have first arisen here and on a greater scale than elsewhere, have been and are being dealt with creatively and energetically. Many of them have been resolved, others have been alleviated, and others are being stubbornly combated. New procedures and technniques have been discovered to tame nature, to increase production, overcome economic differences, guarantee opportunities to the great majority of men and women, create multiple possibilities in the professions and in life in an extremely diversified society, assure political stability and the increasing exercise of freedom, and to make possible disagreement, rectification, innovation, and continuity in a river of collective life that flows on unchanged and unchecked.

The United States is one of the great creations of history, like Rome or the Spanish Empire, realities which we enthusiastically study and understand today. And the United States is being created before our very eyes, at an accelerated rate that allows us to observe it within our lifetime, or even in less than a lifetime. This book shows how in fifteen years, in the space of a generation, enormous changes in all areas and aspects of American life have come about. These changes are all aimed at preserving a kind of life, a life style, and they point to a search for its identity in a program of life. *Geprägte Form, die lebend sich entwickelt,* (coined form, that is developed in living), said Goethe, and this formula would be immeasurably better in defining this condition of American society.

Is this not an intellectually exciting spectacle? Has there been a greater social and historical experiment available for man's contemplation in many centuries? How is it possible, then, that so little is known about the United States? Why is it a subject so thickly covered with generalities, commonplaces, oversimplifications, and, to put it bluntly, lies? How

can we be convinced of the intellectual claims of those for
whom this reality holds no interest? This is one of those
things I cannot understand.

On the other hand, how can those who claim to be pas-
sionately interested in today's problems, who wish to know
them, state them, and resolve them, turn away from the country where, in contrast to other places, these problems have
been the most widely and actively presented; where publicly
and openly and in the most obvious way they have appeared;
and where the most resources and efforts have been devoted
to them? This is the country where many of these problems
have come closest to a solution; or at least, and to the degree
that real problems are unsolvable, they are allowed to continue in their real form and to retain their uncertain essence
within a context that permits them to exist and develop prob-
lematically. How can we believe that those who turn their
eyes from the greatest and most tenacious effort to confront
problems really want to solve the social, economic, educational, political, technical, and religious dilemmas of our day?

Over and again I have expressed my conviction that a great
many things that are considered "American" and are interpreted as signs of "Americanization," are simply *current*
things, things of the twentieth century, that first appear in
the United States with more intensity and luster. This happened in France during the eighteenth century when everything that was not archaic was shortsightedly called "gallicisms" or things French. The present "anti-Americanism"
is disturbing to me, not for what it says about the Americans,
but for what it tells about those who profess and practice it.
As a European I feel wounded by such a reactionary, hermetic, and provincial attitude, an attitude that is not very
intelligent, and this means that it is not very European either.
Anti-Americanism seems to me to signal a spirit of resignation
in Europe and a decline of Europeanism. One may disagree
with the United States on many things. One may take a crit-

ical viewpoint, and these pages are the proof of that. But what one cannot do is to close his eyes to America, pretend it does not exist, and look spitefully somewhere else. Europe has always symbolized creativity, imagination, and hope. It has always looked to the future, searching for new islands or continents among the mists. Whatever we may think about the ship's course, there is no doubt that the United States stands at the prow of today's world. I have often recalled as a symbol of Spain's decline in the seventeenth century, the wonderful image of Don Juan given us by Baudelaire. In the boat that crosses the River Styx on its way to the realm of the dead, leaning on his sword with his eyes fixed on the wake, refusing to look at anything else:

> Mais le calme héros, courbé sur sa rapiěre,
> regardait le sillage et ne daignait rien voir.

Nothing would be more painful to me than a resentful, fearful, distrusting, and diffident Europe with its cape about it, and its back turned to the course of history.

PART THREE

*EPILOGUE:
THE UNITED STATES
IN 1970*

*Translated from the Spanish by
Harold C. Raley*

Three years have passed since I wrote *Analisis de los Estados Unidos*‡—and a generation since I wrote my first book on this topic, *Los Estados Unidos en escorzo*,‡ begun in 1951 and published for the first time in 1956. In the fall of 1967, when Lyndon Johnson was still President and men had not yet reached the moon, I had turned my attention for the second time to the gigantic theme of the United States. I had been observing this country since the days of Truman and the Korean War—a long time by any reckoning! And it becomes even longer if we keep in mind the speed with which change occurs throughout the world and especially in this country.

As I reread my two books three years and four visits after the second one was written, what is my impression of them? On the whole, I would say that they are more valid now than when I wrote them: today the United States resembles much more closely the way I portrayed it earlier. Many features I saw before but which were only beginning to appear are now deeply etched in its face; many of my suspicions of which I was unsure at the time have now been confirmed beyond doubt; some promises have been fulfilled; certain new things I had not foreseen, but which were akin to the spirit I was trying to reveal, have now appeared on the horizon; and certain dark clouds, threatening and seemingly borne closer by the wind, now hover ominously over this land and darken its sky.

There are few things I would feel obliged to rectify; nor would I delete anything, for without antecedents we cannot understand clearly what is presently happening and what will happen in the next decade. Taking my previous writings on

‡ Part II of the present volume—Ed.
‡ Part I of the present volume—Ed.

the United States as a point of departure, since I believe them to be substantially accurate, we must ask in the most precise way possible where the country stands in this autumn of 1970, when Nasser and John Dos Passos have just died; when President Nixon travels in the Mediterranean and the governments of leading countries negotiate with hijackers who capture their planes, blow them up with explosives, and hold the passengers as hostages; when presidential commissions publish their findings on violence, campus unrest, and pornography; when the number of students in universities in the United States has reached seven and a half million; when the average yearly income has surpassed thirty-five hundred dollars; when the American army has entered and left Cambodia on the announced dates; and when fighting continues in Vietnam and at least the pretense of trying to negotiate a settlement of that war goes on in Paris.

If I had to sum up the recent past of the United States in one word, and were it necessary to reduce the sign of the times to three letters, I should select a simple adverb: "Now!" At times the cry becomes, "Right now!" It is heard continuously: "Civil rights, now!"; "Freedom, now!"; "War on poverty, now!"; "Get out of Vietnam, right now!" Sometimes it seems the words are unimportant; the music is what counts. Regardless of what is wanted and even though whatever it is may not be very clear, it is wanted "now." Did we say not very clear? When the cry is heard, usually from small groups: "All power to the people, now!" it would be hard to know what it really means; but it seems that the important thing is the refrain: "Now!"

At first glance this impatient demand seems to indicate a repudiation of the Greek Kalends, a rejection of a tomorrow that never comes. By contrast, it is considered the duty of a

Moslem to make a pilgrimage to Mecca at least once in his life, but since the time is not predetermined, years pass and the majority of believers never go. There are things that are announced, promised, and planned for years, decades, and perhaps even centuries, but which never materialize. If this is the case, is not impatience justified? Are there not many who have grown tired of waiting?

If those who insist on "now!" were the old or at least the mature, this would be plausible; the disturbing thing is that it is the young who say it, those who have not yet waited and who have not had time to wait. Life for them is "now" and "today" because they have hardly known "yesterday." These students and young militant Negroes are probably members of the same generation. Were they Spaniards, I would say they belonged to the generation of 1946; but it may be that the generational scale of the United States, does not coincide exactly with the Spanish.†

The young people of today in the West—and especially in the United States, the prow, as it were, the most advanced portion of the West—do not know how to wait, because they have never waited and because they have always satisfied their desires as soon as they felt them (and sometimes sooner). This is the psychological and sociological explanation for "now!" as a norm and a state of mind. It must be emphasized that this attitude diminishes anticipation and expectation; it dulls the *víspera del gozo*, to use an expression that serves as the title of an admirable book by Pedro Salinas.*

But the seriousness of this "Now!" lies in the fact that it is not only a personal or group attitude, perhaps even a generational mood, or to put it another way, a *spontaneous* attitude; it is also a password that for the reasons just given

† See my book, *El métódo histórico de las generaciones* [English version, *Generations: A Historical Method*, trans. H. C. Raley (University of Alabama Press, 1970)—Ed.]
* Meaning "the eve of joy"—Trans.

readily catches on with today's youth. I would say there is little that is "American" in this attitude. Rather, it goes against the deepest tendency of American life, that since the first years of independence has been a model of patience as well as of efficiency.

Often I have dwelt on the tolerance that the American people have shown toward social ills, and I have spoken about how they accept them up to a point because of a belief that such ills are not without a certain real, albeit insufficient, reason and justification. Ten years ago in the journal *Foreign Affairs*, I published an article in English, "The Unreal America," in which I discussed the usual image of the United States in Europe and Spanish America. I showed how the United States expects society to react in order to correct its own sores and vices, how it expects society itself to produce the "antibodies" that will reestablish the health of the social body. Europeans become annoyed at the tolerance toward certain social maladies that would require a radical cure. Americans prefer medicine to surgery because the latter leaves scars and is dangerous and because it lowers the vitality of the organism. The desire to correct everything "right now," regardless of what it is, is utopian, unreal, and contrary to the American way. It means a turning away from the attitude with which this gigantic creation of history called the United States was made.

There are other aspects to consider, and what I am going to say now will perhaps surprise many. The password "Now!" especially typifies those who are called "radicals" (in Spanish we would call them *extremistas*). This would apply to the entire leftist spectrum of both whites and blacks. But their attitude imitates the reactionary and authoritarian view that has always been evident in some sectors of American life without being able to become predominant. It is the view of those who immoderately espouse the cause of "Law and Order." They are the people who believe that problems can be solved with more and sterner police. If there is juvenile delinquence, they would not seek its causes and try to eventually modify the social conditions of wayward youth. They think it must be stopped "right now" by bringing the full weight of the law and the force of authority to bear on the delinquents. If some unwanted tendency appears within the country, no time should be lost in persuading others that it is bad; it must be immediately and inexorably cut out at the root.

For several decades now such has been the reactionary stance in the United States. Opposing this attitude, there have always been others who make distinctions between things, who see more than the black and white of situations, who realize that things are complex and that mistakes can be made, who believe that errors can be corrected, and who have an abiding faith in man, in his tendency toward perfection, and in his sense of morality. It is disturbing to note that the "radicals" are now copying the reactionaries. The truth is that neither group has accomplished very much in the last two hundred years. Rather, the real accomplishments belong to those who have known how to wait, those who know how long it takes for a tree to grow, those who, instead of shouting, "Right now!", have worked for the day when certain things would be possible. They know that things come about, as men used to say in earlier times, "In God's own good time."

65 VIETNAM

Three years ago I wrote several pages under this same title: "Vietnam." Not a single line of what I said then would need to be changed today. After three years everything concerning a war and a national crisis should have changed, and yet the crucial fact is that the situation remains essentially unaltered. But I can add to my earlier statements.

A different President is in office. Precisely because of Vietnam, Johnson decided not to run again. The war had cast a dark shadow over him, concealing undeniable successes in his domestic policies which someday will again become apparent. Nixon represents the other party, the Republican, whose image has always been associated more with belligerence. Yet it was Nixon who began the withdrawal of American troops, and it is he who has been promising and proposing (and in recent days with more determination than ever) an end to the war.

The truth is that this is also the wish of the vast majority of Americans. It is still not the majority will, however, principally because one of the necessary conditions is lacking: the knowledge of what to do to end the war. Moreover, there are certain groups opposed to ending it.

Nobody believes that the Vietnamese war can end in a victory for the United States. Many think that victory makes no sense whatsoever and that it is not even desirable. Others think the war can come to nothing that deserves to be called a "conclusion." To them the war is *absurd*. Not only is there no enthusiasm for the war; it is also being waged without the feeling that it is a painful duty or an unavoidable task that must be done. Nevertheless, in spite of all this, the war goes on as it did three years ago. The question is: why?

In the order that they present themselves to me, I shall attempt to offer several reasons and explanations that I have sought for a long time concerning this situation. First, it is very hard to stop a military machine once it is in motion. Solely because of its technical apparatus and its inertia, it seems to have a life of its own. In addition, there are economic and personal interests that block an easing of the war and tend automatically to perpetuate it. We should add that there is a feeling within both the American government and those groups that most strongly influence it—although this influence does not extend to intellectual circles—that the United States has obligations to meet in South Vietnam. These groups find the idea of "abandoning" South Vietnam repugnant. Many believe that if the United States were to abandon South Vietnam, its prestige would be undermined and distrust of this country would replace it. This is true, and there are many—for instance in Europe—who critize the presence of the United States in Southeast Asia, but who would be indignant or fearful the day American soldiers left Europe. We should keep in mind that these are the same people who protest the cutback of American forces in Germany or in England.

Another important factor is that many Americans in favor of withdrawal believe that it would have serious consequences —for South Vietnam, that is. And the attitude of the North Vietnamese, who have displayed some of the most ridiculous and lamentable behavior seen in the last ten years, does not help to dispel these reservations.

All these things are seen as obstacles to ending the war by those who believe that the war is in the best interests of the country, that it is necessary and justified, or at least very difficult to end. Such is the thinking of those who with varying shades of meaning are called *hawks*. Let us now examine the problems pointed out by the other side, the open and declared enemies of the war, those who stridently call for an end to the war, those who are referred to as *doves*. The only notable change since 1967 has occurred within this group. Three years ago the government perhaps *would* have liked to end the war, but it still did not actively pursue that wish. Today Nixon is clearly in favor of an end to the war and his public image is more associated with the birds of peace than those of falconry. I believe that today opposition to the war is creating the greatest hindrance to bringing it to an end. It seems to me that if the opposition *wished*, the war could be quickly ended. I am not so certain about what it does in fact want, at least not about what it says it wants. Let me explain.

The activists who demand an end to the Vietnamese War and who give this demand priority in American politics generally go through a series of ideological manipulations that exasperate and disturb the country. Let us see some examples:

(*a*) They completely overlook the existence of South Vietnam. For example, they talk about American "aggression" against "Vietnam," but they never remember how or when the fighting began, where it takes place, or that one group of Vietnamese is fighting against another in the very territory of the South. In other words, to them, "Vietnam" is North Vietnam or at most the North and its staunchest followers.

(*b*) For a long time their opposition took the form of protests against the bombing of the North. In fact, bombing is always atrocious, and besides, the bombardments were the only belligerent actions suffered by the North. Then, two years ago, in October of 1968, the bombing was suspended. Almost automatically the whole matter was forgotten and today nobody points out that what had formerly been considered the most serious aspect of the war has completely vanished.

(*c*) They insist—and rightly so it seems to me—that the government of South Vietnam does not represent the people, that it does not express the will of the country (if such exists), and that it favors and tolerates corruption. But they take it for granted that the government of North Vietnam does represent its country. They never bother to point out that the North is an iron dictatorship, and while they suppose that its people support it, they forget that the people have never had the opportunity to do otherwise, not even to speak out against the government. In brief, they accept without criticism everything the government of Hanoi says about itself, while rejecting everything that Saigon may say, as though the latter government did not exist at all.

(*d*) They strongly protest the cruelty and violent acts committed by the troops of South Vietnam. These are cruelties revealed, proclaimed, commented on, and condemned by the press, radio, television, books, the universities, and the whole country. On the other hand, not even in passing do they mention the cruelties of the North or of the Vietcong. This attitude is so prevalent that it produces the impression of a war that is all in one direction, like a one-way street.

(*e*) The most serious aspect is that in many cases they ask not for peace and an end to the war, but rather the victory of the North over the South or of the Vietcong over the rest of the South. About a year ago, on Moratorium Day, October 15, here at Indiana University with its thirty thousand students, I listened to several thousand of them chant in favor of peace in Vietnam. During the pauses about three hundred members of the SDS (those who for reasons that escape me call themselves "Students for a Democratic Society"), about one per cent of the student body, would shout: "Ho-Ho-Ho Chi Minh—the Vietcong has got to win!" In other words, what these people want is not peace, but rather war as seen from the other side and victory by those who are presently the enemies of the United States.

Unless we are aware of all this, we shall be unable to understand why things have hardly changed in three years and why the fighting continues in Vietnam. The great majority of Americans, on the right and left, conservative or liberal in their thinking, Republicans, Democrats, or independents, young and old, all want the war to end. Most of them want to bring it to a close under whatever conditions possible, almost at any price, because they have the impression that regardless of the serious ills that might be brought on by an end to the war, those very ills are already besetting the country along with the war itself, which is a greater evil than all the rest.

But there are a few small groups in the United States who do not want the war to end, or at least who do not want to see it over unless it leaves other things as dividends. If ending the war means taking an anti-American view, then the country will not accept it. Already there is significant irritation on the part of American workers against student groups who mix the peace movement with aggression against the country and its form of democracy by insulting the very flag for which the workers fought against fascism and national socialism. This is the flag that represents the society to which they proudly feel they belong. Sometimes I wonder what would happen in Moscow if "pacifists" were to gather in front of the Kremlin and burn red flags with the hammer and sickle.

It seems to me that those who toss into the same pot things that are very different and unacceptable to Americans really do not want peace. The search for peace today need not be a divisive enterprise in the United States; on the contrary, it is an undertaking that can arouse the strongest cooperation. There is intense pressure on the government to work for peace. If he is allowed to do so, I believe Nixon will find peace, and not necessarily because this is what he would want—this is another matter altogether—but rather because in 1970 the President of the United States could have no other aim even if he wished.

But I repeat that he will find peace, "if he is allowed to do so." There are a few who do not want peace, others who are unwilling for Nixon to find it, and still others who insist that peace must be accompanied by certain apparently revolutionary things, and who reject the first unless they also get the latter. None of these groups is very large and none has any true power or importance. The real power and importance belong to that much larger group of people who are unaware that they possess either.

66 POLITICS

For complex reasons that would be most interesting to investigate, politics is passing through a phase of mediocrity throughout the world. If we look at the men in office in nearly every country, we note that few of them stand out; in hardly any case do we have a clear idea of *who* and *what* the man really is. In many cases it was elevation to power that made the public aware of the man's existence. Some of these figures are able and deserving men. But this alone is not enough. They lack brilliance, stature, appeal, and the ability to arouse hopes and expectations that, far from being messianic, magical, or doctrinaire, are instead real, which is to say, *political*.

This is painfully evident in the United States. The premature death of Adlai Stevenson, one of the most urbane, discerning, and discreet men I have ever known, and the atrocious, stupid assassinations of John and Robert Kennedy, deprived this country of three outstanding and interesting men, regardless of any reservations about their political personalities. But three men out of a country of two hundred million is a very small number. Even after their disappearance, there should be any number of attractive, able politicians capable of arousing hope and leading people in today's world. Men of these qualities are found in all fields. Why are they missing in politics?

Johnson did his public image irreparable damage with the Vietnamese War, especially in the way he explained the war to the public (see my discussion of this in Chapters 54 and 55). Vice President Humphrey's loyalty to Johnson caused him to be discredited also and denied him any chance to present his candidacy as an alternative to the Johnson policy. Moreover, the Democratic party, which in 1952 made the incredible mistake of sacrificing Stevenson as a candidate against Eisenhower in an election he could not win, made another in 1968 by running Humphrey. Humphrey was not a *new* candidate, and this nullified the undeniably noble and politically intelligent decision by Johnson to withdraw from the contest.

In 1968 an attractive and interesting figure had appeared on the American political scene: Eugene McCarthy, the Democratic senator, who was Catholic and liberal and in so many ways the antithesis of the other McCarthy: Senator Joseph McCarthy. As a reader and contributor to the magazine *Commonweal*, I had long known about Eugene McCarthy, for the magazine had published articles both about and by him. Still, he was not famous and countless Americans did not even know his name, much less what kind of man he was. It was true that among sizable minorities he aroused admiration, loyalty, and hope; but in my judgment he made a serious mistake. That mistake was called Czechoslovakia.

I have discussed at some length the erroneous nature of "anticommunism" (like all "anti-isms," it is intrinsically passive, negative, and parasitic). McCarthy's opposition to the "anticommunist" approach of American policy was essentially correct. Now, the violent end to the "springtime" in Prague, the brutal crushing of timid Czech hopes for freedom by invading Russian troops, was a blow to the views represented by McCarthy. His reaction to the disturbing events in Czechoslovakia was to deny that the invasion had any importance.

But this was a mistake, for indeed the invasion was quite a serious matter. McCarthy should have recognized its importance and he ought to have taken the lead in formulating a proper national reaction based not on "anticommunist" thinking, but rather on an open, active, forceful, and creative policy. His failure to do this led people to become disillusioned with him. As if this were not enough, the leadership of the Democratic party pushed through the nomination of Humphrey as its presidential candidate. McCarthy, understandably hurt, withheld his support almost until the eve of the election. This explains Nixon's narrow victory of only a half million votes. This slight percentage could easily have been swung in Humphrey's favor.

Many Democrats were happy that the party had lost, even if it meant victory for the Republicans. A sizable number of Republicans and Democrats, along with a much larger bloc of independent voters, cast their ballots for Wallace out of spite, knowing that he would not be elected, but unwilling to vote for the official candidates. Of course, spite does not make for interesting politics or policies, and the United States (and the rest of the world) needs policies that will attract. We cannot afford the luxury of mediocre politics in the United States.

Nixon's administration is discreet and moderately effective, good enough "to get by" but nothing more. As I have said before, he cannot supply what the country needs most: an effective rhetoric. To complicate matters, his Vice President, Spiro Agnew, if he symbolizes anything at all, represents an "anti-rhetoric," a rhetoric of negative effects. Everybody jokes about the frequently grotesque alliterations scattered throughout his speeches. They are at once common and obscure, trite and pedantic; quite often his so-called alliterations are words that offer no coherent idea but which simply begin with the same letter. He uses this tactic to scold his political opponents as well as sizable groups within the country (including some of the nation's finest). He does not hesitate to distort things, as, for instance, when he comes up with the concept of "Radical-Liberals" or "Radic-Libs," not withstanding the fact that no such group exists. He appears untroubled that the very name "Radical-Liberal" is a contradiction of terms. The extremist cannot be a liberal any more than a liberal can be an extremist. (I usually define a "liberal" as someone "who is uncertain of what may be considered liberalism".) On the other hand, except for philosophy, which is necessarily radical, that is, an attempt to "get at the root of things," the so-called "radical," in the words of Ortega y Gasset, is "an emerging beast." Agnew's speeches are the very contrary of rhetoric: propaganda. I do not think Agnew has any importance other than that bestowed on him by his office. (I usually define certain Spanish groups with similar influence as "having no motor but holding the wheel.") In other words, such men have no real intellectual stature or prestige of their own, but enjoy instead the power that others have given them. And as long as they have this power they exercise it in such a way as to produce dangerous changes within the social body. Americans are beginning to pray for Nixon's health, for they can imagine what Agnew would be as President.

All this is somewhat disturbing. Dissent and disagreement, which form the substance of American life, are generally not expressed with very much intelligence. The tendency is to criticize *everything*, the good as well as the bad, and perhaps the good more than the bad. Dissatisfied Americans—students, professors, writers—are often blind to their country's highest and rarest values. Much of their criticism is directed toward the "Establishment," and I should like to dwell on this point for a moment.

"Establishment" is a British rather than an American term. Until a few years ago, nobody spoke of an "Establishment" in the United States for the simple reason that there was nothing in this country comparable to the "Establishment" in England. Thus, it is an imported concept and refers to an idea and not to a tangible reality. It is curious to note that those who constantly criticize the American socio-political system never propose another in its place. This is because they have no other. And even if they did, it would be much more vulnerable to criticism. This does not mean, of course, that the American system is faultless: it has countless defects and it has always been criticized for them. The same people who criticize the American system also advocate great changes in South Vietnam. They especially favor "free elections," but they do not propose these same things for North Vietnam, where there is perhaps more reason to ask for them.

This all-inclusive and indiscriminate criticism of the most positive aspects and greatest triumphs of American life irritates the middle class American and causes him to support everything and to reject even justifiable criticism. When violence is joined to criticism, as has occurred in Negro districts and in the universities, the reaction has been more unilateral and less intelligent.

I believe that *actual* violence in the United States is still relatively minor. Aggressive acts committed against people and property are numerous, but within the total volume of this enormous country they amount to only a tiny fraction. Of the more than twenty-two million Negroes in this country, only a few thousand have been involved in violence. Out of some fifteen hundred colleges and universities with more than seven million students, only fifty or a hundred have experienced disturbances, and even in those where trouble has occurred, only a small percentage of the student body was affected and only *for a few days at most* during the last few years. In other words, peace and normalcy have been the rule, and violence the exception. Violence is disturbing as a symptom of a change in attitudes and as a *topic* of discussion. People here and throughout the world talk about violence constantly; they comment on it, condemn it, defend it, and come to the conclusion that it is everywhere.

Violence is becoming less and less the result of spontaneous and eruptive feelings and more and more the product of organization and planning. For example, the explosive summers in black districts, with rioting, burning, looting, and shooting, are becoming less explosive and more peaceful; people are less and less caught up in the collective delirium, frenzy, and rage of other years. On the other hand, the *organized groups* of militants and activists, who use violence in small dosages when and where they can at strategic points, typify the current situation. The same can be said of the universities: certain schools are picked as the scene of riots or, according to the latest trend, bombings.

However, the most serious and dangerous aspect is not the so-called subversion of the Left, but the reaction it is causing. The majority of Americans, acting in good faith and satisfied with the general state of things; who are grateful for the wealth, security, and freedom of their country; who are full of enthusiasm for, and loyalty to, the nation, its history, traditions, freedoms, and flag, are hurt by the immoderate and arbitrary criticism and especially by the insults and violence. The extremist forces of the Right take advantage of the reaction of the majority. (All these terms are rather crude, fit only to describe crude events.) The rightists call on the majority to "close ranks" and to eliminate dissidence in favor of less appealing—and less American—aspects of the United States.

This is exactly what I fear: *a reaction by the real reaction-*

aries. And this reaction is being brought on willingly or unknowingly by a few thousand "leftists," "radicals," and "extremists," who by their organized or spontaneous actions are jeopardizing a system that for all its defects and partial injustices is still superior to any other in existence. It is a system that has always corrected itself, one that has a place for disagreement and a moral awareness of its shortcomings. More than would seem possible, the American system has come ever closer to an ideal of civilized and free life for its citizens.

The bad thing about demagoguery is that it breeds more demagoguery. Lately there are many—on the right and the left—who lack the courage to be anything other than demagogues. They are the people who feel obligated to simplify things and to distort reality and who, by denying that their opponents could be the least bit right, are wrong themselves. The Democratic Convention of 1968 and the trials that followed, the Black Panthers, the Birchers, the militant Negroes who seek their inspiration in Mao (as if their problems had anything to do with China's!), and the Vice President, are all examples of demagoguery. Violence corrodes the principle of peaceful dissent, and unnecessary or unjustified repression makes a mockery of the principle of law and order which in itself is a valid ideal.

American society seems to me to be essentially healthy, although there are unmistakable symptoms of infection. The other McCarthy of the fifties "vaccinated" the United States against demagoguery and extremism. But a generation has passed and today's youth have not been innoculated. Perhaps they still retain a certain "maternal immunity," the "antibodies" transmitted by society itself from an earlier time. But it may be that they need a "booster shot"; perhaps the country as a whole needs another shot of a weakened virus that builds resistance without setting off a disease.

But what the United States really needs is imagination and

a national goal toward which all can enthusiastically strive. It needs the kind of rhetoric that will express what the United States really is, that is, a rhetoric that will tell where its ultimate national aims lie. It needs spokesmen to guide it toward a future based on the real and the possible, and not on utopian and abstract notions that could apply to any situation and for that very reason apply to none. The political will of the United States must deal with things as they really are, but this does not mean that it should leave them as they are. Instead of avoiding its problems, the United States should accept them as a challenge and a means of progressing to something better. Today's youth enthusiastically sing "We shall overcome," and some understand this to mean the victory of one group over another. But a better meaning might be: "We shall all overcome." For this is what is needed: a victory in which there are no vanquished.

67 THE AMERICAN VERSION OF ANTI-AMERICANISM

At the beginning of the 1970–71 academic year, an extensive report dealing with campus disorders was made public. The report was prepared by a Presidentially-appointed committee and was entitled, *The Report of the President's Commission on Campus Unrest*. This document is the result of a unique and characteristic aspect of the United States that most other countries find incomprehensible. The fact that a commission named by the Chief of State would analyze some social and political problem in depth, that it would investigate it from all possible points of view, that it would at times harshly criticize the actions of authorities and recognize that many things are not clear, that it would propose solutions together with their potential effectiveness and limitations, and, above all, that *all this would be made public*, is a spectacle to which we in the rest of the world are not accustomed.

Adherence to the facts, good faith, veracity, and a desire to understand and find justification in diverse points of view, are features of this report. Descriptively, it is a splendid document; I mean by this that it presents the facts accurately, intelligently, calmly, and carefully, and that it does not attempt deliberately to conceal, distort, or omit anything. It should also be pointed out there are no overtones of aggressiveness in the report; instead, it is written with an evident wish not to offend, not to aggravate situations, not to use pejorative language, and as much as possible it tries to respect the dignity of the people involved.

However, there is one aspect that was inexplicably overlooked in what otherwise is a complete and carefully considered study of all aspects of the matter. It is this oversight that I should like to consider.

The report points out that dissatisfaction and unrest have always existed in both American and foreign universities and that there is a long American tradition of dissent, criticism, and nonconformity. The report states, moreover, that unrest in itself *is not a problem*; it is not a matter to be resolved, but an asset to be encouraged and preserved. The things that are new and serious and which demand solutions are the disorders and disruption of university functions, the coercion to which professors, administrators, and students are subjected, the violence, and in extreme cases the burnings and bombings.

When did all this begin? The Presidential Commission's report is quite specific: it all started in 1964 on the University of California campus in Berkeley. It was the "Berkeley invention." "What happened in Berkeley," the Report accurately points out, "was more than the sum of its parts." It was an authentic political innovation that the United States had not seen previously. It consisted primarily of the combination of on-campus matters with the general social and political problems of the country. The Berkeley authorities could deal with the first set of problems, but the off-campus concerns were beyond their powers. The purely academic matters were colored by the emotions aroused by the wider problems. The protest was started by a small group of activist students, and the more radical members assumed the leadership. The latter introduced violence, and this led to the disruption of university functions. The university officials then called in the police, who acted resolutely and with occasional brutality. This outraged many students and professors who had not supported the original protest, but who now joined it. The result was a decline of academic activity and an intensification of political action. In other words, the events led to the politicization of the university.

The so-called "Berkeley invention," popularized by the news media, especially by television, began to spread to other universities. The theme of Vietnam was more important than all the rest in attracting people of a similar attitude; racial problems, civil rights, and poverty were secondary topics varying in importance according to the occasion. Until 1968 the entire process proceeded rather slowly; since that time, that is, since the publication of *Analisis*,‡ this new attitude, this "invention of Berkeley," has come to typify the college community. We saw it first at Columbia University and later at the Democratic Convention in Chicago.

The rationale behind the new attitude is the following: the Vietnamese war, it was first reasoned, was a mistake; from many points of view and for many reasons, it had to be stopped. Then it began to be said that the war was a logical consequence of the American political system. The evil lay not in the war but in "the System," and, as a part of the

‡ Part II of the present volume—Ed.

System, the university should be destroyed or at least drastically transformed. All this meant that even if the war were to end, the position of those who reasoned in this way would not change substantially. The war became simply a detail of no great importance; it could be omitted, as it will be omitted the day it ends, without changing any of the fundamentals.

The Commission's report speaks of the United States as if the country were isolated from the rest of the world and as though the phenomena it describes happened exclusively within its boundaries. In the first place, similar things are presently occurring in the universities of several countries. Leaving aside those universities in countries where no legal political action is possible and where there are no avenues for the expression of grievances—though at the same time there may be sufficient social freedom for protest to be visible (in countries of extreme oppression, protest is simply impossible)—there are many other countries with political freedom and the normal exercise of political activities, where the universities are shaken by agitations that have little or nothing to do with academic matters. In other words, problems are being posed within the universities for which there are no solutions within their confines. It may be that these problems are not expressed through normal political channels for fear the majority would reject the proposed solutions. To put it another way, using the tactics that work best, those concerned with these problems "bring" them to the universities, where they cannot possibly be dealt with adequately and effectively.

In the second place, the extremist criticism of the United States within American universities extends to the structure and organization of the country, the entire range of the laws, usages, customs, values, and way of life that make up American society. In short and above all, campus unrest is, to a high degree, what is called anti-Americanism.

This is exactly how the Presidential Commission's report

looks at it, but the Commission does not draw the most important conclusions. The Commission assumes that the unrest of the students and many professors degenerates into or approaches anti-Americanism through a process of exaggeration and generalization. But it seems to me that this conclusion is drawn because the Commission restricted its inquiry to the United States alone. Their assumption might account for the earlier, sporadic, spontaneous, and isolated unrest that was evident here and there before the "Berkeley invention." But it cannot explain the frequent, serious, and coordinated events that led to the naming of this very Commission. One could say that the latter form of campus unrest is the *American version of anti-Americanism.*

Yet anti-Americanism is not American, but foreign. It did not begin in 1964, but rather much earlier, at least as long ago as 1945. (Another somewhat similar anti-American feeling had been in existence since 1933, when national socialism gained power in Germany.) Anti-Americanism has nothing to do with the war in Vietnam, for it existed several decades before that conflict. It has played a part in the Cold War and has dominated many of the Eastern countries, much of Europe and Latin America, and is now gradually gaining ground in this country. It has reached serious proportions with the younger generation that began to make itself felt in a historical way around 1964.

If one examines carefully what radical students are saying, it can be seen that they are simply repeating with unquestioning willingness what older and more mature enemies of the United States were writing and saying for various reasons decades ago. The arguments of today's American groups are simply the transcription or translation into English of what was formerly being said outside the United States. The concerted efforts of those opposed to the United States make up one of the greatest propaganda machines of all time.

Without an awareness of the origin of current anti-

Americanism, it is very hard to diagnose the causes of campus unrest and to propose effective ways to deal with it. The report is inadequate because it rests solely on intra-American premises and considers only this country in its investigation, whereas the principal causes of the phenomenon lie elsewhere. Why should this be so? Why did such a conscientious and careful committee allow such colossal oversight to weaken its study? The reason seems to me to be the following: there are minorities of the extreme right in this country obtusely obsessed with conspiracy, who try to explain everything in terms of subversive agents and the like. More intelligent Americans are horrified by this kind of explanation. Furthermore, it is evident that the great majority of students implicated in such agitations are not foreign agents or anything of the sort. They are American students and perfectly normal like the rest. The Commission very wisely refused to attribute campus unrest to subversive agents alien to the university community. But the Commission went a step further, and this is where the matter becomes serious. In view of the fact that subversives are not the only, nor even the principal, cause of campus unrest, the Commission hastened to forget it and to shunt the entire possibility aside, failing to realize that such groups do play an important role as catalyzing agents. This does not mean they form an active conspiracy; instead, they exert an influence in other ways: through a process of contagion and the spreading of ideas that "are in the air," their attitudes are imitated and lead to a kind of "mental pollution." Given the opportune moment and with the right catalyst, dark clouds gather and downpours occur which may become deluges that cause destructive floods.

One must not pretend that foreign anti-Americanism explains the entire phenomenon of campus unrest and subversion, but without taking the foreign aspect into account the problem cannot be explained. Foreign influence is apparent at two stages of the process: the beginning and the end. The origin, the seed, the stimulus, as well as the chief beneficiary of anti-Americanism is its foreign counterpart. It may be found both in the planting and the harvesting. In between lies America itself, which exposes its body, its land, its intellectual and economic resources, its freedom, and its uncertainties to the concerted offensive against it.

68 THE SEARCH FOR HAPPINESS

"No protestemos. La protesta mata el contento."
("Let us not protest, for protest kills happiness.")

Unamuno

Among the "self-evident truths" proclaimed nearly two centuries ago in 1776 in the Declaration of Independence of the United States, there is one that holds that all men have the inalienable right to the pursuit of happiness. Life in America has been influenced ever since by this spirit. For in fact, Americans have always believed that man has the right —not to happiness itself, for this would be meaningless, but to search for and to seek happiness. Thus, over a period of two hundred years certain objective conditions have been created in which personal happiness is *possible*. These conditions are what I have referred to as the channel or arena of happiness. Indeed, happiness has always been probable and frequent in the United States, perhaps more so than in most other countries.

Of course happiness is a personal affair. No form of society, no political constitution or government, can guarantee or grant happiness. All they can do is to make it possible and not stand in its way. Yet on the other hand, if we take things in the strictest sense, happiness is impossible (a chapter of my book *Antropología Metafísica* bears the title: "La Felicidad, imposible necesario").* Man is a being who needs to be happy but cannot be; that is, he cannot be so always and forever. But man dwells in what we might call "the element of happiness," he lives immersed in it, and in a limited way he participates in it.

Within the past few years—perhaps the past three to five—a tendency to deny this right has been spreading to many places, including the United States. A lady I have known for many years, and who is too austere for my liking, once said to me: "We have no right to be happy." Expressed in different ways, this is what Western man is hearing. Because so many things are wrong, because there is pain, sickness, poverty, oppression, and vice, some conclude that we have no right to be content, much less happy. Notice that they do not say we *cannot* be happy, but rather that we *should* not be. We must be unhappy, even though our circumstances may be favorable, because there is always someone less fortunate.

The United States cast its lot resolutely on the side of happiness. Indeed, it has carried this choice to its ultimate consequences: it felt it had a duty to be happy, and it considered it a mistake or at least a breach of ethics not to appear to be so.

Today many think they have to protest against everything that is bad, regardless of whether or not it affects them. And since there is always something wrong somewhere, protest becomes a permanent and normal *condition* of life. (Often there are protests against things that are right, but even if this were not so, the result would be the same.) But, as Unamuno —that arch nonconformist and most rebellious of men—used to say, "protest kills happiness." This is precisely the danger that hovers over us all, in the United States and elsewhere.

* "Happiness, A Necessary Impossibility"—Trans. [*Metaphysical Anthropology*, trans. Frances M. López-Morillas (The Pennsylvania State University Press, 1971)—Ed.]

This country has made a gigantic effort to combat the evils, pains, and limitations of life. And it has gone about this task confidently and happily, with a sporting and hopeful spirit. The results of its efforts have been almost improbable. If we compare the true state of current American society with that of any time in the past or with that of any other society of to-day, the comparison is astoundingly favorable to the United States. This does not mean, of course, that there is nothing left to do, or that considerable obstacles, sufferings, and injustices do not remain. Indeed the problems are considerable, but they are incomparable to those of the past or to those of other countries. Furthermore, if this is true today and the United States continues apace, within the foreseeable future all these negative aspects will be reduced much more.

As if this were not enough, the United States, by virtue of this same spirit, has helped to lessen ills throughout a great part of the world. What is referred to almost always with ingratitude or ridicule as "American aid," has become, par-ticularly in the past twenty-five years, one of mankind's greatest claims to honor.

Despite all this, the present American generation, which has just begun to play a role on the stage of history, is being persuaded that it ought not to be happy, not even to the de-gree to which it can be. Under the pretext that not everything is right, it is told it should behave as though everything were wrong. Not only does such an attitude represent a blind alley in a practical sense; it also makes improbable any improve-ment of conditions.

I believe that American youth of today are happy despite these temptations. As soon as they revert to their normal spon-taneity, they turn once again to that arena or element of happiness wherein they ought to live and within which they will experience their own sorrows and those of others. But they are beginning to seek happiness with a troubled con-science; they search less easily, as though they were committing a sin. There is a very real danger in this, for it can compromise and corrode the very fiber of American life.

There is a very serious fallacy in all this which for some strange reason people willingly accept. If happiness could not flourish so long as pain existed in the world, it would have never appeared in the first place—nor could it ever appear—on the face of the earth. It is curious that those who espouse this theory do not invite the whole world to join in a kind of universal mourning, and not certain countries only. For example, the so-called "First World" apparently should suffer because of the sorrows of the "Third World." But the same is evidently not true of the "Second World," whose efforts at conquest are wholeheartedly applauded without any damper being put on its antics. Indeed, the mere questioning of these attitudes is enough to arouse distrust in many quarters.

But that which is properly human is the contrary of the outlook being foisted on us today. Instead of being unhappy because something is wrong, we should be happy—or at least try to be so—even though almost everything is wrong and in spite of all our burdens. Nearly twenty years ago I wrote the following:

> Consider, if you will, a time, not only especially harsh like our own, but one with certain periods that are truly and inescapably atrocious: times of war, of besieged, bombarded, and starving cities, of imprisonment or concentration camps. So many men and women of our time have experienced or are still experiencing these horrifying realities, that personal reminiscences are not out of place. Now then, if we are sincere, we must confess that many times we were happy amidst the atrocious conditions about us. Once we had changed our standards of what was unpleasant and raised our level of tolerance, happiness could be found in muddy trenches, in streets swept by machine-gun fire, in prison, and in the face of enemy rifles. Clearly this is why man can survive many experiences. For man cannot

live without happiness altogether, and we must understand clearly that he can find happiness even in the direst straits. In contrast to the thoughtless cult of anguish, blackness, and nausea, I find the truly human qualities, qualities that lend a certain pride to being human, in man's marvelous capacity to discover delight amid pain, suffering, misery, and fear; and in his ability to see humor even in his own misfortune.

With rare exceptions, today's youth have not had the experiences I spoke of in 1952, when they were either fresh memories or still going on. Today's youth have not learned "to see humor in misfortune," because they have hardly known what misfortune is. They are being urged to do the opposite: they are being asked to declare a state of mourning and to make sadness and protest the rule in the midst of what must be considered—in view of the true state of the world— an incomparable example of well-being, justice, freedom, and prosperity.

These are some of the changes—convergent as one can see— that I have noticed since writing my second book on the United States three years ago. Almost everything *real* is better than before; but there is a budding belief that it is worse, and if people continue to believe it, it *will* be worse.

I ended *Analisis de los Estados Unidos* with my opinion that this country is the "prow" of the Western world.‡ And, as the expression goes, "We are in the same boat." I have high hopes for the whole world in the thirty years we have left in this century. But my hopes are based on certain conditions, and one of these is that the United States must continue to believe that man has the right to search for happiness.

Bloomington, Indiana—Madrid,
October–November, 1970.

‡ Chapter 63 of the present volume—Ed.